Hospitality and Restaurant
ement

NATIONAL RESTAURANT ASSOCIATION®

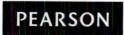

PEARSON

Boston Columbus Indianapolis New York San Francisco Upper Saddle River
Amsterdam Cape Town Dubai London Madrid Milan Munich Paris Montréal Toronto
Delhi Mexico City São Paulo Sydney Hong Kong Seoul Singapore Taipei Tokyo

Pearson

Editorial Director: Vernon R. Anthony
Executive Acquisitions Editor: Alli Gentile
NRA Product Development: Randall Towns and Todd Schlender
Senior Managing Editor: JoEllen Gohr
Associate Managing Editor: Alexandrina B. Wolf
Senior Operations Supervisor: Pat Tonneman
Senior Operations Specialist: Deidra Skahill
Cover photo: (Herrera)
Cover design: Karen Steinberg, Element LLC
Director of Marketing: David Gesell
Senior Marketing Manager: Thomas Hayward
Marketing Coordinator: Les Roberts
Full-Service Project Management: Barbara Hawk and Kevin J. Gray, Element LLC
Text and Cover Printer/Binder: R.R. Donnelley and Sons/Menasha
Text Font: Minion Pro, Myriad Pro Semicondensed

Photography Credits

Front matter: vii (left) Suhendri Utet/Dreamstime; (right) Meryll/Dreamstime; viii (top) Mtr/Dreamstime; (bottom) Stratum/Dreamstime; ix (bottom left) Aprescindere/Dreamtsime; xiii (top left) Justin Baynes; xv (bottom left) Petar Neychev/Dreamstime; 53, 105, 268 Justin Baynes; 61, 125, 209, 255,280 Nikada/istockphoto

All other photographs owned or acquired by the National Restaurant Association Educational Foundation, NRAEF

Copyright Permissions
National Restaurant Association Solutions
175 West Jackson Boulevard, Suite 1500
Chicago, IL 60604-2814

Email: permissions@restaurant.org

10 9 8 7 6 5 4 3 2

PEARSON

ISBN 10: 0-13-211613-8
ISBN 13: 978-0-13-211613-8

ISBN 10: 0-13-272447-2
ISBN 13: 978-0-13-272447-0

NATIONAL RESTAURANT ASSOCIATION®

Contents in Brief

Contents

About the National Restaurant Association and the National Restaurant Association Educational Foundation

Founded in 1919, the National Restaurant Association (NRA) is the leading business association for the restaurant and foodservice industry, which comprises 960,000 restaurant and foodservice outlets and a workforce of nearly 13 million employees. We represent the industry in Washington, DC, and advocate on its behalf. We operate the industry's largest trade show (NRA Show, restaurant.org/show); leading food safety training and certification program (ServSafe, servsafe.com); unique career-building high school program (the NRAEF's *ProStart*, prostart.restaurant.org); as well as the *Kids LiveWell* program (restaurant.org/kidslivewell) promoting healthful kids' menu options. For more information, visit www.restaurant.org and find us on Twitter *@WeRRestaurants*, *Facebook*, and *YouTube*.

With the first job experience of one in four U.S. adults occurring in a restaurant or foodservice operation, the industry is uniquely attractive among American industries for entry-level jobs, personal development and growth, employee and manager career paths, and ownership and wealth creation. That is why the National Restaurant Association Educational Foundation (nraef.org), the philanthropic foundation of the NRA, furthers the education of tomorrow's restaurant and foodservice industry professionals and plays a key role in promoting job and career opportunities in the industry by allocating millions of dollars a year toward industry scholarships and educational programs. The NRA works to ensure the most qualified and passionate people enter the industry so that we can better meet the needs of our members and the patrons and clients they serve.

What Is the ManageFirst Program?

The ManageFirst Program is a management training certificate program that exemplifies our commitment to developing materials by the industry, for the industry. The program's

EXAM TOPICS

ManageFirst Core Credential Topics
Hospitality and Restaurant Management
Controlling Foodservice Costs
Hospitality Human Resources Management and Supervision
ServSafe® Food Safety

ManageFirst Foundation Topics
Customer Service
Principles of Food and Beverage Management
Purchasing
Hospitality Accounting
Bar and Beverage Management
Nutrition
Hospitality and Restaurant Marketing
ServSafe Alcohol® Responsible Alcohol Service

most powerful strength is that it is based on a set of competencies defined by the restaurant and foodservice industry as critical for success. The program teaches the skills truly valued by industry professionals.

ManageFirst Program Components

The NRAEF ManageFirst Program includes a set of books, exams, instructor resources, certificates, a new credential, and support activities and services. By participating in the program, you are demonstrating your commitment to becoming a highly qualified professional either preparing to begin or to advance your career in the restaurant, hospitality, and foodservice industry.

These books cover the range of topics listed in the chart above. You will find the essential content for the topic as defined by industry, as well as learning activities, assessments, case studies, suggested field projects, professional profiles, and testimonials. The exam can be adminstered either online or in a paper-and-pencil format (see inside front cover for a listing of ISBNs), and it will be proctored. Upon successfully passing the exam, you will be furnished with a customized certificate by the NRAEF. The certificate is a lasting recognition of your accomplishment and a signal to the industry that you have mastered the competencies covered within the particular topic.

To earn the NRAEF's new credential, you will be required to pass four core exams and one foundation exam (to be chosen from the remaining program topics) and to document your work experience in the restaurant and foodservice industry. Earning the NRAEF credential is a significant accomplishment.

We applaud you as you either begin or advance your career in the restaurant, hospitality, and foodservice industry. Visit www.nraef.org to learn about additional career-building resources offered by the NRAEF, including scholarships for college students enrolled in relevant industry programs.

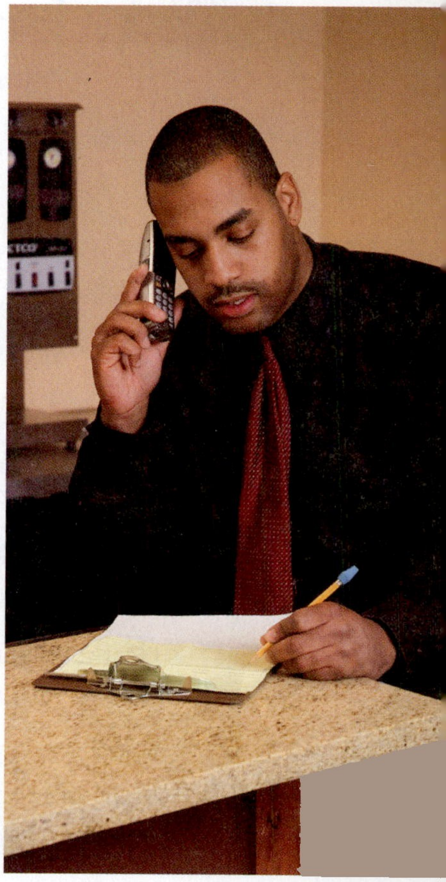

MANAGEFIRST PROGRAM ORDERING INFORMATION

Review copies or support materials

FACULTY FIELD SERVICES
Tel: 800.526.0485

Domestic orders and inquiries

PEARSON CUSTOMER SERVICE
Tel: 800.922.0579
http://www.pearsonhighered.com/

International orders and inquiries

U.S. EXPORT SALES OFFICE
Pearson Education International Customer Service Group
200 Old Tappan Road
Old Tappan, NJ 07675 USA
Tel: 201.767.5021
Fax: 201.767.5625

For corporate, government, and special sales (consultants, corporations, training centers, VARs, and corporate resellers) orders and inquires

PEARSON CORPORATE SALES
Tel: 317.428.3411
Fax: 317.428.3343
Email: managefirst@prenhall.com

For additional information regarding other Prentice Hall publications, instructor and student support materials, locating your sales representative, and much more, please visit *www.pearsonhighered.com/managefirst.*

Acknowledgements

The National Restaurant Association Educational Foundation is grateful for the significant contributions made to this book by the following individuals.

Mike Amos
Perkins & Marie Callender's Inc.

Steve Belt
Monical's Pizza

Michael (Mike) C. Cazel, CSS
Hospitality Safety & Security Services

Heather Kane Haberer
Carrols Restaurant Group

Erika Hoover
Monical's Pizza Corp.

Craig Hudson
Lettuce Entertain You Enterprises

Jared Kulka
Red Robin Gourmet Burgers

Tony C. Merritt
Carrols Restaurant Group

H. George Neil
Buffalo Wild Wings

Marci Noguiera
Sodexo—Education Division

Ryan Nowicki
Dave & Busters

Pen Ann Lord Prichard
Wake Tech/NC Community College

Michael Santos
Micatrotto Restaurant Group

Heather Thitoff
Cameron Mitchell Restaurants

Features of the ManageFirst Books

We have designed the ManageFirst Books to enhance your ability to learn and retain important information that is critical to this restaurant and foodservice industry function. Here are the key features you will find within this book.

BEGINNING EACH BOOK

Real Manager

This is your opportunity to meet a professional who is curently working in the field associated with the book's topic. This person's story will help you gain instight into the resonsibilities related to his or her position, as well as the training and educational history linked to it. You will also see the daily and cumulative impact this position has on an operation, and receive advice from a person who has successfully met the challenges of being a manager.

BEGINNING EACH CHAPTER

Inside This Chapter

Chapter content is organized under these major headings

Learning Objectives

Learning objectives identify what you should be able to do after completing each chapter. These objectives are linked to the required tasks a manager must be able to perform in relation to the function discussed in the book.

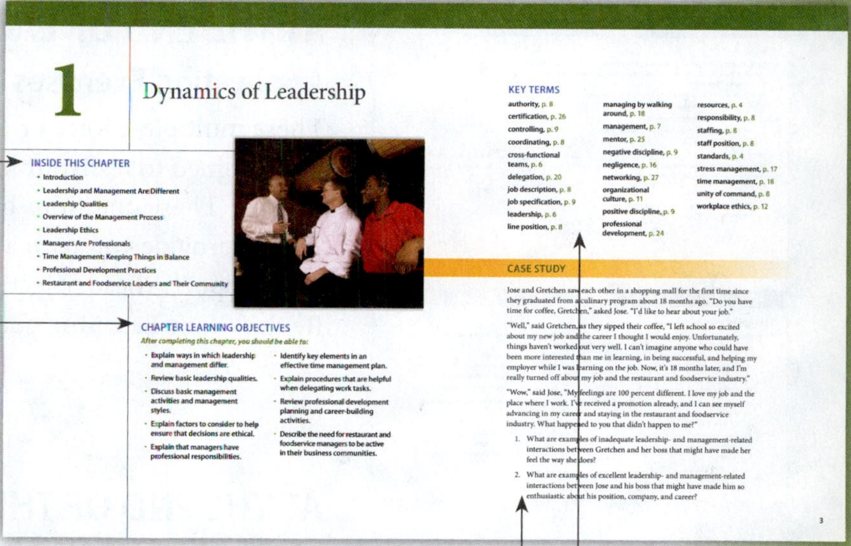

Case Study

Each chapter begins with a brief story about the kind of situations that a manager may encounter in the course of his or her work. The story is followed by one or two questions to prompt student discussions about the topics contained within the chapter.

Key Terms

These terms are important for thorough understanding of the chapter's content. They are highlighted throughout the chapter, where they are explicitly defined or their meaning is made clear within the paragraphs in which they appear.

THROUGHOUT EACH CHAPTER

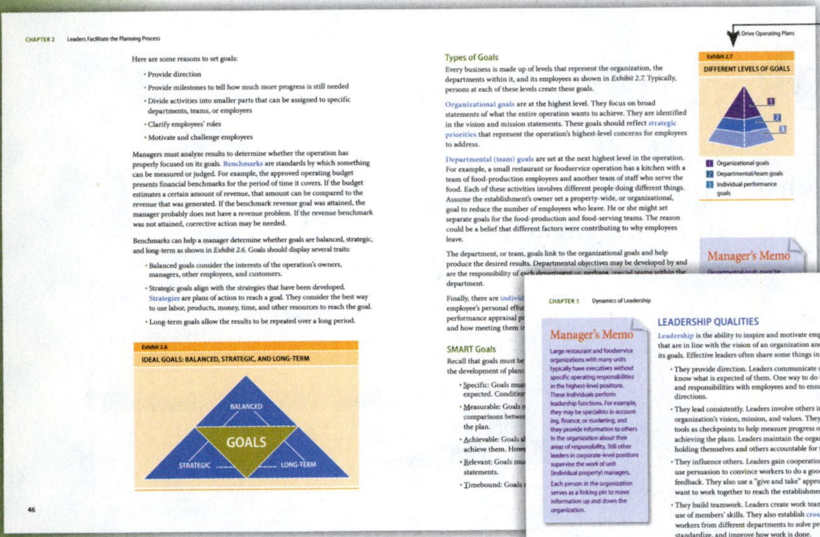

Exhibits

Exhibits are placed throughout each chapter to visually reinforce the key concepts presented in the text. Types of exhibits include charts, tables, photographs, and illustrations.

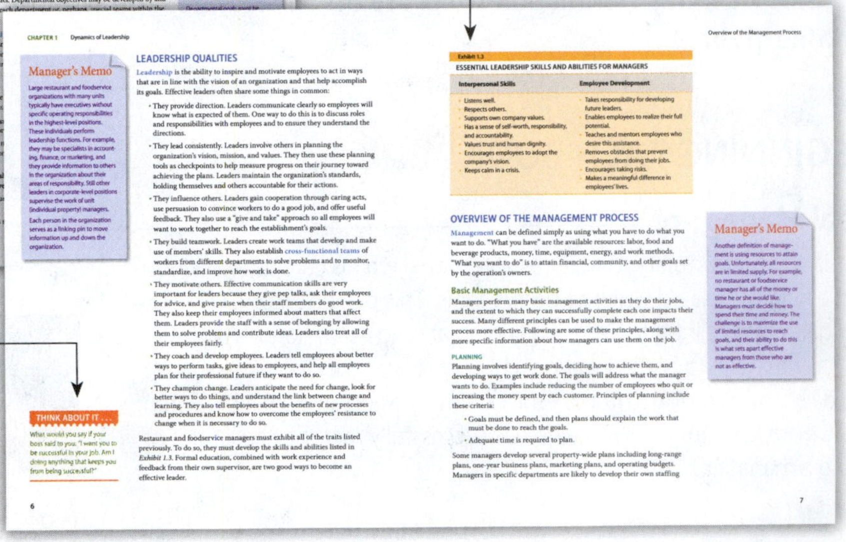

Think About It. . .

These thought-provoking sidebars reveal supportive information about the section they appear beside.

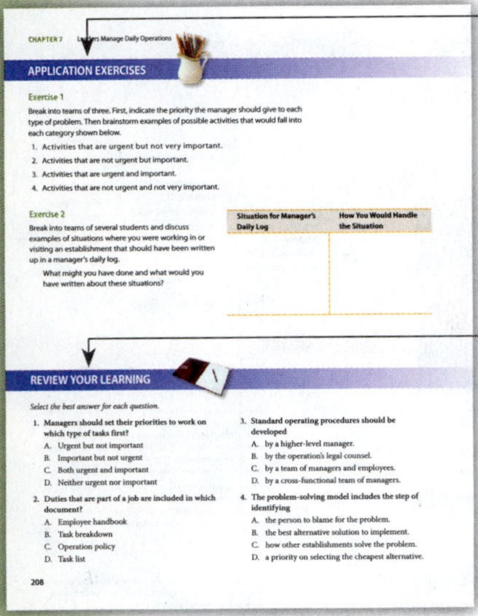

AT THE END OF EACH CHAPTER

Application Exercises and Review Your Learning

These multiple-choice or open- or close-ended questions or problems are designed to test your knowledge of the concepts presented in the chpater. These questions have been aligned with the objectives and should provide you with an opportunity to practice or apply the content that supports these objectives. If you have difficulty answering the Review Your Learning questions, you should review the content further.

AT THE END OF THE BOOK

Field Project

This real-world project gives hou the valuable opportunity to apply many of the concepts you will learn in a competency guide. You will interact ith industry practitioners, enhance your knowledge, and research, apply, analyze, evaluate, and report on your findings. It will provide you with an in-depth "reality check" of the policies and practices of this management function.

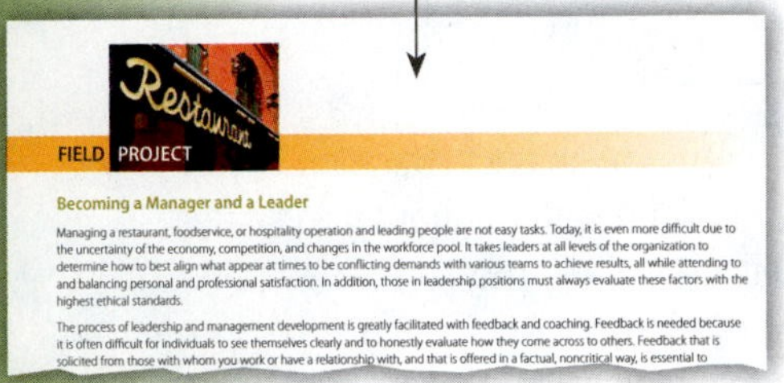

REAL MANAGER

Cain Bassett, FMP

General Manager

Delaware North Companies Inc. Travel Hospitality Services,

Richmond International Airport

Justin Baynes, photographer.

Philosophy: Creating special experiences one guest at a time.

MY BACKGROUND

I grew up in New Orleans, Louisiana, and attended St. Augustine High School and Xavier University. My parents owned and operated Thelma's Restaurant and Bar. As an only child, I spent quite a bit of time with my parents at the restaurant. I can remember wiping down tables, sweeping , mopping floors, and washing dishes as early as seven or eight years old.

Being raised in the restaurant and foodservice business, it was natural for me to pursue this as my dream career. My passion for the business came from watching my parents and seeing the joy and fulfillment they experienced in serving customers.

My first experience as a manager in the industry was actually managing our family business. I quickly learned that the restaurant and foodservice business required dedication, hard work, and a desire to be the best. I have the same attitude about the business today as I had back then.

Believe me, the idea of seeing a business thrive and be successful is a ***real*** adrenalin rush. To play a role in that success is very fulfilling and rewarding. It establishes a sense of pride in a job well done.

MY CAREER PATH

I have worked in all areas of the business—and I do mean all areas! I've been a porter, a dishwasher, a grill cook, a short-order cook, a baking and pastry chef, and an assistant manager. I've worked in marketing and advertising; strategic planning; operations; and multiunit, multiconcept general management. I've worked in the quick-service, casual-dining, and hotel room–service sectors.

I began my professional career in 1978 with Al Copeland Enterprises as an assistant manager of a Popeye's Famous Fried Chicken restaurant. I worked at ACE for over 20 years; the last 10 years were with Al Jr. and his company Spicy Express Inc., rising to the position of area supervisor. During my time there, I was involved in several new concept designs and operational strategies including developing control tools such as sales and labor tracking, sales forecasting, and inventory systems.

Something I always think about: I recall Al Copeland Jr. once telling me that we work on penny profit. *Take care of the pennies and the dollars will take care of themselves.*

Currently, I'm working for Delaware North Companies Inc. Travel Hospitality Services as general manager at the Richmond International Airport (RIC) location. During my time here, I've helped open 10 new restaurants and bars. Having successfully completed management training for national brands such as Applebee's, Caribou Coffee, and Cheeburger Cheeburger, I have been uniquely qualified to lead in this multiunit, multiconcept environment. In 2007 RIC was selected as the first-place winner for highest regards for customer service at a medium-sized airport by *Airport Revenue News* magazine.

Over the course of my career I've attended just about every kind of training you can imagine—from Foodservice Management Professional (FMP), to ServSafe certification, to Dale Carnegie courses, to the Pinnacle Program Series. In addition, I've been through management training programs for a number of national brands, and I'm now a Subject Matter Expert for the National Restaurant Association Educational Foundation.

WHAT DOES THE FUTURE HOLD?

The future appears extremely bright for our industry. As more and more people enter the workforce, dining out and quick-service traffic should continue to thrive. Our business in a way is recession-proof. With most households having a two-family income, dining out or ordering takeout food will become the norm rather than the exception. The challenge is to have a unique quality that sets you apart from the competition.

MY ADVICE TO YOU

This business is not for everyone. The ideal manager should be well grounded in communications and have a strong desire to be successful. Our business requires that you work long hours—10 to 12 hours a day. You must be prepared to work on weekends and holidays and during snowstorms and other acts of nature.

It also requires that you demonstrate a passion for excellence. Great managers are also great listeners and leaders. You must be able to rally your team alongside you to achieve the ultimate goal, which is to "run a perfect shift."

Remember: A career as a manager in the restaurant and foodservice industry can be a memorable and rewarding lesson on how to grow and develop talent. The opportunity exists for you to have a positive impact on the people you manage and come into contact with on a daily basis. As our industry continues to grow, so does the need for capable, qualified managers. We must never forget the business that we are in— "the people business! "

1 Dynamics of Leadership

INSIDE THIS CHAPTER

CHAPTER LEARNING OBJECTIVES

After completing this chapter, you should be able to:

- Explain ways in which leadership and management differ.
- Review basic leadership qualities.
- Discuss basic management activities and management styles.
- Explain factors to consider to help ensure that decisions are ethical.
- Explain that managers have professional responsibilities.
- Identify key elements in an effective time management plan.
- Explain procedures that are helpful when delegating work tasks.
- Review professional development planning and career-building activities.
- Describe the need for restaurant and foodservice managers to be active in their business communities.

KEY TERMS

authority, p. 8
certification, p. 26
controlling, p. 9
coordinating, p. 8
cross-functional teams, p. 6
delegation, p. 20
job description, p. 8
job specification, p. 9
leadership, p. 6
line position, p. 8
managing by walking around, p. 18
management, p. 7
mentor, p. 25
negative discipline, p. 9
negligence, p. 16
networking, p. 27
organizational culture, p. 11
positive discipline, p. 9
professional development, p. 24
resources, p. 4
responsibility, p. 8
staffing, p. 8
staff position, p. 8
standards, p. 4
stress management, p. 17
time management, p. 18
unity of command, p. 8
workplace ethics, p. 12

CASE STUDY

Jose and Gretchen saw each other in a shopping mall for the first time since they graduated from a culinary program about 18 months ago. "Do you have time for coffee, Gretchen," asked Jose. "I'd like to hear about your job."

"Well," said Gretchen, as they sipped their coffee, "I left school so excited about my new job and the career I thought I would enjoy. Unfortunately, things haven't worked out very well. I can't imagine anyone who could have been more interested than me in learning, in being successful, and helping my employer while I was learning on the job. Now, it's 18 months later, and I'm really turned off about my job and the restaurant and foodservice industry."

"Wow," said Jose, "My feelings are 100 percent different. I love my job and the place where I work. I've received a promotion already, and I can see myself advancing in my career and staying in the restaurant and foodservice industry. What happened to you that didn't happen to me?"

1. What are examples of inadequate leadership- and management-related interactions between Gretchen and her boss that might have made her feel the way she does?
2. What are examples of excellent leadership- and management-related interactions between Jose and his boss that might have made him so enthusiastic about his position, company, and career?

INTRODUCTION

Successful restaurant and foodservice operations achieve goals because those in charge are effective leaders and managers. Leaders work with others on their management team to do long-term planning. They must also oversee the work of many employees because the industry is labor-intensive. Computers and machines have not replaced the need for employees to produce and serve food and beverage products to customers.

Restaurant and foodservice leaders must also be effective managers who use basic management principles to meet financial goals without losing sight of required standards. **Standards** are baselines of quality and quantity that can be compared to actual operating results. You can see, then, that the terms *leadership* and *management* relate to different aspects of operating a successful establishment.

Throughout this chapter and book, the term *manager* is used to mean a person at a high level within a restaurant or foodservice organization who directs the work of employees and also manages other nonlabor resources. **Resources** can include food and beverage products, money, time, equipment, energy, and work methods that can be used to reach goals (*Exhibit 1.1*).

Exhibit 1.1

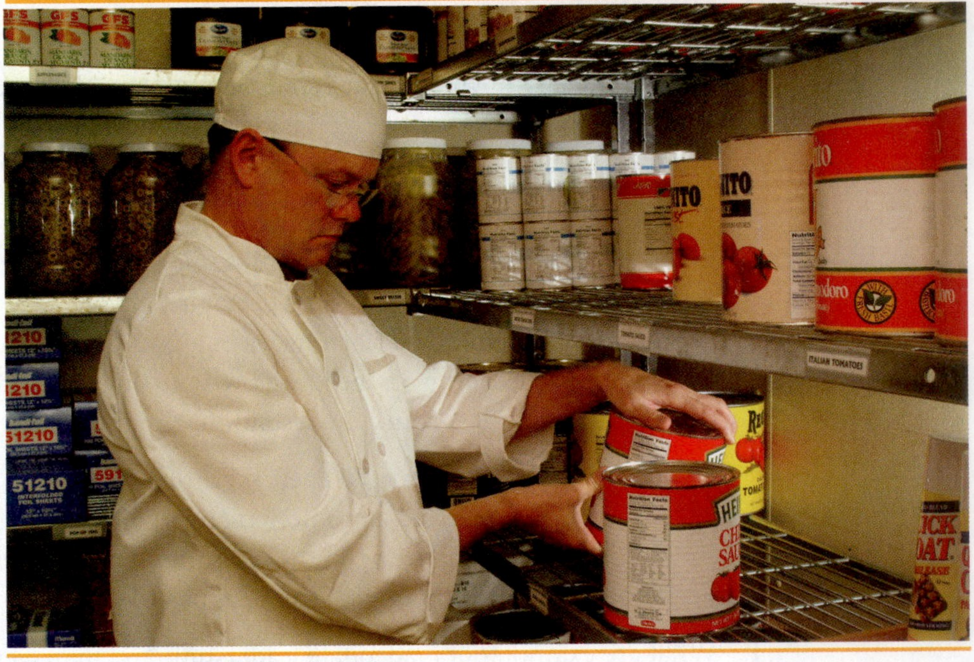

Today's successful managers know how to deal with ethical challenges that occur all too frequently. They do so because they are professionals whose sense of being fair and honest helps them make the "right" decisions when less ethical alternatives exist. The concept of ethics is very important and is discussed later in this chapter.

The best managers also share some additional traits in common with other professionals: They effectively manage time. They know that there are just too many things to do. Managers must do the most important things first. In addition to planning their time, managers must make and implement personal professional development plans. A professional development plan is a schedule or list of training and educational activities. These activities improve their present job skills and knowledge or prepare them for other positions. This enables them to keep up with the fast pace of change in the industry by doing a good job in their present positions or advancing within their careers if they wish to do so.

LEADERSHIP AND MANAGEMENT ARE DIFFERENT

The job of a manager is challenging. A wide range of knowledge and skills are needed to take on the many responsibilities and to perform all of the different tasks that are part of the job. The position requires a person to be both a leader and a manager at the same time. It is useful to address these two different dimensions to understand what is necessary for a manager to be successful. Basically, leadership focuses on the "what" and "why" of the organization, and management deals with "how" these goals can be achieved.

Exhibit 1.2 reviews some of the ways leadership and management differ, and it previews the more detailed discussion that follows in this chapter. It shows that the work leaders and managers do is equally important and essential to the success of the organization. In many cases, restaurant and foodservice operations are small businesses and may not employ executives with a purely leadership role, while other employees handle day-to-day management responsibilities. In most instances, the leader is the manager. As a result, the need to have a "big picture" overview of the business while, at the same time, operating the business is one of the reasons that a manager's job is so interesting and exciting.

Exhibit 1.2

SOME DIFFERENCES BETWEEN LEADERS AND MANAGERS

Component	Leaders	Managers
Goal	Inspire people	Run the operation
Main focus	Lead people	Manage work
Planning responsibility	Develop strategic vision and long-range plans	Develop tactical objectives and one-year plans
Decision making	Facilitate decision making	Make decisions
Problem solving	Create challenges	Solve problems
Employee emphasis	Inspire employees	Manage the employees
Influence on organization	Develop the organization	Maintain the organization
Impact on present situation	Challenge the situation	Accept the situation

Manager's Memo

Large restaurant and foodservice organizations with many units typically have executives without specific operating responsibilities in the highest-level positions. These individuals perform leadership functions. For example, they may be specialists in accounting, finance, or marketing, and they provide information to others in the organization about their areas of responsibility. Still other leaders in corporate-level positions supervise the work of unit (individual property) managers.

Each person in the organization serves as a linking pin to move information up and down the organization.

LEADERSHIP QUALITIES

Leadership is the ability to inspire and motivate employees to act in ways that are in line with the vision of an organization and that help accomplish its goals. Effective leaders often share some things in common:

- They provide direction. Leaders communicate clearly so employees will know what is expected of them. One way to do this is to discuss roles and responsibilities with employees and to ensure they understand the directions.
- They lead consistently. Leaders involve others in planning the organization's vision, mission, and values. They then use these planning tools as checkpoints to help measure progress on their journey toward achieving the plans. Leaders maintain the organization's standards, holding themselves and others accountable for their actions.
- They influence others. Leaders gain cooperation through caring acts, use persuasion to convince workers to do a good job, and offer useful feedback. They also use a "give and take" approach so all employees will want to work together to reach the establishment's goals.
- They build teamwork. Leaders create work teams that develop and make use of members' skills. They also establish **cross-functional teams** of workers from different departments to solve problems and to monitor, standardize, and improve how work is done.
- They motivate others. Effective communication skills are very important for leaders because they give pep talks, ask their employees for advice, and give praise when their staff members do good work. They also keep their employees informed about matters that affect them. Leaders provide the staff with a sense of belonging by allowing them to solve problems and contribute ideas. Leaders also treat all of their employees fairly.
- They coach and develop employees. Leaders tell employees about better ways to perform tasks, give ideas to employees, and help all employees plan for their professional future if they want to do so.
- They champion change. Leaders anticipate the need for change, look for better ways to do things, and understand the link between change and learning. They also tell employees about the benefits of new processes and procedures and know how to overcome the employees' resistance to change when it is necessary to do so.

Restaurant and foodservice managers must exhibit all of the traits listed previously. To do so, they must develop the skills and abilities listed in *Exhibit 1.3*. Formal education, combined with work experience and feedback from their own supervisor, are two good ways to become an effective leader.

THINK ABOUT IT . . .

What would you say if your boss said to you: "I want you to be successful in your job. Am I doing anything that keeps you from being successful?"

Exhibit 1.3

ESSENTIAL LEADERSHIP SKILLS AND ABILITIES FOR MANAGERS

Interpersonal Skills	Employee Development
• Listens well. • Respects others. • Supports own company values. • Has a sense of self-worth, responsibility, and accountability. • Values trust and human dignity. • Encourages employees to adopt the company's vision. • Keeps calm in a crisis.	• Takes responsibility for developing future leaders. • Enables employees to realize their full potential. • Teaches and mentors employees who desire this assistance. • Removes obstacles that prevent employees from doing their jobs. • Encourages taking risks. • Makes a meaningful difference in employees' lives.

OVERVIEW OF THE MANAGEMENT PROCESS

Management can be defined simply as using what you have to do what you want to do. "What you have" are the available resources: labor, food and beverage products, money, time, equipment, energy, and work methods. "What you want to do" is to attain financial, community, and other goals set by the operation's owners.

Basic Management Activities

Managers perform many basic management activities as they do their jobs, and the extent to which they can successfully complete each one impacts their success. Many different principles can be used to make the management process more effective. Following are some of these principles, along with more specific information about how managers can use them on the job.

PLANNING

Planning involves identifying goals, deciding how to achieve them, and developing ways to get work done. The goals will address what the manager wants to do. Examples include reducing the number of employees who quit or increasing the money spent by each customer. Principles of planning include these criteria:

- Goals must be defined, and then plans should explain the work that must be done to reach the goals.
- Adequate time is required to plan.

Some managers develop several property-wide plans including long-range plans, one-year business plans, marketing plans, and operating budgets. Managers in specific departments are likely to develop their own staffing

Manager's Memo

Another definition of management is using resources to attain goals. Unfortunately, all resources are in limited supply. For example, no restaurant or foodservice manager has all of the money or time he or she would like. Managers must decide how to spend their time and money. The challenge is to maximize the use of limited resources to reach goals, and their ability to do this is what sets apart effective managers from those who are not as effective.

plans and employee schedules, training plans, and work area cleaning plans, among numerous others.

> **WHAT'S THE FOOTPRINT?**
>
> Management is a process that will help individuals reach their operation's goals. Plans must be made to help reach those goals. Today's managers understand that concerns about the environment are good for business and should be part of their organization's commitment to be good "citizens" in the community.
>
> Goals that consider the need to "reduce, reuse, and recycle," a slogan used by some environmental groups, can help managers plan for how work will be done and how costs can be controlled. Healthy environmental goals can also influence marketing messages, training program content, and remodeling and construction plans.

ORGANIZING

Organizing is the basic management activity that involves arranging work tasks. Here are some basic organizing principles:

- **Authority**, or formal power, and communication must flow down, up, and throughout the organization.
- Relationships between different organizational levels must be specified. This is frequently done with use of an organizational chart.
- The organization should be designed according to the **unity of command** principle; each staff member should have only one boss.
- Workers in both line and staff positions must be considered. Employees in **line positions** range from the establishment's owner or manager to department heads such as the kitchen or beverage manager to entry-level employees such as servers and bartenders. **Staff positions** refer to technical, advisory specialists such as accountants and purchasing personnel whose jobs are to provide good advice to the actual decision makers employed in line positions.

COORDINATING

Coordinating is the basic management activity that involves arranging group efforts to work together effectively. The following principles help managers let everyone know who is responsible for each job that must be done:

- There is a span of control that suggests the number of employees who can be supervised by one person. Typically, more persons can be supervised when the work is simple and if each worker in the same job performs the same work. By contrast, fewer people can normally be supervised when the work is more complex, and each employee does different work tasks. For example, it is easier for a person to supervise many dish washers than it is for the manager to supervise all of the establishment's department heads.
- Authority should be delegated as far "down" the organization as possible. However, **responsibility** (the obligation that workers have to their own bosses) cannot be delegated. For example, if a manager delegates work to someone, the power needed to perform the assigned work must be given to that staff member.

STAFFING

Staffing involves recruiting new workers, selecting the most qualified candidates, making a job offer, and orienting and training the new employees. Staffing principles are as follows:

- Job descriptions and specifications should be developed for each position and should be kept current. A **job description** indicates the tasks that a person working within a position must be able to perform. A **job specification** indicates the personal requirements needed to successfully do the tasks listed on the job description.

- Effective orientation programs, training for new employees, and professional development programs for all staff members should be in place.

DIRECTING

Directing is the basic management activity that involves supervising the workers. There are two effective principles of directing:

- Knowing how to provide **positive discipline**, or actions that encourage desired worker behavior, and **negative discipline**, or actions that discourage improper worker behavior.
- Varying leadership style, when possible, based on the employees being supervised. Not all employees can be effectively managed with the same leadership style; however, it is sometimes hard for managers to modify their own leadership styles to meet the needs of specific employees.

CONTROLLING

Controlling is the basic management activity that involves determining the extent to which the organization "keeps on track" of achieving goals. Controlling includes these basic principles:

- A formal control process is required. Here is an example of a formal process:

  Step 1: Establish standards (the operating budget estimates that customers will spend $100,000).

  Step 2: Determine actual operating results (the customers actually spent $90,000).

  Step 3: Assess any unacceptable differences (the customers spent $10,000 less than expected).

  Step 4: Take corrective action (develop a program to encourage increased sales).

  Step 5: Determine if the program increased sales.

- Current and accurate operating budgets are required to establish financial performance standards. Budgets are not developed only "because the boss wants it." Instead, they are an important part of a manager's control toolbox and represent a profit plan for the manager.

EVALUATING

Evaluating is the last basic management activity, and it involves determining the extent to which plans are attained. Evaluating principles include the following:

- It must be given a priority. Managers cannot simply evaluate "when they get around to it." Managers must evaluate the extent to which

Manager's Memo

Some managers think controlling involves only physical actions such as keeping beverage storeroom doors locked to prevent theft and portioning food to control costs. In fact, the control process requires a significant amount of planning to establish performance standards and evaluating to assess whether standards are attained. The best managers are able to do a wide range of physical tasks. They can also do all of the many types of office work that requires creative thinking and attention to details.

Manager's Memo

It would be easy and convenient if a manager could manage one activity at a time. Ideally, some time could be spent in planning, such as developing a budget, for example. The manager might help organize procedures in a specific department and then coordinate work efforts between departments. The ideal workday could continue with specific times set aside to staff, direct, control, and evaluate.

Unfortunately, a manager's work is much more difficult. In the real world, the manager must do many things at the same time. For example, managers might (a) plan how all resources can best be used, (b) organize and coordinate work activities and personnel responsibilities between all departments, and (c) make staffing decisions. At the same time, these managers must continue to provide good service to customers, solve employee problems, and make purchasing decisions, among many other tasks.

goals established in basic planning documents have been attained. Examples of basic planning documents include the long-range and one-year business plans, the marketing plan, and the operating budget.

- Employee evaluation is also important, and it occurs when, for example, managers formally assess each worker's performance.

Basic Management Styles

A manager may use different styles of management depending on the situations they face. Four recognized management styles are autocratic, bureaucratic, democratic, and laissez-faire. These are further described in *Exhibit 1.4*.

Exhibit 1.4

DIFFERENT MANAGEMENT STYLES

Management Style	Description	Those for Whom Style Is Most Useful
Autocratic	Characterized by a domineering manager with ultimate authority over employees.	Inexperienced employees performing relatively simple tasks such as busing tables.
Bureaucratic	Characterized by relying on written rules and regulations. Things are always done "by the book."	Employees performing routine work such as bookkeeping.
Democratic	Characterized by treating employees as equals who can contribute to the decision-making process.	Employees who are motivated and experienced in an environment in which cooperation is very important. For example, experienced food servers can work together and help each other keep things going smoothly in the dining room during busy shifts.
Laissez-faire	Characterized by managers who allow employees to do what they want to do.	Consultants and sub-contractors. For example, persons hired to provide pest control services select and apply the chemicals they know to be the best for the specific establishment.

FACTORS INFLUENCING THE USE OF MANAGEMENT STYLES

Factors involved in the specific management style used by a manager include his or her own feelings, personality, knowledge, values, experience, and the types of employees being supervised. Also, the **organizational culture**, or the beliefs, values, and norms shared by workers in the organization that are then passed on to new employees, can influence management styles.

The most effective managers adapt their management style to the situation. Some managers like to delegate work and enjoy involving several employees in a team approach to fixing problems. Other managers like to do things themselves and do not like to interact with employee teams as much. Also, the manager's previous experience and success with a management style usually affects his or her interests in using a basic style or changing it.

The characteristics of the employees being supervised and the type of work being done will likely influence the choice of management style employed. Employees are individuals with different personalities and backgrounds. Some employees will want decision-making responsibility. They will want to help reach the establishment's goals, they will be knowledgeable and experienced, and they will work well under a democratic style. In other situations, less-skilled employees may work better under a more autocratic style.

An establishment's culture, including its traditions and values, can influence the choice of management style because it usually affects a manager's behavior. For example, top-level managers in some establishments stress human relations concerns. Managers in other operations may focus on "bottom-line" financial concerns, even if this reduces the amount of employee participation in decision making. Managers who are most effective are typically those who adopt their organization's unique philosophy and culture.

IMPLICATIONS FOR MANAGERS

How can differing management styles be used in day-to-day operations? First, it is unlikely that a manager would actually use any one of the basic management styles exactly as they were explained in *Exhibit 1.4*. In an ideal work situation, managers would know each employee and understand how each one can best be motivated. Then the manager would use the leadership style that would best create a work environment where motivation can occur.

However, managers are individuals who develop attitudes, beliefs, and personalities based on their own experiences. It is not easy for many managers to learn to use the differing management styles. They can, however, learn about each approach, understand when each might be applied, and try to be flexible as they consider the needs of their employees and differing work situations.

THINK ABOUT IT . . .

Do you think it would be easy to use differing management styles to manage different employees? What impact would high levels of employee turnover have on your ability to get to know your employees?

LEADERSHIP ETHICS

Any discussion of leadership traits and management skills must include ethics. **Workplace ethics** refer to rules of appropriate behavior toward others at work.

Ethics are guiding principles with lasting value that effective leaders use to set the professional tone and conduct in their operations. An individual's ethical behavior is influenced by many factors including his or her cultural background, religious beliefs, personal code of conduct, and personal experiences.

Ethics: A Foundation for Success

Standards of conduct, values, and principles often differ among people. Society, through its body of laws, does not take a position on whether something is right or wrong until it is determined to be illegal. Then, something that is illegal is also judged to be unethical. However, something can be legal (no laws have been broken) but still be unethical. For example, it is legal to share vendors' prices with other vendors and ask for a lower price. However, some managers tell vendors to submit their best price first. They know that many vendors talk to each other in the same way that many managers do. They also know that vendors do not like this practice and may not bid (or submit higher bids) if they do not think the order will be awarded to them.

Manager's Memo

Restaurant and foodservice codes of ethics often include these topics:

- Overview: purpose and goals of the ethics code
- Employees' responsibilities to customers
- Employees' responsibilities to the employer
- Employees' responsibilities to other employees
- Employees' responsibilities to the community and society
- Employees' responsibilities to themselves
- Matters relating to violations of code of ethics

Many operations are guided by written codes of ethics that are designed to remove much of the guesswork about what is right or wrong behavior. These codes act as a safety check to evaluate decisions before implementing them. A code of ethics may include a wide range of topics such as how employees should be treated, statements about employee pay and working conditions, and the use of the organization's resources. Other potential concerns relate to managers favoring relatives who work at the establishment and to providing confidential information to competitors. Still other topics can address acceptance of gifts from vendors and suppliers, conflicts of interest, environmental concerns, and other concerns that impact the operation.

Upholding an organization's code of ethics can directly affect the company's bottom line and profits. Ethical behavior encourages repeat business and a loyal customer base. It is important for establishments to follow a code of ethics because many decisions can directly affect the health and safety of customers, employees, and others. For example, following procedures about holding prepared food safely is one way of behaving ethically. Ensuring that employees wash their hands before preparing food is another action that reflects the ethical principles of managers.

A Closer Look at Ethical Decisions

Here is a list of some basic ethical principles that managers should follow when they make decisions:

- **Honesty**: Do not mislead or deceive others.
- **Integrity**: Do what is right.
- **Trustworthiness**: Supply accurate information, and provide correction for information that is not factual.
- **Loyalty to organization**: Avoid conflicts of interest and do not disclose confidential information.
- **Fairness**: Treat individuals equally; always appreciate diversity.
- **Concern and respect**: Be considerate of persons affected by decision making.
- **Commitment to excellence**: Always do the best job possible.
- **Leadership**: Lead by example.
- **Reputation and morale**: Work to enhance the property's reputation and to improve the morale of employees.
- **Accountability**: Accept responsibility for decisions after they are made.

To determine whether a proposed decision or action is based on sound ethics, a manager should ask the following questions:

- Is the action or behavior legal?
- Will the action or behavior hurt anyone?
- Does the action or behavior represent the company?
- Does the action or behavior make anyone uncomfortable?
- Does the action or behavior show respect for others?
- Have I involved others by asking for their ideas about the situation?
- Is this decision fair?
- Does this decision uphold the organization's core values?
- Would I like to share my decision with my boss, family, or friends?
- Would I like to post my decision on the establishment's bulletin board or report it in the property's newsletter?
- What would others say and think about the details of this decision if it were disclosed to the public?
- Am I confident that my current view of the situation will not change over time?

THINK ABOUT IT . . .

You request a sample of some steaks from a vendor. The vendor provides them, along with "a few more for you to barbeque at your home." Should you accept the samples? Explain.

Effective managers know they are the role models for many behaviors in the establishment, and many employees naturally expect their manager to set the example. Those who consistently see a manager applying proper leadership skills are more likely to want to behave in a similar manner, and the manager's ethical behavior also helps build trust between the manager and his or her staff.

Use of ethical principles to guide decision making allow the manager to merge organizational and personal values as the root for ethical decisions. By consistently using these principles and creating a work environment that emphasizes ethical leadership, a manager can ensure that employees know the importance of making ethical decisions.

MANAGERS ARE PROFESSIONALS

What is a professional? A professional is a person working in an occupation that requires extensive knowledge, skills, and experience. A profession involves membership limited to those with education and experience in a specialized body of knowledge. Membership is usually controlled by licensing, registration, or certification, and is governed by a universal code of ethics.

Successful managers are professionals, and the practice of restaurant and foodservice management requires professionalism. *Exhibit 1.5* shows some characteristics of professional managers.

Exhibit 1.5

CHARACTERISTICS OF PROFESSIONAL RESTAURANT AND FOODSERVICE MANAGERS

Several characteristics describe professional restaurant and foodservice managers:

- Have a positive attitude and pride in themselves and the important work they do.
- Possess the knowledge and skills required to be an expert in their profession.
- Are alert to the need for ongoing education, training, and professional development.
- Contribute 110 percent to help their team meet its goals.
- Are genuinely interested in serving customers.
- Know and consistently attain (or exceed!) their organization's quality and quantity standards.
- Are effective communicators.
- Respect others in the organization.
- Help their employees find pride and joy in their work.
- Follow high ethical standards.
- Admit mistakes and learn from them.
- Follow appropriate personal hygiene and dress standards.
- Have a sense of humor.

More About Professionalism

Professionals are proud of themselves and the work they do. They do their jobs correctly, and they always try to do better and improve their profession in the process. A professional "goes the extra mile," is part of the team, tries to put forth the best possible effort to meet the property's goals, and is truly interested in the employees and customers.

Professional managers know what their own boss expects of them, and they consistently meet, or exceed, these standards. They are effective communicators, and they are concerned about and help resolve problems encountered by other staff members. Professional managers promote mutual respect and understanding between themselves and their employees. Employees should recognize that the boss may not be their friend or "buddy." However, a professional relationship will address job tasks and human relations concerns.

Professional managers know and address what their employees should expect from their employer. A list of some of these expectations is found in *Exhibit 1.6.*

Exhibit 1.6

WHAT SHOULD EMPLOYEES EXPECT FROM THEIR EMPLOYER?

All staff members expect and have a right to expect certain things from employers:

- Fair pay for the work that is done
- Safe working conditions
- Training to meet job standards
- Additional training to maintain performance
- Training that may allow them to be promoted to more responsible positions
- Help ensure that all employees work well together
- An explanation of all policies, rules, and regulations
- A fair evaluation of their work

Managers Must Maintain a Professional Relationship with Their Own Supervisors

It is important for managers to develop a good relationship with their own managers. While much of their communication is with their employees, upward communication with their boss and communication with other managers is also very important.

A manager's discussions with his or her own boss should include discovering what kinds of information the manager wants to share as well as how often to provide it. The type of information needed usually determines its frequency. For example, sales information may be communicated on a daily or weekly basis, while team project goals and results may be shared only once a month.

Effective managers understand the importance of effective communication with their own boss. For example, one strategy may be to set a weekly time to meet with him or her. Topics for discussion can include progress toward operational goals and a review of business performance. They should also ask for feedback about their performance and how they might improve. Before the meeting, they should write down the things they want to share with the boss and the questions they want to ask. These discussion points might become the topics for the meeting. As the boss provides feedback about these topics, the manager must listen attentively and follow up any points with additional questions for clarification.

Exhibit 1.7

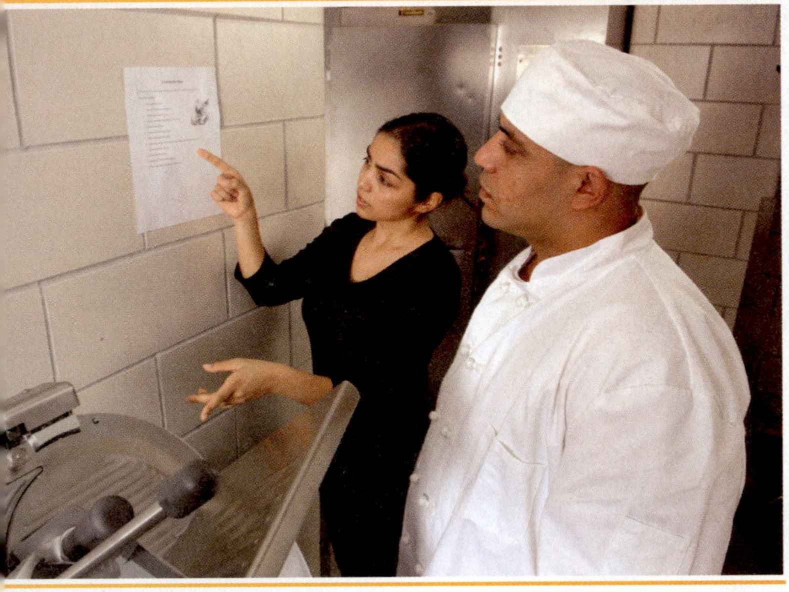

Technical Competence Is Important

Professional managers know that many of the challenges confronting them in their day-to-day work are best met with technical competence. For example, the health and safety of customers and employees are compromised when employees have not been properly trained in the correct food safety practices. This is the responsibility of the manager and his or her team of other managers and supervisors (*Exhibit 1.7*). They are also responsible for attaining financial objectives. In addition to safety and financial concerns, a wide range of other topics are important to managers. They must be knowledgeable about every aspect of their work and develop the appropriate policies and procedures. They must also provide the required training to help all employees consistently meet the operation's quality standards.

Legal Considerations

Legal behavior is determined by the authority of laws, and managers must never overstep the limitations of these responsibilities. Laws protect both employees and customers, and managers and their restaurants can be held legally responsible for their actions. Managers and their employees are expected to perform job duties as they have been taught and as is expected.

No one can be expected to attempt to or carry out a job task for which proper instructions or training has not been provided. **Negligence** is a legal term that indicates a failure to use reasonable care as a manager, and it is grounds for legal action. Professional managers pay attention to details, and they carefully follow each step of written procedures. "Shortcuts" and carelessness are not allowed!

TIME MANAGEMENT: KEEPING THINGS IN BALANCE

Managers must develop and demonstrate leadership and management skills. Doing so many things at the same time can cause intense daily pressures because it often seems that there is not enough time in the day to do everything that must be done. At the same time, everyone recognizes the need for a balance between a manager's professional and personal life.

A manager's professional life can become stressful at times, but there are ways to manage it so that it does not overwhelm other aspects of his or her life. Managers must be able to manage stress, and one way they might do so is by managing time.

Stress Management Concerns

Stress is the emotional and physical strain that a manager experiences when the demands on his or her time exceed that which is available. Stress can be caused by the restaurant or foodservice operation itself and by its employees. Employee-imposed pressures can be created by teams not functioning well, by micromanaging supervisors, and by employees who do not perform up to standards.

Stress can also be self-imposed when, for example, managers try to accomplish too much because they have not set priorities and when they have not developed backup plans for recurring problems such as weather conditions that prevent food deliveries. Self-imposed pressures also occur when managers have unrealistic expectations about what can be accomplished, and when there are communication breakdowns with immediate bosses that yield differences in opinion about goals and activities.

Stress can also be caused by personal factors such as time pressures, loss of a family member, divorce, constant changes, or failure to accept what cannot be changed.

Stress management is a process managers can use to identify what causes them stress in the workplace or in their personal lives. These are some indicators of stress:

- General irritability
- Insomnia (inability to sleep)
- Headaches
- Indigestion
- Pain in neck or lower back
- Changes in appetite
- Changes in sleep patterns

If these indicators appear, managers can try to identify the cause of the stress. One way to identify the cause of stress is to ask these questions:

- Is the stress due to planning or scheduling?
- Are tight timelines causing the stress?
- Is the pressure due to equipment- or facility-related problems?
- Is the pressure related to employee performance?
- Is the pressure being caused by self-imposed, unrealistic expectations?
- Are personal problems interfering with work?

If the causes of stress can be determined, a stress-reduction plan can be designed and implemented, but it will be important for the manager to seek input from people whose opinion he or she values and trusts. These suggestions for coping with and preventing stress can be included in a stress-reduction plan:

- Plan and evaluate daily activities to minimize unanticipated situations.
- Delegate some work to responsible employees.
- Monitor activities by "**managing by walking around**" and by communicating with employees. Managers move around the restaurant or foodservice operation constantly. As they do, they should always be alert to thank employees when they "catch them doing something right." They should correct employees if work is not being done correctly.
- Set realistic goals every day that the manager and his or her team can accomplish.
- Identify company resources, if any, that can assist with managing stress.

Sometimes it is necessary to seek additional help to help deal with stress. Some organizations offer employee assistance programs, stress management courses, and counseling resources to help their managers and other employees deal with stress.

Managers who can effectively balance stress factors are able to maintain a quality of life for themselves that can help to foster the same desired behavior in their employees.

THINK ABOUT IT . . .

What is one thing that you could do to better manage your time? How would that change impact your day or week?

Time Management Concerns

Time management refers to planning and using procedures and tools to increase a person's efficiency and productivity. One critical element in any time management effort is to avoid wasting time on low-priority and unimportant activities.

Although several skills are needed to be an effective time manager, two key skills are the ability to set priorities and to concentrate on one activity at a time. There are other skills needed for effective time management:

- Goal setting
- Planning
- Decision making
- Delegating
- Scheduling

Wise managers are generally aware of all the things they should do during a day, and that allows them to undertake more effective planning, decision making, delegating, and goal setting. This, in turn, enables them to use time more wisely. In contrast, other managers may have good intentions at the beginning of a day and may even write down their plans, but then they allow other things to get in the way.

One way for managers to plan time more effectively is to review the activities they need to complete on a daily or weekly basis and then break these activities into smaller and more controllable tasks. What may appear to be a pile of work that cannot be completed in one day can actually become a manageable flow of work with the most important tasks a lot easier to identify.

After they have created this list of smaller tasks, it is important that they follow through and act on their daily plan. Checking tasks as "done" on their list can provide a real sense of success and motivate them to move on to the next priority. Evaluating how the plans for daily and weekly activities actually worked out is an additional way to improve time management skills.

Many managers use commonly available electronic time management tools to help them organize their time more effectively. However, the principle of planning and then following through on the plan is the same as when a hardcopy personal planner or even a sheet of paper is used.

Time is valuable and not replaceable in a restaurant or foodservice operation. Fortunately, there are ways to schedule time more wisely. The unexpected can happen at any time. When it does, work schedules and productivity can be affected. Experienced managers can anticipate many potential problems and consider them as they develop plans. For example, they may know that the Saturday dinner rush that usually begins about 6:00 p.m. will start earlier than usual if a local college football game ends at 4:00 p.m.

SET PRIORITIES

Some people can keep up with normal workflows and manage anything else with apparent ease. Others are always behind in their work regardless of their best efforts. Most managers fall somewhere between these extremes.

Manager's Memo

You are late for a meeting, and have not had time to say "hello" to the new employee who started today. You must call a sales representative about an equipment item that is under warranty but not working. Also, an employee wants to talk to you right now.

It's 2:00 p.m. You haven't had lunch, and there is a meeting scheduled with your boss about next year's budget at 3:30 p.m. There are a few last-minute changes that need to be made.

You've been told that a regular customer is on the phone with a complaint about last night's dinner, you postponed an employee appraisal session from this morning to this afternoon, and a vendor with an appointment is having her second cup of coffee while waiting for you.

These are all examples illustrating why good time management skills are featured in job descriptions for restaurant and foodservice managers.

Effective managers can do what is expected of them. However, their emphasis on day-to-day activities must be shared with some uninterrupted time that can be used for leadership activities such as developing short- and long-term plans and considering the strategies needed to attain them.

How can they stay focused and find time to address nonroutine activities? One way is to become a time bandit and steal time from other segments of the day. For example, must they attend every meeting to which they are invited? Would a quiet lunch in their office once weekly allow them to be a better planner?

Managers do not need to reinvent the wheel; they can network with others to share ideas and solutions to common issues. Once their plan is in place, they can consider how to make it happen.

Managers should work when they are most productive. If a manager is a morning person, she should start her day early so she can address the most important tasks when she is at her peak. If mornings are not her best time, she should plan her most important tasks for later in the day. If possible, she should adjust her schedule to take advantage of her best work times.

Managers need to recognize that small amounts of time can be used productively. They should not wait for an entire day or week with little else to do before working on a project or long-range goal. They can break the process into smaller, more manageable steps and work on them when a meeting is canceled or when the schedule allows. They should always have a few tasks that they can work on during short free times.

Simple adjustments in how they do things can significantly impact managers' outcomes and reduce daily stresses. It's a matter of time management.

Time management concerns are not always measured by hours or days. Long-term time management is also required for success. Restaurant and foodservice leaders move forward from where they are to envision where they would like to be. That vision provides the direction to set and accomplish goals that might not be considered in the rush of daily job duties.

DELEGATE TO MANAGE TIME

Delegation is the process of assigning authority to employees to do work that a manager at a higher organizational level would otherwise do. It shares authority and entrusts the employees with responsibility to accomplish the tasks that have been assigned to them.

Delegation offers many advantages that include involving the employees more meaningfully in efforts to meet an establishment's goals, improve morale, and help employees reach their full potential.

Managers must ask two critical questions before they delegate: "What activities should, or can, be delegated?" and "To whom should I delegate the activity?"

To answer the first question, a manager should look at the types of activities that might be acceptable for others to do. These tasks seem to be better contenders for delegation than others:

- Fact-finding tasks. The most important parts of problem solving are often to analyze the problem and the alternatives to resolve it. However, managers must typically gather facts before these steps can be undertaken. Can a host summarize information on customer comment cards as an early step in an ongoing effort to address customers' concerns? Can the dining-room manager analyze point-of-sales system (POS) data to look for sales trends?
- Detail work. Time-consuming tasks such as checking dining-room washable flatware inventories (knives, forks, and spoons) to determine if additional purchases are required might be delegated. Perhaps another employee can develop some training materials to supplement a new program that will be implemented in the near future. This will allow the manager to focus efforts on more significant tasks with greater impact on operational success.
- Repetitive tasks. Many routine tasks might be delegated to an employee such as weekly production reports, waste counting and reporting, and sales monitoring. Managers should examine these tasks and determine their suitability to be assigned to employees. Then they need to determine how much training would be required to do so.
- Stand-in tasks. Although managers must attend many important meetings including those to discuss budgets and long-range planning issues, there are likely some other meetings such as those with vendors for routine orders that they might delegate to an employee. This delegation can free up some of their time and also give that employee new ideas about his or her own job growth potential.
- Future job opportunities. One of a manager's key responsibilities is to develop staff, and one way to do so is through delegation. Using the performance appraisal process as a stepping stone, the manager and the employee can determine what possible tasks could be assigned to provide more responsibility or as a stepping stone to management positions.

If a manager determines that a task or project can be delegated, then he or she needs to decide which employee will receive the assignment. The answer to this question is part of the first step in the four-step delegation process:

- Preparation
- Planning
- Implementation
- Assessment and appreciation

Step 1: Preparation

During the preparation phase, the manager must first select the task to be delegated and then clearly define it. Initially, tasks should be fairly simple and straightforward. As an employee develops confidence and skills, tasks can then become more complex.

Exhibit 1.8

The manager might also create a checklist for each task to help make it easy to monitor (*Exhibit 1.8*). Additionally, it will be helpful to outline the results anticipated, resources needed, important information to consider, and the time frame for completion.

Step 2: Planning

The planning phase begins as the manager selects the employee to whom the task will be delegated. These are some factors to consider:

- Does the employee have the qualifications or possess the skills and experience required to accomplish the task?
- What is the employee's availability?
- How much training does the employee need?
- Who would benefit most in his or her development by completing this task?
- Who will contribute most to the operation's productivity if he or she is assigned this task?

The manager should meet with the chosen employee and describe the assignment in detail and outline all the facts and required results. He or she must discuss the resources that will be needed, including other employees, equipment, budget, and additional materials. Any constraints should be identified, as well as how to overcome them.

Another important part of planning for delegation involves determining the level of involvement that the chosen employee can handle. Delegation levels for employees range from the employee waiting to be told what to do and then increasing at various levels of responsibility to an employee who has a high degree of freedom and decision-making authority. (See *Exhibit 1.9*.)

Exhibit 1.9

LEVELS OF DELEGATION

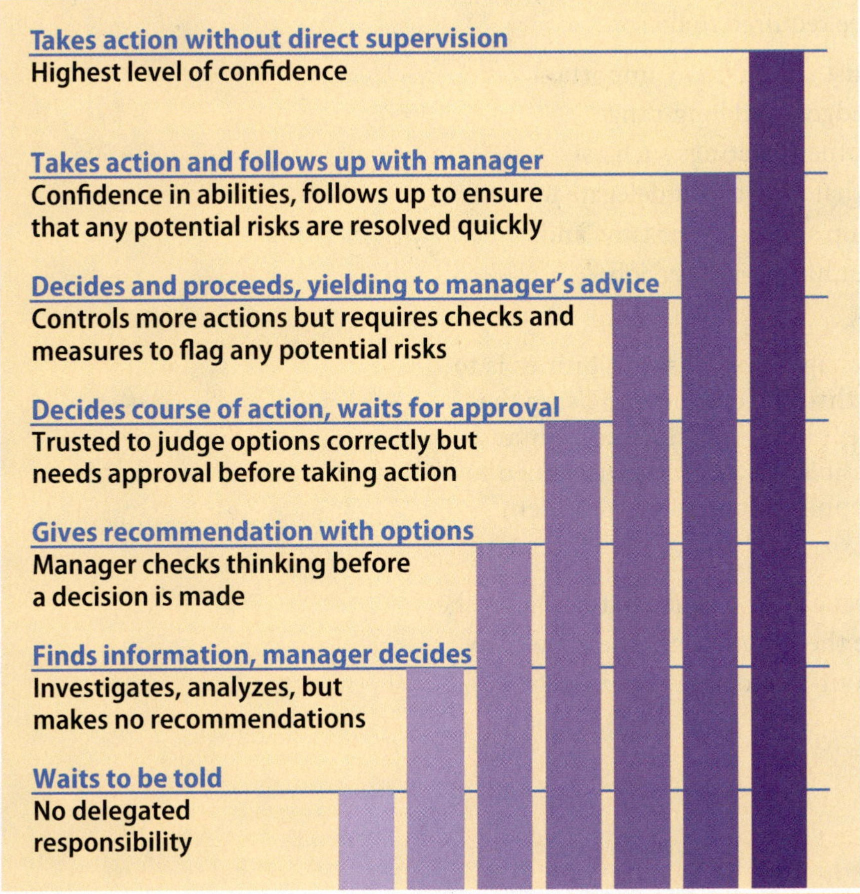
Takes action without direct supervision
Highest level of confidence
Takes action and follows up with manager
Confidence in abilities, follows up to ensure that any potential risks are resolved quickly
Decides and proceeds, yielding to manager's advice
Controls more actions but requires checks and measures to flag any potential risks
Decides course of action, waits for approval
Trusted to judge options correctly but needs approval before taking action
Gives recommendation with options
Manager checks thinking before a decision is made
Finds information, manager decides
Investigates, analyzes, but makes no recommendations
Waits to be told
No delegated responsibility

It is important to discuss the degree of authority the employee will be given to complete the assignment. The manager should also explain why the task is being delegated to the specific person and be sure that all employees who may be affected by the assignment are notified.

Step 3: Implementation

In the implementation phase of delegation the manager assigns the project or task to the employee. As the task progresses, it is important to monitor the situation and discuss any requested adjustments to the original plan. Discussions should include problems or issues and plans to resolve them. Employee feedback, encouragement, and assistance are vital during this phase.

Coaching for employees who still require some direction and support may be necessary, as shown in *Exhibit 1.10.* As a coach, the manager may need to find the balance between telling the employee exactly what to do and offering no support at all.

Exhibit 1.10

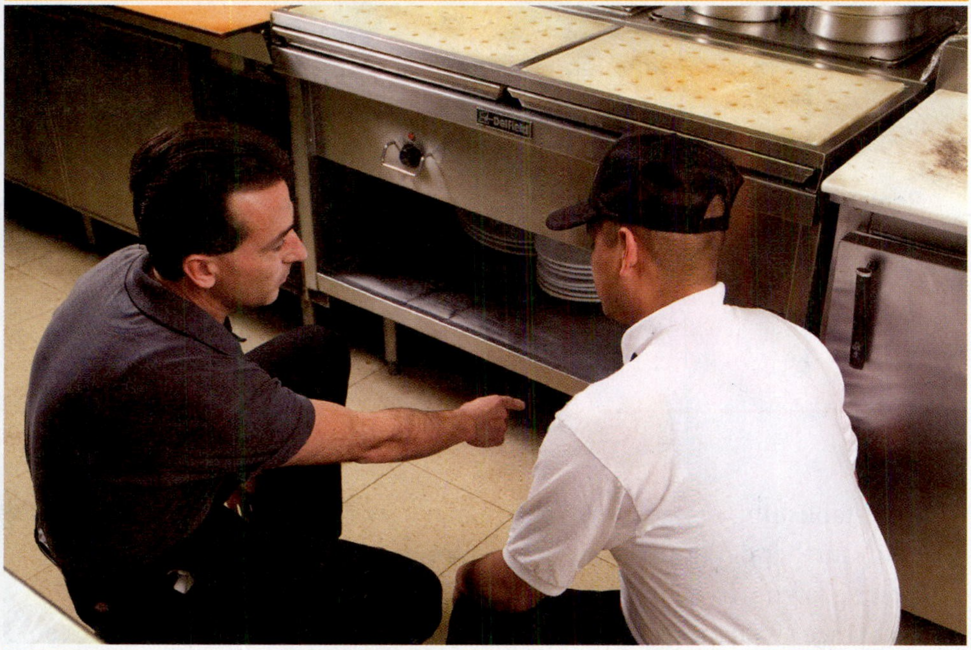

Step 4: Assessment and Appreciation

The final phase of delegation occurs after the task has been completed. A meeting to discuss the results and any lessons learned is important. The manager should thank the employee and acknowledge his or her efforts. Doing so will provide motivation for future assignments and enhance the manager's professional relationship with the staff member.

PROFESSIONAL DEVELOPMENT PRACTICES

As daily tasks become more complex and as the manager acquires more responsibility, he or she will need new knowledge and additional skills to keep pace with these changes. Continuous learning to attain specific career goals is a critical part of a leader's growth.

Professional development is simply the things people do to further their careers. Professional managers consider career advancement goals for 5 or even 10 years in the future. Then they develop plans and take actions designed to reach their goals.

Exhibit 1.11 shows a process to develop and implement a professional development plan.

Exhibit 1.11

IMPLEMENTING A PROFESSIONAL DEVELOPMENT PLAN

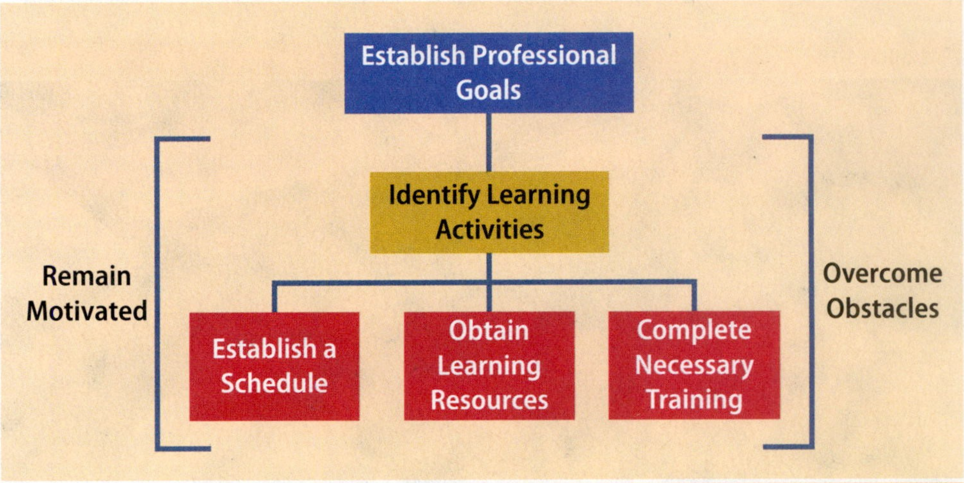

When establishing professional goals, a manager must identify all those goals that will further develop his or her job knowledge and skills and contribute to career growth. To help with goal setting, he or she needs to review past performance evaluations, think about standard or common industry career paths, and talk to other professionals at different organizational levels to obtain advice. The manager must consider what he or she likes to do and does not like to do; not all promotions are beneficial.

The professional goals a manager identifies will most often lead to learning activities that will help him or her reach set goals. He or she needs to research possible learning activities with other professionals, determine which could be useful, and consider the several alternatives mentioned in the remainder of this chapter.

Professional goals can and sometimes do change for personal and professional reasons. Managers should remain flexible and recognize that a review of their career goals and associated learning activities will likely be in order on a routine basis.

A mentor can help them plan career goals and suggest learning activities to achieve them. A **mentor** is someone who can serve as a wise adviser. Ideally, this person will be at a higher position in the company and be willing to serve in this capacity. A mentor can offer insights, serve as a coach, be a sounding board, and provide feedback to the mentee about professional development plans and progress.

Attending continuing education courses through either a local college or university can help a manager remain updated with the latest industry information. Workshops are sometimes offered at conferences that provide continuing education credits as well. These programs may be an important aspect of a manager's professional development program.

Some learning activities such as seeking assistance from a mentor and undertaking special assignments will not cost a manager anything. Others such as attendance at professional meetings; completing residential or electronic training programs or courses; and purchasing leadership, management, and industry-specific books and materials may have associated costs. For these, it will be necessary to determine if the operation's budget includes an allowance for professional development activities. Some operations even grant financial assistance to employees who complete applicable professional development activities.

The most appropriate learning activities should be identified as they consider their goals, budget, and the time they have available to participate. They can then set a priority for the activities based on how well each meets their professional development goals.

It is important to fully participate in and to keep a record of their successful completion of each professional development activity. This information can be used later when seeking promotions, or on their résumé.

Remember that professional goals are not likely to be attained unless an individual is committed to them. The priority that a manager attaches to a plan may be the most important factor in attaining it.

Continuous Improvement Is Essential

Continuous improvement or professional development is essential for success in restaurant and foodservice management, and *Exhibit 1.12* shows many alternatives.

Exhibit 1.12

PROFESSIONAL DEVELOPMENT OPPORTUNITIES

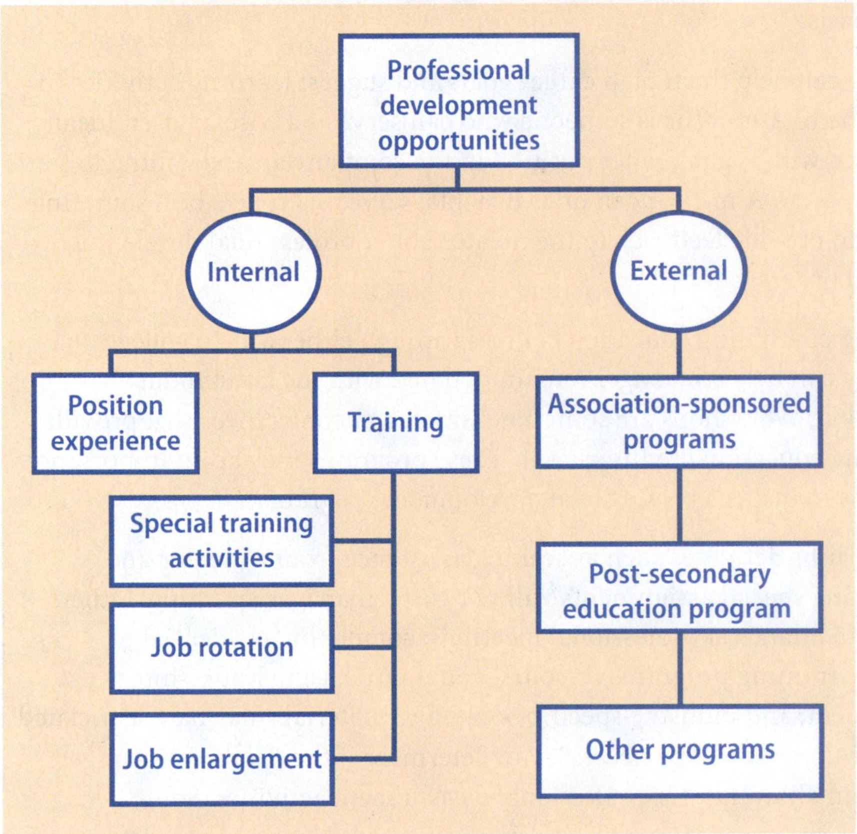

Becoming certified is one key way for a manager to improve himself or herself professionally. **Certification** is a process that requires an individual to demonstrate a high level of skill and to meet specific performance requirements by participating in a rigorous process to become certified.

These are some certification programs for managers in the restaurant and foodservice industry:

- Foodservice Management Professional (FMP)
- ServSafe Food Safety Certificate
- ServSafe Alcohol Safety Certificate
- ManageFirst Professional (MFP) Credential

Certifications are usually administered through professional organizations. Some certification programs require membership in the sponsoring association to become certified while others do not. Many certifications also require work experience as a demonstration of competence in the field.

Membership in professional organizations is another way to remain current with the restaurant and foodservice industry. Weekly or monthly newsletters, workshops, and conferences are just some of the benefits of belonging to a professional organization. The following organizations may be beneficial to join:

- National Restaurant Association (NRA)
- The State Restaurant Association in a person's state
- International Food Services Executive Association
- Women's Foodservice Forum
- American Culinary Federation

In addition, most national organizations have state and local chapters.

Other resources to consider for professional development opportunities include industry publications such as *Nation's Restaurant News*, *Food Management*, *QSR Magazine*, and *Restaurant Business*.

The Internet also provides a wealth of information for restaurant and foodservice management professionals, and it is beneficial to keep up with the ever-increasing variety of electronic resources to further an individual's continuing education.

Remember to Network

Managers must stay connected to their industry, and they can do so, in part, by networking with other industry professionals.

Networking is a process in which several people build relationships to help with career advancement and keep updated about the industry. One method of networking is to attend trade shows and interact with others who are attending. Here are other methods for networking:

- Attending designated networking sessions during conventions, seminars, and conferences
- Participating in community events and sharing information about the restaurant or foodservice operation
- Attending state and local restaurant and foodservice association meetings and social events
- Participating in community career days, forums, charity events, and service projects
- Attending local chamber of commerce meetings
- Volunteering as a community mentor and getting to know key community leaders
- Becoming an active member of a professional restaurant or foodservice organization
- Visiting area competitors and other businesses to establish rapport and identify potential business opportunities

Networking (*Exhibit 1.13*) is also valuable because it helps keep managers current with industry trends. They can develop contacts through memberships in various professional organizations, and they can establish a contact list of peers, vendors, and government personnel.

Exhibit 1.13

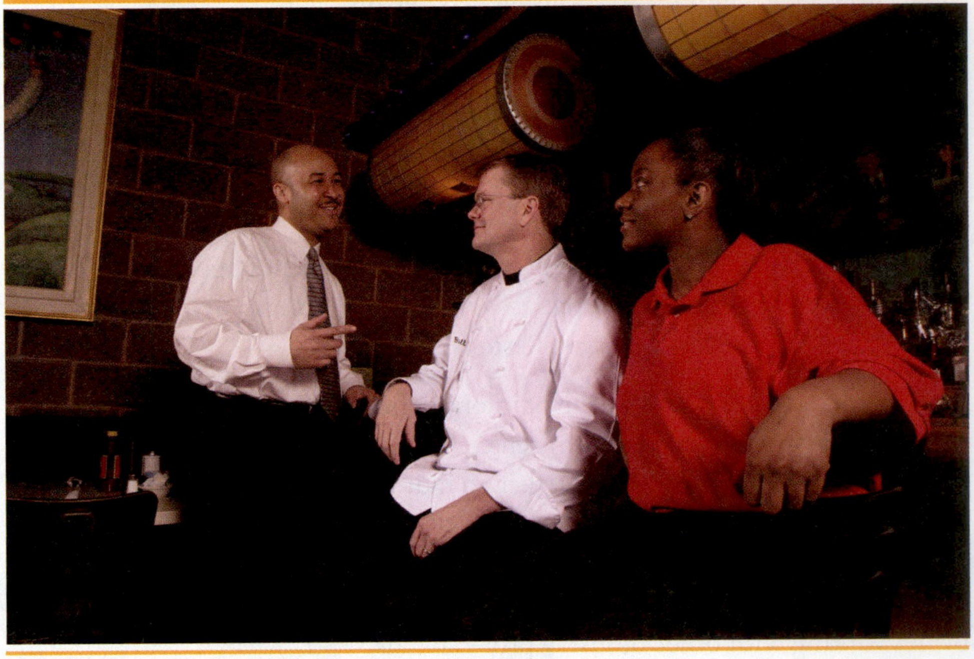

Managers who network can share information, contacts, or opportunities with others in the network and vice versa; for example, they can share best practices with other professionals in their network.

Another networking opportunity occurs when they seek help in dealing with complex problem-solving situations. Colleagues can offer insights and perspectives about challenging situations they may be encountering. This helps them develop a stronger personal relationship that, in turn, can be mutually beneficial to everyone in the network. Networking also promotes important and ongoing conversations within the entire industry.

RESTAURANT AND FOODSERVICE LEADERS AND THEIR COMMUNITY

Professional restaurant and foodservice managers recognize that their business depends on the community in which their property is located. Chances are, many of their customers live in the nearby area, and probably so do most if not all of their employees. They probably purchase most of their food and beverage products and other supplies from businesses in the surrounding area. They know their establishment will be much better off if their community is prospering. Likewise, professional restaurant and foodservice managers are aware that if the local economy is not doing well, if people are moving away, or if there is little community spirit, the operation is not likely to be successful.

For these and related reasons, many managers are active in one or more community-based organizations. When they join these organizations, both their business and the community benefit. Managers can network with other business leaders who share their concerns about creating and maintaining a vibrant community. Membership also gives managers the chance to "give back," share their ideas, and work together cooperatively to help businesses and the community.

Managers Join Community Organizations

Many communities have one or more organizations for business leaders. While they have different names, one common group is a chamber of commerce, which is made up of local organizations with the major objective of promoting interest in local businesses. Membership is voluntary, and this organization is not involved in enforcing local regulations.

Assume that a manufacturing company is considering building a plant in a local area. Chamber members would probably promote this activity. For example, they might work with local government officials to arrange meetings between owners and managers of local businesses and representatives of the manufacturing plant. They might provide tours of the community, answer questions, and "sell" plant officials on the benefits of locating in the community. They might also host the visitors at a meal or banquet function at a local establishment.

Chambers of commerce also promote civic projects. Perhaps they sponsor community cleanup activities or local activities to raise money that will benefit the community. They also represent the business community to local government agencies and provide a "voice" when these agencies consider matters such as taxes, zoning, and other issues of importance to business.

Many communities also have a convention and visitors bureau (CVB). Although they may have other names, the purpose of these organizations is to attract tourists and group meetings to the area. Many businesses including restaurants and foodservice operations and hotels benefit from these visits, and membership in these groups is of great benefit to them.

Managers Participate in Community Groups

It is one thing to join a group and another thing to actively participate in it. Professional restaurant and foodservice managers attend meetings of the community-based organizations to which they belong. They become involved in meetings, participate in the decision-making process, and may even serve on committees or hold office within the organizations.

Manager's Memo

The basic principles of management apply in all businesses. For example, managers in every successful business must plan, organize, staff, direct the work of employees, control resources, and evaluate operating results. While specifics are different, the same basic management principles apply.

Managers should recognize that there is much they can contribute to community-based organizations with members who share their concerns and challenges. The networking that results can benefit everyone.

You have learned that restaurant and foodservice managers do a wide range of different things. Now you are learning that they must also be active in activities outside the operation. Professional managers know they cannot wait to become active in their local business community until they have time or get around to it. They must instead set priorities, manage time, and always do the most important things.

> **Manager's Memo**
>
> Managers join community organizations because doing so benefits their operation and the community. Knowledgeable managers can provide much information and many creative ideas that can help these groups address common problems.
>
> At the same time, the operation can benefit because committees within the groups may have meetings at the establishment. Business leaders may recommend the establishment to others as a venue or an employer.
>
> What are other possible benefits of a restaurant or foodservice manager joining a civic organization?

Their membership and participation in these groups helps build relationships that benefit both the restaurant or foodservice operation and the organization.

Community-based groups often tackle tough questions as they decide what is best for the community and the businesses in it. Since membership is diverse, there may be different opinions about the best course of action. For example, candidates for local or regional elected office may differ on important issues that affect businesses. Members of the organization may then want to consider which, if any, candidate they want to endorse for the office.

Managers should use the same approach in addressing problems posed by these organizations that they use in their own property: help generate alternatives, evaluate them, and decide the best course of action to take. Often there will be agreement; sometimes there will not. Managers should try to take a big-picture view and, whenever possible, think about what is best for the community. In the long run, this approach is better than any other because as the community benefits, so will the operation.

SUMMARY

1. **Explain ways in which leadership and management differ.**

   Leadership focuses on the "what" and "why" of the organization, and management deals with the "how" that is needed to achieve the "what" and the "why."

   Leadership involves long-term planning and directing the work of employees. Management activities involve shorter-term and often day-to-day activities to meet financial goals without losing sight of required standards. Both leadership and management activities are required to operate a successful establishment.

2. **Review basic leadership qualities.**

   Leadership involves inspiring and motivating employees to act in concert with the establishment's vision and to attain its goals. Effective leaders provide direction, lead consistently, influence others, and foster teamwork. They also motivate, coach, and develop their employees and they are the champions of change within their organization.

3. **Discuss basic management activities and management styles.**

   Management is a process that involves several activities. Managers plan in order to define goals, determine how to achieve them, and develop ways to get work done. They organize as they develop and group work tasks, and they coordinate when they arrange group efforts in an orderly manner.

   Managers staff as they implement human resources tasks such as recruiting applicants, selecting qualified candidates, making job offers, and orienting and training staff members to their new positions. The management task of directing involves supervising employees, the task of controlling involves determining the extent to which the organization "keeps on track" of achieving goals, and the task of evaluating addresses whether plans are attained.

Managers can use several management styles based on the situation and the employee involved. The best managers vary their management styles based on the situation.

4. **Explain factors to consider to help ensure that decisions are ethical.**

Managers must determine that proposed decisions are legal and will not hurt anyone. Other factors include determining if the proposed decision best represents the company, will make anyone uncomfortable, and whether their decision will convey respect for others.

Other factors may include the need to involve other persons and to ensure that the decision is fair and upholds the organization's core values. Finally, decision makers can ask themselves if they would like to make their decisions public and whether their view of the situation may change over time.

5. **Explain that managers have professional responsibilities.**

Professional managers share many characteristics with other professionals. They are concerned about doing their job as well as they can and trying to improve their profession in the process. They also understand the need to meet the reasonable expectations of their employees and supervisors.

6. **Identify key elements in an effective time management plan.**

Managers should review activities that need to be completed, set priorities for those that are most important, and develop a daily plan to work on priority activities before doing others. Managers can also evaluate the success of their planning efforts to determine if their time management skills require further improvements.

7. **Explain procedures that are helpful when delegating work tasks.**

A four-step delegation process is helpful. First, in the preparation phase, the manager should select the task to be delegated and determine how it will be monitored. Next, planning is needed to select the employee to whom the task will be delegated. Details of the task should be discussed with the employee, and procedures for determining the employee's level of involvement must be determined.

During the implementation phase, the task is assigned, and the manager monitors the situation as necessary to address any problems. Finally, the assessment and appreciation phase allows the manager to discuss the results, process, and lessons learned as well as provide a sincere "thank you" for a job well done.

8. **Review professional development planning and career-building activities.**

Steps in developing a professional development plan include establishing professional goals, identifying learning activities, establishing a schedule, obtaining learning resources, and completing necessary training.

Continuous learning and improvement are critical for managers to develop into effective leaders. Memberships in professional organizations and certifications are essential in a management's development, as are continuous education courses and workshops. Other sources of industry information can be found in industry magazines and on the Internet.

9. **Describe the need for restaurant and foodservice managers to be active in their business communities.**

   Establishments and the community benefit when the manager is active in civic organizations such as the chamber of commerce and convention and visitors bureau. Managers who actively participate can provide advice to numerous organizations, and the networking that results can provide helpful information and even new business for their properties.

APPLICATION EXERCISE

Your work will be an important part of your life and, hopefully, you will enjoy it. Knowledge of your strengths and personal attributes, or characteristics, can help suggest the types of positions for which you might be most suited.

Explore your personal interests by completing the following exercise:

PART I

List the top three things you do well. These are your strengths.

PART II

Use a chart like the one shown to answer the questions.

Personal Attributes (Characteristics)	How Does This Attribute Help You Do Well?
What are your greatest skills?	
What are your greatest strengths?	
About what do you have the greatest knowledge?	
For what do you have the greatest aptitudes (natural abilities)?	
What things in life do you most highly value?	
What are your interests? (What do you most like to do?)	

PART III

What positions in restaurant and foodservice operations would be of most interest to you based on the previous information. List two to three positions, and then explain what you might enjoy most about each position. Explain your answers.

REVIEW YOUR LEARNING

Select the best answer for each question.

1. **Which activity best describes the primary role of a leader?**
   A. Solving problems
   B. Managing work
   C. Inspiring people
   D. Developing objectives

2. **Cross-functional teams are made up of persons from different**
   A. positions within a department.
   B. departments in the organization.
   C. management levels in the organization.
   D. properties in the organization.

3. **Which is a basic management activity?**
   A. Planning
   B. Coaching
   C. Orienting
   D. Disciplining

4. **A code of ethics is used in an establishment to**
   A. guide decision making.
   B. terminate employees.
   C. promote teamwork.
   D. increase profit.

5. **Which statement is correct about professional managers?**
   A. They should be "buddies" with their employees.
   B. They should use the same management style in all situations.
   C. They know what their employees expect from their employer.
   D. They do not need to be technically competent if their employees can perform required tasks.

6. **Which can help minimize work-related stress?**
   A. Work longer hours to complete all tasks.
   B. Delegate some work to responsible employees.
   C. Focus on customer problems, not employee problems.
   D. Place all blame on incompetent employees.

7. **It is appropriate for a restaurant or foodservice manager to delegate work when**
   A. the manager feels the task must be done correctly.
   B. the task is repetitive and easily mastered.
   C. the manager finds the work unpleasant.
   D. the task requires complex action.

8. **Which can help a manager develop an effective professional development plan?**
   A. Plan to accept any position that is available at a higher organizational level.
   B. Ask the boss what positions require the least amount of time at work.
   C. Determine which positions pay the most money.
   D. Review past performance evaluations.

9. **Learning activities for professional development should be those that**
   A. are least expensive.
   B. require the shortest amount of time.
   C. are related only to the employee's current position.
   D. will contribute to professional knowledge and skills.

10. **When managers help civic groups make decisions, their priority should be what is best for their**
    A. customers.
    B. employees.
    C. community.
    D. operation.

2 Leaders Facilitate the Planning Process

INSIDE THIS CHAPTER

- Introduction
- A Close Look at the Planning Process
- Set the Course of the Operation
- Goals Drive Operating Plans
- Identify Goals with SWOT Analysis
- Develop Operational Goals and Plans
- Leaders Implement Effective Plans

CHAPTER LEARNING OBJECTIVES

After completing this chapter, you should be able to:

- Explain basic principles of planning, with an emphasis on how employees can assist, and procedures useful in managing planning information.
- Describe how a value statement, vision statement, and mission statement are developed and implemented.
- State the importance of SMART goals in the planning process.
- Review procedures for conducting a SWOT analysis.
- Identify how restaurant and foodservice managers use long-range, business, and marketing plans and operating budgets, and explain the relationship among these planning tools.
- Explain the need to consider employees' abilities and to use an organized process in implementing effective plans.

KEY TERMS

benchmark, p. 46
business plan, p. 50
core value, p. 41
departmental (team) goal, p. 47
employee turnover rate, p. 48
income statement, p. 52
individual performance goal, p. 47
long-range plan, p. 49
marketing plan, p. 51
operating budget, p. 52
organizational goal, p. 47
SMART goal, p. 47
stakeholder, p. 43
strategic priority, p. 47
strategy, p. 46
SWOT analysis, p. 48
value, p. 38
value statement, p. 41

CASE STUDY

"I just attended a workshop about developing and implementing restaurant plans," said Sheila. "It was conducted by a retired person who operated several very successful restaurants around the state." Sheila was the general manager of the Pineville Restaurant, and she was talking to Jarrod, the dining-room manager.

"In one way, the speaker made sense, and I can see how planning can help ensure we spend time on priorities. On the other hand, the speaker probably had lots of people in his restaurants who did the real work so he could spend time planning."

"You know," said Jarrod, "we've been talking about planning in one of my college hospitality classes, and the teacher also makes planning sound reasonable. I just don't know how managers have time in the real world to get beyond solving all their daily problems."

1. What would you say to these managers who seem to want to plan but do not know where to find the time?
2. Assume Sheila and Jarrod decided to begin some planning activities. What is the first thing you would suggest they do? Why?

INTRODUCTION

There is a saying, "If you don't know where you're going, any path will get you there." This idea is a good way to begin a chapter on planning. It is easy to say that restaurant and foodservice managers must develop plans and then use their available resources to reach them. It is another thing, however, for some managers to find the time to plan because they are so busy "putting out fires," some of which might have been avoided if plans were in place. Still other managers believe their experience will lead them to success without spending time on planning.

Professional restaurant and foodservice managers do not think this way. Instead, they recognize that success is best ensured when they think carefully about and develop operating plans. They use many principles as they "plan their plans" and as they "work their plans."

This chapter discusses how vision statements and mission statements chart the course for all planning. It also focuses on other planning tools: long-range plans, business plans, marketing plans, and the operating budget.

Leaders must establish goals as part of these plans. They need to understand different types of goals and why they are important.

One of the keys to successful leadership is to involve employees in matters that affect them, as shown in *Exhibit 2.1*. They will be the people who do the work required by plans, so their input can be very useful.

Many restaurant and foodservice managers use a planning method called SWOT analysis. SWOT stands for Strengths, Weaknesses, Opportunities,

Exhibit 2.1

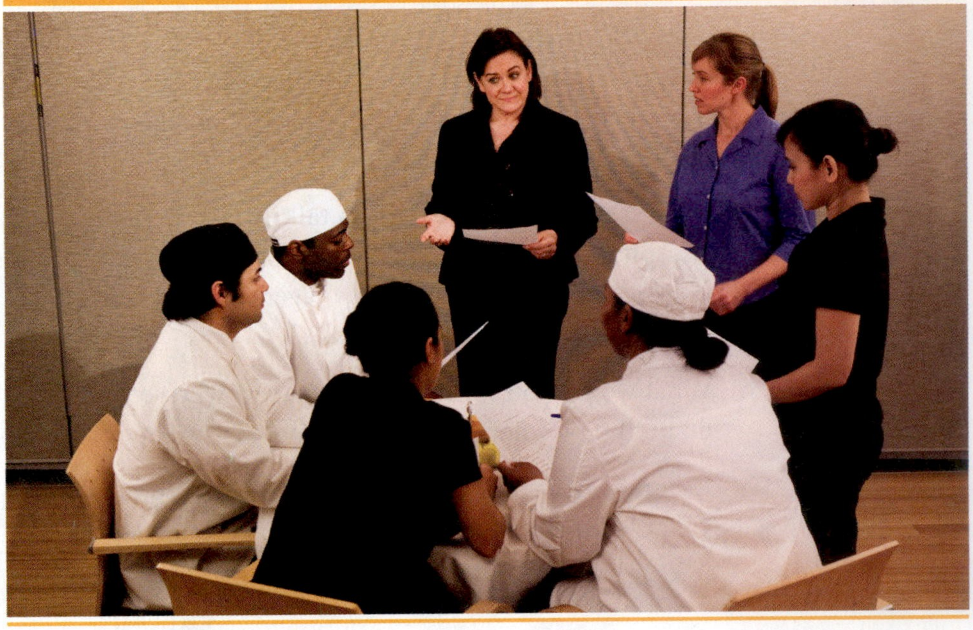

and Threats. When these issues are carefully considered, goals and plans can be developed to maximize the establishment's strengths, capitalize on opportunities, and overcome problems created by weaknesses and threats.

Some operations' teams spend a lot of time developing plans and related goals but much less time implementing procedures to reach them. However, the work really begins once goals are established. The reason can be stated by changing the first sentence in this introduction: "When you know where you are going, you can take the right path to get you there."

A CLOSE LOOK AT THE PLANNING PROCESS

Recall from chapter 1 that planning is a process used to determine goals, decide how to achieve them, and develop ways to get work done. The planning process itself is not especially difficult. It does, however, take time and require creative ideas. It also benefits from suggestions made by members of the operation's team who want to join in the process.

Planning Basics

Several planning principles should be used to ensure the process will be productive:

- Goals first must be defined, then work tasks may be designed and assignments made to reach the goals.
- A formal planning process is needed. This process and several types of plans are discussed later in this chapter.
- All information required for effective planning must be available. While this principle may be obvious, some managers think they protect their position of power by controlling access to information.
- Planning must be done at the right organizational level. One reason is that the required information is more likely to be available. Also, staff members closest to the situation the plan addresses are best able to develop the plan. For example, managers with food-production duties are likely to have many ideas about increasing kitchen productivity but fewer ideas about reducing total costs when the budget is developed. That responsibility rests with the manager and all of the department heads.
- Those affected by plans should help develop them. This principle is related to the preceding principle. If a new work process is being planned, suggestions from the employees who actually do the work can be very helpful. Also, they are more likely to want to use the revised method because it will come from them and not just their managers.

- Necessary resources must be committed to follow up. Planning can often lead to results that require the purchase of new equipment or services such as advertising. Effective planning takes time, and time is valuable. The time spent planning will be wasted if plans are not fully implemented because of cost.

Employees Can Help with Planning

Committed employees want to be involved, and they can help develop plans. Think about a manager's interest in being involved in work decisions and plans that affect him or her. Would the manager want to help if he or she knew the boss respected and valued his or her ideas? Would the plans be better if the manager's ideas were requested and used when appropriate? Would the manager feel important if he or she were asked to help with some planning tasks?

The manager probably would appreciate opportunities to become involved. Those he or she supervises would probably feel the same. Fortunately, there are many ways employees can help with planning.

An operation's basic planning tools include mission statements and budgets. In many establishments, department heads and others develop plans for the operation as a whole. Then, each department or work team develops plans for their area to help the establishment reach its goals.

Entry-level employees can participate in department planning sessions. Their managers will likely benefit from learning employees' ideas about topics like these:

- What can our department do to better serve our customers, or to support the employees who serve the customers?
- What can we do to reduce costs without reducing quality?
- How can we help the operation generate more money while providing value to our customers? **Value** is the relationship between what is paid for something and the quality of the product or service that is received.

Managers can use brainstorming in planning sessions to learn employees' ideas. Brainstorming, as shown in *Exhibit 2.2*, is a method for solving problems in which all group members suggest possible ideas.

When employees help develop the operation's plans, they can begin to align with them and help implement them. Their ideas to make plans work can be of great benefit to managers.

In some establishments, few employees beyond those in management positions understand how their manager decides what is expected of them or what the operation's goals are. All employees should know how their work relates to the short- and long-term goals of their establishment and department. This is easy to accomplish, and it is among the most important responsibilities of every restaurant or foodservice manager.

Manager's Memo

Professional restaurant and foodservice managers know the benefits when employees are committed to the operation. This commitment requires a history of mutual respect between managers and employees. Not surprisingly, this respect must be earned. It evolves over a long period as managers provide opportunities for employees to succeed and reward them for doing so.

When employees are respected by their manager, they enjoy their job more, and they are motivated to do things that benefit the operation. When they are asked to help develop plans, employees recognize that their manager thinks they are important, values their ideas, and needs their help to make the operation successful. Then employees can find pride and satisfaction in their work and make a strong contribution to their team.

Exhibit 2.2

Managing Planning Information

Restaurant and foodservice managers cannot develop effective plans unless they have information to assist with decision making, and ideas about how the information impacts the current and future situations. They must also have creative ideas about how the situation can improve to benefit the operation.

Current and accurate information is the foundation for successful planning. The best managers do not wait until planning begins and then collect as much information as quickly as they can. Instead, they collect four types of information as a routine part of their job:

- **Information about the operation itself:** Restaurant and foodservice managers should talk to their customers to learn their viewpoints. Available marketing information should also be used.

  Revenue is the money generated from the sale of products and services to customers. Operating information about the establishment's revenue and costs is generated for other purposes. These details can be collected to help with planning. Also, available employee information will be useful.

- **Information about the community:** Restaurant and foodservice managers should know about local business conditions and employment rates. This information affects customers' spending habits and the types of employees available. Knowledge of expected population changes, road construction and traffic patterns, and local laws that impact businesses is important. Managers can join other business leaders in groups such as chambers of commerce and can read community newspapers to learn this type of information.

- **Information about the restaurant and foodservice industry:** Local and regional information can be obtained by participating in local and state restaurant associations and other professional groups. Reading industry-related magazines and newsletters can also be helpful for keeping up with industry trends.
- **Information about state, national, and international events:** Remember times when the global recession affected everyone? Even the smallest local business is impacted by what happens around the world. Newspapers and magazines, and news that is constantly updated on electronic media, are among the sources that managers can use to keep up with current events.

THINK ABOUT IT . . .

Managers are very busy. However, keeping up with the news has a direct benefit in their job. What are some examples of news events that might impact a restaurant or foodservice operation?

Reviewing information from external and internal sources is only the first step in managing it. It is important to determine how the information may impact business operations. The restaurant or foodservice manager will have ideas about this, and the management team will likewise have opinions.

People with different backgrounds often have different ideas about what information means. The best plans are often developed from an analysis of available information from different points of view. For example, knowing a foreign airline will begin serving a community may seem to be of no interest to one member of the planning team. However, another member may recognize a possible new market of visiting tourists wanting to sample the operation's unique cuisine.

Restaurant and foodservice managers recognize the benefits of brainstorming about the meaning of available information and using the results in the planning process. A manager's planning goal should not be to "get it over as soon as possible so I can go back to work." Instead, it is important to use time management, interpersonal, and decision-making skills to make the best use of information. The computer-related expression "garbage in, garbage out" applies here. Poor or insufficient information, combined with managers who do not really care, yield plans that were not worth the time or effort to develop.

Exhibit 2.3

No plan can be perfect even if it is based on excellent information. There are always surprises that even the best planners cannot know about. Some managers say that this is what makes the job so interesting.

The best plans do need to be updated and maybe even revised completely at some point. For example labor schedules, shown in *Exhibit 2.3*, are plans that may need to be revised hourly, while operating budgets should be revised when the actual situation changes from what was assumed. However, this not-so-perfect situation is the reason for developing plans, not the reason to avoid planning.

SET THE COURSE OF THE OPERATION

Restaurant and foodservice managers can use a proven "recipe" for success as they move their operation ahead by developing plans and reaching goals. That recipe is made up of several planning tools that are similar to ingredients. Like recipes, planning requires some ingredients to be used before others.

The first three planning tools are the operation's value statement, vision statement, and mission statement. They are the foundation for what the restaurant or foodservice operation will be, and they drive the development of other planning tools. The remaining tools then help managers and their teams determine what they must do every day to move toward what these statements say the business wants to be.

Value Statements

Value statements are a set of standards that guide restaurant and foodservice operations, and they are the foundation for developing the vision statement and mission statement. Value statements help shape the attitudes of the operation's team and define acceptable and unacceptable employee behavior. Value statements reflect the establishment's **core values**: key elements of operation that indicate the most basic reasons the business exists. Core values are typically based on the ideas of respect, caring, responsibility, and honesty, as in these examples:

- Extraordinary customer service
- High-quality, healthy food
- Respect for employees and customers
- Help to the community
- Respect for customers' opinions
- Quality as the highest goal
- Fair treatment of all employees
- Recognition of valuable employee contributions
- Help to employees in developing personally and professionally
- High-quality products and services as a result of teamwork

Value statements guide an establishment's operation by influencing its vision and mission.

THINK ABOUT IT . . .

Some managers focus only on making money. Others believe you cannot make money unless core values drive the business. Money comes as a by-product of values that emphasize customers and employees. What do you think?

Vision Statement

An operation's vision statement is based on its value statements and describes what an establishment wants to become and why it exists. Vision statements aim high and are inspiring. A vision statement is usually expressed in a grand way and uses words or phrases like these:

- Exceeds
- Excels
- Delights
- Puts customers first
- Is extraordinary
- Gets it right the first time

THINK ABOUT IT . . .

"Without a vision, an establishment has no reason to exist." This statement suggests that a vision statement is central to an operation's purpose. Do you agree? Why or why not?

Remember that the operation's vision statement represents its core values. An example of a vision statement that reflects the core value of superior customer service is: "An elegant restaurant where extraordinary service always exceeds the customers' expectations."

After the operation's vision statement is developed, its mission statement can be addressed.

Mission Statement

An operation's mission statement refines its vision statement by stating the purpose of the organization to employees and customers. It tells, in a general way, what the establishment wants to do and how it wants to do it. In other words, it is a guideline to help managers make plans and to guide the decision-making process.

The mission statement should include the target market, products and services, and sometimes the geographic region. One benefit of a mission statement is that it provides a foundation to guide the actions of the managers and their employees.

A well-written mission statement communicates what the operation is striving to do each day. It needs to be clear and concise. Here is an example of a mission statement for a fine-dining establishment:

"The Harbor Bay Restaurant will provide the highest-value dining experience for community residents and business travelers by consistently offering high-quality food served by knowledgeable, friendly staff in clean and relaxing surroundings."

In short, a value statement documents the operation's core values, the vision statement defines what the operation wishes to be, and the mission statement explains how the operation intends to meet its value goals and vision.

Creating the Vision and Mission Statements

Creating a vision and a mission statement requires help from all **stakeholders**: the persons who affect or are affected by the establishment. Stakeholders include owners, managers, supervisors, employees, and customers. The steps in *Exhibit 2.4* show how a restaurant or foodservice team can develop vision and mission statements that will serve as a solid foundation for the business.

Exhibit 2.4

STEPS TO CREATE A VISION AND A MISSION STATEMENT

1. Use the operation's core values to consider its purpose and think about the desired direction for the business.
2. Organize a team of interested persons to discuss general ideas.
3. Work with the team and get their suggestions and ideas.
4. Write a draft of the vision statement based on the ideas.
5. Develop a draft of the mission statement based on the vision.
6. Review and revise the vision and mission statements with further ideas suggested by the stakeholders.
7. Gain approval from the stakeholders.
8. Make copies of the vision and mission statements and distribute them to all stakeholders including employees.
9. Post the vision and mission statements in a common area.
10. Reference the vision and mission statements as a constant reminder of what the operation is trying to do and what must occur for it to be successful.

Manager's Memo

Managers and employees who attend meetings to plan the establishment's vision and mission statements should be free to say what they think and offer ideas that may seem unattainable without fear of being criticized or laughed at.

One tactic that may be helpful is for the leader to ask, "What would our operation be like if it were ideal? What would you see if you left and returned 25 years later, thinking, 'Wow! This place is great! There is no way it could be any better.' What would you be experiencing to believe that the establishment couldn't be any better?"

The answers to questions like these can help planners forget about obstacles and about how things are currently done. They can focus on ambitious ideas that suggest how the operation could move from where it is now to where it could be in the future.

Implementing the Vision and Mission Statements

There is no reason to create vision and mission statements unless they will be used to drive how the establishment is operated. The manager serving as the operation's leader must be a role model. He or she must focus on, talk about, and act according to the vision and mission statements. A real team effort results when everyone agrees with these planning guides and knows their own role in moving toward them. Team members working together can do much more than individual employees working separately.

Here are some ways to make the operation's vision and mission come alive:

- Create a workplace in which these tools are referenced every day.
- Make sure that decisions made help the operation connect with its vision and mission statements.
- Make daily plans that include activities to support the vision and mission.

In today's competitive restaurant and foodservice industry, it is important that managers make the connection between what they want to do attain their mission and how they will do it (develop plans). Then, managers must discover how to communicate the mission to their employees so they will understand its importance and the ways they can help.

Here are some ideas for connecting the vision and mission with daily work activities:

- Include this information in employee handbooks and discuss it more than once during orientation, as shown in *Exhibit 2.5.* Provide examples of how work has been planned with the vision and mission in mind. Communicate the expectation that everyone in the organization needs to support these statements.
- Ensure that all training materials align with and stress the importance of these statements.
- Post the statements where everyone will see them.
- Provide updates at employee meetings about recent examples of actions and successes that directly relate to the vision and mission statements.

The employees' performance drives how the establishment performs, so their roles and responsibilities must be based on the operation's vision and mission. For example, assume the mission statement stresses the importance of high-quality food. To do this, purchasing, production, and service tasks must be designed so that employees successfully prepare and serve high-quality food.

Exhibit 2.5

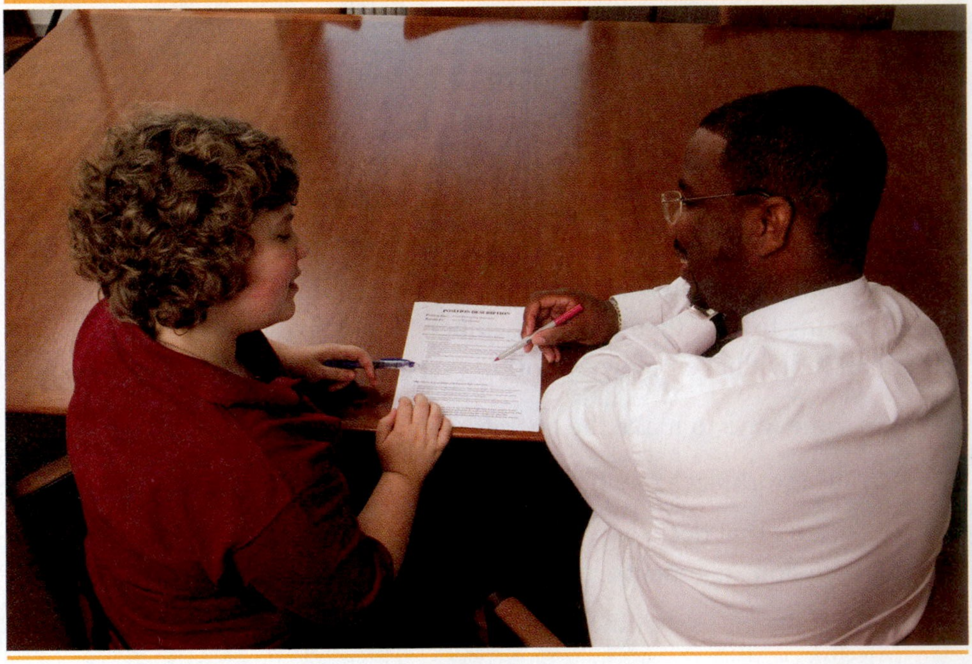

Managers must communicate, clarify, and coach employees to support the vision and mission statement. When they can do so, the employees will be helping the operation succeed.

Employees must be able to perform to standards stated in well-thought-out job descriptions reflecting company values. Standards of quality such as serving and preparing high-quality food must drive the employees' work. They should know that these quality standards are important, and they should also be able to attain the standards.

The manager must select and train the best employees and provide them with the necessary products, tools, equipment, and other resources to meet the quality standards. Then the operation's team can work together to meet the standards in the vision and mission statements.

GOALS DRIVE OPERATING PLANS

Goals are statements of desired results that help an operation measure how well it is doing. In other words, goals are what employees commit to do for their employer. The extent to which goals are reached depends in large part on the employees' knowledge, skills, experience, attitudes, and the amount and quality of resources available for the employees' use.

Importance of Goals

Goals specify desired results. If they are not set, there is no way to compare what actually happens with what the restaurant or foodservice manager wants to happen. For example, assume the operation generated $34,000 for the month. Is that good or bad? This question cannot be answered unless the manager knows the goal was $31,000. With this knowledge, the manager will likely be very pleased. If the goal had been $37,000, the manager would not likely be pleased.

Successful restaurant and foodservice managers focus on goals that define desired results. If managers do not know the desired results, they can focus on only the process. Although process is important, focusing on process because there is no goal is a sign of a manager who is not an effective leader.

For example, assume a manager wants to generate a "reasonable" profit. If he or she develops an effective budget, that planning tool estimates the monthly profit that can be expected. Then the manager can compare the actual profit to the profit goal. Without a profit goal, the manager can only operate as best he or she can and hope that the actual profit is reasonable.

Here are some reasons to set goals:

- Provide direction
- Provide milestones to tell how much more progress is still needed
- Divide activities into smaller parts that can be assigned to specific departments, teams, or employees
- Clarify employees' roles
- Motivate and challenge employees

Managers must analyze results to determine whether the operation has properly focused on its goals. **Benchmarks** are standards by which something can be measured or judged. For example, the approved operating budget presents financial benchmarks for the period of time it covers. If the budget estimates a certain amount of revenue, that amount can be compared to the revenue that was generated. If the benchmark revenue goal was attained, the manager probably does not have a revenue problem. If the revenue benchmark was not attained, corrective action may be needed.

Benchmarks can help a manager determine whether goals are balanced, strategic, and long-term as shown in *Exhibit 2.6*. Goals should display several traits:

- Balanced goals consider the interests of the operation's owners, managers, other employees, and customers.
- Strategic goals align with the strategies that have been developed. **Strategies** are plans of action to reach a goal. They consider the best way to use labor, products, money, time, and other resources to reach the goal.
- Long-term goals allow the results to be repeated over a long period.

Exhibit 2.6

IDEAL GOALS: BALANCED, STRATEGIC, AND LONG-TERM

Types of Goals

Every business is made up of levels that represent the organization, the departments within it, and its employees as shown in *Exhibit 2.7.* Typically, persons at each of these levels create these goals.

Organizational goals are at the highest level. They focus on broad statements of what the entire operation wants to achieve. They are identified in the vision and mission statements. These goals should reflect **strategic priorities** that represent the operation's highest-level concerns for employees to address.

Departmental (team) goals are set at the next highest level in the operation. For example, a small restaurant or foodservice operation has a kitchen with a team of food-production employees and another team of staff who serve the food. Each of these activities involves different people doing different things. Assume the establishment's owner set a property-wide, or organizational, goal to reduce the number of employees who leave. He or she might set separate goals for the food-production and food-serving teams. The reason could be a belief that different factors were contributing to why employees leave.

The department, or team, goals link to the organizational goals and help produce the desired results. Departmental objectives may be developed by and are the responsibility of each department or, perhaps, special teams within the department.

Finally, there are **individual performance goals** that focus on each employee's personal efforts. These goals can be identified as part of the performance appraisal process. Employees must know their personal goals and how meeting them impacts the operation's success.

SMART Goals

Recall that goals must be written so they will be understood and can guide the development of plans to reach them. The best goals are **SMART**:

- Specific: Goals must be clearly stated and indicate exactly what is expected. Conditions needed to reach the goal are important.
- Measurable: Goals must describe measurable results that allow comparisons between the goals and the actual results produced by the plan.
- Achievable: Goals should require an employee or a team to strive to achieve them. However, they must also be realistic.
- Relevant: Goals must relate to the operation's vision and mission statements.
- Timebound: Goals should tell the dates by which they should be reached.

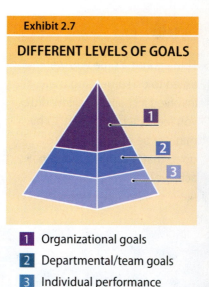

Exhibit 2.7

DIFFERENT LEVELS OF GOALS

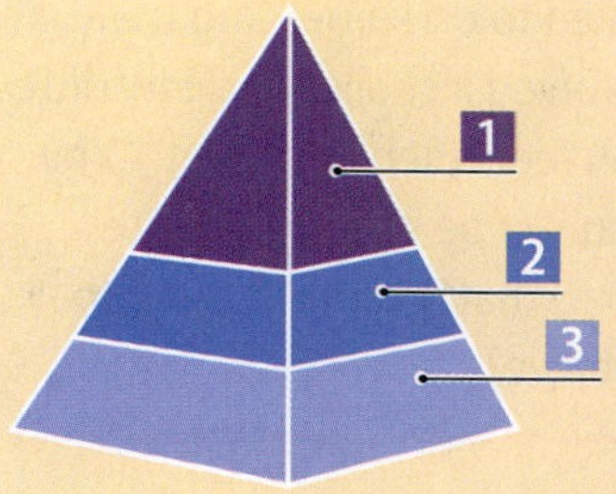

1 Organizational goals
2 Departmental/team goals
3 Individual performance goals

Manager's Memo

Departmental goals must be aligned with organizational goals. The restaurant or foodservice manager must work with the department manager to determine what the department will do to help the establishment reach its goal.

For example, the organizational goal may be to reduce labor costs by a certain amount. The department manager will identify ways to reduce his or her department's labor costs to help reach the organizational goal.

Department managers, in turn, must ensure that their employees clearly understand their responsibility to help reach the organization's goals. Department managers, working with their employees, must develop supportive goals and then assign them to employees or teams.

THINK ABOUT IT . . .

Think about a time you were asked to do something that involved a challenge. How did you feel when you did it? Why might it be useful to create goals that are challenging to achieve?

Here are some examples of SMART goals. Note that they are expressed concisely in one sentence.

- We will decrease customer complaints by 5 percent over the next 3 months.
- We will increase customer counts by 10 percent monthly within 18 months.
- We will be able to use 25 basic conversational phrases in English and Spanish before the end of the current fiscal year.

Writing SMART goals is critical because they help employees and teams know what they need to do. Too often, goals end up being unclear, unrealistic, not measurable, or not related to the vision and mission. Write SMART goals to avoid these problems.

IDENTIFY GOALS WITH SWOT ANALYSIS

Determining goals is an important first step in the planning process. Some situations almost "shout" at managers to set goals addressing them. One example is the failure to pass a local sanitation inspection. Another might be a very high **employee turnover rate** (the percentage of the total number of employees who must be replaced during a specific time period such as a month or a year). Both of these concerns must be taken care of quickly.

Other goals may be hidden among the challenges that confront managers all the time. One way to identify the most important goals among many possible goals is to use SWOT analysis.

SWOT analysis identifies an operation's strengths and weaknesses and examines its opportunities and threats. This helps managers set goals and focus on plans where the business is the strongest and has the greatest opportunities.

SWOT analysis is best conducted by a team that gathers and reviews information and then answers questions such as those in *Exhibit 2.8*. These questions consider the strengths, weaknesses, opportunities, and threats from the viewpoints of the establishment's owners, managers, employees, and customers.

Also think about strengths and weaknesses in relation to competitors. For example, if all of an establishment's competitors insist on having spotless facilities, then a clean establishment is a necessity, not a strength. One way to determine opportunities is to look at strengths with an eye for building on them and look at weaknesses to see if eliminating them can create opportunities.

The answers to questions such as those in *Exhibit 2.8* can help team members discover things they did not know. Then they can use what they learned to make decisions about challenges they can address to move the operation toward its mission.

Exhibit 2.8

SAMPLE SWOT QUESTIONS

Strengths	• What does our establishment do well? • What advantages do we have over other establishments? • What additional resources do we have access to? • What do we do for our customers that exceeds what they expect us to do? • What things do we do better than our competition? • What do other people think are our strengths?
Weaknesses	• What does our operation do poorly? • What could we improve? • What should we avoid? • Where are we wasting money? • What does our competition do better than we do?
Opportunities	• What trends could boost demand for our products and services over the next several years? • What opportunities will occur because of changes in the community? • How might technology help us? • What changes could occur that might benefit our operation?
Threats	• What trends might hurt demand for our products and services over the next several years? • What obstacles are we facing? • Do we have cash-flow problems? • What community situations might threaten us? • What changes could occur that might hurt our establishment?

DEVELOP OPERATIONAL GOALS AND PLANS

As stated, the operation's vision and mission statements are critical to setting the foundation for what the establishment should be. Four specific planning tools help connect the big-picture vision and mission statements with day-to-day operations.

Long-Range Plan

A **long-range plan** is a statement of goals and the activities necessary to reach them that can be used over the next three to five years to move the operation toward its mission.

THINK ABOUT IT . . .

Some managers think long-range planning is a good idea, but then they spend most of their time thinking about current problems or how to react to competitors. Which planning concerns do you think are more important?

Effective planners challenge their teams to think about long-term ways to better meet their mission statement and the concerns identified by SWOT analysis. Then department staff or team members can consider what they can contribute to a property-wide long-term plan.

For example, food-production staff members may believe that a key to providing customer value (a mission priority) is to increase staff efficiency without lowering quality standards. This increased efficiency will help keep menu prices low. Servers may recognize that a better training program will help them more efficiently serve the customers (another mission priority). *Exhibit 2.9* shows a sample format for a long-range plan.

Exhibit 2.9

SAMPLE LONG-RANGE PLAN

Department: Food Production
Goal: Reduce employee turnover to 30% or less within three years

Now	Year 1 Goal	Year 2 Goal	Year 3 Goal
40% Current employee turnover rate	38%	35%	30% Employee turnover rate goal

Department: Dining Room
Goal: Increase positive customer comment score to 95% or more within three years

Now	Year 1 Goal	Year 2 Goal	Year 3 Goal
87% Current positive customer comment score	89%	92%	95% Positive customer comment score goal

Notice that *Exhibit 2.9* shows three-year goals for the food-production and dining-room departments. The manager has agreed that reaching these goals is in line with the property's mission. Now the department heads can meet with their employees to develop and implement business plans to reach these yearly and three-year goals.

Business Plan

A **business plan** is a statement of goals and activities to be addressed within the next 12 months to move the operation toward its mission.

The business plan breaks down the long-range plan into parts that can be achieved during a 12-month period. For example, the food-production department's goal of reducing turnover will involve implementing one alternative during the first year and a second alternative during the second year to further reduce the turnover rate.

Exhibit 2.10 shows a sample worksheet that might be used for a business plan. Note that it allows the planners to indicate the necessary tasks, the staff responsible for each task, and the planned and actual completion dates.

> **Manager's Memo**
>
> Experienced planners know it is one thing to "plan the plan" and another thing to "work the plan." Specific employees or teams should be assigned to work on specific tasks in the business plan. One person should be responsible for completion of the plan and a time schedule for completion must be established.
>
> Those assigned to a task driven by the business plan should be held responsible for this work in the same way that they are responsible for the ongoing work stated in their job descriptions. Their success in each assigned task can be reviewed in formal performance appraisal sessions along with the review of their routine work assignments.

Exhibit 2.10

SAMPLE BUSINESS PLAN WORKSHEET

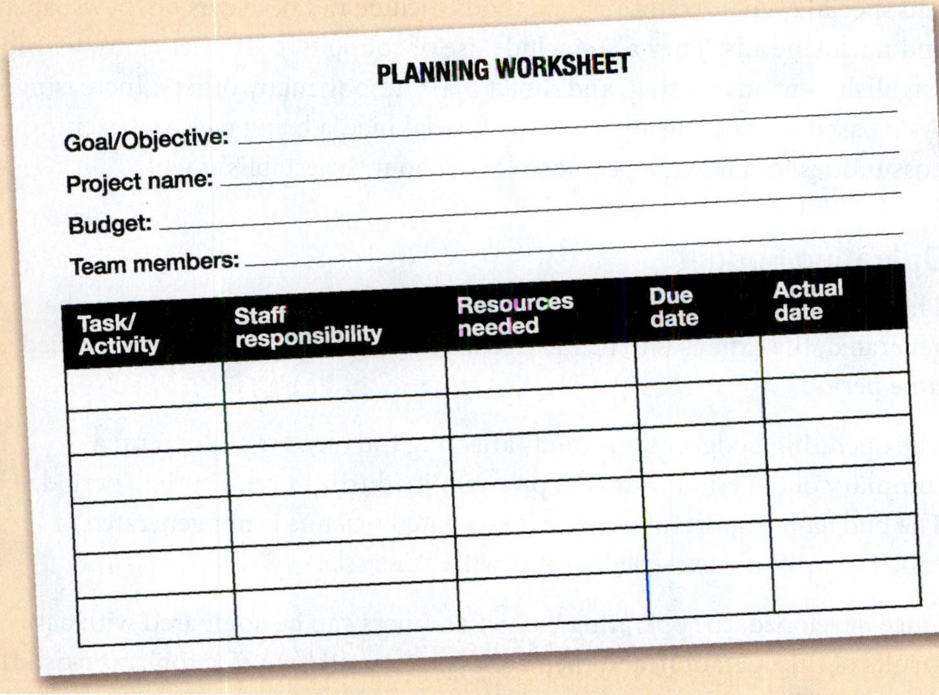

PLANNING WORKSHEET

Goal/Objective: ______

Project name: ______

Budget: ______

Team members: ______

Task/ Activity	Staff responsibility	Resources needed	Due date	Actual date

Marketing Plan

A **marketing plan** is a calendar of specific activities designed to meet the operation's revenue goals. Recall that revenue is the amount of money generated from the sale of products and services to customers. Every for-profit establishment needs revenue to purchase the resources required to serve the customers and to meet the owner's financial requirements. Not-for-profit operations also have financial goals. They may need to generate a profit (often called "surplus") to have funds to purchase items such as additional pieces of equipment. Other possible financial goals may be to break even or to spend no more than a specified amount above revenue that will be covered by an approved budget deficit.

The concept of marketing relates to activities designed to attract, retain, and expand the base of customers that are attracted to the food service operation. A marketing plan provides a yearly road map for restaurant and foodservice managers to plan how to generate revenue by answering the following questions:

- What must be done?
- Who will do it?
- When should it be done?
- How much money is required to do it?
- How will results be evaluated?

One reason marketing plans are needed is that there are many ways to tell existing and potential customers about the establishment's products, services, and special events. Traditional methods include radio, television, newspaper, and magazine ads. They also include use of coupons, customer clubs, within-establishment advertising, and direct mail, among many others. Increasingly, Web-based advertising and the use of social media bring new and exciting possibilities for allowing people to learn about the establishment.

OPEN FOR BUSINESS — BY THE CUSTOMER/ FOR THE CUSTOMER

Just about everyone, including many businesses, uses Facebook and Twitter. Restaurant and foodservice managers can use postings and instant messaging to advertise daily specials, remind club members about how to gain "more points sooner," and even recruit applicants for new and vacant employee positions.

The Web sites of most restaurant and foodservice operations increasingly provide information designed to recruit new customers and invite current customers to visit. The sites also promote products and services to increase the amount of money customers spend during their visits.

Operating Budget

The **operating budget** is a financial plan that estimates the revenue to be generated, the expenses to be incurred, and the profit, if any, for a specified time period.

The operating budget covers items affecting the **income statement**: a summary of the establishment's profitability during a certain time period. The budget is important because if estimated revenue is not generated or if expense limits are exceeded, profits will decrease.

Once developed, the operating budget numbers can be compared with actual results of the operation, and then the manager will know if problems exist. If they do, actions to correct the problems can be taken.

THINK ABOUT IT . . .

Some managers develop planning tools separately, perhaps with different members of the management team. They do not see the importance of using one plan to develop another.

Do you think all the plans are needed, in order? Why or why not?

Putting the Plans Together

Recall the two planning tools that should drive the operation more than any others: the vision and mission statements. The chapter also discussed the four planning tools that connect the vision and mission statements with day-to-day operations: the long-range plan, business plan, marketing plan, and operating budget. *Exhibit 2.11* shows how these planning tools relate to each other and provides an example of how each tool fits into the overall planning process.

Exhibit 2.11

BASIC PLANNING TOOLS

Planning Tool	Example
Vision:	To be the best establishment for business travelers in the community.
Mission Statement:	To meet the dining and small-group-meeting needs of community business visitors by providing desired food, beverage, and small-group-meeting services.
Long-Range Plan:	To provide food and beverage services to 60% of the number of community business visitors identified by the local tourist and convention center within five years.
Business Plan:	To increase the number of community business visitors as identified by the local tourist and convention center by 5% within the next 12 months.
Marketing Plan:	Strategies to increase community business visitor counts and revenue within the next 12 months.
Operating Budget:	Expected revenue from and costs to provide products and services to community business visitors.

The plans in Exhibit 2.11 are shown in order: Each tool must be planned before the next can be addressed.

LEADERS IMPLEMENT EFFECTIVE PLANS

Two strategies are very helpful as plans are implemented. Managers should consider the employees' abilities and use an organized process to implement the plans.

Consider Employees' Abilities

Restaurant and foodservice managers cannot normally do all of the work outlined in a plan. Instead, they must delegate all or some of the plan's tasks to capable employees.

Understanding employees' abilities helps managers determine who might be involved and the extent of their involvement. Here are some questions managers should consider when assigning employees or teams to help with tasks required by plans:

- What are each employee's (team's) strengths and weaknesses?
- Would the employee (team) benefit from a career development challenge?
- Is the employee (team) able to do a good job?
- Can the employee (team) work independently on the assignment?
- Will the employee (team) make a commitment to achieve the goal?
- Does the task require more than one person to work on it?

REAL MANAGER

THE PLANNING PROCESS

My father died in December of 1976; my mother passed away some months later. I attempted to manage and operate our family restaurant; however, at 21 years old, I quickly discovered that it was not as easy as it appeared. I sold the business in 1978 and began working for Popeye's Famous Fried Chicken. I worked at Popeye's for 22 years—the last 10 of which I reported directly to Al Copeland Jr., the son of the founder. I quickly realized that Al Jr. was a stickler for details. Every answer had to be accompanied by a reason for the occurrence. We would have meetings every Monday evening at Al's home. Those meetings, sometimes lasting until 1 or 2 a.m., were very intense, dissecting all aspects of the operation. My working experiences with Al were equivalent to a master's program in all aspects of restaurant and foodservice management. I learned how to read a profit and loss statement and, more important, what action steps to take to bring any line item into budget. My thought process began to change; I began to look at my business in a completely different way. I say that my time working with Al was the most rewarding and educational part of my professional life to date.

THINK ABOUT IT . . .

What benefits are not received by less effective employees? In other words, what reasons are there for staff members to be good employees?

The answer is often "more work"! Managers typically give special projects to the best employees.

What do you think?

- Who should be part of the team assigned to the task? How many employees should be on the team?
- What qualities does each employee (team member) need to work on the task?
- Will the employee (team) be responsible for reaching the entire goal or are there smaller tasks that can be assigned?

After managers understand their employees' abilities and know who might be able to help, it is important to think about these factors:

- **Current skills and knowledge:** Managers must consider whether employees already have the skills needed to reach a goal, or if the assignment can be a chance for the employee to learn. It is hard for staff members to be committed to a goal if the tasks required to reach it are beyond their ability.
- **Ability to cooperate:** Teamwork is not possible without cooperation. Managers must review goals to see if they will require a team approach. If so, the manager will need to select team members who can work together.
- **Accountability:** The term *accountability* relates to how much responsibility a person has for an activity. Managers must decide the extent to which they can hold an employee or a team accountable for plan tasks. However, accountability cannot be totally assigned to another person. If, for example, a boss asks the employee to take on a project, the boss will still be accountable to his or her own manager to ensure the project is done correctly and on time. It is important to consider how committed an individual is to take ownership of goals. Consider these questions to help determine the level of employees' accountability:
  - Do they freely commit to projects?
  - Have they been accountable for past projects?
  - Do they commit to quality work?
  - How disciplined are they in following processes to complete work?
  - Do they accept responsibility readily?
- **Response to change:** Change is to be expected, and some change is likely whenever new goals are set. Some goals involve a higher risk of change than others. However, it is always useful to think about how well employees deal with change.

THINK ABOUT IT . . .

"The greater danger for most of us lies not in setting our aim too high and falling short; but in setting our aim too low, and achieving our mark."

—Michelangelo

How can you set challenging goals?

Use an Organized Process

Knowing how to identify and write effective goals and to develop effective plans is an important part of a manager's job. However, it is only the first step in ensuring that goals will be achieved. Managers must also know how to reach goals.

There are four basic steps in an organized process for reaching goals. *Exhibit 2.12* shows the steps and some useful strategies for each step.

Exhibit 2.12

FOUR STEPS FOR REACHING GOALS

Step 1: Develop the Plan

- Select the most critical SMART goals.
- Develop a project plan for each goal.
- Identify specific activities or tasks that must be completed to achieve each goal.
- Establish dates for milestones (deadlines for specific steps in the plan), follow-up (activities to ensure the plan stays on schedule), and completion (when the project is done).
- Determine who will be responsible for each task in the plan.
- Determine how the results will be evaluated.
- Allow the staff to help develop the plan.
- Communicate the final project plan and goals to your team.
- Indicate that some changes to the plan may be needed.
- Work with employees and teams to incorporate the goals and plan activities into their performance and professional development plans.
- Gain commitment from employees and teams to complete assigned activities.

Step 2: Implement the Plan

- Monitor and chart progress on the plan.
- Review goals to ensure the plan stays on target.
- Follow up on issues that arise and interfere with achieving a goal.
- Continue to communicate progress toward achieving the goal.
- Revise and update the plan if necessary.

Step 3: Evaluate the Plan

- Evaluate results by comparing SMART goals to actual results.
- Communicate success.
- Conduct a recap meeting to discuss what went right and how tasks might have been done differently.
- Recognize and celebrate the good work of the employees and teams.

Step 4: Apply the Results

- Ensure employees know about changes implemented.
- Determine how changes will be announced.
- Provide feedback immediately as well as during performance evaluation and coaching sessions.
- Support the changes and be a role model.

STEP 1: DEVELOP THE PLAN

Each plan should be developed to reach one or more goals. It may not be possible to tackle every goal immediately. If there are too many, the manager should consider which goals are the most critical and which have the greatest chance of helping the operation.

Take the time to think through what must be done to work toward the goal. Each goal may involve a separate project, and a plan is needed for each project to monitor progress.

Recall the sample worksheet for a business plan in *Exhibit 2.10.* It is useful for developing many types of plans.

The manager needs to involve his or her team in the planning process. Doing so can create motivated employees and teams who are committed to working for the desired results.

Once a draft of the plan has been developed, the manager needs to share it with his or her manager, if necessary, and the employees who must implement it. They may all have ideas to make the plan more workable, less time-consuming, and less costly to implement. Also, the manager should emphasize how the plan and its goal support the operation's vision and mission statements.

The manager should work with his or her employees to include the employees' assigned tasks in their performance and professional development plans. Also, he or she should tell the employees that the plan may need further changes if unexpected issues arise as it is implemented.

Manager's Memo

Some plans are not successful. Perhaps the tasks to reach the goal were not the best choices or the plan was not implemented effectively.

The manager should remember that if he or she approved the plan, the responsibility for its completion is shared. The manager had input into it, approved it, perhaps assigned employees to project tasks, and monitored it during implementation.

Employees are not always the cause of a failure to reach goals. The manager can tell the employee his or her help will be needed when other plans are implemented (perhaps with closer supervision). The manager can discuss what did and did not work well, what the employee might have done differently, and how the employee can learn from mistakes.

The employees chosen for the failed project were likely selected because they were committed to the operation and its goals. The manager should do nothing to reduce employees' interest in helping the operation succeed.

STEP 2: IMPLEMENT THE PLAN

It is important to monitor each activity noted on the plan as it is implemented. Due dates help, as do benchmarks that show if progress is being made.

If the project will take a few weeks or longer, the manager will want to review to ensure that the project's priority has not changed. Adjustments and updates to the plan can be made if necessary. Also, he or she should use update meetings with the employees and teams involved. These sessions can provide information about how the project is going. If problems are noted, corrective actions can be taken to get the project back on track.

STEP 3: EVALUATE THE PLAN

When the project has been completed, the manager should evaluate the results by comparing the SMART goal with the situation after the project is complete. If the goal stated that positive customer comments would increase by 5 percent within nine months, did this happen?

For this example, assume the increased positive customer comment score was to result from a new server training program to be developed within four months and delivered over the next two months. The higher customer comments would probably occur during the last three months of the project plan. Changes, hopefully higher, in the customer comment scores could be reviewed as part of the evaluation process.

Exhibit 2.13

Project recap meetings can be used to discuss what went right and what could have been done differently. This information could be useful in the future when projects with similar activities are planned and implemented.

A final evaluation step should be the recognition of success and a sincere and enthusiastic "thank you" as shown in *Exhibit 2.13*. This can occur during a staff meeting, performance review, lunch, or after-work gathering. Employees want to know how they performed and whether their assignment contributed to the project's success.

The manager should also review how the employees' success could be carried over to other situations and discuss how the experience has affected the employees' professional development plan.

STEP 4: APPLY THE RESULTS

New work processes and policies are sometimes rolled out but, over time, managers or employees may begin to make exceptions. When this happens the work leading to the changes is wasted. Managers must work hard to avoid this situation.

An important first step is to ensure that all team members are fully aware of the changes. Effective communication skills are needed to do this.

How should employees be informed about changes? Should a group meeting be held? Should the manager inform department heads, who in turn speak to employees? More than one method may be helpful. For example, the manager can use team meetings, written information, pre-shift meetings, the operation's intranet, bulletin boards, and ongoing reminders during performance appraisal and coaching activities.

Depending on the change, the purpose of the information rollout will be to explain, defend, or teach affected employees about the new way of doing things.

Feedback from information sessions will be very useful to ensure that employees know about the changes and what must be done to implement them effectively. Feedback may occur immediately after information is provided but also will likely occur as managers provide additional training and coaching.

THINK ABOUT IT . . .

Many restaurant and foodservice managers believe that the task of informing employees about changes involves only reinforcement if employees have helped determine goals, develop plans, and complete plan activities.

What do you think?

Sometimes decisions about changes are made at higher levels. In the case of multiunit operations, these changes may affect specific properties differently. The manager's role is to support the changes and help implement them even if they do not agree with them. Remember that managers are role models, and employees will think and act about changes the same way they do.

Also remember that many changes will need further revision. Customer preferences, technology, and creative new ideas may encourage additional change. Not all change is good, but some is. The manager must determine what changes will be helpful and how to apply principles that bring about effective change.

SUMMARY

1. **Explain basic principles of planning, with an emphasis on how employees can assist, and procedures useful in managing planning information.**

   Restaurant and foodservice operations benefit from several types of plans. Employees can help develop and implement plans and can make them better. A wide range of information is important in planning decisions, and this information must be effectively managed.

2. **Describe how a value statement, vision statement, and mission statement are developed and implemented.**

   Several broad planning tools set the foundation for an operation's more detailed planning. These include value statements (standards that guide operations), a vision based on the value statements that describes why an establishment exists and what it wants to become, and a mission statement that states the operation's purpose. Once developed, these planning tools can be used to construct plans that drive day-to-day operations.

3. **State the importance of SMART goals in the planning process.**

   Goals state the desired results that help an operation measure how well it is doing. Goals are an important first step in developing plans. Goals should be SMART: specific, measurable, achievable, relevant, and timebound.

4. **Review procedures for conducting a SWOT analysis.**

   SWOT analysis helps managers identify an operation's strengths and weaknesses and examine its opportunities and threats. Then managers can set goals using this information.

5. **Identify how restaurant and foodservice managers use long-range, business, and marketing plans and operating budgets, and explain the relationship among these planning tools.**

   The vision and mission statements drive four basic types of operating plans. The long-range plan indicates what an operation would like to accomplish over the next three to five years, and the business plan identifies goals for the next 12 months. Marketing relates to activities that attract, retain, and expand the number of customers for an establishment. Marketing plans describe activities to help the operation increase its revenue, and operating budgets estimate revenue, expenses, and profit expected for a specific time period.

6. **Explain the need to consider employees' abilities and use an organized process in implementing effective plans.**

   Plans benefit from considering employees' abilities and using an organized implementation process. Managers must develop, implement, and evaluate the plan and ensure that the results are applied to improve operations.

APPLICATION EXERCISES

You have learned much about the planning process in this chapter. However, effective restaurant and foodservice managers do not know only how to plan; they can actually do the planning. This chapter ends with some activities that allow you to apply basic planning principles to the Anytown Restaurant that you recently started to manage.

Exercise 1: SWOT Analysis for Anytown Restaurant

Anytown Restaurant is located in a small tourist community near the mountains of western North Carolina. It has been in business for about two years and has developed a year-round local customer base made up mostly of retirees. During the tourist season, the restaurant gets many referrals from resorts in the area. Also, the restaurant is close to a major highway, so there is potential to attract those driving along this route.

The restaurant's owner wants to set some goals so Anytown Restaurant can move closer to its vision and mission statements. Assume the vision addresses pleasing customers with great food and service and a welcoming atmosphere. The mission statement is "To provide customers with high-quality, healthy Southern cuisine with superb and courteous service that represents hospitality in the Smoky Mountains."

The restaurant's background is as follows:

- The chef graduated from the Culinary Institute of America and has many years of experience working in fine-dining restaurants.
- The restaurant has a small, select menu of healthy food including game and fish and will create customized menu selections whenever possible.
- More restaurants are opening in the area that offer the same check-average meals (about $30). So far, all of the properties are in town and not located in the somewhat remote natural setting of Anytown Restaurant.
- The restaurant is open for dinner only and has two dining seasons. From September to May it serves about 60 customers each night on Tuesday through Thursday, and 125 on Friday and Saturday. It is closed on Monday. However, it does a brisk holiday business from Thanksgiving through New Year's Day with a 20% increase in business. Customer counts increase by about 25% during the summer months, and the restaurant is open every day during the summer.

- The restaurant has a great staff, but employees are becoming more difficult to recruit because of the restaurant's location and competition from other restaurant and foodservice industry employers.
- Cash flow can be unreliable at times.
- Several retirees have asked if the restaurant does catering.
- The restaurant does not have a lot of information about its competitors.

Break into teams and identify the strengths, weaknesses, opportunities, and threats of Anytown Restaurant. Make any assumptions you wish to help with the SWOT analysis. After you have identified these factors, list the three factors on which your team would focus its planning efforts, and be prepared to explain why.

Exercise 2: SMART Goals for Anytown Restaurant

Review the top three areas identified in your team's SWOT analysis of Anytown Restaurant. Then create three SMART goals for the restaurant. Present your goals to the class, and explain why they are SMART goals.

REVIEW YOUR LEARNING

Select the best answer for each question.

1. Measurable goals allow the organization to

A. determine production levels.
B. create staffing schedules.
C. forecast business needs.
D. identify progress.

2. Which benefit results from involving staff members in the goal-setting process?

A. Requires staff members to be ultimately responsible for goal attainment
B. Determines their interest in management
C. Ensures they will help achieve goals
D. Benchmarks their analysis skills

3. The operation's goals should be driven primarily by its

A. vision and mission statements.
B. competition and employee feedback.
C. employee needs and surveys.
D. business plan and operating budget.

4. What is the benefit to employees who assist with planning tasks?

A. They can develop their knowledge and skills.
B. Their other work assignments will be reduced.
C. They will receive the next available promotion.
D. They will receive fewer additional assignments.

5. Which statement about goals and plans is correct?

A. Marketing plans are not needed if SWOT analysis is done each year.
B. Business plans should cover at least a three- to five-year period.
C. The best goals are those that are easiest to reach.
D. Department goals should help meet organizational goals.

6. What is a strategy?

A. A plan of action to meet a goal
B. A specific goal in a long-range plan
C. A follow-up activity when an action plan is not met
D. Any activity required to implement a training tactic

7. **When is an operation's mission statement developed?**
   A. Before goals are developed
   B. Before core values are assessed
   C. At the same time as core values
   D. Before the vision is determined

8. **When delegating plan tasks, what employee characteristic is most important?**
   A. Years of experience in the industry
   B. Position in the establishment
   C. Tendency to respond quickly
   D. Job skills and knowledge

9. **Which element is present in an effectively developed project worksheet?**
   A. SMART goal to be addressed
   B. Relation to other projects
   C. Amount of teamwork required
   D. Risks if project is not successful

10. **What must employees be told when they are assigned to work on an action plan?**
    A. The penalty if their work is unacceptable
    B. Importance of the plan compared to others
    C. The deadlines to complete each action plan task
    D. That no one else can do the work as well as they can

FIELD PROJECT

Part I

1. Visit the Web site of a restaurant to identify that establishment's mission statement.

2. How might the mission statement help with long-range planning?

3. How might the mission statement help with daily operations?

4. How might a manager share goals from the mission statement with entry-level employees?

5. How might a manager explain that an entry-level employee's job helps the operation to attain the mission statement?

3 Leaders Are Effective Communicators

INSIDE THIS CHAPTER

- Managers Must Communicate
- Overview of the Communication Process
- Communication Challenges
- Effective Communication Skills
- Interpersonal Communication
- Internal and External Communication

CHAPTER LEARNING OBJECTIVES

After completing this chapter, you should be able to:

- Explain why it is important for restaurant and foodservice managers to use effective communication skills.
- Provide an overview of the communication process.
- Discuss common communication challenges.
- Review basic principles useful for business speaking, using the telephone, listening, writing, and controlling nonverbal communication.
- Identify strategies that enhance interpersonal communication.
- Explain practices for developing effective messages and for managing internal and external communication procedures.

KEY TERMS

boilerplate, p. 65
chain of command, p. 68
communication, p. 66
constructive feedback, p. 78
environmental noise, p. 70
external communication, p. 79
feedback, p. 68
interdepartmental communication, p. 82
internal communication, p. 79
interpersonal communication, p. 77
intranet, p. 82
listening, p. 73
message channel, p. 67
message content, p. 67
message context, p. 68
nonverbal communication, p. 67
receiver, p. 69
sender, p. 67

CASE STUDY

"We knew a little bit about what's happening, but not all of this," said Fran, the dining-room server. "The manager said the new salad bar would be installed, but that it would have little impact on the servers because customers just help themselves."

Fran was talking to Matthew, the head cook at Anytown Restaurant. "I'm just as surprised as you are," Matthew said. "I figured we would have to prepare some additional salads and other cold foods. Now I'm learning that a lot of additional items are needed. I think our restaurant manager and dining-room manager just got together during a coffee break and decided to do this. There sure doesn't seem to be much communication about this major change."

1. What do you think is the major problem at Anytown Restaurant?
2. How should the restaurant manager have handled this situation so there would be no surprises for anyone in any department?

MANAGERS MUST COMMUNICATE

Restaurant and foodservice managers spend a lot of time communicating in different ways with many types of people for numerous reasons. However, some managers think that communication is simple. They think, "I have been doing it all my life without any problem."

In fact, it is one thing to simply speak, listen, and write, and another thing to ensure that messages are consistently understood. Managers cannot build teams, strong relationships, and required profits and meet other responsibilities without being good communicators.

Some of managers' on-the-job communication is the same as in their personal lives. Examples include casual conversations with employees about current events or the weather. Stories they share with their softball team may be exactly the stories they discuss with suppliers.

In some situations, communication skills become much more important. For example, when they talk with a customer about falling in the parking lot, there might be legal concerns. When they talk to suppliers about purchases that cost thousands of dollars, communication must be clear.

Restaurant and foodservice managers must know how to be effective communicators because they represent the business to many organizations and persons who affect or are affected by it. They also represent themselves within the professional community and how they communicate reflects on their professionalism.

Managers communicate with many people:

- Employees
- Customers
- Owners (their manager)
- Suppliers
- Community and other officials

Employees have expectations of their managers, who are a primary source of information and a key to their future with the operation. Managers must inform employees about many things such as procedure changes and performance standards. The timing of, consistency of, and process used to deliver these messages affect the workplace.

Managers with effective communication skills can build trust, raise productivity, and help employees stay motivated. Poor communication does the opposite. It can decrease quality and increase turnover rates. It can also create expensive rework because quality standards were not met.

Effective customer interaction is important for success. Managers should try to meet and greet customers when they arrive, check on them during their visit, and if possible be available to thank them when they leave (*Exhibit 3.1*).

THINK ABOUT IT . . .

In today's diverse world, employees speak different languages. If communication problems occur when people speak the same language, what can happen with different languages?

Exhibit 3.1

Managers must also be able to handle customer complaints, answer customer questions, and display an ongoing sense of hospitality. The manager's communication skills influence the customers' views about the establishment. He or she should interact with customers in a way that is consistent with the operation's vision and mission statement.

Managers who practice effective communication and relationship-building skills during the customers' visits will ensure high guest-satisfaction levels. This, in turn, will help increase revenues, profitability, and repeat business.

The need for effective communication between the manager and the owners is easy to explain. The owners want to know how the business is doing, and a comment such as "everything is OK" is not what they expect. Managers communicate using written reports and financial budgets, and at times they provide answers to very detailed questions.

Managers want to know how their own manager views their performance, just as employees want their performance evaluated. The quality and frequency of this communication influences the higher-level manager's view of the manager's success.

Managers must communicate very precisely when they meet with suppliers. The "what, when, and how much" of purchasing agreements can be detailed, and correcting errors can be time-consuming and costly. Managers must understand the legal **boilerplate** on purchase contracts that involve legal concerns such as payment procedures, insurance, and shipping requirements. *Boilerplate* is a term that relates to portions of contracts that do not change when they are used with different parties.

Many restaurant and foodservice managers deal with community and other officials on a frequent basis. Building inspectors, lawyers, and tax officials are among those with whom the manager will likely communicate.

Chapter 1 stated that professional managers try to change their management style with different employees. Managers must also try to alter how they communicate with other persons. The language used in their personal lives must be replaced with business language so there are no communication problems as they interact with a wide variety of people on the job.

OVERVIEW OF THE COMMUNICATION PROCESS

Recall that effective communication skills help ensure the best relationships with employees, owners, suppliers, community officials, and others. When managers understand how the communication process works, they will make their communication better received by listeners or readers.

Communication is the process of sending and receiving information by speech, gestures, or writing to receive a response or action. The communication process involves five elements: sender, message content, message channel, message context, and receiver. The process is shown in *Exhibit 3.2*.

Exhibit 3.2

THE COMMUNICATION PROCESS

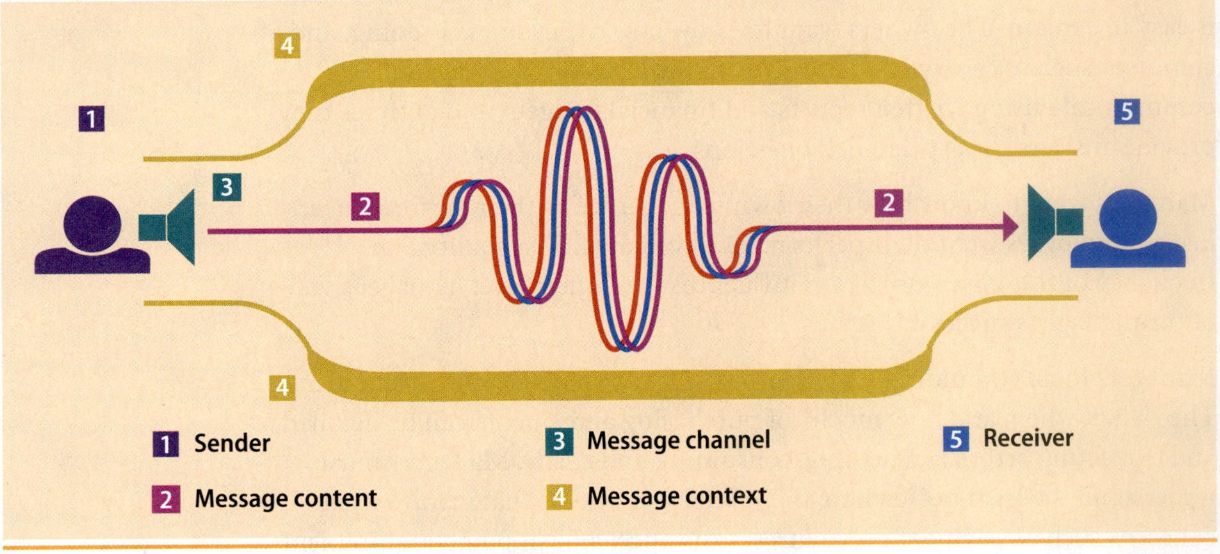

Sender

The **sender** is the person who sends the message to the receiver. A sender should consider some things before sending a message:

- For whom is it intended? (receiver)
- What do I want to say? (message content)
- How will I send it? (message channel)
- What other factors affect the message? (message context)

Message Content

The **message content** is the information sent by the sender to the receiver. Typically, senders send two kinds of messages to receivers:

- Historical information concerns something that has already occurred. Examples include operating information such as number of customers served or labor hours used during a work shift. Other examples are new polices and results of management decisions. Since the information relates to something that has already occurred, no action is normally needed.
- Future-oriented information requires the receiver to do something. A message may ask that someone attend a training program, use standard recipes to prepare menu items, or do certain tasks while someone is on vacation.

Message Channel

After deciding the message content, the sender needs to think about the **message channel**: how the message will be communicated. It can be through spoken or written words, graphics such as diagrams or photos, or nonverbal actions including body motions.

Sometimes words should be used. ("Don't hold the knife that way. Please remember the training about knife handling.") At other times, graphics may be best. ("Here's a diagram of how we will set up the buffet line.") Managers also use **nonverbal communication**, or movements and body language to convey a message, such as using the "OK" sign with their fingers to quickly signal "you're doing a great job." (see *Exhibit 3.3*).

Exhibit 3.3

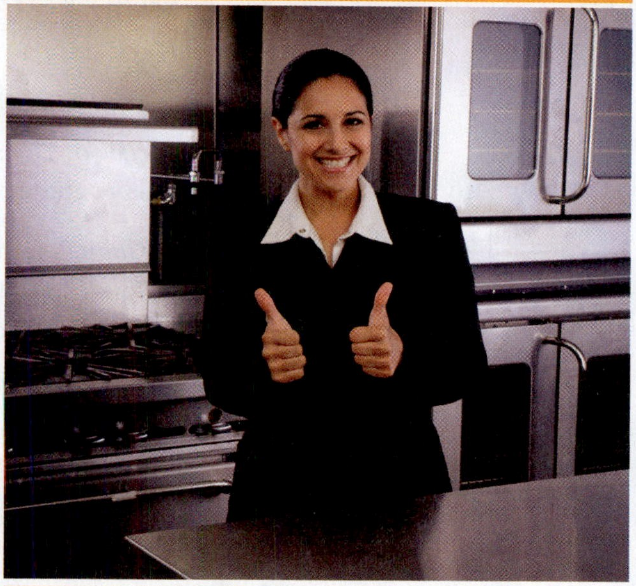

Messages are sent in different directions through the organization. Downward communication from the manager to employees is used to provide directions, ideas, and feedback. **Feedback** relates to how a person responds when he or she receives a message. Upward communication allows employees to provide information to managers. Communication flowing across the organization allows staff in different departments to share ideas. (See *Exhibit 3.4*.)

Exhibit 3.4

COMMUNICATION FLOW

Upward

- Reports to managers
- Schedule requests
- Suggestion-box ideas

Lateral

- Personal networking
- Team meetings
- Communication between department heads

Downward

- Weekly schedules
- Management decisions
- Updates
- Annual reports

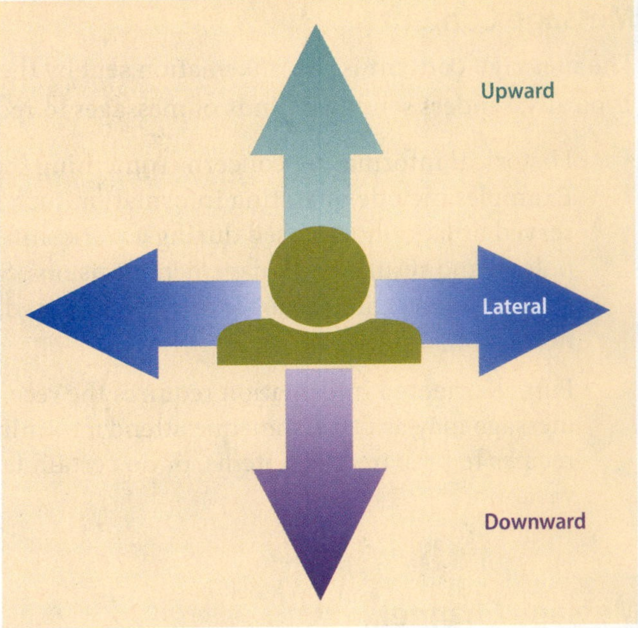

Message Context

A lot of things can happen to a message that can interfere with it being successfully received. The surroundings through which a message travels is called the **message context**. There are three levels to this environment.

As shown in *Exhibit 3.5*, the inner circle of message context deals with the immediate surroundings between sender and receiver. Noise and the fast pace of work are examples of factors in this area.

The middle circle includes factors within the team, department, or establishment. There is a **chain of command** by which authority flows from one management level to the next. It may require employees to send formal messages to the restaurant or foodservice manager through their department head who, in turn, sends them to the manager.

The outer circle refers to broad factors. For example, the operation may have a policy that only certain managers can speak to media reporters.

Managers developing advertising messages must be concerned about any restrictions imposed by society or the media on what they want to say.

Receiver

The **receiver** is the person or persons for whom the message is intended. A person does not just automatically understand and do something when he or she sees, hears, or reads a message. Instead, the receiver must interpret the message to determine what it means. Then he or she can make decisions about what must be done, as well as using words or actions to communicate that the message is understood.

Exhibit 3.5

MESSAGE CONTEXT

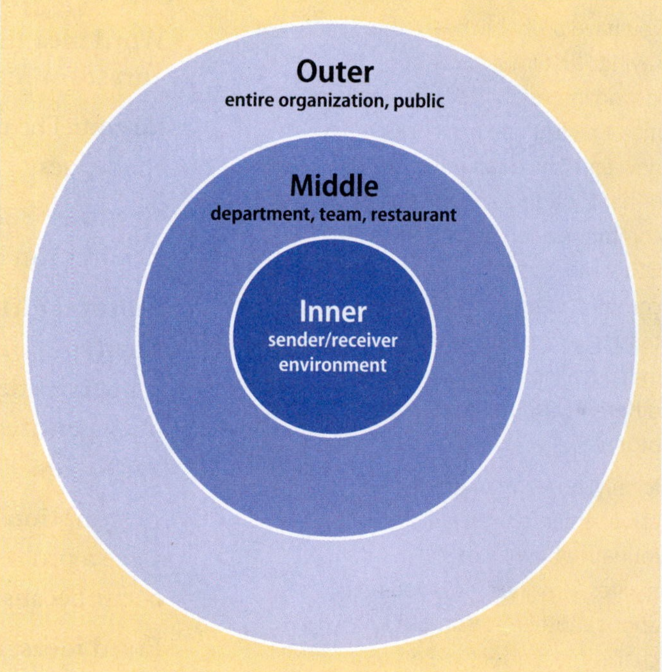

COMMUNICATION CHALLENGES

The ability of a restaurant or foodservice manager to effectively communicate is made difficult by many challenges. *Exhibit 3.6* illustrates that barriers can get in the way of messages sent. These barriers make it harder for messages to be correctly received and understood.

Exhibit 3.6

COMMUNICATION BARRIERS

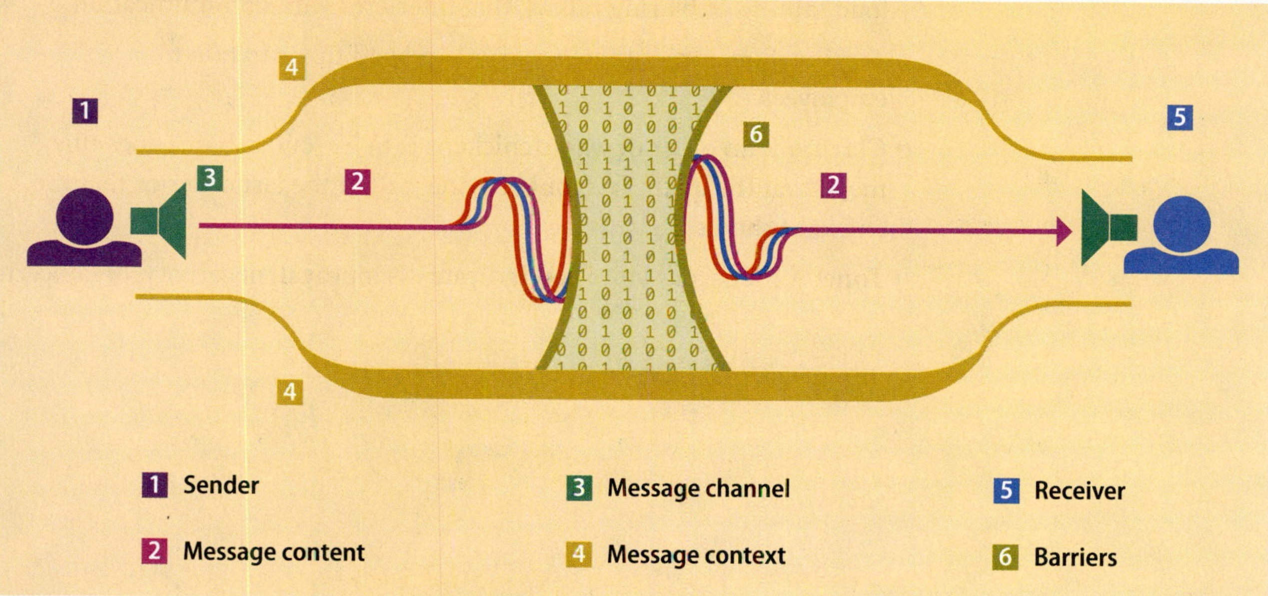

Manager's Memo

You have probably heard the saying "first impressions are lasting impressions." Sometimes a manager's first experiences with a new employee can influence his or her thoughts and affect communication for a long time. Other managers have things in common with an employee. They tend to be friendlier to this individual and may communicate differently than they do with others.

Ideally, how a manager feels about an employee will not influence how he or she communicates. However, how you feel about another person can be a challenge to effective communication. Also, if a manager is happy, frustrated, sad, or stressed, these feelings can influence what or how the manager communicates.

Problems during any part of the communication process can cause a seemingly simple message to become hard for the receiver to understand. Many barriers can interfere with communication effectiveness:

- **Word meaning:** Receivers may not know the meanings of words or phrases or may interpret them differently than the sender.
- **Jargon:** The use of technical language can create communication challenges.
- **Gestures:** Body movements can cause distractions to listening, and gestures can convey different messages to different people.
- **Cultural differences:** The usual distance between two people when speaking differs among cultures. Praising someone in public is not considered appropriate by some. These examples show why managers must have some knowledge about the cultures of their employees.
- **Assumptions:** Some managers assume their team members know how to solve a problem when they really do not. In these cases, problems may occur because the manager did not provide enough information.
- **Fixed ideas:** Managers may think some of their employees "never listen." Then they repeat themselves and cause the employees to lose interest in what they are saying.
- **Opinions:** Some managers hold opinions based on their experiences that may not reflect the current situation. Then their attitudes influence how they send messages.
- **Distracting workplace:** **Environmental noise** is any sound, such as loud talking or blaring radios, that interferes with communication.
- **Timing:** Sometimes there are good and bad times to talk to employees.
- **Clarity:** If an order of whole chickens is to be "cut in half," does this mean that the quantity should be one-half of the last order or that the chickens should be halved?
- **Tone:** A manager's voice can indicate disapproval, negativity, or concern.

EFFECTIVE COMMUNICATION SKILLS

Now that the basic communication process has been described, here are some basic principles that managers can use for speaking, listening, writing, and controlling nonverbal communication.

Speak Like a Pro

Restaurant and foodservice managers speak to many people on an average workday. In today's business environment, most managers use informal communication more often than formal communication.

Successful speakers use basic principles as they deliver their messages to ensure listeners will be receptive and understand them. Many of these principles are shown in *Exhibit 3.7*.

Successful speakers understand their listeners. They know effective communication requires interaction. They also recognize that what they think was clearly communicated may not be what was heard.

THINK ABOUT IT . . .

Sometimes managers know in advance that they will have to talk about serious issues in formal situations. One example may be terminating an employee. What are other situations where managers should plan what to say?

Exhibit 3.7

PRINCIPLES OF EFFECTIVE SPEAKING

Speak Clearly	Use Suitable Language
• Deliver concise messages. • Tell *who*, *what*, *where*, *when*, *why*, and *how*. • Pronounce words correctly.	• Minimize use of jargon. • Define technical terms. • Do not make negative comments. • Do not use slang.
Interact with Listeners	**Remember Nonverbal Communication**
• Verify understanding. • Repeat to ensure understanding. • Create a relaxing environment. • Maintain eye contact.	• Ensure body language does not interfere. • Use appropriate gestures. • Use reasonable facial expressions. • Act like a professional.
Personalize Message for Listeners	**Vary Speech Patterns**
• Consider cultural differences. • Overcome language barriers. • Think about listeners' age and education.	• Change voice tone and pitch. • Pause after important points. • Speak at a steady pace.

Speakers can do several things to help ensure listeners understand their messages:

- Ask questions about the topic and use responses to see if listeners understand.
- Repeat important points using different words.
- Encourage listeners to provide feedback.

Sometimes managers must make formal presentations, such as when they speak to many employees or represent their establishment at a community business meeting. In these situations, they must think about how they will include all needed information in a clear and concise way.

One way to do this is to ensure the presentation covers the five W's and How questions:

- Who?
- What?
- Where?
- When?
- Why?
- How?

Answers to these questions provide the message content. Then it is important for managers to practice the presentation and think about how their voice sounds and whether they use any actions that may distract listeners. Also, managers should think about how listeners can interact with them so the listeners will better understand the message.

THINK ABOUT IT . . .

Some people say the best way to sound friendly on the phone is to smile even though the caller cannot see it.

Do you think this suggestion is a good one? Why or why not?

Use the Telephone Like a Pro

Proper procedures for telephone use should be taught to all employees who must use it on the job:

- Say the establishment's name and your name, and then offer to provide assistance; for example, "Good afternoon, this is Anytown Restaurant, Sasha speaking. How may I help you?"
- Listen carefully to the caller, and be sure to wait until the caller has finished speaking before responding.
- Maintain a positive, polite, and courteous attitude.
- If the caller has a long message, take notes. Be sure to ask the five W's and How questions to take a complete message: who, what, where, when, why, and how.
- Repeat the caller's basic message to ensure you heard everything correctly. Ask questions if necessary.

- If you cannot provide the necessary information, know who can and transfer the call to that person. Before transferring, get the caller's name and phone number in case the call is lost. Do not say "wait a minute" or "hold on." Say something like, "I think Mr. Sanchez is best able to help you; may I place you on hold and transfer the call?"
- Close the conversation by asking the caller if there is anything else you can do: "I am glad I could help, Mrs. Jones; may I help you with anything else?" A polite "thank you for calling" will then be in order.

Sometimes callers become angry or rude. Managers must remember that they represent the operation, so they need to remain polite and in control. Using effective listening skills and trying to put themselves in the caller's place can often help manage these kinds of calls.

Listen Like a Pro

Some people think it is up to the sender to be sure the message is understandable. However, communication is a two-way process. This means the receiver must listen effectively. **Listening** is the ability to focus on what a person is saying to understand the message being sent.

Almost everyone has had the experience of trying to listen carefully but then finding their thoughts move from the speaker to other things. The result is a message that has not been understood. This example shows the need for listeners to focus actively on listening. When they do not, the information being sent (spoken) is lost, and the listener might give the impression of not caring about the speaker or the message.

Effective listening requires the receiver to be involved in the communication process. Here are some aspects of effective listening:

- Maintain eye contact with the speaker.
- Try to avoid interrupting.
- Ask questions for clarification.
- Restate the message to ensure understanding.
- Use effective body language such as nodding the head.
- Lean toward the speaker to indicate interest.
- Take notes if necessary.
- Give the message to others, if necessary, without losing its meaning.

THINK ABOUT IT . . .

"Telephone" is a game where the first child whispers something to the next, and so on, until the last child tells what he or she heard. Usually that message is very different.

This can happen when one employee trains another, who trains another. Ultimately, the task may be done very differently. What can managers do to ensure a consistent training message?

THINK ABOUT IT . . .

Many managers think it is much more difficult to write about something than to talk about it.

Do you agree? If so, why do you think writing is difficult for so many managers?

Write Like a Pro

Written communication, like spoken communication, must be understandable to be helpful. Writing is often more formal than speaking. Managers must be comfortable with all forms of written communication, including business letters, memos, and email. Therefore, an important first step is to know the basic components of a written message:

- **Introduction:** This section is used to capture the reader's attention, state the message's purpose, introduce the message's topic, and tell the writer's point of view.
- **Body of message:** This is an organized discussion of the content.
- **Conclusion:** This section reviews important points and may call for action.

PLAN WHAT TO WRITE

Good business writers plan what they want to say before they begin writing. They also use an organized process to develop their ideas into a clear, concise, and readable document. *Exhibit 3.8* reviews steps in an organized writing process.

Use these ideas to help make your writing more effective:

- Be clear and complete. Sometimes writers leave something out of the message. Review your writing to be sure your ideas are complete and understandable.

Exhibit 3.8

ORGANIZED WRITING PROCESS

1. Think about the reader.
2. Think about what you want to accomplish. Write down what you want to happen as a result of the written message.
3. Identify the message benefits. How will it help the company, the reader, your customers and employees, and you?
4. Think about the situation. Ask yourself the five W's and How questions and write the answers.
   - Who?
   - What?
   - Where?
   - When?
   - Why?
   - How?
5. Identify the topics and group the details underneath them.
6. Order the topics in a logical flow.
7. Write the body of the message first, then the introduction, and then the conclusion.
8. Read the draft of your message. Edit and revise the content and flow to ensure it is easy to read. Check for spelling and correct sensentences.
9. If the document is important, ask someone to read it and make suggestions as necessary to improve it.
10. Write the final draft and distribute the message.

- Be concise. The more you write, the more the reader must read and the more likely that problems can result. Long explanations make messages harder to receive. The best written messages make their points and then move on without using unneeded words.
- Keep it simple. Complex sentences are hard to read. Use short sentences and simple words where possible. If you must use words not used in day-to-day conversation, define them.
- Check your work. If possible, use the grammar and spell-check functions in your computer's word processing program.
- Express a positive attitude. Even if your message must deliver troubling news, perhaps it can review some long-term benefits. No one likes to read negative messages.
- Write often. As is true with most skills, writing skills improve the more often they are utilized.

Emails, faxes, and text messaging are just some ways that technology enables communication. These methods are fairly casual, but managers should use the same basic writing principles that they use with other types of messages.

WRITING PITFALLS

Even the best business writers make mistakes. Try to avoid the following common pitfalls:

- **No planning:** Even if you have little time, think through the message's purpose and main points before you begin writing.
- **Uncertain purpose:** Readers' interest quickly decreases when they do not understand the reason for the written message.
- **Forgetting the audience:** Always remember who will be reading the message. Then you can use the right approach and write a message they will understand.
- **Using an incorrect style:** Write in everyday language and make points the reader will understand. Understanding your readers and why you are writing are important keys to successful writing.

Writing challenges many restaurant and foodservice managers. However, use of the principles just discussed can help capture the readers' attention and ensure they understand the intended message.

Nonverbal Communication

Recall that nonverbal communication refers to a speaker's expressions and movements that tell additional information about the message. It occurs during one-on-one conversations, but it is often most noticeable when someone is giving a speech.

Manager's Memo

Managers should remember that everything they write can be a permanent record of their thoughts. Their written work must meet professional standards because it reflects their operation and themselves.

The amount of time and effort spent on a written message normally increases with its importance. A simple email to inform an employee about a schedule change is important. However, it probably does not require an organized plan of content or review by another person. In contrast, written messages to news media, customers, government officials, and for other important purposes require careful planning and reviewing.

THINK ABOUT IT . . .

How often do you put down what you have written and later reread it to make sure it is clear? Have you ever asked someone to edit your writing? How might these two steps improve your messages?

Exhibit 3.9

EXAMPLES OF NONVERBAL COMMUNICATION

Facial expressions
Crossed arms
Gestures
Back-and-forth pacing
Posture
Touching
Invasion of personal space
Clothing and appearance
Eye contact

An example of uncontrolled nonverbal communication is when a speaker keeps pacing back and forth or gesturing in a certain way. Nonverbal communication also occurs when, for example, a manager is trying to help an employee with something that is important only to the employee. If the manager yawns, stops to make or take telephone calls, or looks at a wristwatch, these actions convey his or her feelings.

So, words are not the only way to communicate. Nonverbal communication can turn any message into a miscommunication.

Exhibit 3.9 shows some examples of nonverbal communication. Managers need to be aware of these things when they are talking.

One way for managers to minimize distracting nonverbal communication is to practice speaking in front of a mirror or ask someone to give them feedback on their delivery. Effective speakers want to know what nonverbal messages they may be using and try to eliminate negative ones.

Exhibit 3.10

Nonverbal signals have different meanings for different cultures. Sometimes, a nonverbal behavior can mean something positive to an individual from one culture and something negative to someone from another culture. In some cultures, the following nonverbal behaviors send a negative message:

- Biting lips—signals nervousness
- Slouching in chair—shows disinterest
- Raising eyebrows—indicates disbelief or amazement
- Gesturing with hands—can be distracting
- Pointing with finger—comes across as scolding or lecturing (*Exhibit 3.10*)

In some cultures, the following nonverbal behaviors can signal something positive:

- Sitting on edge of chair, leaning forward—signals interest
- Smiling—expresses confidence and enthusiasm
- Giving a "thumbs up"—shows agreement
- Winking an eye—indicates recognition

Cultural differences mean that the same behavior can convey multiple different meanings. For example, the sharing of gifts, the need to arrive at meetings on time, and even how one crosses his or her legs when seated can mean very different things in different cultures. Managers must be aware of these factors as they interact with persons of different cultural backgrounds on the job.

INTERPERSONAL COMMUNICATION

Restaurant and foodservice managers do a lot of speaking in one-on-one and small-group situations.

The term **interpersonal communication** means communication between people. It involves speaking to one or a few individuals who are standing or sitting close to each other and providing immediate feedback. Feedback is any reaction of a reader or listener to the words or actions of a writer or speaker.

Interpersonal communication allows the speaker to receive immediate feedback from the listener. At the same time, the receiver can tell whether he or she understands what was said. Then additional information can be provided, if necessary.

Listeners benefit from interpersonal communication because they can quickly express their opinion if it differs from that of the speaker. This two-way "back and forth" conversation is often a very good way to quickly reach agreement or understand reasons for differences.

A Close Look at Interpersonal Communication

Restaurant and foodservice managers must have good "people skills" to get the most from interpersonal communication. They must be skilled at both what they do and what they say.

IMPACT OF MANAGER'S ACTIONS

Effective managers know that actions often speak louder than words. Actions such as conducting themselves in an ethical and professional manner, creating a safe and fun work environment, and remaining humble tell employees a great deal. Many employees make judgments about managers' effectiveness and ethics based on how they act in their leadership role. Employees who observe positive behavior are more likely to set equally high standards for their own actions.

THINK ABOUT IT . . .

Many employees think past actions predict how a manager will react. How does the ability to predict your manager's behavior impact your views about your job?

IMPACT OF MANAGER'S WORDS

Spoken messages impact relationships with employees. Regardless of the message's intent, how a person receives it affects the outcome of the interpersonal communication. If a manager communicates a sense of being concerned about employees, it will improve relationships with staff.

Respecting employees' views is another way to build stronger interpersonal communication. This approach tells them that the manager values their ideas and wants their assistance. Employees view this feedback as meaning their manager is interested in their development and performance.

Types of Interpersonal Communication

Managers should use the best methods of spoken communication to interact with their staff. Common ways include informal chatting and casual conversations to help build a friendly environment. These messages can include nonverbal communication such as a pat on the back, a smile of thanks, or a "thumbs up" to show appreciation and can result in a stronger bond with staff.

Effective managers also provide feedback to support employees. Feedback is easy and fast during interpersonal communication. Also, most employees like ongoing feedback about how they are doing rather than communication limited to yearly performance reviews. The more feedback employees receive, the more they will feel comfortable with it and look forward to the experience. Here are some ways managers can give feedback:

- Offer to provide ideas about or help with tasks.
- Invite employees for a coffee break.
- Point out positive things when providing feedback.
- Thank employees for their efforts even when they can improve.

Most feedback by managers relates to an employee's performance. **Constructive feedback** focuses on specific aspects of performance and can be positive such as emphasizing desired performance, or negative such as addressing performance that should be improved.

Exhibit 3.11 shows some ideas for providing constructive feedback that will make employees want to learn better ways to do job tasks.

THINK ABOUT IT . . .

Both formal, scheduled performance reviews and ongoing informal feedback are needed to let employees know how they are doing. What are some differences between formal and informal feedback? Which do you prefer?

Exhibit 3.11

GUIDELINES FOR CONSTRUCTIVE FEEDBACK

Guideline	Reason
Do not judge too quickly.	To be sure you have all the facts
Keep an open mind.	To base decisions on facts, not emotions
Avoid "talking down" to employees.	So employees do not feel you are acting superior
Be straightforward.	Because employees value direct communication
Be positive.	So employees feel they are not being punished but can use feedback as a learning opportunity
Be patient.	So employees understand you support them for the long term

INTERNAL AND EXTERNAL COMMUNICATION

Managers must have effective internal and external communication skills.

Internal communication relates to messages of all types sent by managers to all employees. In multi-unit companies the term also relates to communication between persons in individual units and others at district, regional, and corporate levels. Effective internal communication helps ensure that all employees in all departments know what is necessary to do their jobs. It is the foundation for teamwork. The internal audience is composed of owners, managers, and employees. They should receive communication that is timely, clear, concise, and informative.

External communication builds the customer base and helps build and maintain the establishment's desired identity throughout the community. The external audience includes customers, news media, community officials including law enforcement and other government employees, and vendors. Potential employees who may want to work at the establishment are also part of this group.

Exhibit 3.12 shows examples of the type of information communicated to internal and external groups.

Manager's Memo

While speaking is the most common type of interpersonal communication, written print and electronic communication can also be used. Examples include thank-you notes and short, encouraging messages.

Managers who use fast, simple, and free or very low-cost ways to provide ongoing communication are maintaining positive relationships with their staff. The result will likely be lower turnover rates and a committed team of employees who want to make their operation successful.

Exhibit 3.12

EXAMPLES OF INTERNAL AND EXTERNAL GROUP COMMUNICATION

Internal Communication Tools	External Communication Tools
Establishment vision and mission statements	Press releases
Establishment goals and plans	Advertisements
Operating procedures such as standardized recipes and checklists for opening and closing	Public relations such as sponsorship of community activities
Policy statements such as dress codes	Publicity such as a major government official dining at the establishment
Human resources materials such as job descriptions and explanations of compensation and benefits	Crisis management materials
Information about employee recognition and awards	Information about environmental and food-related issues

Developing Effective Messages

The process to develop effective organizational messages is similar to the method you learned earlier for developing written messages. This process is reviewed in *Exhibit 3.13*.

Exhibit 3.13

DEVELOPMENT OF ORGANIZATIONAL COMMUNICATION

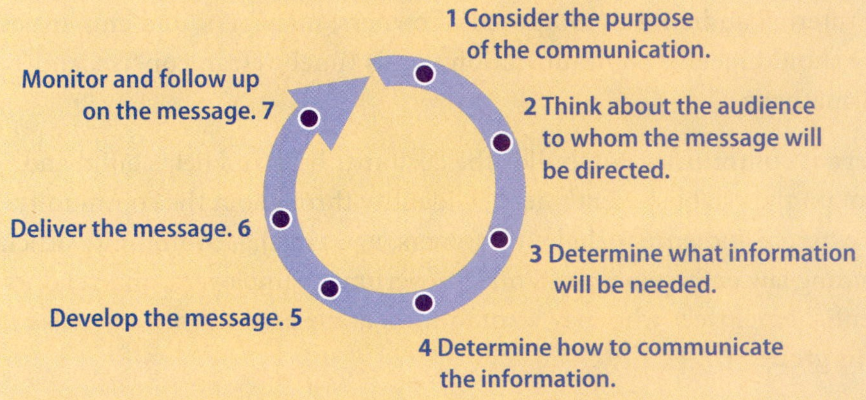

1 Consider the purpose of the communication.
2 Think about the audience to whom the message will be directed.
3 Determine what information will be needed.
4 Determine how to communicate the information.
Develop the message. 5
Deliver the message. 6
Monitor and follow up on the message. 7

MANAGING INFORMATION FOR MESSAGES

Internal or external messages are no better than the quality of the information they contain. Recall from chapter 2 that managers should collect information about the establishment itself, the community, the restaurant and foodservice industry, and global events. Then they and their employees can consider how all of that information may affect their business.

It is not necessary to "start over" collecting information every time a message must be written, a decision made, or a problem solved. Instead, new information is continually obtained and may change what is already known about a situation.

Managers should consider several questions when planning, developing, and processing messages. All of them relate to the major concerns of who, what, where, when, why, and how being emphasized in this chapter:

- Why is a message needed?
- What needs to be communicated?
- What are the best actions? Who needs to know?
- Who should be involved?
- When does the message need to go out?
- Where should the message be sent?

OPEN FOR BUSINESS

WHAT'S THE FOOTPRINT?

Professional managers know that environmental issues increasingly impact every restaurant and foodservice operation. These establishments are affected by regulatory changes including pollution reduction caused by community demands for better air quality. Restaurant and foodservice operations are often blamed for excessive solid waste, commonly thought of as garbage.

An operation's news releases and publicity about efforts to reduce, reuse, and recycle are great examples of external communication tools used to inform the public that the establishment cares about the environment.

- Where will the message be stored?
- How will the message affect operations?
- How will results be evaluated?

The availability of accurate and current information is the foundation for developing any type of communication.

PROCESSING MESSAGES

Restaurant and foodservice managers require an organized way to handle the messages they receive so they can assign a priority to them. For example, messages related to customers and quality concerns normally receive a high priority because they involve the operation's vision and mission. Other examples of priority messages include those from management, those involving financial issues, and those from community officials including health department personnel.

Managers receive many incoming messages during a workday. Preferably, telephone messages should be accepted when they come in. Managers should train employees in specific instructions for telephone use to ensure that all calls are quickly managed when they are away.

Most effective managers try to set aside two or three times during a work shift to view and act on written messages. Other managers manage messages by including when to create them and how to follow up on them on their daily to-do list.

Many messages can be properly addressed without follow-up. However, some messages will require efforts such as developing a report or obtaining information for a reply. Then the manager must decide if the matter requires personal attention or if it can be delegated.

Recall from chapter 1 that some tasks can be delegated, including detailed and repetitive tasks and those involving fact finding. Other tasks might involve representing the manager and tasks that provide educational opportunities for employees.

Records are needed of some types of messages, including those from job applicants and customers planning group events. Managers increasingly use electronic files since many messages that contain backup information are received electronically. Some managers make copies, perhaps for backup purposes, and maintain these in filing cabinets, binders, or in other ways for quick access.

Internal Communication

Successful restaurant and foodservice operations have effective communication between departments and down through the organization to employees.

COMMUNICATION BETWEEN DEPARTMENTS

Remember that communication flows downward, upward, and across a restaurant or foodservice organization. One purpose of information flow across the organization is to encourage and enable **interdepartmental communication**, which occurs between employees in different departments.

Sometimes restaurant and foodservice managers schedule meetings with all employees, possibly at different times, to discuss matters of interest to staff in every department. Examples of topics might be a new performance appraisal system or the rollout of a new customer service training program. These meetings are a good way to ensure all employees learn the same information. However, they can be expensive since the employees will be paid, and they can present schedule challenges.

Exhibit 3.14

Managers may use formal department-head or "executive committee" sessions for several purposes. For example, they can discuss operations-related problems, develop long-range or business plans, or determine how to reduce costs, among many other examples.

Formal communication can also occur between staff other than department heads. For example, entry-level employees may serve on cross-functional teams, and brief meetings held for persons in one department might include employees from other departments (*Exhibit 3.14*). Increasingly, operations may rely on **intranet** systems, which allow employees and teams to use the company's private communications network to share information and ideas. One possible concern with these systems is that messages sent over them provide permanent documentation about the sender's statements.

Careful attention to developing formal communication channels allows communication to flow easily between departments. There should be no "secrets" in the operation, and the free flow of information through effective communication can help prevent departmental "territories" from forming.

THINK ABOUT IT . . .

Communication issues often relate to the teamwork among departments. Concerns can be resolved when everyone works together to determine the best way to reach a goal.

Is teamwork better when communication is effective? Explain your answer.

When an operation has effective ways to communicate between departments, employees in each department will want to resolve problems in a way that is best for the establishment. This is a much better objective than one department "winning" while another department is forced to "lose."

If communication issues do arise between departments, they should be taken care of as quickly as possible. The restaurant or foodservice manager must be involved because he or she manages those who run the affected departments. However, there should be policies, procedures, job descriptions, and experience ("how we have done things before") to help ensure that a fair decision is made.

COMMUNICATION WITH EMPLOYEES

Managers must develop effective communication systems so all team members can quickly learn about changes such as new policies or new goals.

The importance of the information will likely determine the best method to use. Formal and important information such as a new policy might be distributed in one of these ways:

- Through the operation's intranet system
- On the operation's bulletin board
- In a special meeting called by the manager
- In the operation's newsletter

It is important that all employees learn the information at about the same time to reduce the impact of the "grapevine" circulating incorrect information.

Information of lesser importance might be provided by spoken messages from department heads or managers over several shifts. For example, if an establishment will be purchasing new salad bar equipment and making minor changes in dining-room design, all employees will likely want to know whether they are directly affected or not. Face-to-face conversations between department heads and managers, between managers and supervisors, and between supervisors and employees may be a useful way to inform the operation's team.

The examples just discussed involve one-way communication from manager to employees. Other types of information may require feedback. For example, if a new uniform policy is needed, employee feedback may be desired. Discussion meetings might be scheduled with affected personnel or a brief take-home survey might be distributed. Alternatively, a team of employees might be selected to develop recommendations.

Several principles are useful when managers respond to feedback:

- It should be recognized as soon as possible.
- Employees should be genuinely thanked for it.
- If the feedback is useful, employees might be asked about implementation suggestions, and ongoing feedback should be provided.
- If the feedback cannot be used, the manager should explain the reasons. Some feedback should be used, or employees will quickly conclude the manager is "going through the motions" of asking for ideas without really wanting them.

BULLETIN BOARDS: SPECIAL COMMUNICATION TOOLS

Some restaurant and foodservice managers miss a great opportunity to communicate with their team: employee bulletin boards (*Exhibit 3.15*). Some managers think of them as just a place to post employee work schedules and put up materials required by the health department.

Exhibit 3.15

RESTAURANT TECHNOLOGY

Some restaurant and foodservice establishments are now using intranet systems to serve some of the purposes of a bulletin board. The intranet provides exciting opportunities to communicate with employees that are not possible with traditional bulletin boards. For example, there is no space limitation; interesting and colorful graphics can be used; and employees can provide their ideas, suggestions, and other responses directly through the intranet system.

The system also can be used to alert employees about their work schedules and to update them about current events at the foodservice operations. Other uses include reminding employees about meetings and announcing new policies.

However, bulletin boards can also be effective communication tools. They can be used to post operating information such as last week's check average, customer comment scores for food quality, and the cost of dish breakage. This information can even be in the form of a contest won when a team exceeds goals.

Bulletin boards can also feature information about an employee of the month (or other time period), copies of customer comment cards with a public "thank you" for excellent performance, and general news about management decisions.

Information about progress toward long-range and business-plan goals can be posted so employees are aware of the status. This will be of special interest to those who helped with planning tasks.

Managers can request ideas about what employees would like to know. A suggestion box might be placed on or near the board in case employees have questions or comments. Information that is posted should be dated so materials can be removed in a timely manner. Some information, such as that required by law, must remain indefinitely. Other information, such as weekly schedules, might be routinely updated, and still other information can remain as long as there is a reason for having it posted.

Guidelines for posting information should be developed. They could be very simple if all information is posted by the manager and concerns operations-related topics. Guidelines become more important if, for example, employees can post information about employee sports teams, items for sale, and other topics that are less business-related. Perhaps a cross-functional team could provide input, with final details distributed to all employees. When guidelines are clear, employees will have few questions about whether items posted are appropriate.

External Communication

Managers are often challenged to determine the best ways to communicate with persons outside the operation.

EXTERNAL COMMUNICATION METHODS

Examples of ways to communicate information to persons not directly involved with the operation are reviewed in *Exhibit 3.16*.

Restaurant and foodservice managers have an ongoing interest in communicating with those close to their location. Exterior construction and parking-lot maintenance are examples of things that people living or working in the area may wish to know about. New establishment openings require an effective public-communication strategy to reduce fears of increased traffic, noise, or other problems.

Exhibit 3.16

METHODS OF EXTERNAL COMMUNICATION

Print Methods

- Letters
- Direct mail
- Coupons
- Press releases
- Billboards
- Posters and other signage
- Menu clip-ons or information placed on tables
- Newspaper articles or advertisements
- Flyers
- Take-home menus
- Telephone-book ads

Television and Radio

- Public service announcements (PSAs)
- Commercials

Direct Speaking

- In-person sales calls
- Conversations with customers
- Word of mouth
- Community service and other groups
- Telephone

Electronic

- Emails
- Text messaging
- Facebook
- Twitter
- Establishment Web site
- Electronic coupons

COMMUNICATION WITH CUSTOMERS

Restaurant and foodservice managers must communicate with their customers. As a basic guideline, the information can include anything that would interest the guests and benefit the establishment. Managers should constantly ask themselves questions that focus on who, what, where, when, why, and how. Examples include "What do guests want and need to know?" "Why do our guests need to know this?" and "When should our guests learn about this?"

One tool for determining information to provide to potential guests is the marketing plan. Remember from Chapter 2 that the marketing plan is a calendar of specific activities designed to meet the operation's revenue goals. When developed effectively, it provides details about advertising, publicity, press releases, and other information to be communicated to guests and potential guests at specified times.

There are several purposes for information provided to guests while they are at the establishment:

- To educate them about available products and services
- To increase revenues
- To ensure that they have an enjoyable dining experience
- To promote repeat visits

RESTAURANT TECHNOLOGY

Operations increasingly use their Web sites to communicate with potential and actual customers. Menu descriptions, information about future events, notes about the establishment's history, and public-relations information are among the topics found on most Web sites. Comments of past customers, information about recipes for favorite menu items, and details about carryout and delivery services may be posted. Still other examples include nutrition and allergen-related information that would be useful for persons considering a visit to the establishment.

Managers can use and should encourage their employees to use the interpersonal communication skills discussed in this chapter. They can also provide customer-service training programs that provide, among other topics, information about how to communicate with guests.

Menus, interior signage, and tabletop items are examples of written information available to guests when they visit the restaurant or foodservice operation. All information, regardless of how simple it might appear, should be thoughtfully designed and developed to ensure it properly represents the establishment to customers.

Written messages to and from customers should be among the manager's highest priorities. Examples include thank-you letters to regular customers and telephone calls to disappointed customers. Managers can draw on their experience and sense of hospitality as they develop and deliver responses to these routine situations.

Managers should think about routine interactions with customers, plan what they and their employees should do in each instance, and include this information in training programs.

A typical customer experience in a table-service establishment should resemble this example:

- Customers should be warmly and genuinely greeted by the first employees they see. If they are regular customers, employees should know their names and use them.
- When the server first reaches their table, another warm welcome in the spirit of hospitality should be provided ("Good evening; my name is Shirley, and I will be helping you this evening. I'm glad you're here, and we want to make sure you have an enjoyable experience.")
- Attention to details, excellent food and beverage products, and service that exceeds the customers' expectations are all part of the nonverbal communication that emphasizes the team members' concern for their customers.
- Thoughtful final words by the manager, personally if possible, are an appreciated gesture. A flat and insincere "Thanks for coming" should be replaced with something like "Thank you very much for visiting us tonight. We hope you had a great experience and that you will come back again soon." These comments, along with direct eye contact and a handshake, can be an "extra" that sets apart the establishment from its competitors.

Special policies and procedures will likely be important to guide managers as they react to potentially serious issues about foodborne illnesses, slips and falls, or other harmful concerns. Owners and managers should think about these and other common interactions and develop guidelines for interacting with customers.

OPEN FOR BUSINESS: RESTAURANT TECHNOLOGY

Increasingly, potential guests go online to learn others' views about establishments they may want to visit. Managers should closely monitor social media sites that post reviews by the general public.

Here are some points to address when responding to negative online postings:

1. Thank the reviewer for the feedback.
2. Apologize and provide a clear explanation about what caused the problem.
3. Note that specific actions have been taken to avoid a repeat.
4. Offer direct communication with you by email or phone.
5. Quote any positive comments. If the reviewer said the food was good but the service was bad, state you are pleased that the food was good.
6. End by again thanking the reviewer for the feedback.
7. Check for errors. Even with social media, messages should be professional.

Many sites allow the posting of positive comments with permission—a way to turn social media sites into powerful advertising.

The guidelines should be developed and driven by company policies and legal advice as needed. As with other formal written information, the guidelines should consider the five W's and How questions: Who? What? Where? When? Why? and How?

After review and approval by the owner or manager, the guidelines should be given to affected managers with the requirement that they be consistently followed.

Employees must be informed about the guidelines using methods including training programs, employee meetings before work shifts begin, and bulletin boards. They should be made aware of their importance and the need to always involve the proper persons when issues covered by the guidelines arise.

SUMMARY

1. **Explain why it is important for restaurant and foodservice managers to use effective communication skills.**

   Restaurant and foodservice managers must use communication skills on the job to interact with employees, customers, the owner or their manager, suppliers, community and government officials, and others. When they communicate, they represent both their establishment and themselves.

2. **Provide an overview of the communication process.**

   The communication process involves a sender relaying a message through one of a wide range of possible channels within an environment (context) to a receiver. Whether the message is understood relates, in part, to the context of the message and the barriers it encounters.

3. **Discuss common communication challenges.**

   Problems can occur at any point in the communication process, causing a seemingly simple message to be misunderstood. Effective communicators know about these challenges and attempt to avoid them.

4. **Review basic principles useful for business speaking, using the telephone, listening, writing, and controlling nonverbal communication.**

   Messages address the who, what, where, when, why, and how of a situation. Developing spoken messages involves the use of procedures to ensure that the message is clear, listeners "connect" with the speaker, and speakers check listeners' understanding of the message.

   Simple procedures can be used to make sure business telephone calls meet professional standards. They focus on being polite, obtaining accurate information, and providing help for the caller if necessary.

   The ability to listen effectively requires skill and experience. When basic principles are practiced, listeners are more likely to understand spoken messages.

Managers communicate with actions as well as words. Sometimes their nonverbal communication sends messages that do not match what they are saying. Managers should recognize common nonverbal actions and minimize those that create a negative impression.

5. **Identify strategies that enhance interpersonal communication.**

   Most communication for managers involves speaking in one-on-one or small-group situations. The process is often natural, but its effectiveness depends in part on the relationship of manager to employees and the work environment itself. When feedback is given to employees, principles for providing constructive feedback must be used.

6. **Explain practices for developing effective messages and for managing internal and external communication procedures.**

   Managers can use a wide variety of communication tools to send messages to internal and external groups. Basic procedures should be used to develop and process information. The content of messages is no better than the accuracy of the information used to develop them.

   Managers must ensure that there is effective communication throughout the organization. This can be a challenge to ensure the message does not change as it flows between departments and down the organization to employees.

   Managers communicate with persons outside the operation. Special guidelines are needed for serious issues such as foodborne illnesses and accidents, and employees must know and consistently follow them.

APPLICATION EXERCISE

Assume you are the manager of a high-volume restaurant or foodservice operation that employs about 75 full- and part-time employees. You have recently had problems with employees "no-showing" for their work shifts. They did not call to say they could not work, did not alert their supervisor about not being able to work during the shift, and did not show up for work.

You and your management team have developed a policy about no-shows and you will introduce it during two different all-employee meetings.

1. Develop an outline of your presentation to the employees to roll out the new policy. Consider the policy, if any, used where you do or have worked or interview classmates or an operations manager to learn about the policy in use at other establishments. You can also type "restaurant employee no show policy" into your favorite search engine to learn more about the content of policies and to see actual policies from restaurants.
2. When you develop your presentation, focus on the important questions:
   - Who?
   - What?
   - Where?
   - When?
   - Why?
   - How?
3. In addition to developing the presentation's content outline, what are three additional things you would do to prepare for the meeting?

4. What are three things you would do during your presentation to best ensure that it is successful?

5. What are three things you would do after your presentation as follow-up to ensure that the policy is implemented?

REVIEW YOUR LEARNING

Select the best answer for each question.

1. Restaurant or foodservice managers who use effective communication skills will be able to

A. meet profit goals.
B. build employee trust.
C. obtain the next promotion.
D. avoid having to rewrite a letter.

2. Spoken or written words and nonverbal actions are examples of which element of the communication process?

A. Message channel
B. Message context
C. Message barriers
D. Message content

3. What must a message receiver do to understand a message?

A. Interpret it.
B. Agree with it.
C. Trust the sender.
D. Review it two times.

4. Which will help ensure a message is understood?

A. Use technical language.
B. Consider the receiver's background.
C. Deliver messages one-on-one when possible.
D. Repeat the message before the receiver asks questions.

5. Which of the following "W" words should be answered to determine the content for a message?

A. Will
B. Who
C. Wonder
D. Wish

6. Which is a basic writing principle?

A. Ask questions for the reader to answer.
B. Be brief so the reader can ask questions.
C. Always try to express a positive attitude.
D. Include everything possible about the topic.

7. When is nonverbal communication most apparent?

A. In written communication
B. During one-on-one conversations
C. When a person is giving a speech
D. When a person is listening to a speaker

8. Ideally, when should telephone calls be accepted?

A. When they are received
B. During the receiver's free time
C. Two or three times daily in batches
D. In a priority based on whether the receiver knows the caller

9. When should managers respond to employee feedback?

A. As soon as possible
B. Never, unless they have requested it
C. When they have considered if they will use it
D. After they have thought about their relationship with the sender

10. How does a marketing plan help managers decide what information should be provided to customers?

A. It sets a priority on information based on profitability.
B. It provides details about the success of previous communication.
C. It ensures that only "nice to know" information is communicated.
D. It provides details about the type of information to be communicated.

4 Leaders Facilitate Employee Performance

INSIDE THIS CHAPTER

- Motivating Employees
- Employee Development Programs
- Maintaining a Positive Workplace Environment
- The Leader as Coach
- Managing Conflict
- Employee Performance Appraisals

CHAPTER LEARNING OBJECTIVES

After completing this chapter, you should be able to:

- Explain principles to help employees become motivated.
- Review procedures for planning and implementing employee development programs.
- State procedures helpful in maintaining a positive workplace.
- Describe basic coaching practices.
- Identify ways to manage conflict.
- Explain procedures for conducting effective performance appraisals.

KEY TERMS

arbitration, p. 115
coaching, p. 112
conflict resolution, p. 115
cross-training, p. 102
discrimination, p. 111
employee development program, p. 100
esteem needs, p. 93
harassment, p. 107
Herzberg's two-factor theory, p. 94
hostile environment (sexual harassment), p. 110
incentive, p. 92
maintenance factor (two-factor theory), p. 94
Maslow's hierarchy of needs, p. 93
mediation, p. 115
motivation, p. 92
motivation factor (two-factor theory), p. 94
negotiation, p. 115
personnel file, p. 98
physiological needs, p. 93
progressive discipline, p. 113
quid pro quo (sexual harassment), p. 109
safety needs, p. 93
self-actualization, p. 94
sexual harassment, p. 109
social needs, p. 93
zero tolerance, p. 110

CASE STUDY

"Sometimes it doesn't make a lot of sense!" said Nick to Dave. The two restaurant managers were talking to each other during a break at the local restaurant association meeting.

"What do you mean?" asked Dave. "We're talking about employee development programs and how useful they can be."

"Yes," replied Nick, "Don't you think we spend a lot of time planning educational programs for our key employees? Then, when they acquire the knowledge and skills on our time and at our expense, they move on to other establishments. I sometimes think we are really training people for our competitors."

1. What do you think about Nick's views on employee development programs?
2. What can Nick do to keep the employees who successfully complete his educational development programs?

MOTIVATING EMPLOYEES

One of the greatest challenges a restaurant or foodservice manager faces today is motivating employees. Most successful managers know their businesses cannot reach their goals without the ongoing efforts of their staff. How do these managers obtain higher levels of performance from their employees than less successful managers?

The traditional definition of **motivation** is "those factors that cause a person to behave or act in either a goal-seeking or satisfying manner and may be influenced by physiological drives or by external stimuli." Put another way, motivation is the process of providing a person with a reason to do something. In other words, it involves providing **incentives**, which are factors such as recognition or wanting to be part of a group that make employees act in ways that help them reach personal goals.

The Importance of Motivated Employees

What type of employee do managers want to work for them? Do they want employees who show up on time, do exactly what the managers say and no more, and leave promptly at the end of the shift? In fact, these employees would be better than some employees who come to work late, do as little as possible (some of which does not meet standards), and then leave early.

What if managers had employees who were cheerful, liked to do the work and interact with team members, and made suggestions about how to improve tasks? What if the employees wanted to learn more, be promoted, and enjoy a career (not just a job) with the operation? These ideal employees could be counted on to "go the extra mile" and to genuinely like the customers and other employees. It is easy to see that this type of employee is the type that managers want working for them. In fact, it would be great if every employee were like this.

THINK ABOUT IT . . .

How much would you pay to have motivated employees? Good news! Almost every idea in this chapter involves no money. What role do you think money plays in motivating employees?

When thinking about benefits to the operation from having an ideal employee, it is easy to understand the importance of motivated employees. Customers like smiling employees who genuinely want to help them. Employees who are not motivated and do not care are less likely than other employees to meet service standards.

Motivation Concepts

Managers cannot force employees to feel motivated, because employees have a personal interest in doing or not doing something. They can direct employees, but if the employees are not motivated, managers will not get the responses they want. The employees may do the work to minimum standards to keep their job. However, they are not likely to promote teamwork, make suggestions, and be interested in their job. Then customer service, work quality, teamwork, and ultimately profits can all suffer.

While managers cannot force employees to feel motivated, they can create conditions that employees find motivating. Here is the challenge: What motivates one person may not motivate another. People are motivated by different needs including social interaction, job satisfaction, and wanting to feel important. It is important to note that the factors that motivate an employee can change over time.

Everyone is different, and this is why effective managers try to learn about their employees' interests. Then they can begin to learn what can be done to allow the employees to motivate themselves.

To better understand what motivation is and is not, two models are helpful: Abraham Maslow's hierarchy of needs and Frederick Herzberg's two-factor theory.

MASLOW'S HIERARCHY OF NEEDS

Maslow's hierarchy of needs states that people have five basic needs that typically arise in a certain order. As soon as one need is fulfilled to the desired extent, a person is motivated to fulfill the next need. The five needs are shown in *Exhibit 4.1*.

The lowest or most basic needs are **physiological needs**. These needs relate to the body and include food, water, air, and sleep. Employees' physiological needs are met through heating, air conditioning, lighting, meal and rest breaks, and limits on work hours.

When these needs are met to an extent determined by each person, people are motivated to fulfill their safety needs. **Safety needs** concern those things that make people feel secure or keep them safe. These things can be physical such as shelter or a dependable income, or they can be more personal such as freedom from stress. In the workplace, safety needs can be met by factors including fair wages, healthcare and other benefits, safety procedures, and safe operating equipment.

The next level in Maslow's model involves **social needs**, the interest most people have in interacting with others. These needs include love, belonging, and friendship. In the workplace, social needs can be met through friendship, teamwork, and a sense of belonging or acceptance, all of which are encouraged by a welcoming atmosphere.

Esteem needs are at the fourth level, and they focus on how people feel about themselves and how they think others feel about them. Esteem needs in the workplace may be met by recognition, promotions, titles, appreciation, opportunities, and other factors.

OPEN FOR BUSINESS

KEEPING IT SAFE

Professional restaurant and foodservice managers are very concerned about the safety of their employees and customers. They routinely include safety topics as part of the training they give to new employees. When new equipment is installed, they stress safe ways to operate it. As they move around the operation and constantly observe and compare what they see to established standards, managers can point out safety-related issues such as wet floors to avoid slips and falls and unsafe use of knives that results in accidental cuts. Their concern about safety continues as they plan and train employees about what to do in case of accidents, fire, robbery, or natural disaster.

You are learning that employees are themselves motivated, as are all persons, to meet basic safety needs. Now managers can add employee motivation as a reason to continually stress safety concerns on the job.

Exhibit 4.1

MASLOW'S HIERARCHY OF NEEDS

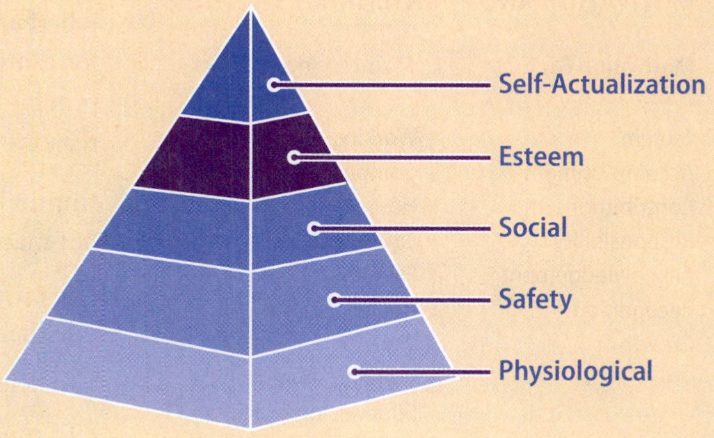

Manager's Memo

Improving maintenance factors is not likely to motivate employees to do better work. Instead, maintenance factors help employees do their basic job, and employees expect certain conditions to be adequate. For example, if you fix the air conditioner in the kitchen, it may prevent employee dissatisfaction, but adequate air conditioning will not motivate employees.

In contrast, if you respect an employee and make him or her feel good about the job, you are creating an atmosphere in which the employee can find satisfaction and motivation in the workplace.

At the highest level is the need for **self-actualization**: the drive to do the very best that one can do. This makes people push themselves, learn new things, and be creative. In the workplace, this need may motivate employees to become the most productive they can be, to produce the best quality work they can, or to develop themselves for other positions.

Each person considers "how much is enough" before he or she becomes motivated to address the next need. For example, the lack of health insurance may cause one person to feel insecure, while another may not be bothered by this. One employee may want to be recognized with a promotion, while another may not care about job titles. Complicating this for managers is the issue that people's needs change; what motivates a person at one time may not motivate him or her later.

HERZBERG'S TWO-FACTOR THEORY

Some people assume that factors that motivate people and those that do not motivate them are opposites. For example, if someone is motivated to work hard to earn vacation time, the same person would not be motivated to work hard if there were no vacation time.

Herzberg's two-factor theory proposes that this reasoning is not correct. This theory identifies two different sets of factors that can motivate and demotivate employees. As their name implies, **motivation factors** are things that motivate people. Things that do not motivate people are called **maintenance factors**. Examples of these two types of factors are shown in *Exhibit 4.2*.

Notice that motivation factors can be personal and difficult to measure. For example, an employee who is concerned about esteem and accomplishment might be motivated to do a good job on a special project. Motivation factors encourage employees to work harder, go beyond the ordinary, and make a real difference in their workplace.

Exhibit 4.2

MOTIVATION AND MAINTENANCE FACTORS

Motivation Factors	Maintenance Factors
• Esteem	• Working conditions
• Accomplishment	• Company policies
• Contribution	• Hours
• Responsibility	• Equipment
• Acknowledgement	• Fair pay
• Recognition	• Health benefits
• Growth	• Time off
	• Working relationships
	• Supervision style

Maintenance factors are things that, if not taken care of, can make employees unhappy and prevent them from doing a good job. If an employee believes he or she does not receive fair pay, for example, this belief will make it difficult or impossible to provide on-the-job conditions in which the employee will find reasons to become motivated.

Improving maintenance factors will not motivate employees, but managers may do so for other reasons:

- To provide the tools, situations, and support employees need to do their work
- To help prevent poor morale and high employee-turnover rates
- To model respectful behavior

Effective managers help their employees be successful by creating a workplace that encourages success. This will be one in which maintenance factors are satisfactory and some motivation factors are present. This type of environment does not just happen. Instead, good managers plan for it, develop it, and maintain it. Helping employees accomplish the things that are important to them helps create that motivational relationship.

Employee Expectations

Employees respond best to managers they respect and trust. Employees come to their workplace hoping to work with managers who have positive qualities. As seen in *Exhibit 4.3*, their expectations fall into three groups: professionalism, personal treatment, and work and task support.

Professionalism refers to employees expecting their managers to demonstrate a high level of skills and knowledge and to exhibit high standards. They want their managers to serve the interests of the customers and their employees and to practice the concepts of leadership, excellence, honesty, and respect for others.

Personal treatment refers to the way managers interact with their employees and the operation's value system that governs their daily conduct. Employees expect their managers to be ethical.

Work and task support deals with work resources, work life, and environment. Employees expect to have the necessary tools and equipment to meet the work standards expected of them. They want their managers to give clear directions about how to do required work. Hazards and risks are always present in a restaurant or foodservice operation, and employees want a safe work environment. Finally, employees need and want support for their own professional development.

Effective managers learn how to meet their employees' expectations. The benefits gained are usually in direct proportion to the amount of time allocated. Managers who develop themselves and their employees and who provide an encouraging work environment are not likely to have motivational challenges. A wise manager knows that he or she is less likely to be promoted unless someone can quickly assume the manager's job duties. This points to the mutual benefit of professional development programs for employees.

Motivation Methods

Exhibit 4.4 on the next page applies some of the ideas just presented. It shows how managers can provide opportunities for employees to move toward their personal goals on the job. The ultimate results of doing this can be a "win-win" for both the manager and the employees.

Exhibit 4.3

EXPECTATIONS OF EMPLOYEES

Professionalism

- Demonstrate knowledge
- Demonstrate leadership
- Practice honesty
- Practice confidentiality
- Practice respect
- Practice moral behavior
- Practice ethics

Personal Treatment

- Practice fairness
- Practice consistency
- Provide support
- Practice compassion
- Provide feedback
- Avoid embarrassing employees

Work and Task Support

- Provide clear directions
- Provide tools and resources
- Encourage professional growth and development
- Include employees in decision-making that affects them
- Provide a safe environment
- Practice reasonable and rational behavior

Exhibit 4.4

MOTIVATION METHODS

Create a sense of engagement.	• Discover what is important to each employee. • Find out each employee's working style. • Explain the role each employee plays in reaching goals. • Make job tasks more interesting by giving employees more responsibility.
Model the desired professional behavior.	• Take time to meet and listen to your staff. • Use proper operating procedures. • Demonstrate cooperation and teamwork. • Be enthusiastic. • Get all the facts and make careful judgments when there is employee conflict. • Respect your employees.
Keep a positive attitude.	• Be hospitable to complaining customers. • When revenue or cost goals are not met, involve employees in creative processes to fix the problems. • Be energetic and passionate about work and the business.
Treat employees with respect.	• Use "please" and "thank you." • Ask employees for their ideas. • Treat employees as you would like to be treated.
Treat employees fairly.	• Treat equal performers equally. • Give all employees opportunities to grow and learn new skills. • Apply all policies consistently.
Get to know your staff.	• Ask employees about their background. • Learn about employees' families.
Encourage open feedback.	• Keep an "open door" policy. • Ask for feedback. • Do not react negatively if someone does not agree with you. • Encourage new ideas and suggestions. • Learn from mistakes; do not punish employees for them.
Encourage involvement and inclusion.	• Create team challenges. • Allow employees to help set their own goals. • Involve employees in decisions that affect them. • Provide staff with a sense of ownership of their work and workspace.
Communicate regularly.	• Give timely updates. • If a learning opportunity is available, communicate it immediately. • Provide information about how the operation makes and loses money. • Explain employees' role in plans for upcoming products and services. • Praise employees for exceptional performance.
Share operations and industry knowledge.	• Share information from the educational programs you attend. • Share industry publications with your employees.
Empower employees.	• Do not manage details that employees can manage. • Identify staff who want to accept responsibilities and delegate various tasks to them. • Allow your employees to do great work by applying their personal creativity to solving problems.
Identify factors that motivate each employee.	• Ask employees what they would like for rewards and recognition. • Create rewards and recognition programs.
Recognize high performance and achievement.	• Celebrate individual and team successes by acknowledging them to all employees. • Send a thank-you note when a job is done well. • Place a note in the employee's file about a job well done.

Basic communication and employee involvement can fulfill many of the needs that motivate employees. Acknowledging people, sharing information, and expressing appreciation and interest are easy, inexpensive, and effective ways to motivate your staff.

ACKNOWLEDGING EMPLOYEES

Showing employees that he or she cares about them is an important but overlooked way for a manager to motivate them. Simple acts like saying hello, calling them by name, and making eye contact can help set a positive tone.

It is important to greet employees every day at the start of the shift, shake hands, and smile. Managers who do not welcome their employees make them feel unappreciated. It is a mistake to give anyone that unintended message.

Saying hello provides an opportunity for the manager to check *in* with employees rather than check *on* them. Then he or she can ask how the employees are doing and confirm they are ready for work.

Make it a habit to say goodbye at the end of the shift. Mention something that went well during the shift and thank them for their help (*Exhibit 4.5*).

THINK ABOUT IT . . .

What do you think about a boss who shows pleasant politeness when you begin and end work? Are there any disadvantages to treating your employees like customers as they enter and leave the establishment?

Exhibit 4.5

EXPRESSING APPRECIATION

Almost every employee appreciates a simple "thank you" for a job well done or for exceptional effort. In addition to saying this informally, place a positive note in the employee's **personnel file**. A personnel file is maintained for each employee and contains confidential documents including their employment application, emergency contact form, disciplinary action history, and current personal information. Personal notes can be useful when formally evaluating the employee's performance, but share the note with the employee immediately.

Some managers have meetings to update their employees about operating information. They also use these meetings to publicly thank individuals or teams. Smaller team or shift meetings provide the same opportunity (*Exhibit 4.6*).

When customers write favorable notes that mention an employee's name, share them with the entire staff by posting them on the bulletin board or reading them at shift meetings. While doing this might embarrass an employee, normally it makes him or her and the rest of the employees feel good. It also encourages everyone to work harder to get recognition.

Exhibit 4.6

SHARING INFORMATION

Most employees like to know what is going on in their operation because it helps them feel secure, valued, and involved. If new things are happening, tell them. If a special group of customers is coming in, let them know. Some managers forget to or do not want to share this information, and they lose a chance to motivate their staff.

Sharing information creates a foundation for involving employees. To get employees to cooperate with new policies and procedures, for example, they are more likely to do so if they understand why the changes are needed.

Sharing information can be a first step in asking for their help in solving a problem. For example, one way to encourage employees to be careful with glassware is to tell them about the cost of breakage. If they understand how breakage takes money away from other things like new equipment or bonuses, they may be motivated to be more careful.

THINK ABOUT IT . . .

Would you like to know about things going on at work? Are there any disadvantages to sharing general information about the business with employees? Why do you think some managers do not do this?

SHOWING INTEREST

Asking someone "How are you?" and listening to the answer shows interest in that person as an individual. Asking "How is it going here?" or "What do you think about that?" shows that the manager cares about their experience at work and is open to learning their ideas.

Caution: Remember that there is a difference between simple interest and harassment, discrimination, or prying. Managers should not ask questions about topics they would not ask in a job interview such as marital status, race, ethnicity, religion, sexual preference, or disability. If unsure about a question, managers should not ask it.

INVOLVING EMPLOYEES

When involving employees in planning and decision making, managers recognize them as valuable persons and team members. They also give them chances for responsibility, contribution, creativity, and growth. In addition, asking for input shows the manager's commitment to teamwork, and involving employees often produces better plans and decisions than when input is not received.

Managers can involve employees in informal discussions, formal committees, projects, and programs. Talk to employees, get their ideas, and consider them before making decisions. Listen to their ideas, thank them, and do not criticize their suggestions.

THINK ABOUT IT . . .

Has someone ever asked you a question and then not paid attention to your answer? How did you know he or she was not interested? How did that make you feel?

Exhibit 4.7

OPPORTUNITIES FOR EMPLOYEE INPUT

• New menu items • New beverage items • Ways to respond to customer complaints • Suggestions to reduce costs • Ways to improve customer satisfaction • Setting of team goals	• Ways to improve the overall operation • Food safety practices • Food handling suggestions • Marketing ideas • Ways to increase customer check average

When customers complain, ask employees for ideas to help solve the problem. Motivated employees who want to help the operation can often make helpful suggestions.

Exhibit 4.7 shows examples of concerns where employee input might be helpful.

EMPLOYEE DEVELOPMENT PROGRAMS

Every restaurant or foodservice employee has more potential that can be developed. Some employees may have difficulty doing some of the tasks in their present position. Other high-performing employees could help the operation and themselves if they learned how to do additional tasks and perhaps be promoted. Managers improve motivation when they help employees improve their job performance.

Who Is Responsible?

At the following times, a manager should try to improve an employee's skills and knowledge:

- The employee has basic skills but could improve productivity with more advanced skills.
- The employee has been given a new job requiring additional skills.
- Changes are planned for the employee's existing job.
- The employee wants to qualify for a different job requiring different skills.

Managers can work with employees to plan and implement an **employee development program**, an organized series of actions planned to expand an employee's skills and knowledge. Actions can include formal activities such as attending a workshop or informal activities such as working on a delegated project.

The responsibilities for employee development should be shared. The operation must provide or allow for development opportunities and often pays some or all of the costs. The manager should help the employee assess needs, suggest development methods, and determine progress. The employee must improve performance and reach goals.

Overview of the Employee Development Process

Exhibit 4.8 shows the steps in the employee development process.

Note that the first step in the employee development process is to establish goals. These should focus on the operation's needs first and then the employee's goals. Frequently, these will be the same, since a motivated employee helps himself or herself while benefiting the company.

An operation's training budget is often a concern when professional development plans are considered. The budget may not be affected at all when, for example, a learning activity involves sitting in on a managers' meeting or

Exhibit 4.8

EMPLOYEE DEVELOPMENT PROCESS

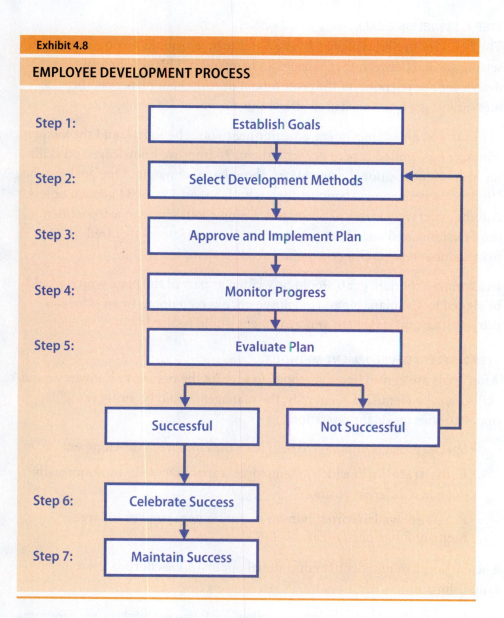

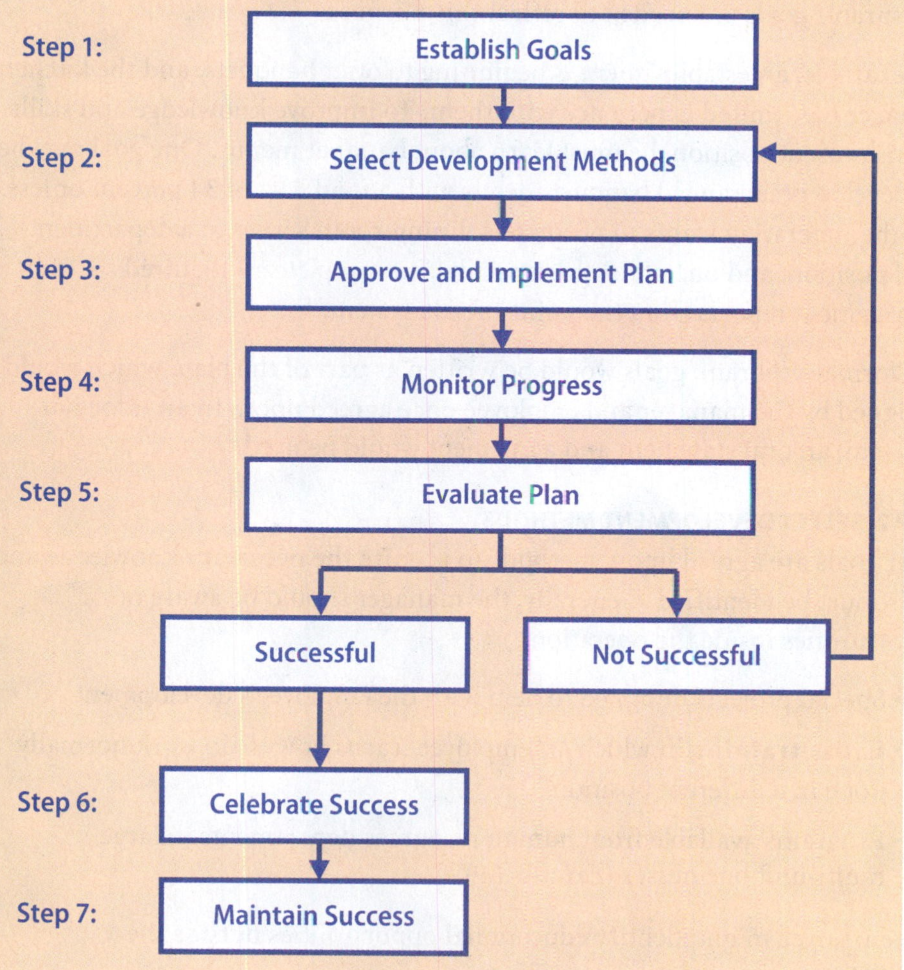

completing a project. The budget will likely be impacted if the activity involves signing up for an online course or attending a restaurant association workshop in another city.

Restaurant and foodservice managers should be aware of the amount budgeted for professional development and then consider priorities when developing plans for specific employees.

Effective managers inform their eligible employees about professional development opportunities that are available based on the plans that have been discussed. Employees should also know that funds are limited and priorities based on the operation's needs will guide decision making.

STEP 1: ESTABLISH GOALS

The first step in the employee development process should involve a goal-setting session between the manager and employee. This session can determine the purposes of the professional development plan. Specific, measurable goals are needed to reflect this purpose.

For example, an establishment is beginning to offer banquets, and the kitchen manager has limited experience with them. To improve knowledge and skills for his present position, he must learn about banquet menus. One goal may be "to develop prearranged banquet menus with a food cost of 34 percent or less." Another operation wants to promote a dining-room server to a department-head position, and one of her goals will be "to complete all required management reports from the point-of-sale system."

In a formal program, goals would be written as part of the plan, which would be signed by the manager and employee once agreed upon. In an informal program, an oral statement and agreement would be used.

STEP 2: SELECT DEVELOPMENT METHODS

After goals are agreed upon, methods to acquire the necessary knowledge and skills must be identified. Generally, the manager should be aware of opportunities inside the operation:

- Special projects designed to help with the employee's development
- **Cross-training** in which an employee learns how to do work normally done in a different position
- Programs available from human resources departments in large multi-unit businesses (*Exhibit 4.9*)

The employee might identify educational opportunities outside the establishment:

- Local trade school, community college, or four-year educational programs
- Trade or professional association resources

- Books, videos, and computer-based training programs
- Educational classes and materials available on the Internet

Exhibit 4.9

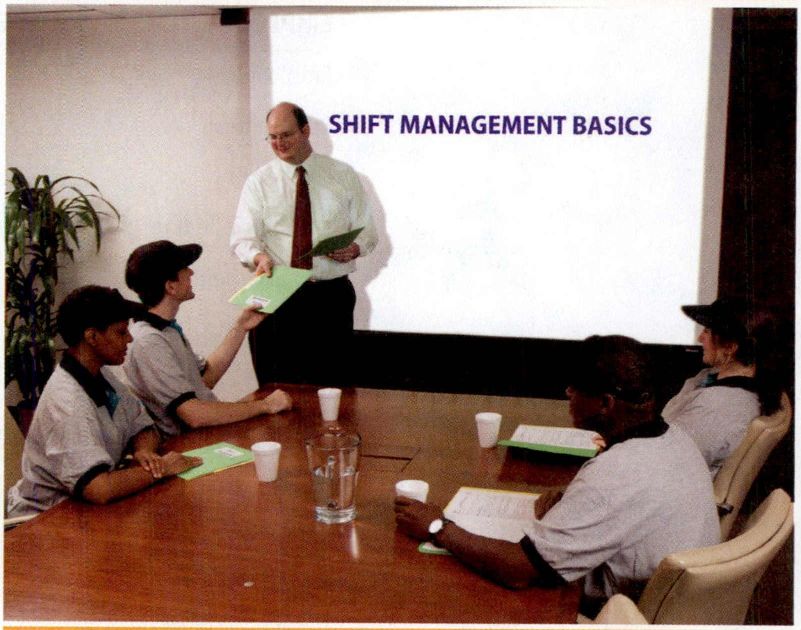

STEP 3: APPROVE AND IMPLEMENT THE PLAN

Several questions should be addressed as the employee development plan is designed:

- How will different activities in the plan be prioritized?
- How much time can the employee spend on each activity?
- How much time will the employee spend on each activity? This question introduces the idea that the employee must be committed to the plan. It also suggests that some personal time away from work might be needed to complete some learning activities.
- What does the operation expect as a result of successful completion of the activity?
- How will the plan be evaluated?

A specific, measurable goal should be established for each educational activity. When this is done, it is easier to evaluate success.

The actual employee development plan can be a relatively short statement including these topics:

- Plan goals
- The plan's time frame
- Development activities
- How success will be measured
- When progress checks will be done

After the development program is planned, it should be implemented. Success will depend on the manager providing the agreed-upon resources and the employee following through with all commitments.

Exhibit 4.10

EMPLOYEE DEVELOPMENT PLAN

Employee: ______________________ Manager: ______________________

Present position: ______________________

Desired position: ______________________

Goal (include time frame to complete plan): ______________________

Development Plan

A. For additional knowledge:

	Knowledge Needed	How to Attain (Development Activities)	Target Completion Date
1			
2			
3			

B. For additional skills:

	Skill Needed	How to Attain (Development Activities)	Target Completion Date
1			
2			
3			

C. Additional development activities:

D. Dates for progress review:

Plan Revisions and Schedule:	Planned	Actual

______________________ ______________________

Employee Date Manager Date

Exhibit 4.10 shows a worksheet that a manager can use to assist an employee interested in developing a plan to attain the knowledge and skills needed for another position. The plan is designed to help prepare an employee for another position. A series of these development plans can be used over time to address transfer or advancement to additional positions.

STEPS 4 AND 5: MONITOR PROGRESS AND EVALUATE THE PLAN

Throughout the program, the manager and employee should meet to discuss progress and ways to overcome any obstacles. The manager should do several things during these sessions:

- Observe the employee's new and existing behaviors.
- Provide feedback about what is observed and whether it is satisfactory.
- Discuss the progress toward the goals and whether it is acceptable.

Formal monitoring of activities can occur at the time of performance review sessions. In some operations, educational development goals are included with performance-related goals and the performance appraisal addresses both types of activities.

Evaluation of progress toward attaining the plan is easier if the developmental activities are measurable. For example, the development plan for a cook might include learning how to precost recipes. A specified number of recipes can be costed, and the cook and manager can then discuss how these calculations impact selling prices and food-cost percentages. Similarly, the dining-room server's ability to complete management reports according to the operation's procedures can be easily evaluated.

STEPS 6 AND 7: CELEBRATE AND MAINTAIN SUCCESS

After activities have been evaluated, the manager and employee can determine whether each activity was successfully completed. If so, they may discuss additional activities or even begin revising the employee's development plan to include additional tasks and responsibilities.

If the planned knowledge or skills goals are not met, it may be necessary to select additional development methods and continue with the development process. The manager will need to determine whether it is more important for the operation to provide additional money for this employee's second attempt or to invest in the educational development process of other employees. This decision will be easier to make as the manager considers the employee's history of attaining career development plans and whether the employee is actually motivated to learn more and to remain with the restaurant or foodservice operation.

The employee may be asked to provide an oral or written summary of the learning experience, which can be useful in determining if the experience might be beneficial for other employees. If applicable, documentation of attendance at educational events such as food vendor shows and local hospitality association meetings can also be requested. Ideally, information learned at these events will be brought back to and be implemented at the restaurant or foodservice operation.

Successful completion of agreed-upon activities should be followed by recognition of success. This may range from a simple "Congratulations; you're the best!" to a job promotion. A record of educational activities in which the employee has participated should be maintained. This information should be part of the employee's personnel file.

The final step noted in *Exhibit 4.8* is to "maintain success." Hopefully, this means that the employee will have enjoyed the professional development process. He or she will want to continue to learn more and advance up a career ladder to increasingly more responsible positions within the organization and the industry.

REAL MANAGER

LEADERS FACILITATE EMPLOYEE PERFORMANCE

Motivating employees is a critical factor in successful restaurant and foodservice management. In the early 1980s, I was working at Popeye's. One of our cashiers particularly stood out. She was smart and hardworking. I mentored her, and she rose quickly through the ranks. One of my proudest memories was seeing her finally able to purchase a home of her own and move her mother and family out of the projects. A true leader strives to promote and reward employee performance.

MAINTAINING A POSITIVE WORKPLACE ENVIRONMENT

When employees feel valued and involved in helping the manager reach goals, they feel better about their workplace. Also, when their contributions are recognized and rewarded, employees will become even more motivated and involved. This cycle of involvement and motivation improves work performance and increases profits.

Building a Positive Workplace Environment

Managers can build a positive work climate in many ways, and focusing on employees is an important part of almost every effort.

FOCUS ON EMPLOYEES

A supportive climate can be built and maintained by spending some time with each employee. Conduct one-on-one sessions for training and performance reviews, and make an effort to help all employees meet their needs on the job.

Nothing can affect an employee's feelings about the work environment more than a manager who does not keep promises. Be honest and upfront about what you can do to satisfy employees' needs. Employees take pride in their work environment when they feel valued and respected, and this personal focus will result in an improved work climate.

MAINTAIN OPEN COMMUNICATION

Open and honest communication between managers and employees is needed to create a positive workplace. Asking for and receiving feedback makes employees feel more involved with operations and improves their attitude about work. In contrast, a lack of openness creates "departmental silos" that discourage communication and teamwork. The term *departmental silos* refers to an emphasis on communication that flows up and down and through each department but not between departments or throughout the organization.

THINK ABOUT IT . . .

"The team functions as a family at work, and managers can help create this environment for their staff."

Do you believe this? Why or why not?

CELEBRATE SUCCESS AND BUILD TEAMS

Improve the work climate by celebrating the successes of employees and teams. Connect celebrations to reaching goals, finishing special projects, and reinforcing desired behaviors. For example, encouraging teamwork among employees and then celebrating it helps create a positive work environment.

PROMOTE DIVERSITY AND FAIRNESS

Modeling the value of diversity goes beyond hiring practices. Follow up on all harassment or discrimination claims that may occur. Employees who observe unfair practices in the workplace do not enjoy their work experience, and this hurts the manager's efforts to improve the work environment.

Successful restaurant or foodservice managers know that diversity adds value to their workforce. The variety of ideas to help with problem solving, the range of available talents, and the employees' ability to anticipate the needs of increasingly diverse customers improve as the diversity of the employee base increases.

All employees meeting reasonable requirements should equally participate in informal and formal professional development experiences and be considered for promotional opportunities if they desire them. Additionally, performance appraisal concerns should address only work or behavior that does not meet established standards that apply to all employees in the same position.

More about the Manager's Role

The manager is a common element in methods of building a positive work environment. The power of the position, however, will go only so far. Managers must take steps to create a positive work climate:

- Have patience. Developing a positive environment takes time. Good managers take the time because they value their employees.
- Make a dedicated effort. People management is a full-time job. Without a focused and ongoing effort, a positive work climate cannot be maintained.
- Show genuine concern. Employees value a manager who values them. Effective managers know that being concerned about individuals as well as work performance produces long-term benefits.
- Set a positive example. Managers should ask themselves, "How do my words and actions help or hurt my employees when they try to do their jobs?" If managers analyze their own behavior and feelings and ensure they present the best image for the operation, they will improve the work climate.

If managers show their own excitement about what the team must accomplish, their employees will display similar energy and excitement about working for the establishment.

Ensuring a Fair Workplace

It is not possible to maintain a positive workplace unless all employees are treated equally. One aspect of this is the prevention of harassment.

Harassment is a form of employment discrimination that violates Title VII of the Civil Rights Act of 1964, the Age Discrimination in Employment Act (ADEA) of 1967, and the Americans with Disabilities Act (ADA) of 1990. **Harassment** is unwelcome conduct based on race, color, religion, sex (including pregnancy), national origin, age (40 or older), disability, or genetic information. Harassment becomes unlawful when (1) enduring the offensive conduct becomes a condition of continued employment, or (2) the conduct is severe or pervasive enough to create a work environment that a reasonable person would consider intimidating, hostile, or abusive.

Antidiscrimination laws also prohibit harassment against individuals in response to filing a discrimination charge, testifying, or participating in any way in an investigation, proceeding, or lawsuit under these laws; or opposing employment practices that they reasonably believe discriminate against individuals, in violation of these laws.

Petty slights, annoyances, and isolated incidents unless extremely serious will not rise to the level of illegality. To be unlawful, the conduct must create a work environment that would be intimidating, hostile, or offensive to reasonable people.

Offensive conduct may include offensive jokes, slurs, epithets (abusive terms), or name-calling; physical assaults or threats; intimidation; ridicule or mockery; insults or put-downs; offensive objects or pictures; and interference with work performance. Harassment can occur in a variety of circumstances, and here are several examples:

- The harasser can be the victim's manager, a manager in another area, an agent of the employer, a coworker, or a nonemployee.
- The victim does not have to be the person harassed, but can be anyone affected by the offensive conduct.
- Unlawful harassment may occur without economic injury to or discharge of the victim.

Exhibit 4.11

Prevention is the best tool to eliminate workplace harassment. Employers are encouraged to take appropriate steps to prevent and correct unlawful harassment. They should clearly communicate to employees that unwelcome harassing conduct will not be tolerated. They can do this by establishing an effective complaint or grievance process, providing antiharassment training to their managers and employees, and taking immediate and appropriate action when an employee complains (*Exhibit 4.11*). Employers should strive to create an environment in which employees feel free to raise concerns and are confident that those concerns will be addressed.

Employees are encouraged to inform the harasser directly that the conduct is unwelcome and must stop. Employees should also report harassment to management at an early stage to prevent it from increasing.

EMPLOYER LIABILITY FOR HARASSMENT

The employer is automatically liable for harassment by a manager that results in a negative employment action such as termination, failure to promote or hire, and loss of wages. If the manager's harassment results in a hostile work environment, the employer can avoid liability only if he or she can prove that (1) he or she reasonably tried to prevent and promptly correct the harassing behavior, and (2) the employee unreasonably failed to take advantage of any preventive or corrective opportunities provided by the employer.

The employer will be liable for harassment by nonmanagement employees or nonemployees over whom it has control such as independent contractors or customers on the premises if he or she knew, or should have known, about the harassment and failed to take prompt and appropriate corrective action.

When investigating allegations of harassment, the federal government's Equal Employment Opportunity Commission (EEOC) looks at the entire record including the nature of the conduct and the context in which the alleged incidents occurred. A determination of whether harassment is severe or pervasive enough to be illegal is made on a case-by-case basis.

SEXUAL HARASSMENT

Similar procedures should be used by managers to help prevent all types of harassment. The following discussion of sexual harassment illustrates methods that can be used to help prevent other types of harassment.

Employers have a legal obligation to protect their employees from sexual harassment. This means managers must protect employees from harassment by coworkers and also by anyone who comes into the establishment, including customers and vendors. Likewise, managers must also protect nonemployees from harassment by employees.

While the law mandates these responsibilities, protecting employees from sexual harassment is also good business practice. Ensuring that employees can work without harassment and know problems will be resolved fairly builds an environment with good morale, low turnover, and high work performance. Managers must understand what sexual harassment is, how to prevent it, and how to respond when it is reported.

Sexual harassment is unwelcome behavior of a sexual nature that interferes with an employee's job performance. The victim of the behavior, not the person who displays it, determines what is "offensive or unwelcome." The issue of sexual harassment is complex because what one person regards as simple teasing might be considered harassment by another.

The law recognizes two types of sexual harassment:

- **Quid pro quo**—This phrase means "this for that" in Latin. It occurs when one person asks for or expects an action of a sexual nature from another person in return for that person's employment or advancement. These conditions include hiring, firing, raises, scheduling, or promotions.

Exhibit 4.12

Unwelcome contact can be considered sexual harassment.

- **Hostile environment**—This relates to an environment that is sexually demeaning or intimidating (creating fear). A person is treated poorly or feels uncomfortable, for example, when people tell offensive jokes of a sexual nature, call others by demeaning names, display sexually explicit or offensive materials, or otherwise behave in ways that are threatening or offensive (see *Exhibit 4.12*).

Men or women who are not the direct target of sexual harassment but who work in environments where sexual harassment is occurring can file "third-party" or "bystander" harassment lawsuits.

Sexual harassment laws originally were intended to protect women from improper advances or intimidation from men. Today, however, persons of either gender can be the victims of sexual harassment or commit sexual harassment.

Managers should encourage normal, friendly interactions and other social behaviors that help create a welcoming environment. Therefore, it is helpful to understand what is *not* considered sexual harassment:

- Normal, friendly interaction
- Nonoffensive joking
- Being polite or nice
- Socializing
- Any behavior that would not offend a reasonable person

Sexual Harassment Policies. Most restaurant and foodservice operations have a **zero tolerance** policy that allows no amount of harassing behavior. The policy typically includes the following types of statements:

- The establishment does not tolerate harassment in any form by any person.
- All persons are responsible for stopping harassment whenever it occurs.
- Harassment should be reported.

The procedures for stopping and reporting sexual harassment vary depending on the operation's location and size and whether it is independently or corporate owned or is a franchise.

Preventing a Hostile Environment. Managers must follow and enforce sexual harassment policies, but their role in preventing a hostile environment includes duties beyond that responsibility:

- Help employees understand what sexual harassment is and how to avoid and deal with it. Educate employees and train them to follow policies and procedures. The training should stress how to say no and communicate discomfort so others will understand when their behavior is unwanted or offensive.
- Encourage open communication. Help employees feel comfortable about bringing issues to the manager's attention. Managers must listen to what employees say and take their concerns seriously.
- Show positive ways to interact with people so the manager's words and actions indicate that harassment is not acceptable.
- Look for signs of harassment and get rid of any items that might offend people, such as cartoons or pictures of a sexual nature. Observe how people interact and stop any improper behavior observed.

If a manager sees signs of harassment, he or she must promptly enforce the policies in a fair and equitable manner. If the manager does not do so in all cases, he or she will create confusion. The manager will also put the operation at risk for claims of **discrimination**: treating persons unequally for reasons that do not relate to their legal rights or abilities. When managers enforce sexual harassment policies and correct behavior, they show a serious intent to protect employees' rights, and most people will behave accordingly.

THINK ABOUT IT . . .

As a manager, what does your behavior say to employees if you tease an employee or ignore harassment?

Managing Harassment Reports. Despite efforts to provide a welcoming environment, sexual and other forms of discriminatory harassment may occur. If a harassment report is made, the operation's policies should be followed. There are some general guidelines to protect the victim and the business. Guidelines vary based on whether an employee or someone else is accused of harassment.

If an employee harasses another employee or anyone else, address the issue promptly and follow these guidelines unless they conflict with company policy:

- Discuss the complaint with the person who reported it to learn more about the situation.
- Collect any evidence of harassment, such as notes or letters.
- Assure the person that the matter will be kept as confidential as possible and that there will be no negative consequences for reporting the situation.
- Inform the employee about the complaint.

- If necessary, change schedules so the parties do not work together.
- Interview any witnesses; do not give them any information. Instead, let them tell their version of the situation in their own words.
- Interview the accused employee with a witness present. The manager explains what he or she understands about the situation, and asks the employee what he or she believes happened. The manager may need to talk further with the complaining party or witnesses to clarify the situation.

After the investigation is complete, the manager consults with the appropriate person, such as his or her manager, and takes whatever action is reasonable. Each case is different, so any action taken should be reasonable for the situation. It is often wise for the manager to seek competent legal counsel to ensure that all planned corrective actions are within the law.

When an employee makes a harassment report about someone who is not an employee, such as a vendor or customer, the manager must promptly explain the harassment policy to the accused person, indicating that everyone who comes to the establishment must follow this policy. The manager needs to remain professional and focus on the behavior and not the individual.

THE LEADER AS COACH

Experienced restaurant or foodservice managers know that coaching is one of the best ways to improve employee performance. **Coaching** involves informal efforts to improve job performance. The process takes considerable listening skills, patience, and focus, but effective coaching produces improved performance that is worth the effort.

The Coaching Process

Steps in the basic coaching process are shown in *Exhibit 4.13*.

Much coaching is done as restaurant and foodservice managers "manage by walking around." As they do so, they can compare an employee's performance to expected performance as described in a job standard such as standard operating procedures (Step 1).

When employees are observed doing something right, managers should reinforce their performance (Step 2). This can be a simple comment such as "Great job!" or "That's a tough task, and you always do it correctly; thanks!"

Sometimes, managers will note employees doing something incorrectly. In this case, coaching involves correcting negative performance. A manager might, for example, tell why the action is incorrect, show the employee the correct way to do it, or inform the employee's manager who can help the employee improve.

Exhibit 4.13

STEPS IN THE COACHING PROCESS

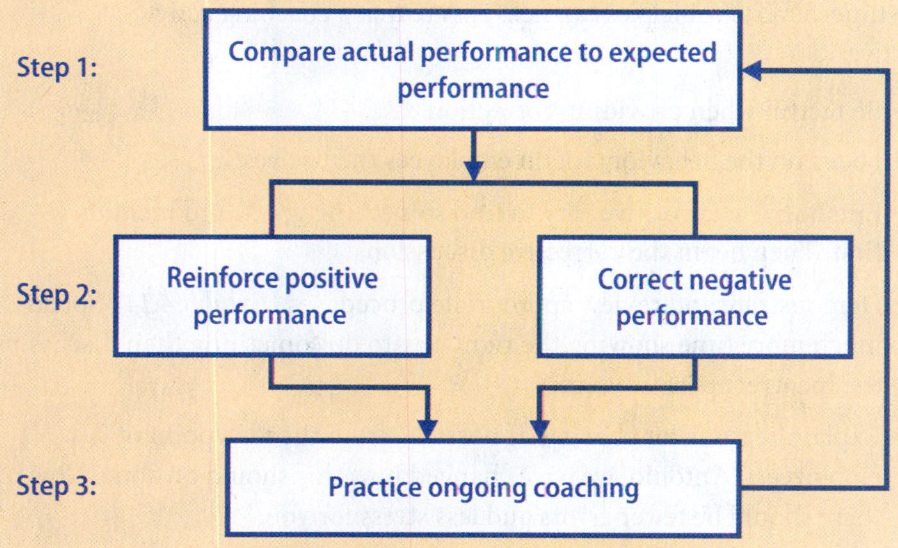
Step 1:
Compare actual performance to expected performance
Step 2:
Reinforce positive performance
Correct negative performance
Step 3:
Practice ongoing coaching

Correcting errors should normally be done in private or at least quietly at the workstation. Remember: The purpose is to correct proper performance, not to embarrass or punish the employee.

If an informal coaching discussion does not correct the problem, a second coaching session may be needed. The manager may need to revise his or her coaching technique to make it more effective. Also, the manager might help the employee plan a more formal employee development program as discussed earlier in this chapter.

If coaching reveals that the employee does not want to do the task, the manager may decide to move from coaching to **progressive discipline** efforts. Progressive discipline involves a series of punishments that become more serious as unacceptable performance continues.

Step 3 in *Exhibit 4.13* suggests that the manager should perform ongoing coaching. This means that the process of comparing actual to expected performance should continue, as well as reinforcement or correction.

The manager acting as a coach provides input and makes suggestions for changes. He or she also provides feedback about the employee's ideas and responses, and helps the employee improve performance. These actions are not simply giving orders and criticizing mistakes.

Coaching is not a one-time activity. It involves a commitment to help an employee grow and an interest in helping the employee determine how to accomplish this. The function of the coach is to think about how to help employees solve their own problems.

THINK ABOUT IT . . .

Sometimes coaching sessions and even formal training are not able to help an employee learn a task. What would you do if the employee was an above-average worker in every task except one?

Coaching Principles

Coaching helps employees learn how the manager views their work on a timely and ongoing basis. Employees like this input, there is no expense, and it takes little time. Several principles can help ensure that a coaching activity is effective:

- Be tactful when providing correction.
- Focus on the behavior, not on employees themselves.
- Emphasize the positive. Try to find something good, and mention it first. Then begin the corrective discussion.
- Demonstrate and review appropriate procedures (*Exhibit 4.14*). Spend much more time showing the right way to do something than discussing the incorrect performance.
- Explain reasons for changes, if possible, from the viewpoint of employees: "Antonio, we have changed how this should be done. Now there should be fewer errors and less stress for you."
- Maintain open communications with staff members. The manager should support ongoing coaching discussions to reduce concerns such as "Now what does the boss want to talk to me about?"

Exhibit 4.14

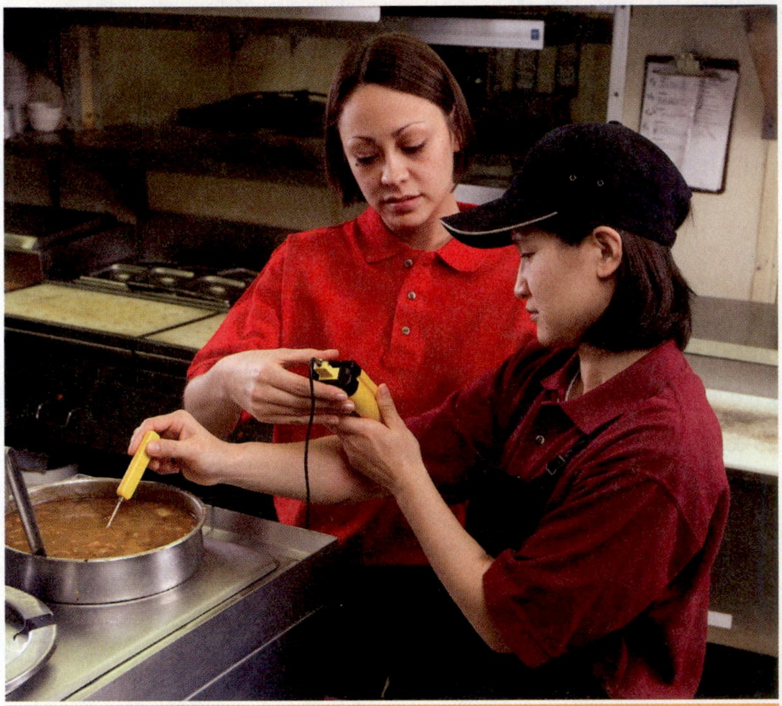

- Conduct discussions of negative behavior in private. Praise employees for proper performance in public and have performance improvement conversations in private.
- Evaluate employees' work by comparing their performance against standards. The review of performance should consider how an employee's performance compares to what is expected, not how it compares to others' performance.
- Direct positive reinforcement to all employees who correctly perform a task, not to just the best employees.
- Ask employees how they think work can be improved. A coaching discussion can be another opportunity to obtain useful ideas from employees.

THINK ABOUT IT . . .

Consider these two comments:

"This is an easy thing to do, and I don't know why you can't do it."

"It's a little tough to do this step correctly; let me show you."

Which comment is a more effective coaching technique? Why?

MANAGING CONFLICT

Restaurant and foodservice managers must sometimes deal with conflicts that arise among employees. Therefore, they must know and practice skills of conflict resolution in the work environment. **Conflict resolution** refers to processes that encourage finding solutions to problems before more formal grievance procedures are needed.

Conflict Resolution Strategies

Typically, conflicts occur because of disagreement about a work situation or personality clashes between employees. An effective conflict resolution process can develop understanding and cooperation that leads to an agreement that works for those involved. The process should allow employees to avoid embarrassment or other situations that might interfere with solving the problem.

Managers can use several forms of conflict resolution strategies:

- **Negotiation:** discussion between involved persons with the goal of reaching an acceptable agreement
- **Mediation:** a process in which a neutral third party facilitates a discussion of difficult issues and makes suggestions about an agreement
- **Arbitration:** a process in which a neutral third party listens and reviews facts and makes a decision to settle the conflict

Exhibit 4.15

RESOLVING EMPLOYEE CONFLICTS

1. Identify concerns as well as all persons involved and their feelings about the situation or individuals.
2. Determine the facts.
   a. Define the conflict and impact of the problem.
   b. Verify the sources and facts of the conflict.
   c. Review and enforce operation policies.
   d. Identify other persons who should be involved, such as higher-level managers.
   e. Interview all involved persons separately.
3. Develop a resolution that best meets the needs of all parties.
   a. Work together to identify critical factors.
   b. Ensure that the resolution complies with existing policies and is fair, legal, and will resolve the issue.
   c. Confirm that all parties are comfortable with the resolution.
4. Communicate the resolution.
   a. Be sure all involved parties are aware of the resolution.
   b. Be sure all parties understand the resolution.
5. Document the agreement reached.
   a. Accurately record all important information and resolution details.
   b. File the information in employee files or another place where it can be reviewed if necessary.
6. Follow up on the agreement.
   a. Discuss any other details to ensure the issue is resolved.
   b. Monitor the agreement if necessary.

All three forms of conflict resolution follow similar basic steps that are reviewed in *Exhibit 4.15*. Ultimately, the best process to use is one that results in a solution the concerned persons can accept and feel good about. Additionally, allowing employees to resolve conflict with one of these methods gives them greater control over their own work situation.

The steps in *Exhibit 4.15* can be used to review how an employee conflict might be resolved. Think about an example in which there is uncertainty about whether keeping the salad bar clean is the responsibility of kitchen or dining-room personnel.

- **Step 1. Identify concerns:** Food-production and dining-room employees indicate they are very busy during rush times and do not have time to maintain the salad bar.
- **Step 2. Determine the facts:** Staff members in both departments are very busy during rush periods. However, there are serious food safety and cleanliness issues and, since there are no existing policies, the matter must be resolved.

- **Step 3. Develop a resolution:** The establishment manager meets with the kitchen and dining-room managers, and all recognize the problem is serious. All three managers agree that an emphasis on teamwork can solve the problem.
- **Step 4. Communicate the resolution:** Currently employees from both departments help refill salad-bar items. The policy will be revised to note that whoever brings items to the salad bar will take a few moments to clean up spilled items. All food-production and dining-room staff will be trained in proper cleanup.

  All managers including the establishment manager will also clean up the area when necessary. The dining-room manager will be responsible for supervising the area and performing cleanup duties until someone is available to assist.
- **Step 5. Document the agreement reached:** A new policy will be announced at food-production and dining-room department and preshift meetings. Procedures will be included in training material that will be discussed at a department-head meeting so all managers understand the new process.
- **Step 6. Follow up on the agreement:** Managers will closely monitor the salad-bar situation to determine if cleanliness standards are met, and will suggest corrective actions if they are not.

EMPLOYEE PERFORMANCE APPRAISALS

Employee performance appraisals are a critical aspect of an environment that enables employees to stay motivated. They are very important for several reasons.

Employee appraisals allow managers to interact with employees for specific purposes:

- Discuss past performance
- Establish new performance goals
- Review job-related issues
- Talk about employee development opportunities
- Document performance

Performance appraisals typically focus on performance, important issues and facts, and agreement about performance opportunities and goals. An operation's policy usually indicates how often formal performance appraisals should be conducted.

Exhibit 4.16

PERFORMANCE APPRAISAL PROCESS

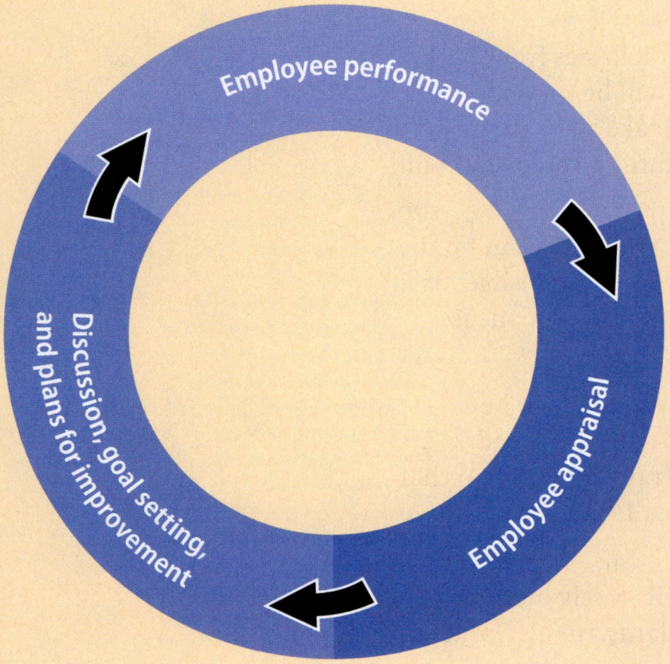

Performance Appraisal Procedures

As seen in *Exhibit 4.16*, the performance appraisal process is cyclical: A review of past performance is followed by its evaluation, which is followed by goal setting for future performance.

Too many managers approach the appraisal process in a hurried manner and focus on the most recent examples of an employee's performance. Add in a lack of ongoing feedback and little emphasis on goal setting, and it is easy to see why many employees have negative feelings about appraisal meetings.

Effective restaurant and foodservice managers understand the importance of performance appraisal to the development of their staff and operation, so they know evaluations must be done carefully and correctly.

Several steps should be followed to ensure the appraisal process is productive and helps everyone gain the most benefits from the meeting.

STEP 1: PREPARING FOR THE MEETING

Set a time and place for the appraisals meeting and notify the employee in advance. The employee will want to prepare for it just as the manager must.

Gather the facts needed to evaluate the employee's performance. Review the employee's file and ask team leaders who work with the employee for their input. At the same time, the employee should complete a self-evaluation to discuss during the meeting. It should focus on the employee's strengths, opportunities, accomplishments, and future development goals.

Use these suggestions to prepare for the performance appraisal session:

- Review job descriptions, current development plan goals (if any), project reports, employee file information, and any other related performance data.
- Focus on performance measures and not personality traits.
- Review the employee's background including skills, training, and attendance records.
- Identify the employee's performance strengths and areas needing improvement.
- Gather information about performance from all of his or her managers.
- Identify areas in which you think the employee can improve during the next appraisal period.
- Give the employee a self-evaluation form and request that he or she complete it and bring it to the meeting (*Exhibit 4.17*).

Exhibit 4.17

SAMPLE EMPLOYEE APPRAISAL FORM

Employee name: Sam Bradley Position title: Bartender

Appraisal period: From 1/1/2012 to 6/30/2012 Today's date: 7/5/2012

PART I: PERFORMANCE OF JOB TASKS

Job Description Task	Performance (*circle one:* 1 = unsatisfactory; 5 = exceptional)				
1. Stocks bar at beginning of shift	1	2	3	4	5
2. Prepares drinks according to standard recipes	1	2	3	4	5
3.					
9.	1	2	3	4	5
10. Follows postshift cleanup procedures.	1	2	3	4	5

PART II: JOB-RELATED BEHAVIORS (*circle one:* 1 = unsatisfactory; 5 = exceptional)

1. Cooperation	1	2	3	4	5
2. Attitude	1	2	3	4	5
3. Dependability	1	2	3	4	5
4. Judgment	1	2	3	4	5
5. Job knowledge and skills	1	2	3	4	5
6. Interpersonal relationship	1	2	3	4	5
7. Other: ______________	1	2	3	4	5

PART III: IMPROVEMENT and PROFESSIONAL DEVELOPMENT

A. Last Period's Goal	Achieved	Not Achieved	Comments
1.	❑	❑	
2.	❑	❑	
3.	❑	❑	

B. Next Period's Goal	How Success Will Be Measured
1.	
2.	
3.	

PART IV: COMMENTS

Supervisor:	Employee:

Signatures:

______________________________ ______________________________

Supervisor (Date) Employee (Date)

Exhibit 4.18

STEP 2: CONDUCTING THE MEETING

The performance appraisal session allows the manager and the employee to have an open discussion about how the employee has performed since the last appraisal meeting (see *Exhibit 4.18*).

Start by asking for the employee's view of his or her performance. Also, ask about challenges to performance or reaching goals and ask if he or she has any questions. After the employee has provided his or her views, managers should share feedback about the employee's strengths and opportunities.

After both employee and manager have discussed the employee's performance, gain agreement about past performance and how the employee will improve. The manager must be sure to ask how he or she can help.

An employee development plan should be discussed. Goals should be considered, and the employee can refine them further to include timelines and resources needed.

There are strong reasons to involve the employee in the goal-setting process during performance discussions:

- Involvement creates ownership for the employee's development.
- The goal-setting process can be a motivation tool to help develop the employee's leadership skills.
- The employee gains a better understanding of how he or she is helping the operation reach its goals.
- The process allows the employee to find pride in his or her work.
- The manager gains information about the employee's views.

Use these principles when conducting a performance appraisal meeting:

- Create an open and friendly atmosphere.
- Explain that employee input is desired.
- Try to put the employee at ease.
- Discuss job requirements, strengths, and opportunities and compare the employee's actual performance against goals set for this appraisal period.
- Be prepared with questions to engage the employee.

- Take notes during the meeting.
- Encourage the employee to suggest ideas for an employee development program, and offer suggestions.
- Reach agreement on goals, a schedule, and any needed resources.

STEP 3: CLOSING THE MEETING AND FOLLOWING UP

The manager closes the meeting by providing a summary, and asks the employee about any comments or suggestions. The manager tells the employee that he or she will support the employee's development plan and offer ongoing assistance as the plan is implemented.

End on a positive and friendly note, and let the employee know if any follow-up meetings are needed. Document the meeting, including a summary of past performance, information about the employee development plans, and any commitments. Be sure to give the employee a copy of the summary report.

A final activity in the performance appraisal process is for the manager to think about how he or she managed the meeting and consider whether there are things he or she could have done better. This analysis can help the manager plan and conduct future performance appraisals.

DISCUSSING PERFORMANCE PROBLEMS

Discussions about performance problems can occur during informal coaching sessions, in special conversations, or as part of a performance appraisal meeting. The time spent meeting about the issue, and the type of meeting, depend on how serious the problem is.

If an employee fails to follow standard operating procedures (SOPs) a six-step process can be used to address this problem:

- **Step 1:** Compare observed performance with SOPs. These job standards are the basis for training employees to do specific tasks and are the benchmarks that actual performance is compared to.
- **Step 2:** Identify gaps between observed behavior and the SOPs. A gap can be relatively minor, such as an error in folding a napkin, or very serious, such as putting a soiled preparation knife in the pot-and-pan sink.
- **Step 3:** Determine the reason for the gap. Perhaps the employee did not know (a training problem), forgot, or does not care (a discipline issue).
- **Step 4:** Correct the negative behavior. A simple coaching conversation or retraining may be the first step in a progressive discipline program. The decision about the method to correct the problem will be based on how serious the gap is and on the manager's view of why it occurred.

- **Step 5:** Monitor employee behavior to ensure the problem is corrected. Managers can do this by observing how work is performed as they move throughout the restaurant or foodservice operation, with coaching conversations, or by addressing the situation during performance appraisal meetings.
- **Step 6:** If the performance problem is not corrected as the result of these steps, follow-up disciplinary action may be needed. This will be determined by operation policies and by the factors creating the performance problem.

The basic message in a discussion to correct performance problems should be that the manager and employee will be partners in improvement plans. The manager should ensure that the approach used to correct the problem is one that eliminates misunderstandings and makes clear what is expected of the employee.

SUMMARY

1. **Explain principles to help employees become motivated.**

   Motivation is the process of giving employees a reason to do something. Motivated employees promote teamwork, make suggestions, and are interested in their jobs. Effective managers know about and learn to meet their employees' expectations. There are many ways managers can encourage motivation, and most center on recognizing the value of employees and treating them respectfully.

2. **Review procedures for planning and implementing employee development programs.**

   Managers should work with employees to help them improve their performance and gain the knowledge and skills required for future positions. The process involves setting development goals, identifying development opportunities, approving and implementing the plan, and monitoring and evaluating its progress.

3. **State procedures helpful in maintaining a positive workplace.**

   Managers who maintain a positive workplace establish the groundwork for effective motivation. They focus on employees, maintain open communication channels, and celebrate success. They also build teams, promote diversity and fairness, and ensure a fair workplace by prohibiting any type of harassment.

4. **Describe basic coaching practices.**

   Coaching involves informal efforts to improve performance. Effective managers compare actual to expected performance. Then they reinforce positive performance publicly and correct negative performance in private. The coaching process is ongoing as managers monitor the work of staff.

5. **Identify ways to manage conflict.**

   Typical conflicts occur because of personality clashes or disagreements about work situations. Procedures to resolve conflicts involve identifying the conflict and all persons involved, along with their feelings about the situation. Then managers should determine facts, develop a resolution that meets the needs of all parties, and communicate and document the resolution, following up as necessary.

6. **Explain procedures for conducting effective performance appraisals.**

   Employee appraisals help managers discuss past performance, establish new performance goals, discuss job-related issues, and talk about employee development programs. The process involves meeting preparation, conducting and closing the meeting, and following up as necessary. Managers may also discuss performance during informal coaching sessions or in special conversations.

APPLICATION EXERCISES

Exercise 1

Work with classmates or interview several friends who have jobs. Each person should review the following list and decide which of the 10 possible motivators would be the most important to him or her. Create a table similar to the one shown. Assign 10 to the most important item, 9 to the next, and so on. Put your ranking in the Individual column.

Then, as a group, add up the individuals' weights for each factor and divide by the number of students in the group. This will show the average score for each factor. Place this number in the Group column.

1. Are there major differences in the individual and group rankings?
2. If so, what does this mean?

WHAT DO PEOPLE WANT FROM THEIR JOBS?

Factors	Individual	Group
High wages		
Job security		
Promotion in the company		
Help with personal problems		
Stimulating work		
Personal loyalty of manager		
Tactful discipline		
Appreciation of work done well		
Positive working environment		
Feeling of being involved		

Exercise 2

Work with a classmate. One student should role-play the part of an establishment manager building an employee development program, and the other should be an employee. The manager should make sure that all elements of the goal-setting session are considered and should base feedback on personal work experience. The employee should respond based on personal background, work experience, and career goals.

After 10 minutes, switch roles and conduct a goal-setting session for the other person. Then share your goals with the class.

Exercise 3

Effective leaders are excited about their work, and they spread their enthusiasm to their employees. One way to create a positive work climate is to think positively. If you model traits that employees value and expect in a manager, your staff will begin to exhibit these behaviors as well.

Work in groups to brainstorm answers to these questions:

1. How can managers improve their employees' enthusiasm during daily work activities?
2. How can managers tell if their employees are excited about their jobs?

REVIEW YOUR LEARNING

Select the best answer for each question.

1. **Which statement about motivation is correct?**
   A. When managers direct work, they are motivating employees.
   B. Managers motivate when they create conditions employees appreciate.
   C. All employees in an operation are motivated by the same factors.
   D. Good managers always know what motivates all of their employees.

2. **Which is the most basic level of need according to Maslow's hierarchy of needs?**
   A. Safety needs
   B. Social needs
   C. Esteem needs
   D. Physiological needs

3. **What can a manager do to show interest in employees?**
   A. Discuss the same type of topics you would discuss in a job interview.
   B. Talk about almost any type of personal matter; employees are a family.
   C. Talk to employees about anything that is not directly job related.
   D. Encourage staff to talk about personal matters; it increases productivity.

4. **What should managers do as they prepare for an employee performance appraisal session?**
   A. Ask their boss to suggest correct performance scores.
   B. Review the employee's personnel file and job description.
   C. Prepare an outline that emphasizes the employee's weaknesses.
   D. Think about the employee's personality and how it impacts the job.

5. **Which statement is true about employee development programs?**
   A. They can help motivate employees.
   B. They should be used only for managers.
   C. They should be used only for long-term employees.
   D. They should mandate that employees remain in the operation.

6. **How can a manager build a positive work environment?**
   A. Develop a restaurant or foodservice policy that requires it.
   B. Pay employees more than staff at other establishments.
   C. Make sure that managers set a good example.
   D. Focus primarily on preventing sexual harassment.

7. **Employees who are not a target of sexual harassment but work where it is occurring can file what type of lawsuit?**
   A. Quid pro quo
   B. Third-party
   C. Hostile environment
   D. Innocent victim

8. **An advantage of effective coaching is that it**
   A. saves time because discussions can be held at the workstation.
   B. helps employees learn how the manager views their work.
   C. allows employees to defend what they are doing.
   D. reminds employees about "who is the boss."

9. **Which conflict resolution strategy allows a neutral third party to make suggestions about an agreement?**
   A. Negotiation
   B. Arbitration
   C. Litigation
   D. Mediation

10. **According to Herzberg's two-factor theory, which is a motivation factor?**
    A. Hours
    B. Work breaks
    C. Safe conditions
    D. Responsibility

FIELD PROJECT

Part II

1. Visit a local establishment to observe manager and employee interactions.
2. Does the establishment create a safe and fun environment for entry-level employees? How?
3. Do the managers show they respect their employees? Explain.
4. Note how the managers motivate their employees.
5. How does the establishment recognize its employees' achievements and encourage them to be successful?

5 Leaders Facilitate Teamwork

INSIDE THIS CHAPTER

- Teamwork and Success
- Common Restaurant and Foodservice Teams
- Stages of Team Growth
- Building Effective Teams
- Setting Team Goals
- Managing Team Projects

CHAPTER LEARNING OBJECTIVES

After completing this chapter, you should be able to:

- Explain why teamwork is important to the success of restaurant and foodservice operations.
- Review common types of restaurant and foodservice teams.
- Describe the five stages of team growth and development.
- Discuss basic principles helpful in building and maintaining effective teams.
- Explain basic procedures for setting team goals.
- Identify procedures for effectively managing team projects.

KEY TERMS

adjourning (team development), p. 134
cross-functional team, p. 132
debrief meeting, p. 144
forming (team development), p. 133
functional team, p. 132
high-performance team, p. 137
norming (team development), p. 134
performing (team development), p. 134
problem-solving team, p. 132
self-directed team, p. 132
storming (team development), p. 134
supervisor, p. 136
table turn, p. 144
team, p. 128
teamwork, p. 128
work ethic, p. 137

CASE STUDY

"I've never seen anything like this in my life!" said Peter to Shari-Ann, who nodded in agreement. Peter and Shari-Ann were longtime cooks at the College Town Restaurant, and they were on their coffee break.

"It's been only about six weeks since the new restaurant manager started working here along with that kitchen manager and that dining-room manager that he brought in," continued Peter.

"Yes," Shari-Ann said, "and have they ever made some changes around here! Remember how all of us cooks used to get together and plan daily specials and help resolve problems in the kitchen? It was nice because we would all have a chance to make suggestions about how the operation could get better."

"Yeah, that lasted one day under the new bosses," replied Peter. "Now, we are basically just told what to do. We aren't supposed to know or care about what's happening in any other department. Their motto seems to be 'Just do your own job and don't worry about anybody or anything else. Let us manage everything.' "

"Well, Shari-Ann," replied Peter, "I've had enough. I've started to look for a new job."

1. What do you think is the main problem at the establishment?
2. If you were giving advice to the new restaurant manager, what would it be?

TEAMWORK AND SUCCESS

Leaders in restaurant or foodservice organizations, both large and small, are looking to the power of teams to help accomplish tasks. Competitive pressures are driving leaders to rely on collaborative work teams to react rapidly to customer demands and the business climate.

In today's competitive restaurant and foodservice industry, managers must learn how to direct and coordinate effective team behavior and team results to have a successful and enduring organization.

THINK ABOUT IT . . .

Think about the skills sports coaches need to inspire and teach team members to work together to reach goals. How could you apply these team leadership concepts to the operation of a restaurant or foodservice establishment?

To carry out activities in an establishment, a manager can use a variety of team types. This chapter looks at those different types and discusses the advantages and disadvantages of working with teams. Leveraging teams means getting people to work together as a unit. As teams make progress on their assigned tasks, they move through various stages of growth. This growth pattern is presented along with factors that support or hinder the building and sustaining of a team.

Finally, advantages are described for including teams in goal setting for projects. As part of setting goals, effective managers and their teams use a systematic process to complete projects, which will be reviewed as well.

What Is a Team?

A **team** is a group of people who work together to complete a task or reach a common goal. Teams are important in the restaurant and foodservice industry. Even though one person can, and should, make a difference to an operation's success, no one person has enough knowledge, creativity, and experience to tackle today's complex business problems alone.

Members of a team work together and have common goals. The act of cooperating and working together to complete tasks and reach common goals is called **teamwork**, and teamwork is absolutely essential to the success of all restaurant and foodservice operations.

ADVANTAGES OF TEAMS

Effective teams offer many benefits to restaurant and foodservice managers. These typically include greater productivity and better assurance that products and services will consistently meet required standards. Other benefits include more effective use of limited resources, including time and money.

THINK ABOUT IT . . .

Have you ever heard someone say, "I'd rather do this by myself so I will know it is done right"? As a manager, how do you get employees to work as members of a team?

Team members who work closely together generally have increased creativity and great ideas. These advantages are very useful as employees make decisions, solve problems, and help plan how to deliver products and services. Professional managers know that the quality of teamwork relates directly to the quality of the customer experience that is provided.

Teamwork offers many other benefits:

- **Positive work environment:** Team members feel a closer connection to their coworkers, managers, the operation, and its goals. This promotes a sense of common purpose and focuses the team's efforts more effectively. Teamwork also reinforces the contributions each member makes to the establishment.
- **Open communication channels:** Teams help break down barriers that can exist between departments or groups. For example, an establishment has customer complaints about slow service. The cooks may blame this on servers who make mistakes when taking and submitting orders. The servers may blame the cooks for producing requested items too slowly. In contrast, members of a cross-functional team of cooks and servers can make suggestions that range across departmental lines (see *Exhibit 5.1*). Their emphasis will be on fixing the problem, not on blaming others.
- **Employee support systems:** Teams can help their members feel less stress when something goes wrong. Team support can also make it easier for an inexperienced member to tackle an assignment without fear. He or she will not have to worry if the work will get done, because other members are there to help and to teach. This support creates greater opportunities for more employees to be successful. Also, more employees can receive recognition for their contributions to team tasks.

Exhibit 5.1

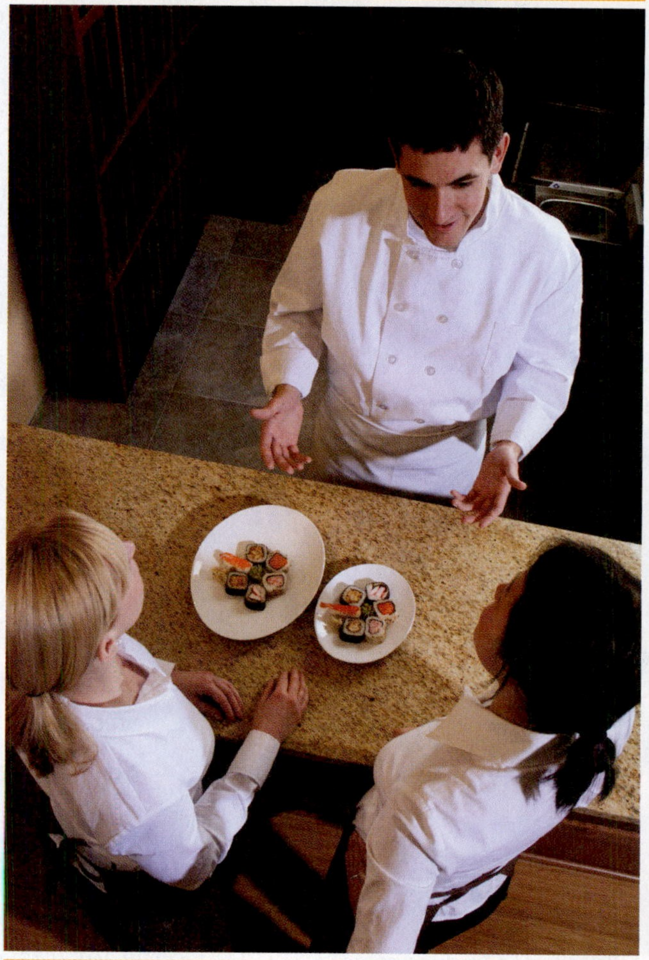

- **Workplace diversity:** The ability to blend a diverse workforce together to complete tasks and solve problems can help everyone value the talents and differences that each member brings to the job.

Finally, the combination of these advantages can help reduce employee turnover, which is a serious challenge in some establishments.

PITFALLS OF TEAMS

There are also some potential problems related to working in teams. Here are some suggestions for minimizing them:

- **Taking too long to make a decision:** A manager can quickly make a decision if asked for advice. One challenge in using teams is the amount of time the group may need to think and make suggestions. Understanding how to conduct meetings and knowing when to make team assignments can reduce the time needed. Also, an ongoing emphasis on connecting the work with the operation's tasks and goals helps managers and teams focus on the same priorities.

- **Mishandling team disagreements:** Working in teams can create conflict for some employees. Although disagreements between some members may make others uncomfortable, some conflict can lead to a broader understanding of work challenges and how to overcome them. If a conflict arises, managers should help their team members stay focused on project issues rather than personalities. If a conflict turns personal, a manager should get involved to ensure that the team remains effective.
- **Working inefficiently:** Selecting a team to tackle a task that might better be done by one person can result in some employees questioning the need for more persons on the task. How many servers should fold napkins and how many cooks should pre-prep a single entrée item? The wrong answers to these questions can lead to unmet goals and ineffective team interactions. It is a manager's responsibility to know when use of a team is the right strategy to complete tasks and accomplish goals.
- **Avoiding responsibility:** Employees may not want to participate in a team project if they think it will fail, because that will mean they also failed. Managers must encourage trust and communication within the team to ensure the team's success.

THINK ABOUT IT . . .

Consider the saying "If everyone is responsible, no one is responsible"? If the manager tells cooks to "reduce costs" without further details, who is responsible for failure?

Do the advantages of teams outweigh the possible disadvantages? The benefits or drawbacks depend on the manager's ability to determine the best way to use teams to reach specific goals.

TEAM MEMBER SKILLS

Team members must have the right blend of skills if their teams are to be effective. In other words, not every person on a team must have the ability to do all tasks. However, collectively the team must be able to do all of the required tasks.

When team members collectively have the necessary skills, the individual strengths of each member increase and so does the probability that the team will be successful. One of a manager's responsibilities is to select team members whose skills complement each other.

For example, some cooks may be very skilled at food-production tasks but feel uncomfortable interacting with guests. Other cooks may enjoy carving a roast or preparing omelets on a buffet line. The food-production team can then meet its responsibility to produce and serve food for the buffet.

Three complementary types of skills are needed for successful teams:

- **Adequate technical abilities:** The type of problem assigned to a team dictates the technical abilities that are needed. Abilities may be required in several areas depending on the tasks to be done. For example, when a new menu is planned, a team of food-production, service, and higher-level management staff will likely be needed. This team will better know what customers want than will a team made up of persons from just one of these groups.
- **Problem-solving skills:** These skills will be used by a team to identify the causes of a problem and the potential solutions and trade-offs of resolving it.
- **Interpersonal skills:** Team members who communicate effectively and help others stay focused on goals are critical to success. Team members with these skills help create an environment of openness and trust, and this allows the team to move toward its goals.

COMMON RESTAURANT AND FOODSERVICE TEAMS

As this chapter has stated, successful operations must have effective teams, and complementary skills are important in helping teams be successful. This section discusses several of the teams needed to effectively manage a restaurant or foodservice establishment.

Employees Are on Many Teams

Many people think that an employee belongs to just one team, such as the lunch server's team or the cook's dinner team. However, most if not all employees are members of several teams:

- **The restaurant or foodservice team:** Every employee is part of the operation and has a responsibility to meet the goals of the business.
- **A department team:** A group of employees, such as those involved with food production or dining-room service, must have the knowledge and skills to fulfill their department's contribution to reaching the operation's goals.
- **A work-shift team:** Employees in the food-production department work on different shifts when the establishment is open for several meal periods each day. Employees on this team are responsible for food production and service during a specific time period. However, the lunch-production team may also do pre-prep work for the dinner team. Also, work schedules may require cooks to sometimes work on different shifts and therefore on different production teams.

Exhibit 5.2

- **One or more workstation teams:** An employee working in the production department may work with a team of cooks to pre-prep for dinner and then work with different employees on the cook's line during the actual time of meal service.
- **Other teams:** An evening-shift food-preparation employee may have other duties not directly involved with food production. These duties may be ongoing or last only until a specific project is completed. For example, he or she may serve for two months on a cross-functional team that studies how dining-room service can be made more efficient. The same employee may serve on an ongoing advisory team to the kitchen manager to provide employees' views about matters suggested by the manager.

It should be clear that it is difficult to talk about an establishment's organization or operation without talking about employee teams.

Types of Teams

All of the restaurant and foodservice teams just discussed can be categorized into four types:

- **Functional teams** that perform the routine tasks that are part of their job description (*Exhibit 5.2*).
- **Problem-solving teams** created for the specific purpose of solving an immediate problem.
- **Cross-functional teams** with employees from different departments who focus on solving problems that impact their areas and the operation as a whole.
- **Self-directed teams** that are small groups of employees who manage many daily issues within their functional team with little supervision. For example, a team of experienced servers might decide who will do setup and cleanup tasks and how customer tables will be assigned. Self-directed teams are used when team members have the experience to complete most of their tasks with little supervision. *Exhibit 5.3* reviews each type of team and provides examples of their activities.

Exhibit 5.3

BASIC TYPES OF TEAMS

Type	Description	Example
Functional team	A team of employees from the same area or department who perform the routine tasks in their job description	The servers on the evening shift perform before-opening duties, serve guests, and perform closing duties.
Problem-solving team	A temporary team of employees selected to solve a specific problem	A dining-room manager selects a special team of servers to make suggestions for the service of a large group that reserves the entire establishment on a normally slow evening.
Cross-functional team	A team of employees from different departments who consider problems that impact their areas and the operation as a whole	A multiunit establishment has determined that many customers want healthier meals. A team made up of a nutritionist, restaurant managers, food-production personnel, and a marketing director will plan new menu items.
Self-directed team	A small group of employees who manage many daily issues within their functional team with little supervision	The training director for a quick-service restaurant chain decides that her training managers can handle more responsibility. The team begins planning for training needs and monitoring progress using weekly update meetings and ongoing discussions to brief the director.

STAGES OF TEAM GROWTH

Nearly 50 years ago in 1965, Dr. Bruce W. Tuckman, an educational psychologist, published his theory of the four stages of group development. This model, still in use today, divides the process into four stages: forming, storming, norming, and performing.

Forming

In stage one, **forming**, team members are getting to know each other and learning what they will have to do to reach their assigned goals. Members are discovering the best ways to work with each other. They are also learning about what they can and cannot do as the limits of group behavior are determined.

During the forming stage, the team also assesses the manager's role and leadership. At this time, the manager must assume a large role in directing the team's progress. For example, he or she must state what needs to be done, establish guidelines, and provide specifics on the five W's (*who, what, where, when, why)* and how, to explain tasks. At this stage, team members are focusing on becoming a contributing part of their team.

THINK ABOUT IT . . .

When a team focuses less on individual performance and more on working together, members build team confidence, resulting in better products and services. How can a confident team help provide better products and services?

Storming

In stage two, **storming**, the reality of what the team is expected to do becomes clearer. Also, some conflicts between team members may begin to surface. Typically, this is the most difficult stage for teams to get through because power clashes and competition between team members are common.

Also, some team members may become impatient with their team's progress and may try to do things by themselves rather than working together. At this time, the manager must use a coaching style of leadership. He or she can explain tasks as often as necessary and persuade team members to work together.

Norming

In stage three, **norming**, team members settle their differences and develop more trusting relationships. The team realizes the benefits of working together and helping each other achieve success. The members understand the team's needs and accept the team's ground rules and the role that each person plays in reaching team goals.

In this stage, conflict decreases as team members develop more confidence in their ability to work together and accomplish the task. The manager supports the team by providing encouragement, listening more than telling, and promoting team discussions.

Performing

In stage four, **performing**, the team members begin to depend on each other. They can effectively analyze and solve problems together. They accept each other's strengths and weaknesses and adapt to meet the needs of each member.

During this stage, the team becomes productive and adds value to the operation. Now the manager no longer needs to provide as much direction but can begin to delegate and can monitor the team's progress with update meetings.

Adjourning

In 1977, Dr. Tuckman, working with Mary Ann Jensen, added a fifth stage to his group development model. This final stage of team development is called **adjourning**. Adjourning occurs when the team has achieved its purpose and members move on to other tasks. Unless the establishment closes, a functional team will not go through this stage.

However, some members of functional teams may be promoted or transferred. Other members will leave, and new employees will join the team. These individuals will likely have many of the feelings described as they adapt to their new team. However, existing team members can assist them.

The work of problem-solving and cross-functional teams can adjourn. Then employees may become part of different teams working on other special projects. Managers should understand that some team members will feel stress during adjourning, especially if the team has worked together for a long time. The best managers sincerely thank members of adjourning teams and invite them to work on other teams when the need arises.

Putting It All Together

Exhibit 5.4 reviews the feelings and actions of teams as they go through the four main stages of team development.

Exhibit 5.4

STAGES OF TEAM DEVELOPMENT

	Forming	Storming	Norming	Performing
Team feeling	• Excitement • Optimism about the future • Pride in being selected • Wondering about personal role in the team • Wondering about the future • Questioning why team members were selected	• Resistance to approaches different from what the team uses • Attitude changes about the team and work assignments • Questioning parts of assigned work • Increased tension • Jealousy • Loss of interest	• Expressing constructive criticism • Membership acceptance • Relief that things are going smoothly • Understanding how members contribute to the team • Acceptance of membership • Sense of common purpose	• Knowing how group processes work • Understanding each member's strengths and weaknesses • Satisfaction with progress • Trust • Close attachment to members • Enjoyment of work
Team behavior	• Friendly • Agreeable • Deciding how to accomplish the task • Determining acceptable team behavior • Information gathering • Handling complaints about the organization • Discussing task barriers	• Arguing • Choosing sides • Perceived "pecking order" • Power struggles • Lack of progress	• Attempts to get along • Avoiding conflict • Discussing how the team works • Establishing and monitoring team rules • Expressing ideas and suggestions	• Changing behavior to fit with the team • Working through team problems • Friendliness • Flexibility • Humor • Ownership of results
Leadership style	• Directing	• Coaching	• Supporting	• Delegating

THINK ABOUT IT . . .

Team members relate differently as teams develop. How do you think the process would affect you if you started at a new establishment and all teams were in the performing stage?

BUILDING EFFECTIVE TEAMS

The time required for a team to move through the four development stages varies, but the manager should play a key role in each. His or her efforts will help change the individual focus of each member to a more cooperative team effort.

Principles of Team Building

Managers can support team building and development in several ways:

- Communicate effectively and clearly with the team.
- Select the appropriate leadership style for each stage of a team's development. (See *Exhibit 5.4*.)
- Conduct team-building exercises so team members understand the development process. The activities selected should help the team achieve goals and not be "just-for-fun" events.
- Understand and explain the role of the team in helping the operation reach its goals. This is necessary because a team that does not know its role will not perform as effectively.
- Apply effective management skills to support the team. Knowing that every team will go through the same basic developmental stages—some more successfully than others—means that strong leadership by the manager is essential.

Manager's Memo

Effective team leaders in every department of an establishment encourage their team members to be service-minded. First, they serve as role models by exhibiting attitudes, words, and actions that emphasize customer service. Second, they provide customer service training whenever it is needed. Third, they reward team members who excel at customer service. One example is when they observe an employee going out of his or her way to help a customer and they say "Great job!" Another example is when they provide favorable input about the employees' customer service skills during performance appraisals.

Focus on Team Leaders

Successful teams do not happen by chance. **Supervisors** are first-rung managers who direct the work of entry-level employees on their teams. These team leaders must establish and maintain a work environment in which their team members work together effectively. They must identify and make the best use of each member's strengths, and this requires coordination. Effective team leaders consistently demonstrate several traits:

- They have great interpersonal (people) skills. They develop a team emphasis that gives a priority to team-building activities.
- They allow team members to make decisions. When possible, they share management responsibilities with team members who have the knowledge, skills, and experience necessary for the tasks at hand.
- They allow team members to establish or at least contribute to team goals and the process for measuring progress toward the goals.
- They request comments from team members about work improvement strategies, productivity, and other matters affecting goals.
- They link the team with other managers to gain commitment to the project and access to the resources necessary to attain goals.

- They maximize morale levels, minimize unnecessary turnover, and wisely use limited resources.

Successful team leaders know their operation's mission statement, and they share it with their team. They work with their department head to determine the best ways for their team to support the operation's and the department's mission statements. This process allows team members to know how they, their team, and their department contribute to the establishment's mission.

Effective team leaders set expectations and monitor performance as work progresses. They ask team members for suggestions about corrective actions that will help the team better reach goals. By involving the team, they ensure the strategies for addressing departmental challenges are better accepted and team members have a high interest in their success. Team leaders also ensure that team members are skilled and knowledgeable by providing access to training and professional development opportunities.

Manager's Memo

The best team leaders give their employees the authority to make decisions within their areas of responsibility. This gives the team a sense of ownership for their decisions. Leaders also know how to manage information and provide it as necessary to help their team plan and monitor progress toward their goals. Good leaders encourage team members to offer diverse opinions and ideas, and they encourage communication, networking, and feedback in team discussions. They also reward their team when new ideas are successfully implemented.

High-Performance Teams

A **high-performance team** is one whose members have an intense interest in making decisions and developing plans to help the operation reach its goals. Members of high-performance teams set performance goals and develop work procedures and methods that help attain them. They recognize they are accountable to their manager to reach the goals they have developed. They also have the necessary work ethic to continue efforts to reach goals until they are successful. The term **work ethic** refers to following a set of values based on the idea that there are benefits to work that include strengthening character.

High-performance teams are self-directed because they propose challenging goals and suggest ways to reach them. Team members often learn the best operating procedures as they work closely with others during work shifts.

Members of high-performance teams trust, respect, and support each other. You learned in chapter 4 that managers who trust, respect, and support employees provide opportunities for staff to become motivated. This same concept applies to members of high-performance teams: they are motivated to attain the team's goals. They actively work with each other and are willing to help each other whenever assistance is needed. They encourage each other by asking for advice or providing assistance when asked. They commonly have a sincere interest in improving the quality of their teamwork as well as the quality of their team's output.

Restaurant and foodservice managers should work with high-performance teams during the storming and performing stages of team development. That is when procedures and standards are being established, and what managers do then helps establish expectations.

THINK ABOUT IT . . .

Managers who build high-performance teams develop challenges, overcome difficulties, and encourage team members to excel. Explain why these are or are not reasonable strategies in today's restaurant and foodservice management environment.

The leaders of high-performance teams do several things as they develop these teams:

- Work with the team to develop clear and measurable goals.
- Work with the team to determine the best ways to reach these goals.
- Work to build trust and to allow team members to find pride and satisfaction in their work.
- Select team members with the best knowledge and skills for the task, and then work with these staff members on an ongoing basis to improve their abilities.

Team Management Challenges

Teams are sometimes confronted with problems that hinder their effectiveness. These problems can be created by the managers themselves or can involve conflicts between team members.

MANAGEMENT CHALLENGES

Several factors can impact a team's effectiveness:

- **Poor management style:** Although managers must be involved throughout the team's development, the use of only one management style over all the stages does not normally produce a high-performing team.
- **High employee turnover:** If team members change frequently, it becomes harder to develop the relationships that encourage members to work closely together.
- **A focus on relationships instead of goals:** For example, a manager might engage in too many team-building exercises to get the team started. This strategy might make some team members incorrectly think the manager is more concerned with interpersonal relationships than reaching goals.

CONFLICT CHALLENGES

Conflict within teams occurs when team members have differences of opinion about goals, procedures to attain them, or other matters that hurt successful performance. Sometimes, for example, the diversity that is a strength of teams can also produce conflict within the team.

The conflict can occur because of communication problems, how the team is organized, or personal differences, among other reasons. Communication problems include poor listening skills, failure to share information, and confusion about assignments or procedures. Team organizational problems can occur when employees enter or leave the team. Other problems arise when, for example, there are different levels of participation. Personal concerns include how team members feel about themselves and each other.

There are other reasons for conflict between team members:

- Unclear deadlines
- Poor instructions
- Too much to do and too little time
- An overemphasis on cost rather than results
- Unclear team member responsibilities

Managers can use five basic strategies to manage conflict within teams:

- **The direct approach:** The manager quickly identifies the issues and deals with them in the manner that he or she believes to be best.
- **Bargaining:** A "give and take" approach is used. While this can be helpful, many times the result is that everyone is equally dissatisfied.
- **Enforcement of team rules:** Although basic rules are important, this problem is often created when one team member does not want to participate fully. The manager might want to find another team for the person causing the problem.
- **Retreat:** A manager could avoid the problem or work around it. This method is useful only if the problem is minor.
- **Conflict management as a team:** When team members agree to address the conflict together, they can often develop plans that all team members can agree to.

One method for managing team conflict successfully uses a three-step approach:

Step 1: Address the problem on a person-by-person basis. The manager can informally talk to the employees involved in the conflict and see if they can work it out.

Step 2: As a one-on-one mediator, the manager can gather information, talk with team members, and consider the problem in the context of meeting the needs of the customers, team, and establishment (*Exhibit 5.5*).

Exhibit 5.5

Manager's Memo

Negotiation is often an effective way to manage conflict when it involves equal parties who are dependent on each other. Managers who are effective negotiators have certain skills:

- Recognizing areas of understanding and differences
- Working with all parties to develop a common statement about the nature of the disagreement
- Listening to what each person is saying and understanding the emotional factors behind the words
- Resolving the problem after all information about the issue is known

Step 3: If the first two steps do not work, a team meeting should be held. Its purpose should be to identify the facts and relate the problem to the needs of the customers, team, and establishment. Then the manager should try to arrange a team decision to which all members will agree.

Many managers use a questioning process as they meet with team members who have disagreements. For example, Linda received a promotion to dining-room supervisor and Jessica thinks she should have received the promotion. The two employees seem to disagree about everything from schedules to responsibilities to ideas for work improvements.

The restaurant manager and dining-room manager might meet with the two employees and have an objective and frank discussion addressing the following questions:

- What does each of you think is the main problem?
- What does each of you think the other person does that makes the problem worse?
- What does each of you want or need from the other person?
- What does each of you think you do that contributes to the problem?
- What is the first thing each of you can do to help resolve the problem?

Linda and Jessica should both be asked to answer each question while the other person listens. Then the two managers can lead a discussion that yields an agreed-upon understanding of what the problem is. If both parties will admit partial responsibility, they can work toward agreeing about what can be done to resolve the problem.

Manager's Memo

The team members and their managers need to agree on goals.

Think about a team of servers working the evening shift. Most team members have been at the establishment a long time. The dining-room manager will not need to give each team member constant instructions ("Go to table 4 first, then fill the water on table 6, etc."). Team members will know these details.

However, how will the manager and team members know if the shift was successful? Will "success" be achieved if there are no complaints? If the manager does not get angry with any server?

Employees want to know how their managers feel about their work. This information can be provided during coaching and performance appraisals. However, teamwork is required in addition to individual success. This can be addressed at team or pre-shift meetings, and even by offering contests in which all servers can win by meeting or exceeding predetermined goals.

SETTING TEAM GOALS

Teams must have goals for the same reason that individual employees do. Goals provide a purpose for work, and they are used to help determine whether that purpose was achieved.

Goal Setting

Restaurant and foodservice teams at any of the four stages of development need goals to be effective. Then team members will understand what the team must do, and members can suggest ideas about the best ways to reach the goals.

One way to have agreement about team goals is to allow each member to provide input. If all team members and their managers can agree about the goals, the team will be off to a good start.

Types of Team Goals

Chapter 2 explained that best goals are SMART:

- Specific: Goals must be clearly stated and indicate what is expected.

- Measurable: Goals must be measurable to determine the extent to which goals are attained.
- Achievable: Goals should be reasonable so they are attainable.
- Relevant: Goals must relate to the operation's vision and mission statements.
- Timebound: Goals should tell the dates by when they should be reached.

Managers must work with team members to develop SMART goals for their team just as they should interact with individual employees to develop goals for them.

Effective teams develop three types of goals:

1. **Team-building goals:**
   - *Getting to know each team member.* Teams are most effective when the members discover each other's backgrounds, skills, and work styles.
   - *Learning to work together.* Teams need to identify the strengths of each member and set processes in place to work efficiently together.
   - *Setting ground rules.* Members need a common understanding of how the team will conduct itself and what is acceptable and unacceptable behavior. Some of the topics for discussion are meeting attendance, promptness, courtesy, assignments, and breaks.
   - *Using decision-making processes.* One problem with ineffective teams is that decisions just seem to happen. Teams need to discuss how decisions will be made to avoid future conflicts.

   Here is an example of a SMART goal related to team-building: "The team will review and revise, if necessary, the decision-making process discussed in the training and agree on the process to be used by July 15."

2. **Information goals:**
   - *Getting updates from team members on progress.*
   - *Learning about the tools used to support the team's tasks.*
   - *Communicating with other employees and teams.*

   An example of a SMART goal involving information might be as follows: "The team will meet at least once every two weeks to share information and update project plans."

3. **Work-related goals:**
   - *Developing plans and procedures to reach goals.* Without a road map, teams can flounder. The team leader should discuss work procedures with team members. Breaking the process into smaller steps and assigning duties will help the team members cooperate. Teams should continue to review and revise these plans as they move toward reaching their goals.

- *Understanding the tasks and each team member's responsibilities.* Team members should be able to ask questions about their tasks and the expectations of those who make the assignments.
- *Identifying the business needs supported by the goals.* Managers must be able to explain how the team's goals relate to business needs. If they cannot or do not, team members will have difficulty trying to reach these goals because they will not see the reason for their assignment.
- *Understanding the process that will be used.* Team members need to understand the overall process and know the specific steps that are their responsibility.
- *Identifying the resources that are needed.* Team members should discuss resources that might be needed sooner rather than later in the decision-making process. This discussion ensures that necessary resources will be available when needed.

Here is an example of a SMART goal applicable to specific work tasks: "Team members will review the proposed changes to the operating procedure and make any suggestions for improvement at a group meeting on January 17."

Busy teams doing many things will benefit from the use of SMART goals to drive their activities. Often, goals can be stated and agreed upon in an informal process. This is acceptable as long as the agreed-upon goals drive the activities needed to attain them.

Benefits and Challenges of Team Goals

Teams that participate in developing goals are typically more effective than teams that do not. Members are more likely to support goals when they feel they have helped define them. Assisting with goal setting also increases a member's opportunity for success, and that builds confidence in his or her own ability to accomplish goals.

Managers must provide ongoing leadership of and communication with their teams. If they do not, a team can misunderstand the value of its contribution. Rewarding the team, for example, with personal thank-you notes for participation in the goal-setting process supports feelings of accomplishment.

Several factors can hurt the ability of a team to set team-building, information, and work-related goals:

- A trusting environment is needed for teams to flourish. Teams can fail in goal setting if personal interests conflict with project goals or the operation's mission statement. Identifying ways to eliminate these obstacles through team-building activities can help.

- Poor communication can affect goal setting. It can also affect the ability to meet goals if it results in team members not helping each other.
- The lack of a strong connection between project goals and business needs can slow the goal-setting process. Managers should examine goals to ensure they link to the operation's needs.

THINK ABOUT IT . . .

The term *groupthink* describes what happens when team members shape their own opinions to match what they think are the opinions of other group members. What can be done to mitigate the impact of groupthink?

MANAGING TEAM PROJECTS

Basic principles should be used to manage projects whether they have been assigned to specific employees or to teams. Too often, however, a "Ready, Fire, Aim" approach encourages teams to take action even if that action may not be the best thing to do.

Planning Projects

Planning is the first step in managing any project. An important first task is to ensure that the project's goals are linked to an identified business need. Providing input about proposed goals helps the team create a solid footing from which plans can be developed.

Teams should ensure that SMART goals (those that are specific, measurable, achievable, relevant, and timebound) have been developed. Team members may also have useful ideas about planning to reach the goals, determining the resources that are needed, improving work methods, and ensuring that plans are practical.

During the planning stage, managers should also consider whether the team needs any special training to be successful. If training is needed, it should be scheduled before the team starts to implement its plan. The final step before moving to the next phase is for the team to communicate its suggested plans to the manager and other affected persons. With changes, if any, and approval, the project plan then can be implemented.

Manager's Memo

Brainstorming is a way to collect ideas in which each team member makes suggestions without comment from the others. The team leader can ask a question such as, "What can we do to speed up our dining service without hurting our quality? Table turns?" Then each team member can make one suggestion, which the leader writes down. When no one has any further suggestions, the members can review the ideas and determine which might be most useful. Many times the best idea is a combination of two or more suggestions.

A brainstorming session should encourage everyone to provide ideas; the more ideas the better. One of the most important benefits of a team arises when its members work together to suggest how to manage challenges. Then they can also work together to solve the problem, perhaps in another brainstorming session. ("What is the best way to implement our idea?")

Implementing Projects

Once the team has determined its approach, members know their roles and responsibilities, and necessary resources are available, the plan can be implemented. During this phase, the manager must monitor the team's progress. If a new team has been brought together to address a specific problem, some of the issues that can occur during early stages of team development may apply.

If early challenges arise, the manager should ask the team to evaluate how it can become more effective. The manager can also redirect some of the team's efforts to minimize any conflicts.

Communicating project updates is very important to let everyone know the team's progress. If there are setbacks or unexpected problems, the team can receive advice from the manager and others and take actions to get back on course.

Evaluating Projects

During the last phase of project management, the team and manager determine whether the project's goals have been achieved. As you have learned, this is relatively easy to do if goals have been stated in ways that can be measured. Consider, for example, a goal regarding table turns. **Table turns** are the number of times a table is used during a specific meal period. Compare the goal "We will speed up table turns" to the goal "We will increase our table-turn rate to 2.75 by December 1."

Another aspect of the project evaluation can focus on how well the team functioned together. A debrief meeting can be conducted for this purpose. A **debrief meeting** is a session in which the team leader asks all team members to evaluate all aspects of a project after it is completed.

For example, members can be asked to evaluate how effective the team was in performing tasks. What would they do again? Are there things they would change? If so, what would they change?

Questions about team interaction are also important. Since employees will continue to work in one or more teams, it is important to explore how they interacted with other team members.

Finally, the team leader should recognize and celebrate the success of the team and its members. This celebration can be conducted during the debrief meeting or at another time.

SUMMARY

1. **Explain why teamwork is important to the success of restaurant and foodservice operations.**

   A team is a group of persons who work together to reach a goal. Restaurant and foodservice employees are grouped into teams with specific responsibilities that involve working closely with other teams.

   Effective teamwork can increase productivity and better ensure that products and services meet standards. Also, resources can be used more effectively, problem solving will improve, and creativity and innovation during planning will be greater. Managers using teams recognize that decisions can take longer, disagreements may arise, some tasks are better performed by individuals, and some employees may not wish to participate in team projects. To be effective, the team's members must have adequate technical abilities, problem-solving skills, and "people" skills.

2. **Review common types of restaurant and foodservice teams.**

   All employees of an operation comprise one team. This team is broken down first into departmental teams, further into teams with specific responsibilities, and finally into teams of individuals who have common responsibilities during specific work shifts.

   There are three basic types of teams: functional teams that perform routine tasks, problem-solving teams to resolve immediate problems, and cross-functional teams that work to resolve issues impacting several departments. The fourth type of team, self-directed teams, makes many decisions with little supervision.

3. **Describe the five stages of team growth and development.**

   In stage one, forming, team members get to know each other and learn what must be done to reach goals. During the second stage, storming, team members become much clearer about their responsibilities and some conflicts between team members may surface. In the third stage, norming, team members settle personal differences and develop more trusting relationships. The fourth stage, performing, evolves when team members begin to depend on each other and can analyze and solve problems together. A fifth stage is called adjourning and occurs when a team's work is completed and the team is disbanded.

4. **Discuss basic principles helpful in building and maintaining effective teams.**

   Managers play a key role in developing effective teams. They must communicate effectively, use appropriate leadership styles, conduct team-building exercises, and explain the team's role in helping the operation reach goals. They must also apply effective management skills to support the team.

   High-performance teams are those with very committed members who are allowed to plan ambitious goals, make decisions, and work hard to reach "stretch" goals.

   Team leaders have excellent interpersonal skills and allow members to make decisions that contribute to reaching goals. They also request comments from members about work methods and work with the team and other managers to help ensure their teams are effective.

   Teams do not work well when a poor management style is used, there is high employee turnover, or there is a focus on relationships instead of goals.

   Conflict between team members must be effectively managed. Strategies include the direct approach in which the manager decides how to resolve it. Other strategies involve bargaining, enforcing team rules, or ignoring the conflict. The best tactic is often to allow team members to work together to resolve the conflict.

5. **Explain basic procedures for setting team goals.**

   Goals provide a purpose for work and also help determine whether that purpose was achieved. Employees are likely to accept team goals if each team member has provided input in their development.

   There are three basic types of team goals, which involve team building, gathering and communicating information, and understanding what must be done and the best ways to do it. Goals are most effectively developed when there is a trusting environment, effective communication, and a strong connection to a business need.

6. **Identify procedures for effectively managing team projects.**

   Projects should be planned with SMART goals. Team members must know their roles and responsibilities and be assured that necessary resources are available. Managers must monitor the team's progress, address any challenges that arise, and resolve employee conflicts.

   Project evaluation is important to help determine whether goals have been achieved. A debrief meeting can be conducted to learn how well the team worked together.

APPLICATION EXERCISE

You are the kitchen manager at the Ocean Retreat Restaurant and are experiencing a problem that has almost gotten out of hand. As background, three cooks are normally working at the close of the evening shift and are involved in kitchen cleanup duties.

The kitchen closing team also includes one dish washer who cleans up that area, mops the floor, and does related duties. You have hired a new dish washer for this hard-to-fill position who does great work, but he must leave shortly before 11:00 p.m. to catch the last bus home. This is not usually a problem, but when it is, it is a big problem!

You thought that any remaining dish-washer tasks could be done by the remaining cooks, but they claim the dish washer works slowly to avoid completing his assignments. You have reviewed his work and, while he is a little slow, all cleaning standards are met when he completes a task.

The cooks say they do not want to continue doing the dish washer's closing duties and are suggesting that cleanup work be deferred to the morning dish-washing shift.

1. Five basic strategies to manage conflict within teams were discussed in this chapter. Which one would you use? Why? (Hint: *Consider whether aspects of one or more strategies could be used to develop a customized approach.*)
2. A three-step method for successfully managing team conflict was also presented. What are examples of actions you might take and questions you might ask during each of the steps?

   Step 1: Talk informally with each employee.

   Step 2: Be a mediator.

   Step 3: Conduct a team meeting.

REVIEW YOUR LEARNING

Select the best answer for each question.

1. **What principle is important when developing a project team?**
   A. Remember that some employees may not want to participate if failure will reflect on them.
   B. The more employees involved in the project, the better will be the outcome.
   C. Try to select team members who have similar and equal skills.
   D. It is always best to select the most experienced employees.

2. **Which type of team performs routine tasks that are part of the members' job descriptions?**
   A. Problem-solving team
   B. Cross-functional team
   C. Self-directed team
   D. Functional team

3. **A "give and take" approach is an example of what basic strategy to resolve conflict within teams?**
   A. Direct approach
   B. Bargaining approach
   C. Retreat approach
   D. Enforcement approach

4. **Which is a characteristic of a high-performance team?**
   A. The members are self-directed because they propose challenging goals.
   B. The members must include only the most experienced employees.
   C. The members do not need goals because they are highly focused.
   D. The members are very knowledgeable and do not need advice.

5. **Which effort is a team-building goal?**
   A. Learning how to analyze an operating budget
   B. Identifying business needs supported by goals
   C. Getting updates from members about progress
   D. Learning to work together effectively

6. **At which stage do team members begin to recognize the benefits of working together?**
   A. Forming
   B. Storming
   C. Norming
   D. Performing

7. **Which leadership style is most useful for teams in the performing stage?**
   A. Coaching
   B. Supporting
   C. Delegating
   D. Directing

8. **Including teams in the goal-setting process offers which major benefit?**
   A. Gaining the team's acceptance of the goals
   B. Reducing costs related to attaining the goal
   C. Shortening the time needed to reach the goal
   D. Decreasing the time a team spends in storming

9. **During the planning stage of a team project, team members can assist with**
   A. ensuring alternatives are both feasible and practical.
   B. confirming the project is done at the lowest cost.
   C. talking to customers about project outcomes.
   D. monitoring each other's participation.

10. **The importance of discussing lessons learned during projects is to**
    A. consider if similar projects can be done without a manager.
    B. discover ways to shorten the team development process.
    C. identify members who did not contribute adequately.
    D. determine how members worked with each other.

6 Leaders Manage Employee Work Schedules

INSIDE THIS CHAPTER

- The Need for Effective Work Schedules
- Determining Budgeted Labor Cost
- Creating a Master Schedule
- Developing a Crew Schedule
- Distributing and Adjusting the Crew Schedule
- Monitoring Employees during a Shift
- Analyzing After-Shift Labor Information
- Work Schedules for Managers

CHAPTER LEARNING OBJECTIVES

After completing this chapter, you should be able to:

- Explain the need for effective work schedules.
- Discuss basic procedures for determining budgeted labor cost.
- Describe how to create a master schedule.
- Explain how to develop a crew schedule.
- Describe procedures for distributing and adjusting the crew schedule.
- Identify common practices helpful for monitoring employees during work shifts.
- Explain methods for analyzing after-shift labor information.
- Review basic concerns in developing work schedules for managers.

KEY TERMS

- contingency plan, p. 170
- crew schedule, p. 150
- cross-training, p. 160
- employee absence policies, p. 164
- Fair Labor Standards Act (FLSA), p. 165
- Family and Medical Leave Act (FMLA), p. 164
- floater, p. 170
- fringe benefits, p. 151
- labor cost, p. 150
- line-up meeting, p. 171
- management schedule, p. 174
- master schedule, p. 152
- no-show, p. 166
- overtime (legal), p. 174
- overtime (scheduling), p. 166
- point-of-sale (POS) system, p. 155
- salary, p. 151
- sales forecast, p. 154
- sales history, p. 154
- scheduling, p. 150
- shift leader, p. 170
- time-off request policy, p. 162
- variance, p. 172
- wages, p. 151

CASE STUDY

"Don't blame me," said Jervon, the kitchen manager at John's Steakhouse. "I work with what I get," he continued, "and lately we haven't been getting good cooks in here. It takes a lot of time to train new employees, redo recipes when they mess them up, and teach them how to work in the kitchen."

"It's not acceptable to make these kinds of excuses without telling me what we can do to correct the problem," replied Ruth, the operation manager. "We have reduced the labor hours for almost all other positions to give to you as many extra hours as we can while still considering budgeted labor cost goals," she continued. "What can you do and how long will it take to reduce kitchen labor hours to the level we discussed when the budget was developed, while still meeting our quality standards?"

1. What is the main labor-related problem at John's Steakhouse?
2. What would you do if you were Ruth to help bring kitchen labor costs within budget standards?

THE NEED FOR EFFECTIVE WORK SCHEDULES

Restaurant and foodservice managers must schedule the right number of employees in the right positions at the right times to produce products and services meeting expected quality standards. They must do this while considering the labor cost they will incur while the employees are working. **Labor cost** refers to the money and fringe benefit expenses paid to the employees for the work they do.

Managers must use an effective **scheduling** process to determine which employees will be needed to serve the expected number of customers during specific times. The **crew schedule** that results is a chart that informs employees who receive wages about the days and hours they are expected to work during a specific time period (usually a week).

The crew schedule is not just a list of employees' names and times. Instead, it is a well-thought-out plan that considers the expected volume of business, the employees required, and the expected labor cost. The crew schedule also recognizes that the employees have personal lives. It tries to balance the needs of the operation and its customers with the needs of its employees.

Unfortunately, the best-planned crew schedules may need to be changed because of unexpected business volume and employee-related problems. Backup plans consider these types of events to minimize problems that impact customers.

Several steps should be followed in a specific order to manage employee work schedules:

- **Step 1:** Determine budgeted labor cost.
- **Step 2:** Create a master schedule.
- **Step 3:** Develop a crew schedule.
- **Step 4:** Distribute and adjust the crew schedule.
- **Step 5:** Monitor employees during shifts.
- **Step 6:** Analyze after-shift labor information.

This chapter discusses how to complete each of these steps.

DETERMINING BUDGETED LABOR COST

The first step in developing an effective employee schedule is to determine how much money can be spent for labor during each work shift. This amount is found in the approved budget. Managers should not spend more for labor than the amount in the budget, and meeting this goal begins when the employee schedule is planned.

Managers must know the amount of labor cost that has been budgeted and use this information to develop employee schedules. When they do this, there is better assurance that the actual labor cost will be within budget standards.

THINK ABOUT IT . . .

A budget is planned for a 12-month period. How can planners know in October what the revenue and expenses will be next November? How can managers who are planning schedules use dated financial information?

The process for determining the amount that can be spent for labor should relate to the approved operating budget. Consider Demond, manager of The Surfer's Grill. His establishment is open for dinner seven nights per week and serves customers from 5:00 to 10:00 p.m. Demond and his management team developed an operating budget for the current year. They built the budget by estimating revenue and expenses for each month separately and then combining the monthly budgets to obtain the annual, or yearly, budget.

Since Demond's budget was planned in the late fall for the next year, its financial estimates can be outdated when the actual month arrives. For example, if the budget for September of year two was planned in November of year one, the September year two information will be 10 months old by the time September of year two comes to pass. Therefore, Demond and his team must update each budget using past, current, and even future estimates of the number of customers to be served based on many factors that are discussed later in this chapter.

Demond's approved budget allows him to spend $38,900 for employees receiving wages for the 30 days in June. **Wages** are monetary compensation for employees who are paid based on the number of hours they work. This budgeted labor cost will be adjusted, if necessary, based on more current financial information and then will be used to drive the development of the employee schedule.

Demond's budget estimates **fringe benefits** separately from wages. Fringe benefits are monies paid indirectly in support of employees for purposes such as vacation, holiday pay, sick leave, and health insurance. This means Demond's schedule for employees who receive wages does not need to consider the cost of fringe benefits paid to these employees.

The employee schedule being developed will also not include the monies or fringe benefits paid to managers who receive a **salary**. A salary is a fixed amount of money for a certain time period that does not vary, regardless of the number of hours worked.

The Surfer's Grill serves dinner every day, and the employee schedule is planned on a weekly basis. The amount that Demond can spend on employee wages on an average day in June is easy to calculate:

June labor (wage) budget ÷ Days in June = Average daily wage
$38,900 ÷ 30 = $1,297 (rounded)

Manager's Memo

The process being discussed to develop a master schedule relates the forecasted number of customers to the labor hours required to produce the meals for the customers. Some managers use a slightly different approach.

They calculate the forecasted revenue and relate that to the number of labor hours required to generate the revenue. This second method still requires knowledge about the number of customers that are expected. The number of customers is then multiplied by the check average: the amount that is spent by an average customer. For example, imagine that a restaurant or foodservice operation serves 2,100 customers during July and generates $25,200 in revenue. The average customer, then, spends $12:

$25,200 ÷ 2,100 customers = $12

When the master schedule is developed, the manager would calculate the amount of revenue expected and use that revenue target to plan the master schedule.

If the *average* hourly wage rate (not including benefits) is approximately $12, Demond can schedule no more than 108 hours for employees who receive a wage for an average day in June:

Average daily wage ÷ Average hourly wage rate = Average hours per day for employees who receive a wage

$1,297 ÷ $12 = 108

His labor budget also suggests that no more than 756 waged hours can be worked in an average week:

Average hours per day × Days open per week = Average hours per week for employees who receive a wage

108 × 7 = 756

The previous calculations will be very helpful to Demond as he develops his schedule for employees who receive wages. He knows the amount he can spend for wages each day ($1,297). He also knows the average number of hours he can schedule per day for employees who receive wages (108 hours) and per week (756 hours).

It is important to note that the concept of "average" in these calculations means more labor hours can be scheduled when more customers are expected, and fewer labor hours can be scheduled when customer counts are forecasted to be lower. "Average" also means that some employees can be paid more than $12 per hour, and some, including tipped servers, will be paid less than $12 per hour. Also, recall that the establishment's manager, Demond, is developing a schedule for employees who receive wages. Employees who receive a salary are carried in a separate labor expense account, as are employee benefits expenses.

CREATING A MASTER SCHEDULE

After the manager knows the number of labor hours that can be used without exceeding the labor budget, a master schedule can be created. A **master schedule** considers the expected number of customers and spreads out the number of hours allowed by the budget between the different positions in the operation. This plan shows the number of employees that will be needed in each position and the total number of hours that employees in these positions will need to work.

A master schedule has two primary purposes:

1. To help ensure that the correct number of waged employees are available so customers will receive prompt, efficient service and properly prepared food
2. To plan waged labor expenses so the budget goals can be met

Exhibit 6.1 shows a master schedule that Demond developed for one dinner shift at The Surfer's Grill. Remember that his establishment is open for dinner seven nights each week. He develops a separate master schedule for each

Modern **point-of-sale (POS) systems** make it easy to track customer counts. POS systems collect information about revenue, number of customers, menu items sold, and a wide range of other information. The system then generates numerous reports that provide information helpful for management decision making.

Accurate historical sales information is important. Inaccurate information can cause too many employees to be scheduled, which increases labor costs beyond budget goals and reduces profit. Inaccurate information could also result in too few employees being scheduled. This will result in poor service, customers who do not return, and customers who tell others about their bad dining experience.

Sales Forecasts

Sales forecasts that are as accurate as possible are critical to developing a good master schedule. Past sales records are used as a baseline which is then increased or decreased based on current, local, and national trends.

As the projected number of customers increases, the number of employee hours required will increase. As estimated customer counts decrease, the number of employee hours required will decrease.

A master schedule is created with the idea that a certain sales level is most likely to be reached. As estimated customer counts change from that norm, either up or down, the master schedule should be adjusted.

For example, if a new office park is slated to open across the street, then lunch sales would be projected to show an increase over last year. If a manufacturing plant in town is expected to shut down, the operation would probably lower its projections because some residents would not be dining out as often.

Experienced restaurant and foodservice managers know that many factors impact how many customers will visit their property on a given day or for a specific meal period. The master schedule should reflect the expected customer count as closely as possible because the crew schedule must provide the right number of labor hours to serve the customers.

Here are some examples of factors that will influence customer counts, and that should be considered when the master schedule is developed:

- **Holidays:** Some holidays tend to increase customer counts, and for others, the establishment should close because of almost no business. For example, Mother's Day is the highest-volume day of the year for many operations, while many properties close on Christmas Day. Thanksgiving is a good holiday for some establishments but not for others. Knowing the operation's past sales history for each holiday and adjusting the master schedule accordingly will allow the establishment to do the best on each day of operation.

Manager's Memo

POS systems provide customer and other data for different periods such as yearly, monthly, weekly, daily, by meal period, and even hourly or in 15-minute periods. Yearly and monthly data are used for budgeting and income statement purposes. Weekly sales information is used for purchasing and scheduling. Daily, meal-period, and hourly or part-hourly data are also used for employee scheduling and for production planning. In establishments without POS systems, sales history information comes from a manual tally of information on guest checks or from cash register readings.

- **Seasonal adjustments:** The weather often plays a critical role in customer counts. Extreme heat or cold will normally cause sales to drop. Hurricanes, tornadoes, and snowstorms all affect sales. In severe cases, the establishment may have to close. Other seasonal adjustments include the holiday shopping season, which typically increases sales, and income tax time, when sales in some operations slow down.
- **Advertising and promotions:** These factors are known in advance, so their impact can be considered when the master schedule is planned. Hopefully these events cause sales to increase, and managers should plan for more employees to serve additional customers. On the other hand, if competitors have a well-planned promotion, customer counts could be reduced, and this should be reflected in the master schedule.
- **Community activities:** Fairs, festivals, and athletic events will all get people out into the community. Depending on the location of the event, these activities can increase sales. The best managers know what is happening in their communities and how it will impact their business.
- **Economy:** Restaurant and foodservice operations are affected differently by the economy. In tough economic times, business may slow in fine-dining operations and pick up in more casual service properties. When the economy is growing, most establishments may enjoy increased business. The economy is an important concern when the master schedule is planned.

Trends

Managers should study more than just the previous year's information when forecasting future revenue. They also need to consider current trends. Local trends are more important than national ones, but the economy, unemployment rates, and other national and even international events will all affect customers' desire or ability to eat out.

An example of how managers make revenue projections can be helpful. In the following example, the managers of an upscale establishment are developing revenue projections for next year's budget. Information about budget revenues and labor costs will be used, in part, to develop the master schedule. The establishment is close to a small coastal city in Florida and receives most but not all of its business from the town's residents.

Exhibit 6.2

The managers consider some of the factors that affect their planning:

- A major hurricane recently damaged many of the area's vacation homes and resorts. As a result, tourism is projected to be down next year.
- A national retailer is opening a store close to the establishment next September. The managers expect revenue to increase because of the new store, but they have also learned the city is considering widening the street in front of the establishment. This construction may affect revenue levels because potential customers may have difficulty driving to the establishment (*Exhibit 6.2*).

The managers do simple research on the possible impacts of the hurricane and the new store:

- A manager who is in charge of an establishment in a nearby city said her operation had an eight percent revenue increase after a large store opened in the neighborhood.
- The local chamber of commerce expects a 20 to 30 percent decrease in tourism through May but then expects it to quickly return to normal.
- The chamber of commerce also reports that a county-wide fair with fireworks and a major country music star will be held in July at a location close to the restaurant.
- The mayor's office thinks the city council will approve the road construction, which will most likely start in January and last for four months.

Exhibit 6.3 shows the managers' revenue projections for next year based on what they have learned. Notice how their research affects each month's numbers.

Exhibit 6.3

SALES PROJECTIONS FOR THE NEW YEAR

Month	Sales Projection	Reason
January	Down 10%	8% cut because of the beginning of street construction and 2% due to tourism drop.
February	Down 15%	13% due to construction, which will now be in high gear, and 2% due to tourism drop.
March	Down 15%	Same reasoning as February.
April	Down 15%	Same reasoning as February.
May	Down 2%	Construction should be complete; 2% drop due to reduced tourism.
June	Up 5%	A major promotion to celebrate the end of construction will increase sales 7%, less 2% due to tourism drop.
July	Up 10%	Fairgrounds celebration; tourism back to normal.
August	Same as last year	
September	Up 10%	Retail store grand opening will create more establishment customers.
October	Up 8%	Business spike expected from retail store.
November	Up 8%	Same reasoning as October.
December	Up 10%	Retail store 8%, plus 2% due to new promotion.

The managers know that the information they are working with is as accurate as it can be. However, they also know that new retail stores do not always open on schedule and road completion projects are not always completed on time. It is important to receive information updates and be able to quickly modify plans, if necessary.

Customer Service Needs

Restaurant and foodservice managers must estimate the number of customers they will serve on a monthly basis to develop the operating budget and on a daily basis to create the master schedule. If an establishment serves two meals daily such as midday and evening meals, a separate master schedule may be required for each meal period. The purpose of the master schedule is to determine the number of employees in each position that must be scheduled for each meal period.

It would be easy if the number of customers arriving to be served was approximately the same each hour. In fact, many establishments have a customer volume that varies greatly during a meal period. How can a manager develop the master schedule and the resulting crew schedule without knowing the number of customers to be served each hour or other time period?

The answer goes back to the POS system that can provide customer-count information by any time period requested. Also, managers typically know that, for example, they might be fairly "slow" during the first hour of a shift and perhaps during the last hour of the shift, with the majority of customers arriving between those two time periods.

Using POS information and the manager's operating experience, the number of customers expected per hour can be determined. With this information known, the number of employees required for each position in the master schedule can be determined.

Returning to Demond at The Surfer's Grill, the master schedule in *Exhibit 6.1* indicates that he is estimating 160 customers for the evening meal on 6/11. How were the numbers of employees in each position determined, and how did he know to schedule them for the hours shown?

For example, if the establishment opens for dinner at 5:00 p.m. and closes at 10:00 p.m., the last guests may be seated up to 10:00 p.m., and they will still be dining after the operation stops seating additional customers. Notice that Demond has scheduled three server hours before 5:00 p.m. to get ready for customer service. He has also scheduled three server hours for after 10:00 p.m. to clean up and get ready for the next evening shift.

On a typical dinner shift, only a few customers are served during the first hour. Then business increases until only a few are seated shortly before 9:00 p.m. Most of these customers have left by 10:00 p.m. and cleanup can begin.

Exhibit 6.4

CUSTOMERS SERVED PER HOUR AT THE SURFER'S GRILL

Date: 6/11 **Total no. of customers expected:** 160

Time	% of Total Customers	No. of Customers
5:00–6:00 p.m.	15%	24
6:00–7:00 p.m.	20	32
7:00–8:00 p.m.	25	40
8:00–9:00 p.m.	30	48
9:00–10:00 p.m.	10	16
	Total no. of customers	**160**

Demond's review of recent POS system information and his long-term experience at The Surfer's Grill allow him to create estimated percentages of customers per hour, as shown in *Exhibit 6.4*. Demond is then able to translate those percentages into the number of total customers for each hour.

Demond used the information in *Exhibit 6.4* to develop the master schedule. Note that in *Exhibit 6.1* during the 5:00 to 6:00 p.m. time period he has scheduled only two servers, and they are the same two servers who came in before opening.

The last hour of service, 9:00 to 10:00 p.m., is normally a slow serving time. Demond has kept four servers during this period because as the customer count decreases, the servers will be able to begin some end-of-shift tasks that will not be obvious to customers. These servers will also be available as needed for final cleanup duties after the last customers leave.

The same type of factors used to plan server hours for the 6/11 dinner shift are also used to plan the number of hours required for the other positions. Note again that Demond is determining the required number of hours for each position without indicating the specific employee to fill the position.

The Master Schedule and the Budget

The draft of the master schedule should be compared with the average number of hours employees receiving a wage can work per day while staying within budget standards.

Recall that Demond can schedule, on average, approximately 108 hours for employees receiving wages each day. *Exhibit 6.1* indicates that Demond was considering using only about 102 hours on 6/11. Shouldn't he schedule more hours?

THINK ABOUT IT . . .

Some managers schedule as few employees as necessary. Other managers think, "I have made my best judgment but will schedule a few extra hours just in case." What would you do?

Remember that the budget standard is an average: Demond should schedule more than 108 labor hours on shifts forecasted to be busy and fewer labor hours when fewer customers are expected.

Demond's sales forecasts indicate that the evening being scheduled will be a slow night. He knows that his production and service standards will be met if he serves about 160 customers and schedules approximately 102 labor hours. His plan is to "save" the additional labor hours. Then he can use them for the nights he thinks will be busier and require more labor hours for all positions.

Managers developing master schedules may be able to use one employee to fill more than one position during slow serving hours or entire meal periods. If they do so without affecting the quality of production or service, labor hours can be saved that can be reassigned to busier work shifts.

Exhibit 6.5

For example, perhaps a host and a cashier position can be combined during slow periods, or perhaps a bartender can function as a lounge server during slow times. Also, a cook who has received food safety training may be able to assume a dish-washer position during very slow shifts. Also, dish washers might be trained to do some basic vegetable and other pre-preparation work to replace a cook for a few hours or an entire slow shift (*Exhibit 6.5*).

The examples just described show benefits of **cross-training**, or coaching an employee to do tasks that are not normally part of his or her position. This is just one tool of many that experienced managers can use while always striving to meet customer- and profit-related goals.

DEVELOPING A CREW SCHEDULE

The master schedule is used to prepare the crew schedule. However, planning the crew schedule involves more than just inserting a specific employee's name into each line of the master schedule. Instead, managers must consider many factors as they match necessary positions in the master schedule with specific employees in the crew schedule.

First, there should be a balance between the needs of the establishment and its customers and the needs of its employees. The operation will need employees at the times noted on the master schedule. However, the crew schedule should be developed with flexibility in mind.

What happens when an employee requests a day off for an important personal occasion such as a child getting married or a religious celebration? It can be stressful for a manager to learn an employee cannot, or will not, work a shift when he or she is really needed. Many of these situations can be avoided with clear policies and open, two-way communication.

Communication and Crew Schedules

Communication plays an important role in scheduling employees. Most employees want to see the operation do well. They realize a team effort is needed to ensure success: If the operation is successful, they will continue to have jobs. Therefore, it is important to keep employees informed about what is going on.

Employees should be told about plans such as a change in the menu or hours of operation or an upcoming promotion expected to increase business. The servers would probably not request time off during these periods because of the potential for increased tips.

Likewise, they should learn about potential decreases in business caused by, for example, road repaving in front of the establishment. Perhaps a line cook may decide to go on vacation that week. This would be a win–win situation for both the employee and management. One fewer line cook could be scheduled, and that person could have a well-deserved break.

Open communication will not solve all scheduling problems, but it will help solve some of them. Most employees who know what is going on in an operation are more likely to schedule their personal time around events affecting their work.

Manager's Memo

Developing a master schedule may look complicated, time-consuming, and perhaps not very practical. In fact, managers of many small operations do not need to develop a formal master schedule because their employees normally work specific shifts each week. These managers may view historical sales information, make updated sales forecasts, and then develop a crew schedule based on their experience.

A master schedule should be developed for all work shifts. However, since forecasted customer counts are often very similar, the staffing plan suggested by a basic master schedule can be repeated for each similar work shift.

Managers of many operations create a master schedule electronically with spreadsheet software and use their experience about normal business flow during specific meal shifts to determine the labor hours needed.

Remember that the basic purpose of a master schedule, however it is developed, is to ensure that the proper number of employees will be available when needed while staying within the budgeted labor cost goal.

Time-Off Requests

Restaurant and foodservice managers should establish and circulate a **time-off request policy** that tells the procedures and guidelines employees should follow when they want time off from work.

VACATION REQUESTS

Managers must follow their property's policies for granting vacation time to employees. Employees should also be aware of policies from discussions at orientation and training sessions and from the current employee handbook (*Exhibit 6.6*).

One good way to determine when vacation time is available for your employees is to determine which weeks during the year could have heavy revenue volumes. These weeks could be "blocked off" the vacation calendar and request form. Some managers also allow no more than a specified number of persons from a department or other work area to take time off at once.

Vacation requests are normally fulfilled according to seniority: employees working for the operation the longest have first choice. Vacation request forms should be submitted in writing and in advance. Then managers will have time to prepare for the absence. Managers who have cross-trained their employees will have fewer problems dealing with employees away from work.

Exhibit 6.6

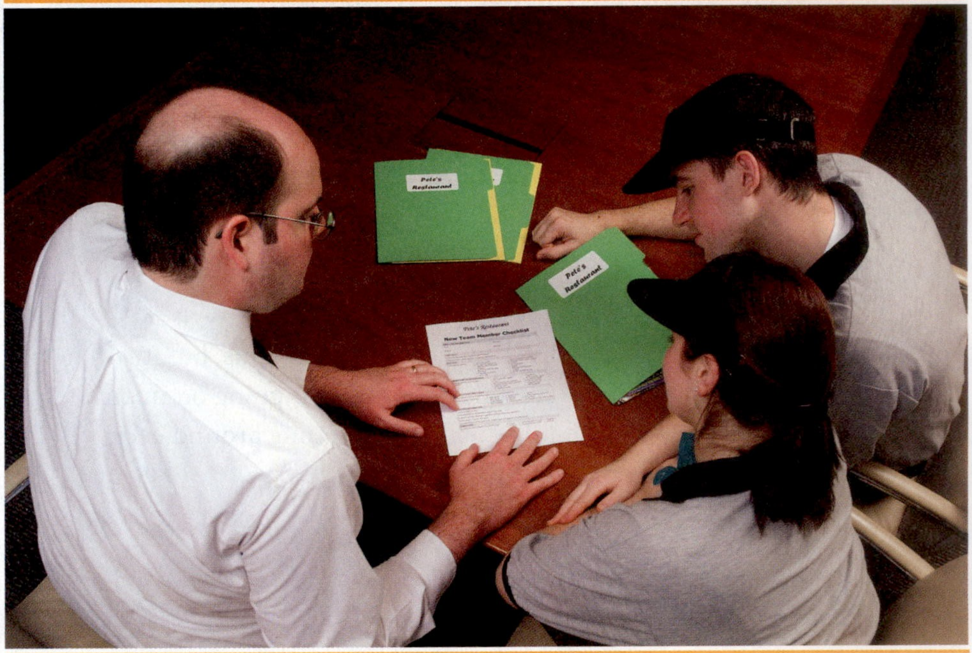

DAY-OFF REQUESTS

Guidelines are also needed for employee day-off requests. Since these requests are usually for only one or a few days, receipt of the requests at least one week before the schedule is developed may be acceptable.

Managers should also think about how many employees in a department or work area can be off at one time. If a conflict occurs, a guideline should be in place about whether requests will be honored on a seniority or "first come, first served" basis.

Day-off requests are normally not an issue unless there is a major event such as a prom or concert in the community. These times are when a well-thought-out and consistently applied policy is needed.

Special concerns are likely to arise for holidays. Some managers develop an annual schedule of holiday shifts such as the sample seen in *Exhibit 6.7*. However, special exceptions should be made for employees requesting time off for religious holidays.

Manager's Memo

Experienced restaurant and foodservice managers know it is sometimes easier to develop a time-off policy than it is to enforce it. Employees do have important events that occur in their personal lives, and sometimes these events are more important to them than their job.

Part-time employees in communities with low unemployment rates, for example, may have little problem obtaining work from another employer. Managers would like to allow these employees time off at their preferred times. However, positions must be filled and the operation's needs as well as those of the employees must be considered.

Sometimes managers must make tough decisions. If they do not, the operation is likely to have, in effect, no policy at all. Managers want to avoid comments such as "You let Allie off last week and we all had to work harder. Now I'm asking for time off and you refuse it. That's not fair!"

Exhibit 6.7

SAMPLE HOLIDAY SCHEDULE

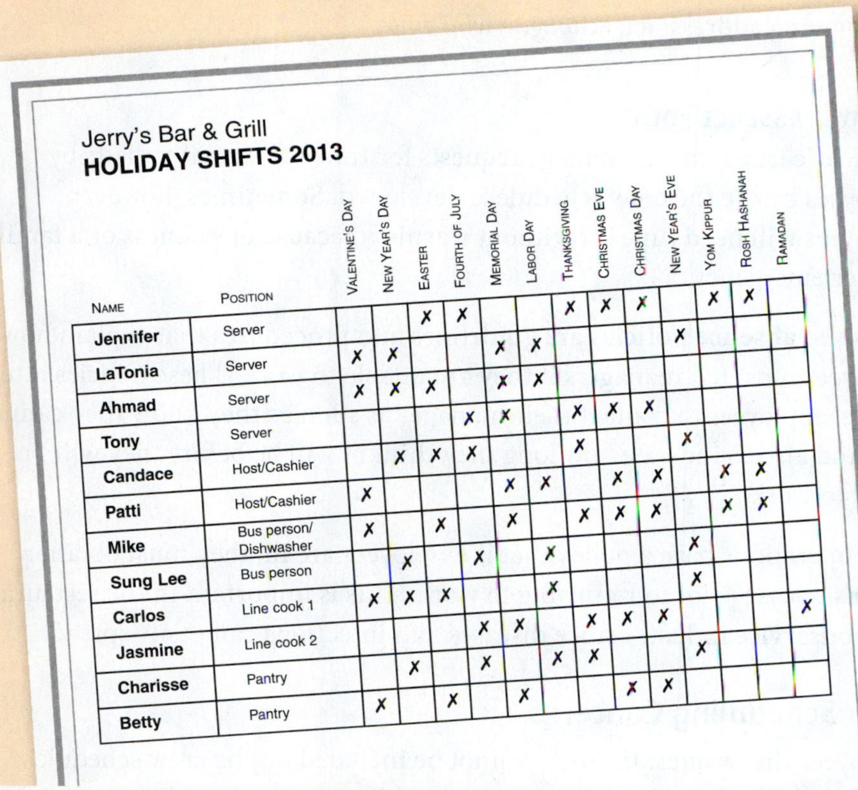

Jerry's Bar & Grill
HOLIDAY SHIFTS 2013

Name	Position	Valentine's Day	New Year's Day	Easter	Fourth of July	Memorial Day	Labor Day	Thanksgiving	Christmas Eve	Christmas Day	New Year's Eve	Yom Kippur	Rosh Hashanah	Ramadan
Jennifer	Server			X	X			X	X	X		X	X	
LaTonia	Server	X	X			X	X				X			
Ahmad	Server	X	X	X		X	X							
Tony	Server				X	X		X	X	X				
Candace	Host/Cashier		X	X	X			X			X			
Patti	Host/Cashier	X				X	X		X	X		X	X	
Mike	Bus person/ Dishwasher	X		X		X		X	X	X		X	X	
Sung Lee	Bus person		X		X		X				X			
Carlos	Line cook 1	X	X	X			X				X			
Jasmine	Line cook 2				X	X		X	X	X				X
Charisse	Pantry		X		X		X	X			X			
Betty	Pantry	X		X		X			X	X				

FAMILY AND MEDICAL LEAVE ACT

The **Family and Medical Leave Act (FMLA)** is a federal law that allows eligible employees to take off an extended amount of time for medical and other personal reasons. The FMLA applies to businesses employing 50 or more persons. An employer that is covered by the act must grant an eligible employee up to a total of 12 weeks of unpaid leave during a 12-month period for the following reasons:

- The birth of a child and to care for the newborn child within one year of birth.
- The placement with the employee of a child for adoption or foster care and to care for the newly placed child within one year of placement.
- To care for the employee's spouse, child, or parent who has a serious health condition.
- A serious health condition that makes the employee unable to perform the essential functions of his or her job.
- Any qualifying exigency arising out of the fact that the employee's spouse, son, daughter, or parent is a covered military member on "covered active duty."

The act provides that an employee must, on returning to work, be given the same position at the same rate of pay as when he or she left. For a complete discussion of the FMLA, consult the U.S. Department of Labor's Web site at the following address: *www.dol.gov/whd/fmla*.

EMPLOYEE ABSENCE POLICY

You have learned how to manage requests for time off formally made by employees before the crew schedule is developed. Sometimes, however, employees will need time off without warning because of sickness or a family or other emergency.

Employee absence policies are guidelines and procedures that explain how employees must tell managers if they are unable to work. These policies often require employees to contact their manager as soon as they know they cannot work and also to indicate how long they think it will be before they will return to work.

Many operations have a policy that if employees are ill, they must obtain a doctor's release prior to returning to work. This is important in the restaurant and foodservice industry since diseases and infections can easily spread.

Other Scheduling Concerns

Employees that request time off cannot be included on the crew schedule. There are other factors that managers should consider when they review the master schedule and begin to plan the crew schedule.

USING EMPLOYEES EFFECTIVELY

Most operations have some great employees, some good employees, and some employees whose skill levels need to be improved. Each employee's abilities should be considered when managers schedule employees for specific shifts. For example, those whose skill levels need improvement might be placed with other employees who can mentor and help them.

More experienced and productive employees are often scheduled during times of high business volume. However, it is not a good idea to schedule the best employees on one shift and leave the other shifts with a weaker crew. It is also wise to plan training sessions for slower days and meal periods.

BUILDING FLEXIBILITY INTO THE SCHEDULE

Every employee will not be available every day for every shift. Sometimes arrangements are made when an employee is hired; for example, a server could request Tuesday and Thursday evenings off to attend a college class.

Some operating factors may have to be considered when the crew schedule is written because they were not considered when the master schedule was planned. For example, perhaps many large food deliveries are received on Fridays because the weekend shifts are the busiest. Who is going to receive them, and how much time will be needed? Can someone do this work and still complete their other responsibilities? What if equipment is out for service; will that lower productivity? These are examples of the challenges that might need to be considered when the crew schedule is developed.

Employee training may be another concern. Perhaps a recently hired employee who must be trained will be scheduled, or another staff member must relearn a specific task. A lead employee who is mentoring this person may be taken away from regular tasks, and perhaps an additional person will need to be scheduled to maintain efficiency.

Employee meetings are another activity that sometimes is not considered on the master schedule. If managers want to conduct a meeting, that time should be set aside on the crew schedule.

SCHEDULING MINORS

Legal concerns become important when employees are less than 18 years old. The **Fair Labor Standards Act (FLSA)** is a federal law that sets minimum wage, overtime pay, equal pay, record keeping, and child-labor standards for covered employees. Additionally, the act prohibits persons younger than 18 years old from operating power equipment.

According to the FLSA, 14- and 15-year-olds may work the following:

- Nonschool hours
- Three hours on a school day
- Eight hours on a nonschool day
- Eighteen hours in a school week
- Forty hours in a nonschool week

OPEN FOR BUSINESS

RESTAURANT TECHNOLOGY

Effective scheduling is essential for managers who want to maintain production and service quality while paying attention to labor costs. "Off-the-shelf" software packages are available to help managers with their scheduling responsibilities and so much more. For example, applications allow employee scheduling to be combined with time clocks. Managers can see who has checked in, and employees can be refused access until a specified time before they are scheduled to check in. In addition, they cannot check out beyond a specified time after their scheduled check out times.

Electronic scheduling enables managers to track absences, manage overtime, and send completed schedules to their employees with messages if they wish to do so. Information can also be used for online payroll processing, including with third-party payroll processing businesses.

The FLSA also stipulates that work may not begin before 7:00 a.m. or end after 7:00 p.m., except from June 1 through Labor Day, when nighttime work hours are extended to 9:00 p.m.

The FLSA has major implications for establishments that hire minors, and the person responsible for preparing the crew schedule must know the law. Some state laws also regulate the work of minors, and managers must follow the laws that have the highest minimum standards. For more information about the FLSA, review the information at the Department of Labor's Web site: *www.dol.gov/whd/flsa.*

PAYING OVERTIME

Overtime refers to the number of hours of work, usually 40, after which an employee must receive a premium pay rate. This rate is usually 1.5 times the basic hourly rate. Some employees may have to be paid overtime because of customers arriving at the establishment near closing time, preventing those scheduled to leave early from doing so. Others may work overtime because another employee did not report to work and did not inform the manager that he or she would be a "**no-show**." This term applies to employees who, when they are scheduled to work, neither tell managers they will not work nor report for their assigned shift. However, overtime should never be planned into a schedule because it is a waste of payroll dollars.

PLANNING FAIR AND REASONABLE SCHEDULES

Those planning crew schedules should not take advantage of their best employees. For example, if the operation is busiest on the weekends, the excellent nontipped employees should not be scheduled to work every weekend unless they prefer this schedule. In other words, they should not be "punished" for being good at their jobs.

Those planning crew schedules should also recognize that employees who work at the beginning and end of shifts likely have some pre-shift set-up and after-shift cleanup duties. Different employees in the same position should normally be scheduled in a way that all employees will share in these duties.

More about Crew Schedules

After the manager has developed the master schedule and considered the factors just discussed for specific employees, the crew schedule can be developed.

Operation manager Demond at The Surfer's Grill modifies the basic master schedule for each of the dinner shifts being planned for the week of 6/11. His worksheet for all of the shifts during the week is shown in *Exhibit 6.8*.

Exhibit 6.8

CREW SCHEDULE WORKSHEET FOR THE SURFER'S GRILL (6/11–6/17)

Note: All start times listed are p.m.	**1**	**2**	**3**	**4**	**5**	**6**	**7**	**8**
Server	**Monday 6/11**	**Tuesday 6/12**	**Wednesday 6/13**	**Thursday 6/14**	**Friday 6/15**	**Saturday 6/16**	**Sunday 6/17**	**Scheduled Hours**
Kimo	3–10		3–10	5–10	3–10	3–10		33
Janet	4–11	4–11	4–11	5–10			4–11	33
Talisha	6–11	7–11	7–11	5–10	7–11			22
Kylie	6–11	7–11	7–11		7–11	4–11		24
Todd		3–10		3–10	3–10	5–11	5–11	33
Claudia			6–10	6–10	5–10	5–10	5–10	23
Lee					7–11	7–11	7–11	12
								180
Host								
Morris	4–11		4–11		6–10	6–10	4–11	29
Herman		4–11		4–11	4–11	4–11	4–10	34
								63
Bus Person								
Ron	4–10	4–10	4–10	4–10	4–10			30
Shanna	5–11				5–11	5–11	5–11	24
Jack		5–11	5–11	5–11		6–10	6–10	26
								80
Dish Washer								
Shane	3–11	3–11	3–11	3–11	3–11			40
Raul	5–12	5–12	5–12			3–11	3–11	37
Paula				5–12	5–12	5–12	5–12	28
								105
Bartender								
Nate	4–10	4–10	4–10		4–10	4–10		30
Alice		5–11		5–11	5–11		4–10	24
Carol	5–11		5–11	4–10		5–11	5–11	30
								84
Cook								
Lenny	1–9	1–9			1–9	1–9	2–10	40
Pedro	2–10			2–10	2–10	1–9	2–10	40
Allie	4–12	4–12	4–12	4–12	4–12			40
Melissa	4–12	4–12	4–12	4–12	4–12			40
Joe		5–11	1–9		5–11	5–11	5–11	32
Bill			5–11	1–9		5–11	1–9	28
								220
						Total waged labor hours		**732**

When reviewing *Exhibit 6.8*, note that the schedule for Monday shows the employees who are scheduled for the time blocks required by Demond's master schedule for The Surfer's Grill shown in *Exhibit 6.1*. The weekly schedule also considers all special requests made by employees for the week.

Before Demond circulates his crew schedule, he wants to confirm that the number of scheduled labor hours does not exceed the standard labor costs: 756 hours. The process used to determine budgeted labor costs were shown earlier in the chapter.

Demond has scheduled 732 waged labor hours, which is 24 labor hours less than the goal:

$$756 \text{ hours goal} - 732 \text{ scheduled hours} = 24 \text{ hours less than goal}$$

Now that Demond is satisfied that the labor standard will be met if the actual hours worked does not exceed the scheduled hours, he can distribute the crew schedule.

DISTRIBUTING AND ADJUSTING THE CREW SCHEDULE

Crew schedules should clearly indicate these details:

- Dates and days of the week covered by the schedule
- Employees' names
- Scheduled days to work and to be off from work
- Scheduled start and stop times (indicate a.m. and p.m.)
- Date of schedule preparation and name of the manager preparing it

Crew schedules should be distributed approximately 7 to 10 days before the first day of the schedule period. Demond also posts the schedule on the employee bulletin board.

Exhibit 6.9 shows a crew schedule developed from the crew schedule worksheet shown in *Exhibit 6.8*. It includes all of the information just noted that should be included on a crew schedule.

Distribution of Crew Schedules

Crew schedules can be distributed to employees in several different ways. In some properties they are posted on employee bulletin boards and in other central locations. They also can be included with paychecks. Increasingly, managers email schedules or make them available on the operation's intranet system. An intranet is a network of computers for a single organization that can be at the same or different locations.

Exhibit 6.9

CREW SCHEDULE FOR THE SURFER'S GRILL (6/11–6/17)

	1	2	3	4	5	6	7
Server	**Monday 6/11**	**Tuesday 6/12**	**Wednesday 6/13**	**Thursday 6/14**	**Friday 6/15**	**Saturday 6/16**	**Sunday 6/17**
Kimo	3–10 p.m.		3–10 p.m.	5–10 p.m.	3–10 p.m.	3–10 p.m.	
Janet	4–11 p.m.	4–11 p.m.	4–11 p.m.	5–10 p.m.			4–11 p.m.
Talisha	6–11 p.m.	7–11 p.m.	7–11 p.m.	5–10 p.m.	7–11 p.m.		
Kylie	6–11 p.m.	7–11 p.m.	7–11 p.m.		7–11 p.m.	4–11 p.m.	
Todd		3–10 p.m.		3–10 p.m.	3–10 p.m.	5–11 p.m.	5–11 p.m.
Claudia			6–10 p.m.	6–10 p.m.	5–10 p.m.	5–10 p.m.	5–10 p.m.
Lee					7–11 p.m.	7–11 p.m.	7–11 p.m.
Host							
Morris	4–11 p.m.		4–11 p.m.		6–10 p.m.	6–10 p.m.	4–11 p.m.
Herman		4–11 p.m.		4–11 p.m.	4–11 p.m.	4–11 p.m.	4–10 p.m.
Bus Person							
Ron	4–10 p.m.	4–10 p.m.	4–10 p.m.	4–10 p.m.	4–10 p.m.		
Shanna	5–11 p.m.				5–11 p.m.	5–11 p.m.	5–11 p.m.
Jack		5–11 p.m.	5–11 p.m.	5–11 p.m.		6–10 p.m.	6–10 p.m.
Dish Washer							
Shane	3–11 p.m.	3–11 p.m.	3–11 p.m.	3–11 p.m.	3–11 p.m.		
Raul	5 p.m.–12 a.m.	5 p.m.–12 a.m.	5 p.m.–12 a.m.			3–11 p.m.	3–11 p.m.
Paula				5 p.m.–12 a.m.	5 p.m.–12 a.m.	5 p.m.–12 a.m.	5 p.m.–12 a.m.
Bartender							
Nate	4–10 p.m.	4–10 p.m.	4–10 p.m.		4–10 p.m.	4–10 p.m.	
Alice		5–11 p.m.		5–11 p.m.	5–11 p.m.		4–10 p.m.
Carol	5–11 p.m.		5–11 p.m.	4–10 p.m.		5–11 p.m.	5–11 p.m.
Cook							
Lenny	1–9 p.m.	1–9 p.m.			1–9 p.m.	1–9 p.m.	2–10 p.m.
Pedro	2–10 p.m.			2–10 p.m.	2–10 p.m.	1–9 p.m.	2–10 p.m.
Allie	4 p.m.–12 a.m.	4 p.m.–12 a.m.	4 p.m.–12 a.m.	4 p.m.–12 a.m.	4 p.m.–12 a.m.		
Melissa	4 p.m.–12 a.m.	4 p.m.–12 a.m.	4 p.m.–12 a.m.	4 p.m.–12 a.m.	4 p.m.–12 a.m.		
Joe		5–11 p.m.	1–9 p.m.		5–11 p.m.	5–11 p.m.	5–11 p.m.
Bill			5–11 p.m.	1–9 p.m.		5–11 p.m.	1–9 p.m.

Date Prepared: 6/1 **Prepared By:** Demond

Adjustments to Crew Schedules

Proper scheduling will help ensure that all positions will be filled as needed; however, problems may still arise. Employees or family members can become ill, and a wide range of other issues can cause them to miss work.

A **contingency plan** is a document that outlines actions to take in the event of an emergency or an unexpected event. This plan can involve several elements:

- Cross-training employees
- Identifying shift leaders
- Using floaters

CROSS-TRAINING EMPLOYEES

All staff positions in an operation should have several employees trained to perform that job. As previously mentioned, cross-training involves developing employees' abilities to do tasks other than the ones they regularly do. While they may not do a specific job every day, cross-trained employees can do that job if the need arises.

Cashiers could be trained as servers and hosts; servers could be trained as cashiers and hosts (*Exhibit 6.10*). A baker could be trained for pantry and line-cook functions, and a line cook could learn how to do pantry and baker duties. As more employees are cross-trained for more positions, managers have more flexibility to reassign positions when there is a need to do so.

IDENTIFYING SHIFT LEADERS

Shift leaders are employees who receive wages and, in addition to their regular tasks, train new employees, answer work-related questions, and perform other functions assigned by managers. For example, an exceptional server could be paid at a higher hourly rate to serve as a server shift leader. A shift leader can help supervise employees if the on-shift supervisor becomes busy with an emergency.

Exhibit 6.10

Shift leaders are common in quick-service restaurants. They are chosen because they are good employees who always follow company policy, meet or exceed company standards, and show some leadership ability. A shift leader position can be a stepping-stone into a management position.

USING FLOATERS

Floaters are employees who can perform more than one job on a regular basis. They are used to fill in for employees taking time off. For example, a floater in a kitchen might work the line-cook position two days, pantry two days, and baker one day to cover those positions for the regular employees.

Floaters are different from employees who have been cross-trained. Floaters do different tasks on a daily basis, whereas cross-trained employees normally do their regular tasks but sometimes do different tasks. Both are valuable because of the flexibility they provide if another employee cannot work a shift.

MONITORING EMPLOYEES DURING A SHIFT

You have learned that managers consider quantity and quality standards when planning the master schedule and crew schedule. However, it does little good to do this planning unless there is follow-through while the employees are working.

Managers can use several methods to stress the need to meet standards during work shifts. Those in charge of dining-room service can emphasize the need to meet sales and service goals during line-up meetings with service employees. A **line-up meeting** is a brief training session held before the work shift begins. For example, the kitchen manager can reinforce production quality goals for the department.

Line-up meetings are often used to update employees about business expected during the shift, daily specials, and other operating concerns. However, emphasizing goals that connect the mission statement to daily operations can set the pace for performance during the shift.

Managers can also observe employees throughout the shift. An earlier chapter discussed "managing by walking around" to note potential problems and coaching to address them. Managers will also observe employees doing things correctly and should use positive feedback for reinforcement.

Professional managers allow their experience to guide them as they monitor quality during work shifts. For example, some managers of table-service restaurants say they can judge the effectiveness of service by the amount of water in customers' water glasses. If water glasses are full, service is as it should be. If water glasses are not full, servers do not have time to fill them, and this suggests problems may be occurring.

Kitchen managers make use of their own experience to monitor quality. They use temperature and taste checks, comparison of production plans with quantities of food produced, and constant vigilance about food safety to ensure that standards are being met (*Exhibit 6.11*).

Some managers schedule meetings only when there are problems. While such meetings are necessary, other meetings to plan and evaluate goals and to thank employees for meeting or exceeding standards are also important.

THINK ABOUT IT . . .

In some establishments, employees who begin work but are asked to clock-out early because of low customer counts are paid a minimum amount for being available. Why do you think some managers do not do this?

Exhibit 6.11

ANALYZING AFTER-SHIFT LABOR INFORMATION

Professional restaurant and foodservice managers know that the control of labor costs involves more than just planning an employee schedule that meets labor cost standards. They must also analyze actual labor costs after work shifts are completed to learn how well their plans worked out.

Labor costs for employees who receive wages are managed by using the labor cost standard in the approved operating budget. If the budget goal is not met, the difference between the budgeted expense and the actual expense is called a **variance**.

Exhibit 6.12 shows Demond's analysis of waged labor hours for the week of 6/11. It is the same as his worksheet in *Exhibit 6.8* except that he completed columns 9 and 10 after the week ended.

When reviewing *Exhibit 6.12*, focus on the last three columns:

- Column 8 shows the number of hours scheduled for each employee.
- Column 9 shows the number of hours actually worked by each employee. This information is taken from employee time records.
- Column 10 shows the variance or difference in the number of scheduled and actual hours for employees in each position.

The bottoms of columns eight and nine show that while 732 labor hours were scheduled for all employees, 763 hours were actually worked. This created a variance of 31 hours:

$$763 \text{ actual hours} - 732 \text{ scheduled hours} = 31 \text{ hours more hours than scheduled}$$

Is this variance significant? A quick calculation will answer this question. Remember that the average hourly wage not including fringe benefits is $12:

$$\text{Hours variance} \times \text{Average hourly rate} = \text{Additional labor cost}$$
$$31 \times \$12 = \$372$$

If that number of hours variance continued for the entire year, it would cost the establishment $19,344:

$$52 \text{ weeks} \times \$372 \text{ per week} = \$19,344 \text{ per year}$$

Also, because some employee benefits are tied to wages, these costs would also increase.

When reviewing *Exhibit 6.12*, note that the cook Pedro worked 42 hours and will be paid $28.50 for each overtime hour:

$$\text{Hourly pay} \times \text{Premium pay rate} = \text{Hourly overtime pay}$$
$$\$19.00 \times 1.5 = \$28.50$$

THINK ABOUT IT . . .

Every dollar of excessive cost reduces profit by a dollar. However, when reducing labor cost, managers must remember that standards cannot be lowered. What would you do to bring the labor costs in line?

Exhibit 6.12

REVIEW OF SCHEDULED AND ACTUAL LABOR HOURS AT THE SURFER'S GRILL (6/11–6/17)

Server	Monday 6/11	Tuesday 6/12	Wednesday 6/13	Thursday 6/14	Friday 6/15	Saturday 6/16	Sunday 6/17	Scheduled Hours	Actual Hours	Variance
	1	2	3	4	5	6	7	8	9	10
Kimo	3–10		3–10	5–10	3–10	3–10		33	32	
Janet	4–11	4–11	4–11	5–10			4–11	33	35	
Talisha	6–11	7–11	7–11	5–10	7–11			22	22	
Kylie	6–11	7–11	7–11		7–11	4–11		24	27	
Todd		3–10		3–10	3–10	5–11	5–11	33	35	
Claudia			6–10	6–10	5–10	5–10	5–10	23	25	
Lee					7–11	7–11	7–11	12	14	
								180	**190**	**10**
Host										
Morris	4–11		4–11		6–10	6–10	4–11	29	38	
Herman		4–11		4–11	4–11	4–11	4–10	34	20	
								63	**58**	**(5)**
Bus Person										
Ron	4–10	4–10	4–10	4–10	4–10			30	32	
Shanna	5–11				5–11	5–11	5–11	24	29	
Jack		5–11	5–11	5–11		6–10	6–10	26	29	
								80	**90**	**10**
Dish Washer										
Shane	3–11	3–11	3–11	3–11	3–11			40	40	
Raul	5–12	5–12	5–12			3–11	3–11	37	37	
Paula				5–12	5–12	5–12	5–12	28	30	
								105	**107**	**2**
Bartender										
Nate	4–10	4–10	4–10		4–10	4–10		30	32	
Alice		5–11		5–11	5–11		4–10	24	26	
Carol	5–11		5–11	4–10		5–11	5–11	30	31	
								84	**89**	**5**
Cook										
Lenny	1–9	1–9			1–9	1–9	2–10	40	40	
Pedro	2–10			2–10	2–10	1–9	2–10	40	42	
Allie	4–12	4–12	4–12	4–12	4–12			40	40	
Melissa	4–12	4–12	4–12	4–12	4–12			40	40	
Joe		5–11	1–9		5–11	5–11	5–11	32	36	
Bill			5–11	1–9		5–11	1–9	28	31	
								220	**229**	**9**
							Total hours	**732**	**763**	**31**

It is also important to note that the 763 labor hours worked were greater than the 756 hours that can be worked on average to stay within budget standards. Recall that Demond only scheduled 732 labor hours because he was expecting fewer customers than average.

Demond must give a high priority to finding out why the number of additional labor hours is so high. He should meet with his department heads and review the information in *Exhibit 6.12*. Every position except host required more labor hours than scheduled.

Demond and his team may determine that there are some reasonable explanations for the increased number of labor hours. For example, more customers may have been served than expected. If so, Demond may need to do a better job of forecasting customer counts when labor schedules are developed.

Demond may also discover that several training programs were conducted and these hours were not considered when the schedule was planned. Supervisors should indicate when activities such as training and nonroutine cleaning are planned so these hours can be included in the schedule.

There may also be unexplainable excess in the labor hours. Then a careful analysis is needed to identify and correct the problems. Demond and his management team must quickly determine the problems causing the variance and correct them to bring labor costs back under control.

The approach outlined in this chapter to managing labor costs expands the concept of overtime. From a legal view, **overtime** refers to hours for which a premium wage must be paid. However, it is also helpful to think of another type of "overtime": the number of labor hours worked in excess of scheduled hours.

WORK SCHEDULES FOR MANAGERS

Work schedules must also be developed for managers, and a **management schedule** showing days and times managers are expected to work can be used. Like the crew schedule, it is developed in part with information from the master schedule.

A management schedule should be developed using the process just discussed for planning the crew schedule:

- Develop the master schedule. Think about the need for managers to supervise planned production and service volumes and other routine and special activities.
- Follow the operation's policies for requesting time off.
- Schedule managers fairly.

Three special concerns must be considered when managers are scheduled:

1. Most managers receive a salary and are not held to a specific number of hours worked. However, salaried managers can still have scheduled hours, and unreasonable demands should not be placed on them.
2. Management schedules can include "on call." Sometimes managers are contacted on their days off to solve operating problems. This interrupts their personal time and can lead to frustration and burnout. To prevent this, a manager can be scheduled to be on call in case a problem arises. The on-call list should be rotated so all managers can enjoy time away from work. For example, when the kitchen manager is off duty, the dining-room manager can be alerted about a kitchen problem. If unable to resolve the problem, he or she may contact the general manager, who is on call, for a solution.
3. At least one manager should be on duty whenever employees are working in the establishment. Then if an emergency occurs, he or she can take action. Additionally, many states require that at least one person on the premises be trained and certified in food safety and sanitation principles.

Exhibit 6.13 shows how a management team might be assigned to ensure coverage during a week. Imagine the establishment is open for lunch and dinner, and the schedule is for one week. The schedule is changed frequently so all managers can have different days to work and different closing shifts.

Exhibit 6.13

SAMPLE MANAGEMENT SCHEDULE

Position	Monday	Tuesday	Wednesday	Thursday	Friday	Saturday	Sunday
General manager	Off	11 a.m.–7 p.m.	3:00 p.m.–close	9 a.m.–7 p.m.	3 p.m.–close	11 a.m.–7 p.m.	Off
Assistant general manager	9 a.m.–6 p.m.	Off	Off	4 p.m.–close	4 p.m.–close	4 p.m.– close	9 a.m.–6 p.m.
Executive chef	10 a.m.–8 p.m.	Off	Off	10 a.m.–8 p.m.	1 p.m.–8 p.m.	10 a.m.–8 p.m.	10 a.m.–8 p.m.
Culinary shift leader	Off	9 a.m.–7 p.m.	9 a.m.–6 p.m.	1 p.m.–close	Off	Off	4 p.m.–close
Dining-room manager	4 p.m.–close	4 p.m.–close	1 p.m.–9 p.m.	Off	Off	4 p.m.–10 p.m.	4 p.m.–close
Bar manager	4 p.m.–close	Off	Off	4 p.m.–10 p.m.	4 p.m.–close	4 p.m.–close	4 p.m.–9 p.m.
Service shift leader	Off	11 a.m. – 8 p.m.	11 a.m. – 8 p.m.	2:00 p.m.–close	9 a.m.–4 p.m.	9:00 a.m.–8 p.m.	Off

SUMMARY

1. **Explain the need for effective work schedules.**

   Managers must schedule the right number of employees in the right positions at the right times to produce products and services meeting quality standards. They must do so while not exceeding budgeted labor cost standards.

2. **Discuss basic procedures for determining budgeted labor cost.**

   An approved operating budget indicates how much can be spent for waged labor. This amount can be used to determine the average daily wage and the average waged hours per day and week. Managers should schedule waged hours in a way that will not exceed these allowable hours.

3. **Describe how to create a master schedule.**

   A master schedule allows managers to determine the number of employees needed in each position and the total hours that persons in these positions should work. Information used to develop a master schedule includes sales history data, sales projections, and current trends.

4. **Explain how to develop a crew schedule.**

   A crew schedule is prepared with the general information in the master schedule. Guidelines must be in place for employees to request time off for vacations and other days off. Planners must also know requirements of the Family and Medical Leave Act (FMLA), and employees must follow policies when unable to work.

   Managers must consider how to use employees effectively, how to build flexibility into crew schedules, and how to schedule minors. Overtime should not be scheduled.

5. **Describe procedures for distributing and adjusting the crew schedule.**

   Crew schedules should be distributed on a timely basis. Posting on an employee bulletin board, including with paychecks, and using email and intranet are some ways to distribute the schedule.

6. **Identify common practices helpful for monitoring employees during work shifts.**

   Managers should emphasize the need to meet sales, production, and service goals during line-up meetings, coaching, and routine meetings. Managing by walking around and careful observation of employees, food quality, and service levels are all important.

7. **Explain methods for analyzing after-shift labor information.**

   Managers should compare the number of labor hours scheduled with the actual hours worked. When actual labor hours exceed planned hours, corrective action is often necessary.

8. **Review basic concerns in developing work schedules for managers.**

   Salaried managers can have scheduled hours, although they may work longer than waged employees. These schedules can include "on-call" alternatives so most managers will not be interrupted during their personal time. Management schedules should ensure that at least one manager is on duty whenever employees are working in the establishment.

APPLICATION EXERCISE

A master schedule for the Blue Diamond Café is shown below. The establishment is open from 8:00 a.m. to 2:00 p.m., Monday through Saturday. The customer count is approximately the same each day. Based on the master schedule, create a crew schedule using this information:

SAMPLE MASTER SCHEDULE FOR THE BLUE DIAMOND CAFÉ

Date: Total No. of Customers Expected:

Time	**6:00 a.m.**	**7:00 a.m.**	**8:00 a.m.**	**9:00 a.m.**	**10:00 a.m.**	**11:00 a.m.**	**12:00 p.m.**	**1:00 p.m.**	**2:00 p.m.**	**Total Hours**	**Rate**	**Total Payroll**
Customers			20	30	30	65	75	70	25			
Position												
Server A		x	x	x	x	x	x	x		7	$ 6	$ 42
Server B						x	x	x	x	4	6	24
Server C			x	x	x	x	x			5	6	30
Server D					x	x	x	x		4	6	24
Server E						x	x	x	x	4	6	24
Host/Cashier A			x	x	x	x	x			5	12	60
Host/Cashier B						x	x	x	x	4	12	48
Bus person A			x	x	x	x	x	x		6	10	60
Bus person B						x	x	x	x	4	10	40
Dish washer A		x	x	x	x	x				5	11	55
Dish washer B					x	x	x	x	x	5	11	55
Line cook 1	x	x	x	x	x	x				6	19	114
Line cook 2		x	x	x	x	x	x	x		7	19	133
Line cook 3					x	x	x	x	x	5	19	95
Pantry A	x	x	x	x	x	x				6	19	114
Pantry B						x	x	x	x	4	19	76
Total												**$994**

- Brad cannot work on Wednesdays because of classes.
- Amanda cannot work on Thursdays.
- Christie cannot work on Mondays or Tuesdays.
- Chenise is 17 years old.
- Micah will be late this Friday because of a dentist's appointment.
- Juan can work mornings only on Tuesdays.

Compare your schedule with others in the class.

1. What factors did you consider as you planned the schedule?
2. What difficulties did you have, if any? How did you resolve them?
3. Do you think the employees will be satisfied with their schedule? Why or why not?

SAMPLE CREW SCHEDULE FOR THE BLUE DIAMOND CAFÉ

Name	Position	Monday	Tuesday	Wednesday	Thursday	Friday	Saturday
Shawna	Server						
Fran	Server						
Fred	Server						
Chenise	Server						
Sally	Server						
Brad	Host/Cashier						
Micah	Host/Cashier						
Mike	Bus person						
Bob	Bus person						
Derek	Dish washer						
Jillian	Dish washer						
Denise	Line cook						
Juan	Line cook						
Amanda	Line cook						
Christie	Pantry						
Zelle	Pantry						

REVIEW YOUR LEARNING

Select the best answer for each question.

1. **What is a crew schedule?**
   A. A list of days and times that managers must work
   B. A list that includes only days and times that nonservice employees must work
   C. A list of days that employees have requested for vacation time
   D. A list of days and times that employees receiving wages will work

2. **Approximately how many hours can employees receiving a wage work during an "average" day when the average daily wage is $875 and the average hourly rate is $13?**
   A. 22
   B. 48
   C. 67
   D. 83

3. **A master schedule for a work shift indicates**
   A. positions that are needed.
   B. names of employees needed.
   C. customer counts per hour.
   D. budgeted labor cost.

4. **Premium rate of pay must be given to employees who work when?**
   A. Sundays and holidays
   B. Five or more days in a row
   C. More than 40 hours weekly
   D. Four hours as scheduled

5. **The Fair Labor Standards Act (FLSA) prohibits minors from**
   A. exceeding minimum wage.
   B. earning overtime.
   C. working on school days.
   D. using power equipment.

6. **How many days in advance of the use should a crew schedule normally be posted?**
   A. 3 to 5
   B. 5 to 7
   C. 7 to 10
   D. 10 to 14

7. **How are shift leaders paid?**
   A. Wages
   B. Salary
   C. Salary plus incentive
   D. Salary plus bonus

8. **When is a line-up meeting held?**
   A. On the first day of every month
   B. When there is an emergency
   C. Before the shift begins
   D. After the shift is over

9. **What is the difference between a budgeted expense and an actual expense called?**
   A. Overrun
   B. Forecast
   C. Variance
   D. Error

10. **What is the minimum number of managers that must be on duty when employees are working?**
    A. One manager on-site
    B. One manager in the kitchen and one in the dining area
    C. No managers if the establishment is not open for business
    D. No managers unless customers are present

7 Leaders Manage Daily Operations

INSIDE THIS CHAPTER

- Managers Establish Priorities
- Managers Develop Operating Tools
- Managers Resolve Operating Problems
- Managers Report to Upper-Level Managers
- Managers Plan for Emergencies

CHAPTER LEARNING OBJECTIVES

After completing this chapter, you should be able to:

- Describe how restaurant and foodservice managers should establish priorities.
- Describe procedures used by restaurant and foodservice managers to develop and use two important operating tools: policies and procedures.
- Explain a basic approach that managers can use to resolve operating problems.
- Describe how restaurant and foodservice managers should develop and submit reports to upper management.
- Review procedures that restaurant and foodservice managers should use to plan for and manage emergencies.

KEY TERMS

action plan, p. 193
alternative (problem-solving), p. 193
cause, p. 192
competitive bids, p. 183
contact list, p. 205
critical incidents, p. 199
emergency, p. 202
evacuation, p. 204
legal liability, p. 196
manager's daily log, p. 196
media policy, p. 205
petty cash fund, p. 195
policy, p. 183
preventable emergency, p. 202
preventive maintenance, p. 182
problem solving, p. 191
standardized recipe, p. 186
standard operating procedure (SOP), p. 186
subpoena, p. 197
suggestive selling, p. 189
task analysis, p. 186
task breakdown, p. 186
task list, p. 186
unpreventable emergency, p. 202

CASE STUDY

Alana and Vernette are managers at Pomme de Terre Café and are discussing some employees they recently hired.

"I used to think it was better to hire experienced servers because they would require less training," said Alana, "but now I'm wondering about that. The last two servers we hired have lots of previous experience. However, they always want to do things the way they did them in other restaurants. They don't seem interested in following our procedures."

"Yes," replied Vernette, "I've noticed that too. I think that 'No experience preferred' is the best way to handle our search and selection procedures in the kitchen."

1. What is the main problem that Alana and Vernette have as they train and supervise new employees?
2. Who do you think would be better new employees: those who did or did not have previous experience in the position for which they were hired? Why do you think so?

MANAGERS ESTABLISH PRIORITIES

Restaurant and foodservice managers must be able to do many things at the same time. There is no such thing as a "typical" day. Most managers do the best they can to estimate the number of customers to be served, to have the right amount of food products available, and to schedule employees to prepare and serve the customers. However, many things can happen.

For example, there may be a weather problem that was not expected, causing customer counts to go down. Maybe for some unknown reason a lot more customers decide to visit the establishment than were expected. Employees may call in sick or even quit without telling the manager. There may be equipment problems, even in operations with good **preventive maintenance**. Preventive maintenance programs involve procedures to follow the manufacturer's instructions about how to keep equipment in good working order.

Employees or customers may become ill while they are at the establishment (*Exhibit 7.1*). Food delivery trucks may be delayed, or products that were ordered may not be on the trucks. Then managers must quickly arrange to obtain necessary products or to plan menu substitutes. Emergencies of several types can occur without warning, and professional restaurant and foodservice managers must be ready for these.

It should be no surprise to learn that managers determine their priorities based on the operation's goals. These goals, in turn, are driven by the operation's values, mission statement, and long-range and business plans. This approach helps place the mission statement into the planning of daily operations. In other words, what managers do every day will lead the operation toward attainment of its goals.

Manager's Memo

No one can know exactly what is going to happen at any given time. However, experienced managers develop plans that consider what they expect will happen. For example, they schedule employees according to the times when most customers normally visit the property. They set rules for customer reservation systems that allow the normal amount of time between table turns. They have procedures in place to help ensure that the right quantities of food and beverage products are available when needed. They develop standardized recipes to best ensure that products will always look, taste, and smell the way customers expect them to.

These and many other plans minimize surprises, but they do not prevent unexpected challenges. The best-prepared managers are still confronted with problems that must be managed on the spot with little time to think about what to do. The ability to deal with unexpected problems sets apart the best managers.

Exhibit 7.1

Sometimes managers have trouble knowing the difference between tasks that are urgent and tasks that are important. While important tasks are significant, urgent tasks require immediate action. Some managers think that all tasks that are urgent must be done "right now." However, they need to think about the relative importance of their tasks and then do those that are more important before addressing those that are less important.

One way to set priorities is to classify tasks based on their importance and urgency. Work on tasks in the following order:

1. Give priority to tasks that are very important and very urgent. Examples might be to finish a budget due tomorrow or to communicate frequently with the kitchen and dining-room managers as setup is done for tomorrow's Mother's Day buffet—the busiest meal period of the year.
2. Work on tasks that are very important but not urgent. The best example for many managers is long-range and business planning. There are few things more important than planning for the operation's future; however, this is frequently not an urgent task and is put off to another time.
3. Deal with tasks that are not important but urgent. Examples may include returning telephone calls and email messages. A good approach is to set aside blocks of time for these tasks rather than to be interrupted when doing more important activities.
4. Handle tasks that are neither important nor urgent. Tasks such as editing a preventive maintenance report and reading outdated trade magazines should probably not be done at all, or certainly only when tasks in the previous three categories have been completed (and in almost all establishments, this situation will never occur).

Manager's Memo

Some managers do long-range planning when they "get around to it." Their belief is that they must take care of all the daily business first and then do planning activities.

The approach discussed in this chapter recognizes that a manager's best plans sometimes may need to be set aside during work shifts to take care of unexpected issues. However, it also focuses on the need to develop plans for "normal" operations to minimize time spent on problems that might not have occurred with proper planning.

Planning does not stop surprises in daily operations, nor does it eliminate emergencies. It does, however, help the manager spend as much time as possible on tasks that help move the operation toward its goals.

MANAGERS DEVELOP OPERATING TOOLS

Restaurant and foodservice managers should make use of two powerful tools to help them with their ongoing leadership tasks: policies and procedures. Policies and procedures are rules that guide employees. If they are well developed and implemented, they can help promote the consistent, standardized, and quality-driven work that must be done every day to make the operation successful.

THINK ABOUT IT . . .

Some managers set priorities and do all they can to stick with them. Other managers think there are so many "surprises" during the day that planning is a waste of time. What do you think?

Policies

A **policy** is a planned course of action for an important activity and provides a general strategy for managing that activity. Policies guide managers as they make decisions about issues that occur frequently.

For example, how many weeks of vacation does an employee receive if he or she has worked at the establishment full time for three years? Is it always necessary to get competitive bids when meat orders are placed? **Competitive bids** involve requesting prices for items of the same quality from a specified number of vendors to determine the lowest price. Policies that indicate two weeks of vacation and a requirement for competitive bids make questions about these issues easy for managers to answer consistently.

Policies connect the establishment's mission to its daily operations. They identify expected outcomes and establish responsibility, and they provide clear direction to employees to help them with their work. Policies are written expectations about the conduct and actions of all employees.

Managers should ensure that these actions are taken regarding policies:

- Well-written policies are developed and implemented.
- Employees receive proper training so they know about and can follow policies.
- All policies are routinely reviewed, revised if necessary, and monitored to ensure they are followed.

There may be property-wide policies that apply to all employees, with specific requirements for employees in each department. For example, the operation's vacation policy may call for a certain number of allowed vacation days, but different procedures may be used in each department to request them.

Some policies are used throughout the operation to address general issues such as what to do in the event of a fire. In an independent establishment, these should be approved by a manager, but approval of a higher-level manager may be required in a restaurant chain. Some policies relating to safety and health are developed to address requirements of governmental agencies. If there are questions about them, the governmental officials should be contacted.

POLICY DEVELOPMENT BASICS

The development of useful policies requires careful planning that begins by defining the policy's purpose. Ineffective policies are easy to recognize and, unfortunately, many operations have some. They are unclear and not useful because they do not provide reasonable direction and explanations. In other words, they do not tell employees what they need to know. However, if policies are well developed, the information helps guide the manager and employees as decisions are made and as actions are evaluated.

Writing a policy does not require a high level of writing skill. Instead, a manager must understand the policy development process and be able to communicate information in a meaningful way. A team effort is very helpful. The operation's managers and supervisors can provide input, and lawyers who know about labor law can advise when necessary.

Many operations use the same format for all of their policies. A sample is shown in *Exhibit 7.2*.

Exhibit 7.2

SAMPLE POLICY FORMAT

Policy Name	**Employee use of phones**
Purpose	Provide a guideline for the use of personal cell phones and all other electronic communication devices at the establishment.
Scope	This policy applies to all operation employees present at the establishment while not on approved personal breaks.
Policy Statement	The policy of Pomme de Terre Café for employee use of cell phones at the establishment when not on personal breaks is as follows: 1. Personal cell phones may not be used during work times and must be turned off and kept in employee lockers during work shifts. 2. Exceptions, for emergency purposes only, may be granted by the manager. 3. No still or video pictures may be taken at any time without the prior consent of the manager. 4. No communication of any confidential information to any party at any time is permitted by use of personal cell phones or by any other means. 5. Employees who violate this policy will be subject to disciplinary action based on the establishment's progressive discipline policy. **Approved By:** H. Hammel, Operation Manager **Approval Date:** 6/6

Developing a good policy begins with a statement about its purpose. The next part of the policy can indicate for whom it is intended. The policy itself can then be explained in a simple and logical sequence. If a timeline is needed, it should be included. The final part should indicate the name and position of the manager who approved the policy.

IMPACTS ON OTHER DEPARTMENTS

Policies made for one department may affect other departments. For example, a dining room policy requiring salad bars to be set up by a specified time requires the food to be available from the kitchen. Consult with all parties involved when developing or revising policies so everyone who is affected is aware of and agrees with them. This is usually best done when a team of managers work together to develop them.

KEEPING POLICIES CURRENT

Existing policies must be kept current, and modern technology makes this easy to do. They should be routinely reviewed to ensure they reflect actual work practices. Then revisions can be made as needed to help the operation keep up with changing times. New policies should be developed in a timely manner.

Exhibit 7.3

Standard Operating Procedures

A **standard operating procedure (SOP)** is a written description or list of steps that tell how to correctly perform a task. A task is one responsibility in an employee's position. For example, a cook may have the responsibility to prepare entrées. The entrée preparation task can be broken down into procedures that may be involved in several tasks (the correct use of a tabletop mixer, for example) or steps listed in a **standardized recipe** to prepare one entrée item. A standardized recipe is the set of instructions that should be used to produce a food or beverage item. If followed, the recipe will ensure that the operation's quality and quantity standards for the item are met (*Exhibit 7.3*).

SOPs must be reviewed and updated as necessary. Customer complaints, unexpected costs, quality problems, and employee feedback can help identify areas of concern. Priorities should be established, and a process to revise procedures should be implemented. Drafts of procedures should be reviewed and ideas should be received from affected employees before final approval by the restaurant or foodservice manager.

The process of developing and revising SOPs is ongoing as menu items and service procedures change, as customer preferences evolve, and as new equipment is purchased. However, the use of approved procedures is an important aspect of ensuring quality in daily operations.

Sometimes SOPs are developed just to improve a specific step in a task. At other times, job tasks are developed basically by putting procedures together or revised, for example an SOP might be made for purchasers buying fresh seafood because of increasing spoilage. Once developed, this procedure can be included in the purchasing task.

A second approach is to determine how an entire task should be done and then develop the SOPs that make up the task. For example, a standard operating procedure could be developed to indicate how bottled wine should be presented and served to customers. This is done in a process called task analysis.

Manager's Memo

You have learned in earlier chapters that the best restaurant and foodservice managers want their employees to make decisions to improve operations. Now you are learning that the same managers develop procedures that indicate how tasks should be done. Should employees have some say in how work should be done, or shouldn't they?

The answer to this question is simple: Employees should have input when procedures are developed. After they are developed, every employee should consistently use them unless the manager and his or her team agree that the procedures should be changed.

Task Analysis

Task analysis is a process for identifying each task in a position such as cook or server and determining how the procedures in a task should be done. Its purpose is to focus on the workplace knowledge and skills required to perform each task. Done correctly, task analysis becomes the foundation for developing standard operating procedures that will be taught in training programs. Task analysis can also be used to decide how experienced employees can do things in better ways.

The first step in task analysis is to prepare a **task list** that indicates all tasks included in a position. The second step is to develop a **task breakdown** that explains how to perform each of the procedures that make up the task. When these are developed and included in training programs, employees' work is more likely to be done correctly. Then many problems that can occur in daily operations will be avoided.

Task List

Managers use several activities to develop a task list:

- Ask supervisors and experienced employees to describe the work done by someone in the position during a normal shift.
- Review existing position descriptions to learn about the responsibilities indicated for the position.
- Use a simple questionnaire that asks, "What do you and others in your position do as part of your job?"
- Observe staff members as they work. Compare and contrast what they actually do to what they said they would do.

After the tasks in a position are known, SOPs to complete each task must be determined.

Exhibit 7.4 shows a sample task list for a bartender position at Pomme de Terre Café.

Manager's Memo

A good SOP is a simple guideline that helps employees understand their job. It should be written in clear and concise language. Slang terms and technical jargon should be avoided. If abbreviations must be used, their meanings should be included. Remember that written procedures will most often be read and used by those with less experience than the writer. The goal is to create a document that tells employees how to do a task or improves their understanding of a work process.

Exhibit 7.4

SAMPLE TASK LIST FOR BARTENDER POSITION AT POMME DE TERRE CAFÉ

Position Tasks
1. Inspect the bar prior to opening to ensure that adequate supplies are available.
2. Request additional supplies as necessary and stock the bar.
3. Follow setup procedures including checking and obtaining glassware and paper supplies.
4. Prepare garnishes, mixes, and premixed drinks.
5. Greet customers.
6. Mix, prepare, and serve drinks to customers, and mix and prepare drinks ordered by food servers and beverage servers according to the recipes approved by the beverage manager.
7. Collect checks and payment for drinks served.
8. Report complaints to a manager as soon as they occur.
9. Maintain and clean bar area and equipment.
10. Carefully follow all laws and operation policies and procedures regarding alcoholic beverage service and inform manager if continued service to specific customers is in question.
11. Serve drinks to customers seated at lounge tables in the absence of a beverage server.
12. Continually practice beverage and revenue control procedures.
13. Thank customers and invite them to return.
14. Maintain records of liquors, beers, and wine to ensure bar stock is maintained at all times.
15. Maintain daily inventory and records indicating drinks in the greatest demand.
16. Clean and lock up the bar area according to SOPs.
17. Attend staff meetings as required.

Approved By: Macie Smith, Operation Manager
Approval Date: 6/11

TASK BREAKDOWNS

A task breakdown indicates the SOPs that are required to perform each task. For example, a storeroom clerk may have to "Properly rotate food products so the oldest items will be issued first" (*Exhibit 7.5*). To do this, the storeroom clerk will need to determine the quantity of each product needed, know correct product placement locations, move products from the receiving area to the storeroom, and do all of these procedures in a way that recognizes basic safety and sanitation principles.

Exhibit 7.5

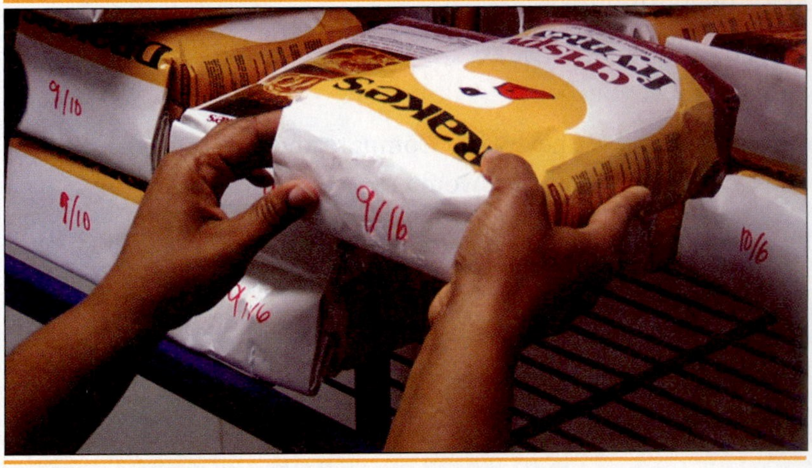

Should the managers or the employees determine how each procedure should be performed? If not these individuals, who will decide? The trainers? The trainees themselves? None of these choices will ensure that procedures to consistently attain the quality and quantity standards will be developed and used. Therefore, it is much better when procedures are defined and implemented by a team of managers and employees.

How are task breakdowns written? The same basic process is used that was used to develop the task list. In other words, experienced staff can be interviewed, and available information such as existing task breakdowns and training documents can be studied. Employees can be asked to write out, in order, the steps needed to perform a task. They can also be observed, and brainstorming sessions can be used to identify the best ways to perform each task.

The SOPs that are developed should completely explain how the task should be done. They should also be easy to understand and consider the knowledge and skills needed to perform the task.

A simple way for managers to develop a task breakdown is to observe an experienced employee doing the task and write down what they observe:

- Record each activity (step) in sequence.
- Ask the employee and a manager to review the notes.
- Make any necessary changes to reach agreement about how the task should be done.

Exhibit 7.6 shows a sample task breakdown for serving a bottle of wine to customers.

Exhibit 7.6

SAMPLE TASK BREAKDOWN AT POMME DE TERRE CAFÉ

Task: Serving a Bottle of Wine

Step No.	Step
1.	Present wine list.
2.	Assist customer with wine selection.
3.	Take wine order.
4.	Obtain proper wine glasses and place on table.
5.	Obtain wine that was ordered and bring to table.
6.	Present wine bottle to customer.
7.	Open wine bottle.
8.	Pour small amount of wine in customer's wine glass.
9.	Allow customer to taste wine.
10.	Pour wine (if acceptable) or obtain second bottle (if unacceptable).
11.	Refill wine glasses as necessary.

Note that each step for serving a bottle of wine is listed in proper sequence in *Exhibit 7.6*. In some establishments, SOPs could be much more detailed. For example, Step 1 might be expanded to include information about **suggestive selling**, a strategy for encouraging guests to order products or services they may not have been aware of or intending to purchase. Step 9 could be expanded to indicate how to determine which customers should be served before other customers at the table, how to present the wine, if requested, to each guest, and exactly how to pour the wine.

Once the SOPs are developed, they should be used for training new and existing employees. Also, restaurant and foodservice managers can evaluate whether SOPs are being followed correctly in daily operations as they "manage by walking around" and observe how tasks are being done.

Policies Drive SOPs

Policies and standard operating procedures often are included in an employee handbook for manager and employee reference. *Exhibit 7.7* shows a sample policy and procedure for checking the identification (ID) of a customer ordering alcoholic beverages.

Exhibit 7.7

SAMPLE STANDARD OPERATING PROCEDURE

Policy: All customers ordering an alcoholic beverage will be asked to show proper identification (ID) that will be checked thoroughly and properly according to a specific standard operating procedure.

Standard Operating Procedure

1. Greet the customer politely.
2. Politely ask the customer for an ID.
   - Ask the customer to remove the ID from his or her wallet and look for signs of tampering such as bubbles, creases, improper thickness, or ink signatures.
   - Greet the customer using the name on the ID.
3. Verify the following on the ID:
   - The ID is valid.
   - It has not been issued to a minor.
   - It is genuine.
   - The ID belongs to the customer.
4. If the ID is OK, serve the customer.
5. If there are concerns about the ID, seek further verification:
   - Ask for a second ID.
   - Compare the customer's signature to the ID signature.
   - Ask the customer questions that only the ID owner could answer.
6. If the ID is OK, serve the customer; if the ID is not OK, refuse service and follow the establishment's procedure for refusal of service.

Approved By: A. Samuels, Operation Manager
Approval Date: 2/22

Manager's Memo

Most managers monitor their food cost by using a food cost percentage:

Food cost ÷ Food revenue = Food cost percentage

If a food cost percentage is too high, the problem is frequently thought to be in the back of the house. For example, the purchase costs are too high, there is inventory theft, or portion sizes are too large.

Sometimes this approach does not define the problem. A food cost percentage can be too high because the revenue is too low due to theft or embezzlement: the crime of stealing money or property from the person or business who lawfully owns it. In this case, the high food cost percentage is not occurring because the food cost is too high, but because the food revenue is too low. Finding ways to reduce food cost will not increase the revenue, and the problem will continue.

This example shows that it is critical to properly define a problem before solving it.

MANAGERS RESOLVE OPERATING PROBLEMS

Managers handle problems during almost every work shift, and they must do so quickly and correctly. If not resolved, problems can become more challenging for managers to solve. Therefore, managers must be able to implement effective problem-solving strategies.

Managers rarely have all of the information needed to be 100 percent certain of their decisions. Therefore, they must be comfortable with the uncertainty and risks that are involved with many decisions.

In rare cases, one possible solution to the problem is to do nothing. For example, a contract with a vendor is ending, and the last delivery is late. There is little need to discover why and then correct the problem.

However, in most cases, problems that are either unsolved or incorrectly solved can cause negative results:

- Poor employee morale and high turnover
- Customer dissatisfaction
- Lost revenue, increased costs, and decreased profits
- Continuing problems for the operation

Managers must recognize a problem when it occurs, define and properly resolve it, and quickly implement a solution.

A Problem-Solving Model

Problems arise during almost every shift in every establishment. Fortunately, most can be resolved by considering existing policies and procedures. Some problems, however, create special challenges and require creative ways to address them.

Problem solving involves a well-thought-out process that uses a logical series of activities to determine a course of action. While various common methods are used, the one shown in *Exhibit 7.8* combines useful steps from several and provides a practical plan that busy restaurant and foodservice managers will find useful. The steps in *Exhibit 7.8* begin with establishing what the problem is.

Exhibit 7.8

PROBLEM-SOLVING MODEL

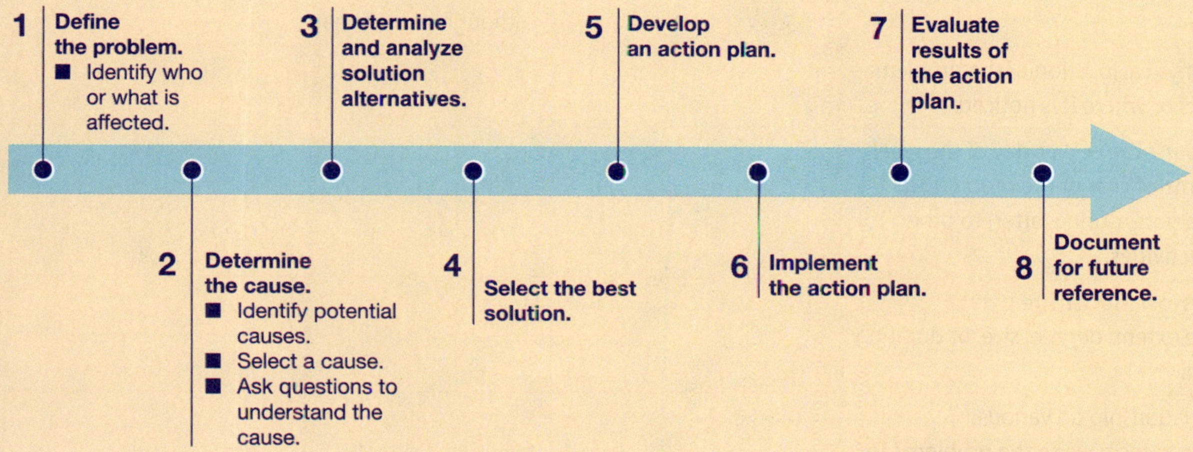
1 Define the problem.
■ Identify who or what is affected.
2 Determine the cause.
■ Identify potential causes.
■ Select a cause.
■ Ask questions to understand the cause.
3 Determine and analyze solution alternatives.
4 Select the best solution.
5 Develop an action plan.
6 Implement the action plan.
7 Evaluate results of the action plan.
8 Document for future reference.

STEP 1: DEFINE THE PROBLEM

Before a problem can be solved, it must be carefully defined. If it is not, a manager can waste time determining a solution that will not be helpful. The best way to define a problem is to think about who or what is affected through a questioning process. It is also helpful to think about what the situation would be like if there were no problem. The answer to this question can help determine whether the action plan that is developed (see Step 5) is successful. Depending on the problem, groups of persons including employees, managers, owners, customers, or even the public could be asked to help explain the problem.

STEP 2: DETERMINE THE CAUSE

Problems can have one or more **causes** (the actions or situations that create the problem). They are often procedure breakdowns or human errors. Restaurant and foodservice operations are made up of a series of complex systems including those for purchasing, production, customer service, cash handling, cost control, and scheduling. Problems can occur when one or more of these systems break down or were not carefully developed in the first place.

When problems are caused by human error, a manager must question the people affected by the problem to determine its cause. Managers can use tools such as the Problem–Cause Box in *Exhibit 7.9*. Be careful not to accuse or blame anyone when asking these kinds of questions.

Exhibit 7.9

PROBLEM–CAUSE BOX: ASK THE RIGHT QUESTIONS

	Is	Is Not	Therefore
Problem? ______________________	Where, when, to what extent, or regarding whom does this problem occur?	Where, when, to what extent, or regarding whom does this problem *not* occur, though it might have?	What might explain the pattern of the problem?
Where? The physical location of the problem—where it occurs or where it is noticed.			
When? The hour, time of day, day of the week, month, and time of year of the problem; its relationship (before, during, after) to other situations or activities.			
What Kind or How Much? The type of problem—the extent, degree, size, or duration of the problem.			
Who? What relationship do various individuals or groups have to the problem? To whom, by whom, near whom, and so on does the problem occur?			

STEP 3: DETERMINE AND ANALYZE SOLUTION ALTERNATIVES

An **alternative** is a possible solution to a problem. The list of alternatives should be as long as needed. Do not think about whether an alternative is ideal; if it can potentially be helpful, put it on the list. One alternative that should always be considered is to do nothing. Sometimes solutions are found for problems that will go away, for example a "problem employee" is resigning next week. On the other hand, doing nothing when there is a big problem or putting off solutions for another time will allow the problem to continue.

After the alternatives have been generated, they must be analyzed to determine which, if any, will help resolve the problem. Several key questions should be asked for each alternative:

- What will happen if we use this alternative? Who will be affected and how? Will the alternative help more than any other alternative?
- Is it cost-effective? Will the solution cost more than the problem? Can the alternative be revised to cost less and still fix the problem?
- Is it reasonable? Does the alternative have a good chance of succeeding?
- Will everyone accept the alternative? If not, the alternative will be difficult to implement.

STEP 4: SELECT THE BEST SOLUTION

After the impact of proposed alternatives is known, the list of possible solutions should be reduced. Hopefully, there will be only two or three alternatives left. The analysis of the remaining alternatives should then continue. Ask the tough questions and dig deep to find the best alternative to eliminate or reduce the problem. Remember that an incorrect solution will create the need to repeat the problem-solving process, and the negative impact of the problem will also continue.

STEP 5: DEVELOP AN ACTION PLAN

After the solution has been chosen, an action plan must be developed. An **action plan** is a series of steps that will be taken to resolve the problem.

THINK ABOUT IT . . .

Albert Einstein said, "We can't solve problems by using the same kind of thinking we used when we created them." Why ask questions to find a solution? Why use a team to problem solve?

Manager's Memo

With a little experience using this problem-solving method, managers will find it to be a practical way to resolve many daily problems. When a problem is noticed, the process begins, alternatives are identified, and solutions are considered.

All too often in the fast-paced restaurant and foodservice industry, a snap decision about a critical problem leads to disaster:

- The problem can get worse and even become a crisis.
- Employee morale can decrease. Problems can create stress for employees, and this can lead to frustration and create other problems including increased employee turnover.
- Reduced revenue may result. Revenue-related problems must be quickly resolved because the entire operation can be affected both immediately and in the longer term.
- Increases in costs may occur. This can occur from a problem with a procedure that creates waste or allows theft. Increased costs lead to reduced profit or, worse yet, a loss.

STEP 6: IMPLEMENT THE ACTION PLAN

Communicate the action plan and its expected outcomes to everyone involved so they know what must be done and how they will be impacted.

STEP 7: EVALUATE RESULTS OF THE ACTION PLAN

Was the action plan effective? Thinking about the answer to the question posed in Step 1, "What would the situation be like if there were no problem," can help in the evaluation process. If the problem has been resolved, the action plan was successful. If the problem still exists, the alternatives to resolve the problem must be reconsidered or the action plan will need to be revised. Then the problem-solving process must be continued until the issue has been corrected.

STEP 8: DOCUMENT FOR FUTURE REFERENCE

It is useful to record the problem and solution and keep the information on file. Before beginning another problem-solving activity, managers can review this file for similar events that may be helpful in resolving the new situation.

Exhibit 7.10 shows how a manager can use the problem-solving method to resolve a common problem in daily operations.

This problem-solving approach is very useful for problems that occur in daily operations. It also applies to longer-term problems such as marketing concerns about how to increase revenue and operating issues relating to higher-than-normal costs. The steps can be done quickly, perhaps with participation from team members when necessary. As the challenge becomes larger and the results of not correcting the problem become greater, it is likely that more time and effort will be needed to ensure that the problem-solving process is successful.

Exhibit 7.10

PROBLEM SOLVING IN DAILY OPERATIONS

Where Do We Get More Lettuce?

Step 1: Define the Problem

Juan, the manager, has just learned that there will not be enough lettuce for tonight's dinner production. Juan recognizes two problems: Why did we run out of lettuce, and what do we do right now? The problem is easy to state: There is not enough lettuce.

Step 2: Determine the Cause

Juan realizes that it is critical to determine why the establishment ran out of lettuce. However, that issue can wait until a decision is made about where to obtain more lettuce.

Step 3: Determine and Analyze Solution Alternatives

Juan and the kitchen manager have a quick conversation and consider the following alternatives:

- Call the vendor and ask him or her to deliver more lettuce. While it is too late for the delivery truck to make a run, the salesperson might be able to deliver more lettuce today.
- Send an employee to the grocery store to purchase lettuce at retail price.
- Send an employee to the local buyers' club where a discount can be received for large purchases.
- Contact a nearby unit in the restaurant chain to see if that property can provide the needed lettuce.

The situation is fairly urgent. The two managers decide not to contact the vendor because the vendor's location is in another town. They know they can buy the lettuce at either a retail store or a buyers' club, and the price will be lower at the buyers' club. They decide to first contact the nearby unit in their restaurant chain and, if that is not a possibility, to send an employee to the buyers' club.

Step 4: Select the Best Solution

The nearby restaurant in the chain does not have enough additional lettuce, so a kitchen employee who drives a pickup truck will be sent to the buyers' club. No check or currency will be needed because the establishment has an account, and the store's manager will be notified that an employee is on the way to purchase one case of lettuce.

Step 5: Develop an Action Plan

The kitchen employee is asked to go to the buyers' club and told he will be paid $15 from the establishment's petty cash fund to reimburse for gas. A **petty cash fund** is a predetermined amount of money that is used to make relatively infrequent and low-cost purchases for an establishment.

Step 6: Implement the Action Plan

The employee leaves for the buyers' club, the manager calls the buyers' club, and the kitchen manager makes different assignments so food production can continue until the lettuce arrives.

Step 7: Evaluate Results of the Action Plan

After the problem has been corrected, the manager evaluates the solution to determine if it was successful. The results on lettuce stock levels, cost, and any time spent implementing the solution are evaluated.

Step 8: Document for Future Reference

The next morning the kitchen and operation manager meet to determine why they ran out of lettuce. Purchasing, inventory management, issuing, and food preparation activities are analyzed. They discover that two cases had been marked with the wrong date when they were received, so they were not issued in the order they were received. These cases were later thrown away by a kitchen employee when he noticed the case contents did not meet the property's quality requirements. Actions taken to resolve the problem include reminding all employees that no food can be thrown away, even if spoiled, without notifying the kitchen manager.

THINK ABOUT IT . . .

No manager is perfect. Sometimes risks must be taken and tough choices or unpopular decisions made. Do you think experienced managers will more often make the right decisions than inexperienced managers? Why or why not?

MANAGERS REPORT TO UPPER-LEVEL MANAGERS

Effective communication is a key to maintaining a positive relationship with upper-level managers. Upper-level management has delegated the authority to perform certain tasks such as to lead the operation during specific work shifts. Management will want to know how well revenue and labor goals, among others, were attained. The on-time completion of a daily log and other reports will provide this information.

The best upper-level managers know that they must help those whom they supervise to be successful. Lower-level managers help themselves and their own managers when they use procedures that maintain positive relationships with upper-level managers. There are numerous ways to do so:

- Be competent: Always apply the knowledge and skills required to do the job correctly.
- Note what other higher-level managers do and how they act to mirror the actions important in the corporate culture.
- Follow the proper work practices. For example, meet deadlines, look for opportunities to help the operation be successful, and help improve the performance of line-level employees.
- Help employees find pride and joy in their work and practice effective team leading skills.

Managers must report information about daily operations to upper management; this task is an important part of a manager's responsibility. This communication is necessary to help ensure that all managers have all the necessary information available to make operating decisions. Information must be provided according to schedules developed by higher-level managers and should not be considered something for the manager to do at his or her leisure.

Exhibit 7.11

Manager's Daily Log

The **manager's daily log** contains information that affects the operation. It tells what happened during each shift and is useful for reviewing situations and noting problems (*Exhibit 7.11*), and for capturing facts that can protect the establishment from legal liabilities. A **legal liability** occurs when an establishment is legally responsible for a situation.

Managers may record a variety of information in this log:

- Unusual changes in menu item sales or customer counts
- Unusual events
- Employee or customer accidents
- Reports of possible foodborne illness
- Incidents of unusual employee interactions
- Weather and other business-related forecasting information
- Information needed by managers of future shifts
- Communication or teamwork problems on the shift
- Employee tardiness, attendance, and absenteeism
- Future challenges that may need to be addressed
- Any critical incidents
- Other information required by the owner or higher-level managers

RECORDING INFORMATION IN THE LOG

The main purpose of the manager's daily log is to share information. Some information will help managers ensure smooth operations in the short term whereas other information will be useful to managers and owners in the long term. Therefore, the log must be available to various people. In addition, when there is a potential legal or other complaint, the log is subject to a **subpoena**: a legal notice that requires certain documents be provided to a court of law.

Managers should not make personal comments and other entries in a manager's daily log if they cannot be supported by facts. They should include only information that can be defended and explained if required by lawyers or a court, and they should always follow the operation's guidelines for making log entries.

The types of information that should be recorded in a log fall into two main categories: operating information and critical incidents, or events that need to be recorded for historical purposes in case of a potential claim or lawsuit.

Operating Information. Most information in a log will be about day-to-day operations. This operating information may have either a positive or negative effect on the business and includes both routine and unusual situations.

Manager's Memo

Large restaurant and foodservice operations must typically track much information and use several types of daily manager's logs. However, managers in smaller properties use simpler methods. For example, perhaps the daily reservation journal serves as the manager's log. Also, one simple log may be used for entries by all managers. The log summarizes the most important financial information such as total shift revenue and customer counts and total labor hours on a by-position or by-department basis.

Exhibit 7.12 shows a sample daily manager's log.

While *Exhibit 7.12* shows sample entries about staffing issues, information about individual performance, attitudes, and disciplinary actions should not be part of a public record. If such issues occur, record them in the employee's file or other private logs kept in a secure location. Follow the operation's guidelines for recording these situations.

Exhibit 7.12

SAMPLE MANAGER'S DAILY LOG

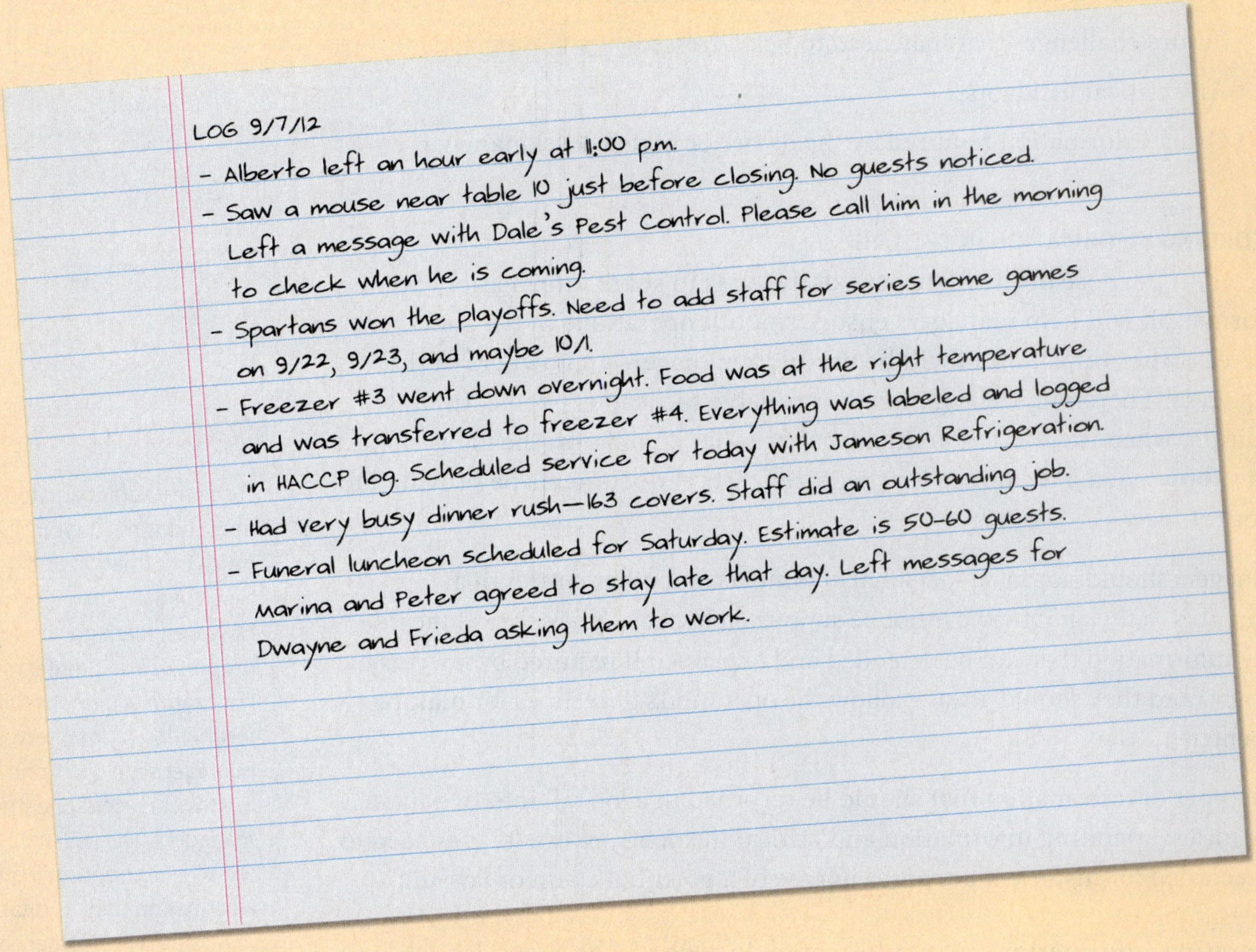

LOG 9/7/12

- Alberto left an hour early at 11:00 pm.
- Saw a mouse near table 10 just before closing. No guests noticed. Left a message with Dale's Pest Control. Please call him in the morning to check when he is coming.
- Spartans won the playoffs. Need to add staff for series home games on 9/22, 9/23, and maybe 10/1.
- Freezer #3 went down overnight. Food was at the right temperature and was transferred to freezer #4. Everything was labeled and logged in HACCP log. Scheduled service for today with Jameson Refrigeration.
- Had very busy dinner rush—163 covers. Staff did an outstanding job.
- Funeral luncheon scheduled for Saturday. Estimate is 50–60 guests. Marina and Peter agreed to stay late that day. Left messages for Dwayne and Frieda asking them to work.

CRITICAL INCIDENTS

One purpose of the manager's log is to record **critical incidents**: events relating to food safety, security, police, or emergency services.

There are four main categories of critical incidents:

- **Accidents:** Slips, falls, or other mishaps involving injury or the potential for injury, even when no injuries are visible and the persons involved say they are unhurt.
- **Incidents:** Situations in which a person or persons become involved in unacceptable behavior in the establishment or on the establishment's property; for example, fights.
- **Emergencies:** Situations that involve urgent medical or security threats, such as a customer who collapses or a robbery. An emergency may or may not include rescue squads, 911 or similar emergency calls, and hospital visits.
- **Reports of food problems:** Reports or occurrences of possible allergic reactions, foodborne illness, or foreign materials in food.

The facts relating to critical incidents must be recorded in detail at the time of the incident. The general facts about the incident are usually included in the manager's daily log, with full details recorded in other documents or kept in private files.

Consider these examples of critical incident entries in a manager's daily log:

- Ten-year-old boy ran into lobby door and bruised forehead, 4:50 p.m. Checked forehead, and it seemed to be fine. Gave boy and his eight-year-old sister some promotional helium balloons.
- Yelling in the break room, 10 a.m., between Sam and Jean.
- Man choked on roast beef sandwich, 11:20 a.m., table 7. His companion performed Heimlich maneuver. Man is OK. See incident report.
- Customer found piece of plastic in her salad. Talked with guest; she was fine. Gave her a new salad. Checked back at the end of the meal and brought dessert to her and her friend. See incident report.

Each operation should have guidelines for managing and recording critical incidents. Many operations use a critical incident form to record the details. *Exhibit 7.13* shows a form with information that should be recorded to fully explain a critical incident.

Exhibit 7.13

SAMPLE CRITICAL INCIDENT FORM

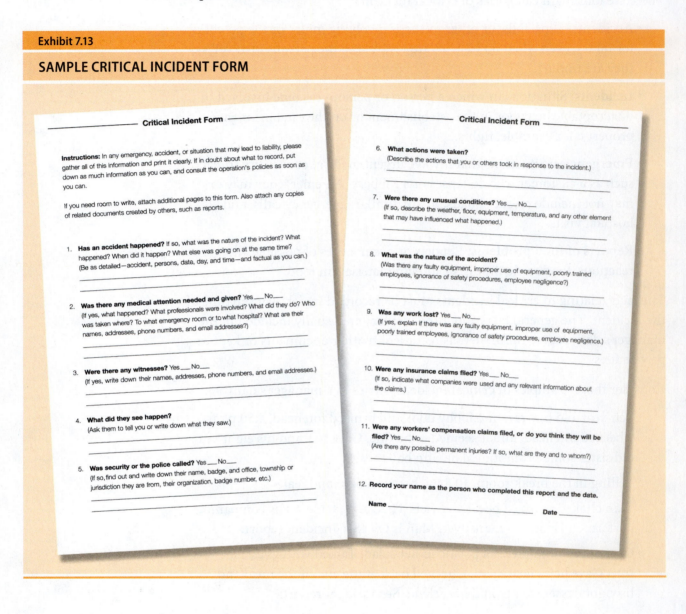

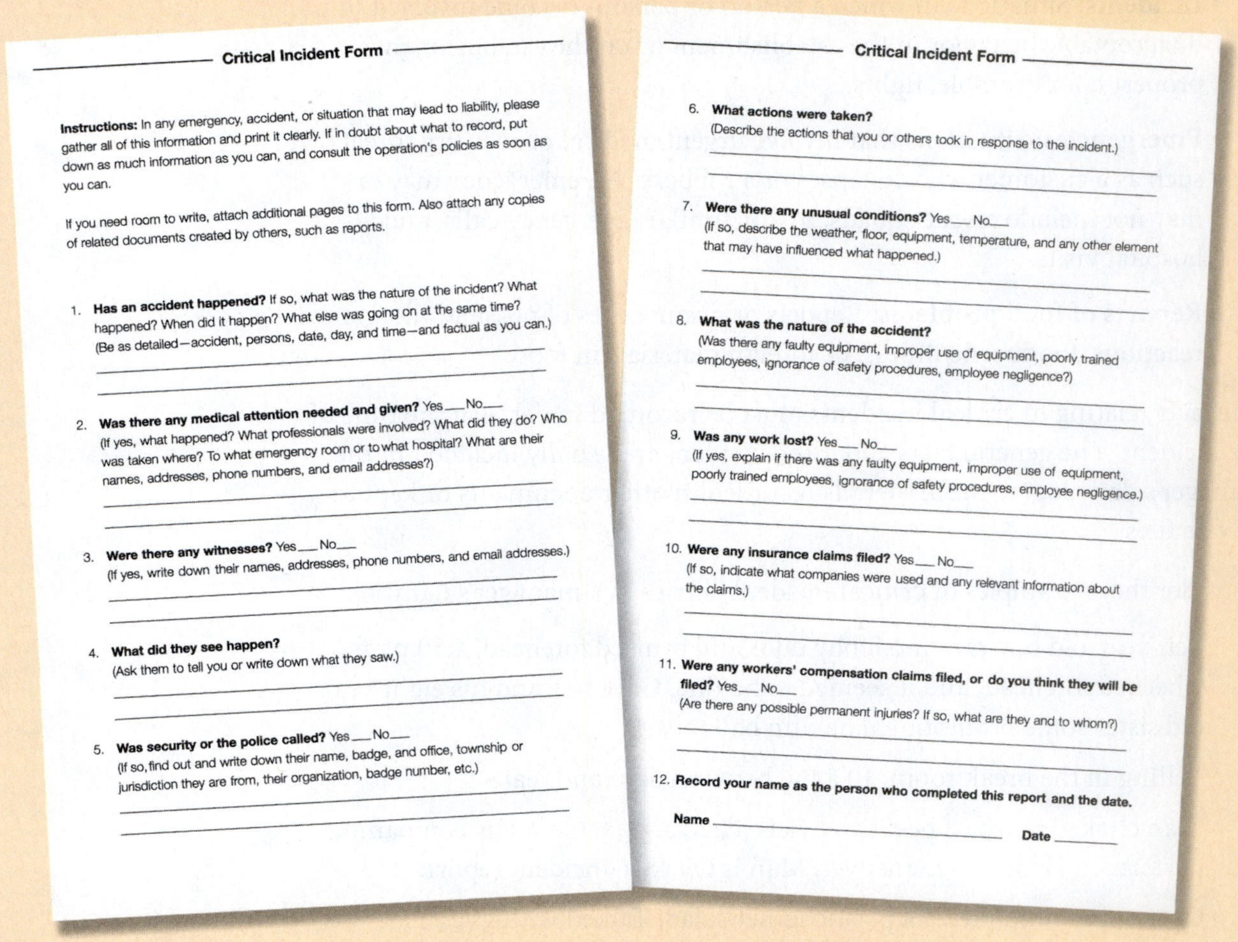

Critical Incident Form

Instructions: In any emergency, accident, or situation that may lead to liability, please gather all of this information and print it clearly. If in doubt about what to record, put down as much information as you can, and consult the operation's policies as soon as you can.

If you need room to write, attach additional pages to this form. Also attach any copies of related documents created by others, such as reports.

1. **Has an accident happened?** If so, what was the nature of the incident? What happened? When did it happen? What else was going on at the same time? (Be as detailed—accident, persons, date, day, and time—and factual as you can.)
2. **Was there any medical attention needed and given?** Yes__ No__ (If yes, what happened? What professionals were involved? What did they do? Who was taken where? To what emergency room or to what hospital? What are their names, addresses, phone numbers, and email addresses?)
3. **Were there any witnesses?** Yes__ No__ (If yes, write down their names, addresses, phone numbers, and email addresses.)
4. **What did they see happen?** (Ask them to tell you or write down what they saw.)
5. **Was security or the police called?** Yes__ No__ (If so, find out and write down their name, badge, and office, township or jurisdiction they are from, their organization, badge number, etc.)

Critical Incident Form

6. **What actions were taken?** (Describe the actions that you or others took in response to the incident.)
7. **Were there any unusual conditions?** Yes__ No__ (If so, describe the weather, floor, equipment, temperature, and any other element that may have influenced what happened.)
8. **What was the nature of the accident?** (Was there any faulty equipment, improper use of equipment, poorly trained employees, ignorance of safety procedures, employee negligence?)
9. **Was any work lost?** Yes__ No__ (If yes, explain if there was any faulty equipment, improper use of equipment, poorly trained employees, ignorance of safety procedures, employee negligence.)
10. **Were any insurance claims filed?** Yes__ No__ (If so, indicate what companies were used and any relevant information about the claims.)
11. **Were any workers' compensation claims filed, or do you think they will be filed?** Yes__ No__ (Are there any possible permanent injuries? If so, what are they and to whom?)
12. **Record your name as the person who completed this report and the date.**

Name __________ **Date** ______

Basic details should be recorded for each critical incident:

- Description of the situation and people involved, including names, date, and time.
- Names and contact information of witnesses.
- Any other important information such as employees following or not following normal procedures.

- The names and badge numbers of any police who come in response to the incident. When someone is sent to the hospital, the name of the hospital, ambulance company, and persons who operated the ambulance should be recorded. It is not necessary, however, to record all the information that may be necessary on hospital, insurance, or other legal forms.

This detailed information should be placed in a confidential file that will not be read by other employees and managers.

Critical incidents that involve unacceptable or excellent employee behavior may also be recorded in other private logs or in employee files. Always follow the operation's requirements for managing, recording, and reporting critical incidents.

Reports to Upper Management

Recall that managers in charge of daily shifts use a manager's daily log to report important information to others, including upper-level managers. This information is very important and will be used to monitor and make decisions about operations.

Restaurant and foodservice managers should know what information their own managers want. Much, but not all, of this information will be financial data. Information about critical incidents will also be important. Note: *Much of the financial information in these reports can also be used by the management team for budgeting, problem solving, decision making, and other purposes.*

Managers in multi-unit restaurant or foodservice organizations will likely need to develop a detailed list of information on a by-shift, daily, or other basis. Much of the financial information may be sent electronically from the operation's point-of-sale system to the organization's central offices. This is often sent in a template, or format, determined by upper-level managers. For example, spreadsheets are often used to report revenue and cost information on a daily, weekly, monthly, and year-to-date basis.

Managers must learn what information is desired by upper management and then develop a process to collect it and send it on a timely basis. Managers need to keep copies of all reports sent to upper-level managers and be prepared to answer any questions about the information in the reports. Questions can be minimized by ensuring the reports clearly explain the data presented. This is important because critical-incident reports often describe unusual situations.

Operation guidelines will indicate persons to whom upper-level management reports should be sent. These reports should be treated confidentially and should be shared only with those permitted by company guidelines.

MANAGERS PLAN FOR EMERGENCIES

> **Manager's Memo**
>
> Unresolved problems can create some emergencies. For example, if managers ignore an unsanitary condition in the kitchen, a foodborne-illness outbreak could occur. An unsanitary condition is a problem, but a foodborne-illness outbreak is an emergency.
>
> Not all emergencies result from unsolved problems. Sometimes they just happen. Tornados, hurricanes, floods, and other natural disasters do not result from problems in the operation. In these cases, managers can concentrate only on minimizing effects by properly handling the unexpected event.

An **emergency** is a sudden or unexpected situation that can cause injury, death, or property damage, or interfere with normal activities. Managers must know how to effectively manage emergencies to minimize the chance of disastrous outcomes.

Restaurant and foodservice emergencies can affect owners, managers, employees, customers, and the public (sometimes all at once). Establishments can often survive emergencies that are handled properly and, in a severe situation, a proper response can even save lives.

Some managers think that because emergencies occur without warning, they cannot be planned for. However, professional managers prepare for them with detailed plans. An establishment's reaction to an emergency must be planned before the event happens. A priority must be placed on actions that can protect people, help emergency services resolve the immediate problem, and calm the situation.

The key to managing emergencies is to have a plan before the emergency occurs and to practice it. Then if an emergency does occur, managers and employees will know what to do.

Types of Emergencies

Emergencies can be preventable or unpreventable. A **preventable emergency** is one that may be prevented from happening, such as a fire or foodborne illness. An **unpreventable emergency** is one that cannot be prevented, such as a natural disaster.

Exhibit 7.14 shows some of the most common types of preventable and unpreventable emergencies that impact restaurant and foodservice operations. It also provides a summary of actions that can be taken to manage the emergencies.

Exhibit 7.14

COMMON TYPES OF RESTAURANT AND FOODSERVICE EMERGENCIES

Fire	Many fires can be prevented. Proper installation of equipment and fire suppressant systems in the kitchen hood and easily accessible placement of fire extinguishers can prevent most fires from spreading. Periodic checks of electrical and gas systems can prevent many fires from starting. Only in rare cases, such as a lightning strike, can a fire not be prevented.
Foodborne illness	Most foodborne illnesses can be prevented. Managers should be trained and certified in food safety and should implement training programs so employees will correctly handle and store food. The use of a Hazard Analysis and Critical Control Point (HACCP) program within the establishment is also beneficial. The HACCP system is used to control risks and hazards during the flow of food through a restaurant or foodservice operation.
Armed robbery	Armed robberies cannot be prevented, but they can be deterred. Most robbers are after a quick and easy strike and will survey a location before they rob it. They are primarily after cash; therefore, money should be handled properly. If customers pay cash, the cashier station should be away from the front door and periodic drops should be made into the safe. A video surveillance system is also a good deterrent. An effective control system would involve servers collecting payment from guests and turning in their receipts after their shift. This way, the money is dispersed throughout the operation because some servers will be in the dining room taking orders and others in the kitchen picking up orders. Accounting for cash should be done in the manager's office, and the cash that is collected should immediately be put into a locked safe. In the event of a robbery, employees should never resist a robber. Procedures should emphasize the safety of employees and customers.
Gas leak	Although rare, gas leaks can be deadly, but they are preventable. Gas equipment should be properly installed by a licensed technician. All gas lines and couplings should be inspected monthly. Pilot lights should be inspected daily to ensure they are working properly.
Terrorist attack	Terrorists can contaminate the water or food supply. The U.S. Department of Homeland Security has named restaurants and hotels as "soft" targets of terrorists. Regrettably, at this time there is no way to prevent a terrorist attack or to know what form it will take. Managers and employees should be alert and report any suspicious activity to the authorities. Also, they should purchase all food and beverages from vendors that they know and trust.
Natural disaster	While some advance notice may be given about natural disasters, many occur with little warning. Managers should learn whether their area is likely to experience certain types of weather, such as hurricanes or tornados, and prepare as best they can if an event is forecast (e.g., boarding up windows and securing fixtures and furniture). Managers must rely on their emergency management plans to help ensure the safety of customers, employees, and property.

Written Emergency Plans

Emergencies can happen quickly such as fires, explosions, or robberies, or they can occur over several hours or more as in the case of a foodborne-illness outbreak. They can also occur over many months or even years, as in the case of lawsuits.

KEEPING IT SAFE

Portable fire extinguishers can be used for two different purposes: to control or put out small fires and to keep exit routes clear of fire.

Some employees feel a false sense of security when fire extinguishers are available. In fact, there is much risk involved because fires can increase in size quickly and block the exit route of the person using the extinguisher. Also, portable extinguishers have limited contents that can be used up in a few seconds.

Before a fire extinguisher is used, it is important to make a quick risk assessment:

- Is the fire too big?
- Is the air safe to breathe?
- Is the area hot or smoky?
- Is there a safe way out?

The employee must quickly answer these questions to determine if it is safe to stay and use the fire extinguisher. Managers should train employees to be very careful and conservative as they make this almost instantaneous decision.

THINK ABOUT IT . . .

If every employee understands emergency management procedures, can any employee represent the organization during an emergency? What image do you want the public to have of your operation during an emergency?

Effective managers do not think about what to do when emergencies happen. Instead, they develop plans for them and communicate the plans to everyone before they occur. Emergency plans should include a written policy that clearly identifies how to handle each type of potential emergency. The policy should include this key information:

- A list of roles and responsibilities of those who will be part of the plan.
- A list of key contacts.
- Procedures for sharing information.
- A requirement that news media be referred to a specific contact person such as the owner or corporate offices. Employees should not talk to the media, and media should not normally be allowed on-site.
- Responsibilities for completing paperwork.
- Plans to provide training in emergency plans to all employees.

Some emergencies will involve evacuation. An **evacuation** is the process of removing customers and employees from the building when an emergency occurs. Managers cannot usually do this alone, but responsibilities for assisting should be delegated to a position, not a specific employee. Employees change, especially with multiple shifts, while positions do not. To ensure an evacuation is done successfully, the plan should include the following steps:

- A drawing should be made of the establishment showing all exits, routes to access those exits, and alternate routes in case an exit is blocked. The drawing should be posted throughout the building.
- When an emergency occurs, call the emergency number in the area without delay and tell the location, explain exactly what the problem is, and indicate the approximate number of people involved.
- A manager should be designated to secure all cash and other valuables if it is safe to do so.
- A manager or lead employee should be designated to meet arriving emergency personnel and repeat information about the problem and number of persons involved.
- A location outside the building should be designated for everyone to assemble. This should be located some distance from the establishment, perhaps in the parking lot of a neighboring business.
- Employees and customers should immediately be evacuated in a calm and orderly manner. Servers should be instructed to lead customers seated at their stations to the assembly area. A chef or lead cook should be designated to make sure everyone is evacuated from the kitchen and

back-of-the-house areas. Another employee should be designated to check the restrooms and assist anyone there in leaving.

- All employees should practice the plan on a regular basis, and it should be part of the orientation and training procedures for all new employees.

The roles and responsibilities required to follow through on the emergency plans should be in writing. Remember to indicate the responsibilities by position, not by employee name.

Other Emergency Concerns

The establishment should maintain a current list of key contacts next to every phone. A **contact list** includes key persons to be notified in the event of an emergency. Other useful contacts are the fire department, police, health department, an electrician, a plumber, and a security company, if applicable.

Another policy to define in advance of an emergency relates to how information will be shared. Restaurant and foodservice managers should always cooperate fully with local government officials. However, some managers are concerned about fines or other penalties if they are in some way responsible for all or part of the emergency.

Local health departments, fire code inspectors, and other officials protect citizens' interests. By cooperating with these officials and sharing information, managers enable them to complete their tasks quickly and efficiently and correct the problem so it does not recur.

What Information to Share with the News Media

Restaurant and foodservice managers must be careful as they consider what and how much emergency information to share with the news media. Many large organizations have media relations departments to assist with the management of news media during emergencies.

Only one person should interact with the media, and this person should be designated in the operation's media policy. A **media policy** is a strategy developed to guide interactions with newspaper, television, and radio reporters about the establishment's response to an emergency.

The person representing the establishment to the media will depend on the emergency. If it is a lawsuit, the legal firm representing the operation would be the logical voice. If the emergency involves destruction of property or a customer illness, an owner or manager would be the most likely spokesperson. When talking to the media, the spokesperson should be brief and focus on the positive to get customers back into the establishment. In no case should employees be allowed to talk to the media. They should be instructed to refer all questions to the designated person. The way the designated spokesperson interacts with the media will help in the establishment's recovery efforts.

If possible, the media should be kept off the property, and they should not be allowed to take photos or videotape. However, they can do so from the street or other public spaces.

More about Policies and Paperwork

THINK ABOUT IT . . .

Why would it benefit a restaurant or foodservice manager to practice ways of communicating with the news media before an emergency occurs?

An operation needs a written policy for all aspects of managing emergencies. It should be included in the employee handbook and addressed in every employee's training. Role-play activities can be used in management training to ensure everyone is prepared to act in any emergency.

All employees need to know "who is responsible for what" so they can fulfill their responsibilities if an emergency occurs. They should be trained so they can react quickly. In an emergency, the stress level is high, so the establishment will benefit from a trained and prepared staff.

After an emergency is over, there will be paperwork to complete. Forms from government agencies, insurance companies, and in the case of a chain operation, reports to the home office will most often be required. A meeting with everyone involved should also be held to evaluate the plan that was used. Did things happen as expected? What did not work as well as it should have? What needs to be improved?

Unfortunately, the effectiveness of an emergency plan, even if it is practiced many times, is unknown until it is needed. After the meeting, any policy affected by changes should be rewritten based on what was learned.

SUMMARY

1. **Describe how restaurant and foodservice managers should establish priorities.**

   Restaurant and foodservice managers do many things, and they must establish priorities. One guideline is to give priority to tasks based on the operation's goals. Another is to classify tasks based on importance and urgency and then do the most important (not necessarily the most urgent) tasks first.

2. **Describe procedures used by restaurant and foodservice managers to develop and use two important operating tools: policies and procedures.**

Policies help managers make consistent decisions about issues that occur frequently. Policies should have a clear purpose. When practical, a team effort to develop policies is useful.

Procedures tell how to correctly perform a task. When possible, they should be developed with team input. Standard operating procedures (SOPs) should be easy to understand and should consider the knowledge and skills required to perform the task. Policies and procedures should be carefully written, featured in employee training, and kept current.

3. **Explain a basic approach that managers can use to resolve operating problems.**

A basic eight-step process can be used to resolve problems. The problem-solving model begins with (1) defining the problem, (2) determining its cause, and (3) determining and analyzing solution alternatives. The approach continues with (4) selecting the best solution, (5) developing an action plan, (6) implementing the plan, (7) evaluating the results of the plan and (8) documenting the problem and solution for future reference.

4. **Describe how restaurant and foodservice managers should develop and submit reports to upper management.**

Managers use procedures to maintain positive relationships with their own bosses. Effective communication is a key to this.

Managers can use a manager's daily log to report to other managers and improve communication between shifts. This report will include financial and operating information including an overview of any critical incidents.

Managers must be aware of other information, much of which is likely to address financial issues, that is desired by their own manager. They must then develop a process to collect and route this information to their manager on a timely basis.

5. **Review procedures that restaurant and foodservice managers should use to plan for and manage emergencies.**

While managers cannot know when emergencies will occur, they should plan for the most common types. Restaurant and foodservice emergencies may include fire, foodborne illness, armed robbery, gas leaks, and natural disasters.

Emergency plans should indicate the responsibilities of employees in certain positions and include procedures for evacuation from the building.

Restaurant and foodservice managers should develop a media policy that indicates how an appointed person should interact with the media in response to an emergency.

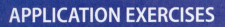

APPLICATION EXERCISES

Exercise 1

Break into teams of three. First, indicate the priority the manager should give to each type of problem. Then brainstorm examples of possible activities that would fall into each category shown below.

1. Activities that are urgent but not very important.
2. Activities that are not urgent but important.
3. Activities that are urgent and important.
4. Activities that are not urgent and not very important.

Exercise 2

Break into teams of several students and discuss examples of situations where you were working in or visiting an establishment that should have been written up in a manager's daily log.

What might you have done and what would you have written about these situations?

Situation for Manager's Daily Log	How You Would Handle the Situation

REVIEW YOUR LEARNING

Select the best answer for each question.

1. Managers should set their priorities to work on which type of tasks first?

A. Urgent but not important
B. Important but not urgent
C. Both urgent and important
D. Neither urgent nor important

2. Duties that are part of a job are included in which document?

A. Employee handbook
B. Task breakdown
C. Operation policy
D. Task list

3. Standard operating procedures should be developed

A. by a higher-level manager.
B. by the operation's legal counsel.
C. by a team of managers and employees.
D. by a cross-functional team of managers.

4. The problem-solving model includes the step of identifying

A. the person to blame for the problem.
B. the best alternative solution to implement.
C. how other establishments solve the problem.
D. a priority on selecting the cheapest alternative.

5. **Which of the following are needed in action plans to resolve problems?**
   A. Policies
   B. Costs
   C. Goals
   D. Steps

6. **When analyzing different alternatives to solve a problem, which is the best solution?**
   A. Least expensive
   B. Least complicated
   C. Most immediate
   D. Most likely to work

7. **Information posted in a manager's daily log should**
   A. include facts to protect the operation from legal liabilities.
   B. consist of problems that involve financial matters.
   C. include in-depth descriptions of critical incidents.
   D. focus on data that will help managers in the long term.

8. **Responsibilities for assisting in an emergency should be delegated to a specific**
   A. employee.
   B. manager.
   C. department.
   D. position.

9. **Procedures for emergency evacuations should**
   A. be handled by the manager on duty.
   B. be delegated by position, not by employee.
   C. ensure customers leave before employees.
   D. require an order by a police or fire official.

10. **The establishment's contact person for an emergency should be**
    A. the same person regardless of the type of emergency.
    B. the employee who made the call to emergency services.
    C. the manager of the department affected by the emergency.
    D. the person identified in the operation's media policy.

FIELD PROJECT

Part III

1. Interview the manager of a local establishment in order to learn how he or she resolves operating problems.

2. How does the manager identify potential causes of problems that have never occurred before?

3. How does the manager decide whether to personally resolve an issue or enlist employee assistance?

4. How does the manager evaluate potential solutions to solve problems?

5. If the manager has used the advice of entry-level employees about a problem solution and it did not work, what did the manager say to those employees?

8 Leaders Manage Meetings

INSIDE THIS CHAPTER

- The Need for Effective Meeting Management
- Planning Effective Meetings
- Conducting Effective Meetings
- Meeting Evaluation and Follow-Up

CHAPTER LEARNING OBJECTIVES

After completing this chapter, you should be able to:

- Explain the need for meetings to be effectively managed.
- Describe procedures for planning effective meetings.
- Explain procedures for conducting effective meetings.
- Suggest procedures required to evaluate and follow up on meetings.

KEY TERMS

- action item (meeting), p. 223
- action meeting, p. 213
- agenda, p. 217
- brainstorming meeting, p. 213
- emergency meeting, p. 213
- facilitator, p. 219
- ground rules (meeting), p. 221
- information meeting, p. 212
- minutes, p. 223
- problem-solving meeting, p. 212
- Robert's Rules of Order, p. 212
- status quo, p. 222
- tabled (agenda item), p. 220
- warm-up activity, p. 221

CASE STUDY

"I just hate going to these weekly manager meetings," said Rosetta. She was speaking to Fernando, a fellow manager at the Blue Bay Restaurant.

"I agree," replied Fernando, "It's almost like we're being punished for being promoted to manager."

"That's a good way to say it, Fernando," continued Rosetta. "We already know what will happen. First, the boss will say how bad our financials were last week; then he will go on a by-department basis through the entire restaurant to indicate how the people in that unit spent more than they should have and negatively affected our results. The meeting will end with a statement about going back out there and doing better this week."

"That's exactly what has happened in the past, and it's exactly what will happen again at tomorrow's meeting," said Fernando. "We have lots of ideas to help this place. But we never get a chance to present these suggestions because we focus on what has happened in the past rather than what we can do in the future."

1. What is the main problem with the meetings conducted by the manager of the Blue Bay Restaurant for the managers?
2. What are the two most basic things you would suggest to improve these meetings?

THE NEED FOR EFFECTIVE MEETING MANAGEMENT

Managers must communicate with their employees about many things. Most frequently they do so on a face-to-face basis. Sometimes these individual conversations are with those whom they directly supervise. At other times they want to provide a message that a large group of employees, or perhaps all of the employees, should know. When this occurs, managers can communicate in writing with an announcement on the employee bulletin board, by email messages, and by written information provided in memos that supervisors may review during employee meetings.

At other times, important information that everyone should know is best discussed in a group meeting. Some meetings are conducted frequently, such as line-up meetings before employees begin work. Planning meetings to develop departmental strategies to complement the operation's long-range plans may occur frequently for a relatively short period of time. Still other meetings such as discussing business expansion plans or rolling out a new menu may be held infrequently but are still very important.

There are time and cost concerns about meetings. Employees may need to be away from their work, or must come to work early or leave work later to attend meetings. Employees are typically paid for their attendance at meetings, so the sessions must be cost-effective: The benefits of the group message must be greater than the costs to present the message. Therefore, it is important to confirm the necessity of meetings. Their objectives must be important, and the manager must believe that a meeting is the best way to attain the meeting's objectives.

Restaurant and foodservice managers may plan and conduct meetings that range from very informal employee updates (*Exhibit 8.1*) to formal meetings that use **Robert's Rules of Order.** Robert's Rules of Order is a set of rules for conducting meetings in an organized way that allows everyone to be heard and to make decisions without confusion. To learn more, enter "Robert's Rules of Order" into a favorite search engine.

Types of Meetings

Meetings are held for many different reasons. A meeting is an assembly of two or more people for the purpose of discussing or making decisions about one or more topics. There are different types of meetings, but restaurant and foodservice managers are typically involved in four types:

- **Information meetings:** These meetings share communication such as project reports and updates or are used for orientation and training.
- **Problem-solving meetings:** Problem-solving meetings are held to consider and resolve one or more problems. These meetings may involve discussing, analyzing, and reviewing alternatives, and deciding what actions should be taken.

Exhibit 8.1

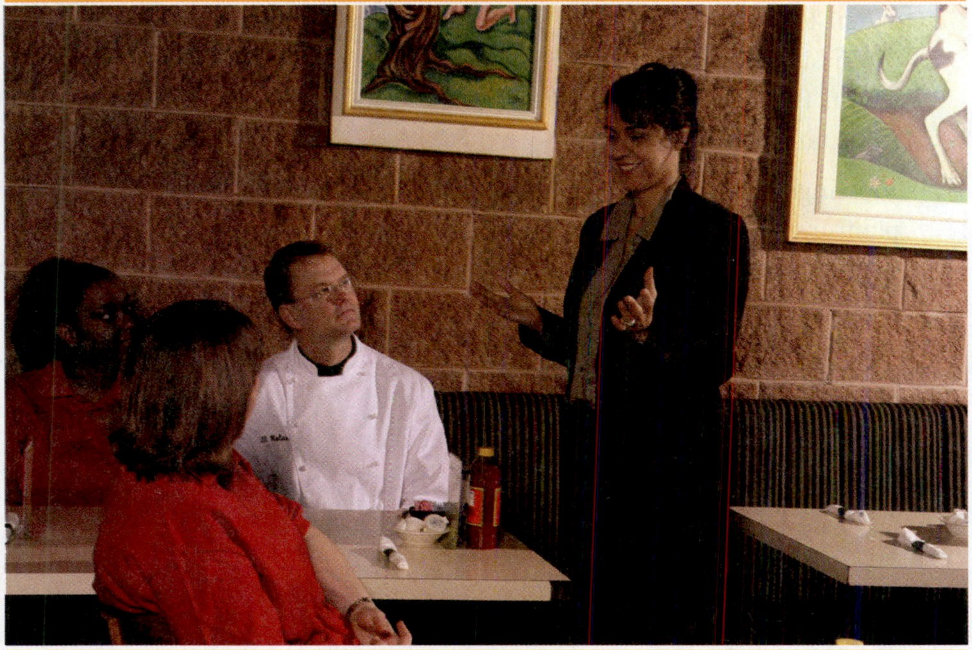

- **Brainstorming meetings:** Operations hold brainstorming meetings for developing a list of ideas or creative solutions to an issue confronting the operation. The purpose of these meetings is to collect ideas, not to make a decision. Participants may analyze the impact of the alternatives suggested, gather additional information, and discuss ideas with their employees.
- **Action meetings:** Action meetings are brief meetings often involving just a few employees that address and resolve a problem so action can be taken right away. The goal of the meeting is to decide and commit to action. An **emergency meeting** is a type of action meeting that occurs when some type of emergency has occurred and immediate action must be taken.

Avoiding Problem Meetings

The poor impressions some employees have about meetings can be a challenge for managers. These views will not likely change unless managers learn why employees do not like meetings and eliminate these problems.

The reasons many people dislike meetings are varied:

- The person holding the meeting fails to explain the meeting's goals. Meetings that do not stick to planned topics leave attendees wondering what exactly the meeting is about, why they are participating, and what role they will play in the meeting. In addition, issues not related to the goal of the meeting can easily distract from the effectiveness of the meeting.

Manager's Memo

Meetings attended by employees and their managers can be difficult to conduct for several reasons. First, employees may not want to talk out of fear that they will say something their manager does not like or something he or she wanted to bring up later. Second, employees may disagree with their manager but not say so during the meeting out of fear that he or she will get angry.

1. What would you be afraid to talk about at a meeting attended by your manager?
2. Would you be afraid to say something in disagreement with him or her? Why or why not?
3. Do you think other people feel the same way you do?

- Many participants do not take meetings seriously and do not prepare for them. They arrive late, leave early, and do not pay careful attention to discussions. This can be a problem especially if employees do not see results from previous meetings and if employees have lost the expectation that meeting problems will be addressed.
- Meetings are too long. Too often meetings drag on because of lack of planning or lack of an effective leader who can keep things moving.
- Meetings can cause stress. Many employees believe they have more than enough work to do during their shift. What if they are required to attend a meeting during the work shift and also to complete all of the work normally required? Many employees think their manager does not care or understand what they must do when they return to work. This is especially true if employees are required to attend a large number of meetings.
- Some of the same people dominate the meeting. There are always a few people who want to be heard more than others. These persons affect the interests of other attendees in participating.
- The information presented at meetings is confusing. Many times employees leave meetings with different views as to what happened, and then no productive results can be implemented.
- Many people do not say what they really think during meetings. This problem can occur when the person conducting the meeting does not want to or know how to encourage participation. Other reasons include attendees dominating the discussion and employees not feeling secure saying what they think.

Knowing some of the reasons employees become frustrated with meetings, managers need to consider these factors when planning and conducting meetings at their establishment.

PLANNING EFFECTIVE MEETINGS

Some employees would probably admit that attending meetings is one of their least favorite job-related activities. Given the poor image that meetings sometimes have, how can a manager plan and conduct meetings that employees will agree are important and useful?

Overview of the Meeting Process

Exhibit 8.2 provides an overview of steps in the meeting process. Review it briefly to learn about the four steps that must be completed in sequence to best ensure that a meeting will be successful.

As shown in *Exhibit 8.2*, there are four steps involved in an effective meeting. The fourth step is not usually necessary unless a meeting on the same topic will be held.

THINK ABOUT IT . . .

How are meetings viewed in the organizations where you have worked? What do you dislike most about meetings?

Exhibit 8.2

THE MEETING PROCESS

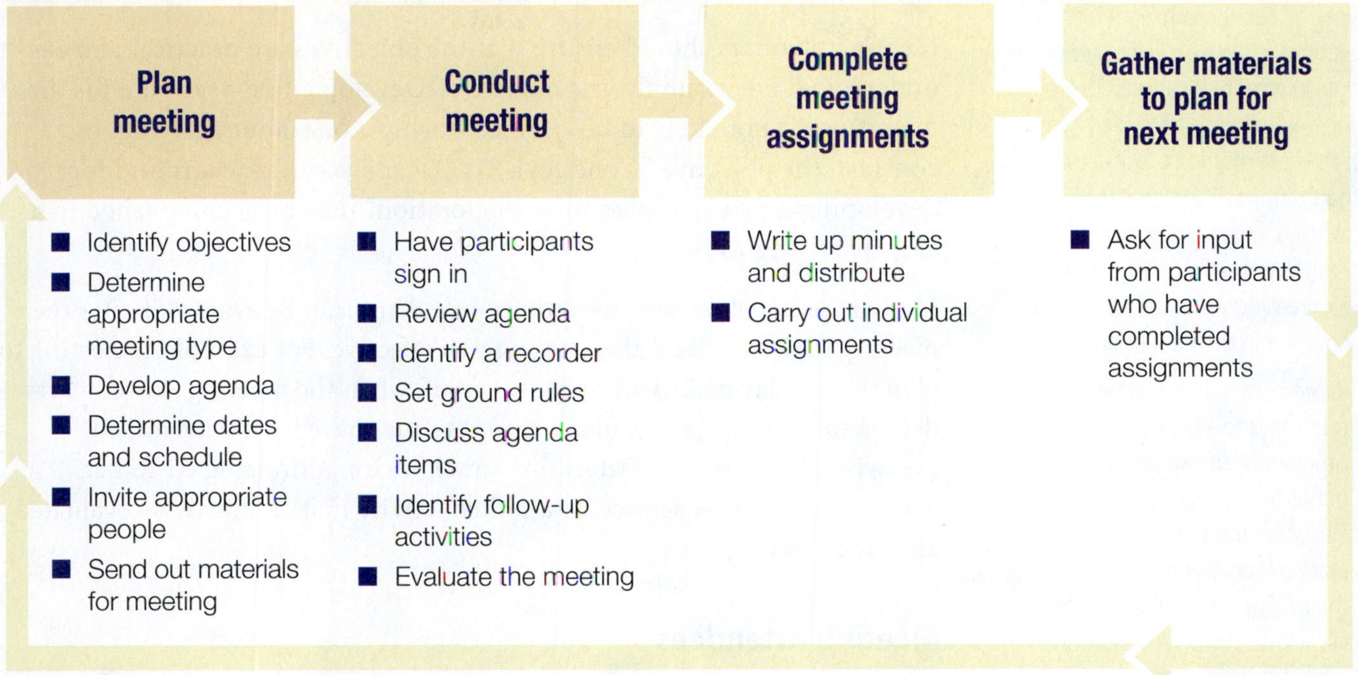

Plan meeting
Conduct meeting
Complete meeting assignments
Gather materials to plan for next meeting
Identify objectives
Determine appropriate meeting type
Develop agenda
Determine dates and schedule
Invite appropriate people
Send out materials for meeting
Have participants sign in
Review agenda
Identify a recorder
Set ground rules
Discuss agenda items
Identify follow-up activities
Evaluate the meeting
Write up minutes and distribute
Carry out individual assignments
Ask for input from participants who have completed assignments

Unfortunately, some managers believe they are too busy to get ready for meetings. They may also share some of the poor impressions about meetings discussed previously. They may just be going through the motions of having meetings because they must do so or they think meetings are needed once in a while.

They may also be unaware of basic principles for planning and conducting a business meeting. All of these problems can make meetings unsuccessful and contribute to employees' dislike of them.

As shown in *Exhibit 8.2*, the first step in managing a meeting is to plan it. Doing so involves considering the details of a meeting before it begins. Then the meeting planner and the participants will know what should occur during the meeting. Planning involves use of some basic activities to help ensure that the desired outcomes are achieved.

Meeting Objectives

Meeting planners should identify the business objectives to be accomplished at the meeting. These objectives will drive the rest of the planning process, beginning with the type of meeting that is needed to accomplish them. For example, the yearly budget, staffing needs, employee turnover rates, special events, or promotions would be topics for an information meeting.

An effective meeting planner will also receive input from the management team and employees involved to ensure that the meeting is necessary. A meeting is likely to be unsuccessful if its objectives are not agreed upon.

THINK ABOUT IT . . .

What is the single largest contributing factor to poorly run meetings? Why? What message does it send when a manager is not prepared for a meeting?

> **OPEN FOR BUSINESS — RESTAURANT TECHNOLOGY**
>
> Technology enables meetings to be held with participants in remote locations. These can be very helpful, for example, for those in multiunit foodservice organizations. Traditional telephone conference calls are still useful, but meeting participants are increasingly interacting with each other in online meetings:
>
> - Video conferencing allows attendees to see and hear each other without expensive video or hardware systems.
> - Desktop meetings such as "Webinars" allow attendees to use their computers, for example, to view slide show presentations while listening to the presenter by telephone.
> - Participants can collaborate with each other while working together in real time sharing keyboard inputs and mouse controls.
> - Attendees can chat with each other or with specific participants.
> - Participants can save, post, replay, or email information from technology-assisted remote meetings.
> - Drawing tools are available to allow participants to graph, highlight, and indicate items of interest to their fellow participants on computer screens.
>
> To learn more about online meetings, use your favorite search engine to query the phrase "online meetings."

Obtaining input helps attendees understand the meeting's purpose and agree that it is important. If attendees have this agreement, they will be more interested in attending and actively participating in the meeting.

Meeting planners should ensure that the objectives are practical and easy to understand. For example, the objective "Develop a five-year plan for the operation" is not likely to be attained during a one-hour meeting. In contrast, the objective "Conduct a SWOT analysis as background for developing a five-year plan for the operation" may be accomplished in a single meeting.

Many meeting objectives are activity-based and can be evaluated after the meeting to determine if the meeting was effective. For example, a meeting to plan the holiday party will be successful if, when the meeting is over, party details such as date, time, menu, and activities have been determined. Likewise, the objective "Determine strategies for addressing customer concerns about slow service" is another activity that can easily be evaluated after the meeting.

Meeting Attendees

Meeting planners must determine who should attend the meeting, and this relates to the type of meeting and its purpose. It is important to invite only those employees who are essential to the purpose of the meeting. Also, it is not always necessary that all affected employees attend an entire meeting. For example, perhaps some employees are impacted by only one or two topics that will be discussed. They might be invited to the beginning of the meeting when these concerns are addressed, and they could leave after those discussions are ended.

Employees appreciate their manager's leadership skills, which are evident when meetings consider the needs of those who attend them. Employees like it when meetings are focused and include only those who need to be there. They will recognize that the manager respects their time and will be more likely to want to attend meetings that affect them.

Meeting Frequency

The type of meeting can dictate how often it is held. For example, many managers want regularly scheduled staff meetings. These tend to be information meetings that provide attendees with timely updates about revenue, promotional campaigns, customer-related issues, and general information. These meetings also offer an opportunity to recognize teams and individuals for work well done.

Managers should not normally mix too many types of meetings into a single meeting session. First, it is unlikely that the same individuals will need to be involved in discussions about multiple topics. Also, the meeting might be very long. It is usually better to have shorter meetings focused on similar issues and objectives than to combine a number of items into one longer meeting.

Developing the Agenda

The next step is to develop the meeting agenda based on its objectives. An **agenda** is a list of topics that will be considered at a meeting. The topics are created by considering the meeting's objectives and any input gathered from participants. The agenda becomes the road map for conducting the meeting. A sample meeting agenda is shown in *Exhibit 8.3*.

Meeting managers must consider the following items when they plan an agenda:

- Name or type of meeting—for example, staff, status, progress, or budget.
- Date, time, and location of meeting.
- Names of persons who should attend.

Manager's Memo

The sample weekly staff meeting agenda shown in *Exhibit 8.3* is formal hard copy. Some managers, especially in small operations, may hand-write agenda topics. Also, they may not need to list attendees if, for example, the meeting involves all department personnel who are well known to the manager.

What other suggestions can you make for a meeting agenda that is practical for managers in small-volume operations?

Exhibit 8.3

SAMPLE MEETING AGENDA

WEEKLY STAFF MEETING

Date:	10/11/12
Time:	4:00–4:30 p.m.
Location:	Banquet room
Attendees:	Jesus Fernando, Jorgé Hernandez, Kristy Lee, Lawrence Towns, Clayton Smith, Janet White, Tony Zardini
Materials:	Ideas for new menu items
Meeting objective:	Update service staff about reception details, new menu items, and vacation schedules

Agenda Topics	Presenter	Time
Review of previous items	Jorgé Hernandez	5 minutes
Overview of meeting	Jorgé Hernandez	5 minutes
Item 1: Schedule for Wright wedding reception	Jorgé Hernandez	5 minutes
Item 2: New items for winter menu	Tony Zardini	5 minutes
Item 3: Vacation scheduling for November and December	Clayton Smith	10 minutes

Action item: #3: Clayton to collect all vacation requests before 11/17 and develop tentative vacation schedule before 11/22.

Next staff meeting: 10/18/12

THINK ABOUT IT . . .

Some informal meetings may not require documenting attendees. Other meetings may do so to verify that employees received important information. When would you record or not record the names of attendees at a meeting?

- Materials needed.
- Meeting objectives.
- Agenda topics driven by the objectives. One early topic is often a review of action items from the previous meeting. For example, it may be important to determine their status or to confirm the completion of action items.
- Specific topics by presenter. If there is more than one presenter, list the specific topic each presenter will address.
- Time limit for each agenda item. Sharing information takes less time than discussion or activities. Schedule the time required while keeping the meeting as short as possible.
- Action items. Assignments, if any, will need to be made with specifics including who will be assigned, what each person is supposed to do, and when the assignment should be completed.
- Date and time of the next meeting, if necessary.

Manager's Memo

Among the types of meetings employees typically dislike are those scheduled on an ongoing basis. For example, department heads may meet with the manager once every two weeks to discuss "what's going on." Problems sometimes arise when there is no real news to share. Managers may think that other attendees will conclude they are not doing their job, and others will think they are letting their team down. This situation results in each manager making a report on topics that are not of real concern.

Since time is so important and because managers and their team members are so busy, those planning meetings should consider a policy of "need to know" rather than "nice to know" and schedule meetings only when there is important information to share.

Scheduling the Meeting

After the meeting's objectives and agenda are planned, its time, length, and date become important. Since the time for each agenda activity is known, it should be relatively easy to determine how much time will be required for the meeting.

Few operations have dedicated rooms for meetings, although properties with banquet spaces might use that space. The meeting's time and location become important concerns because employee meetings may need to be held in the dining room using dining-room tables and chairs. This limits most meetings and certainly those involving a large number of employees to times when customers are not being served. Can meetings be scheduled before customers arrive or after customers leave? How is a meeting time scheduled when a large number of employees must attend, and they work on different shifts and different days? These are the kinds of challenges that managers face when they schedule meetings.

Managers must consider the schedules of the attendees and their own time requirements when deciding the best meeting time. For example, the amount of expected business will be an important factor for all meetings. Employees who may spend relatively little pre-prep time on normal shifts may be very busy preparing for other shifts with many more expected customers. Meetings scheduled during these times cannot be successful.

If there are some participants who must attend the meeting, managers will need to schedule the meeting for times they are available, and this sometimes requires that multiple meetings be scheduled. Once details are finalized, managers need to complete and distribute the meeting agenda to the participants along with any other meeting materials.

Before-Meeting Activities and Assignments

Meeting planners must determine whether there are any before-meeting activities that must be completed by the participants. These activities can range from selecting, duplicating, and circulating reading materials that will be discussed, to requirements that some attendees complete tasks and report the results at the meeting.

These questions can help determine the type of before-meeting activities needed:

- What pre-activity or assignment needs to be completed?
- Does the activity need to be completed before the meeting, or can it be done during the meeting?
- Does this activity support one of the objectives of the meeting?
- Will all participants need to complete the activity? If not, who must do so?
- How much time is needed to complete the activity?
- What knowledge and materials are required to do the activity?
- Is follow-up on the pre-assignment included in the meeting agenda?

After the manager has determined the need for any before-meeting activities or assignments, applicable information can be included and distributed with the agenda. The manager may want to indicate why the activity is needed and, if necessary, how participants with assignments should contact the meeting planner if there are questions.

Exhibit 8.4

CONDUCTING EFFECTIVE MEETINGS

Focus on the Meeting Leader

The key to effective meetings centers on the person who is conducting it, so it is important to understand the role that a meeting facilitator can play. A meeting **facilitator** is someone who runs a meeting. Whether the manager serves as the facilitator or asks someone else to manage the meeting, a facilitator's major responsibility is to keep the meeting focused and moving toward its objectives (*Exhibit 8.4*).

THINK ABOUT IT . . .

"Meetings don't go off topic. People do." How does stating the purpose of the meeting at its beginning and throughout the meeting as necessary help in focusing the conversation?

A meeting facilitator has other responsibilities as well:

- Determining whether any issues need to be tabled. An agenda item is **tabled** when it is held over for another meeting.
- Informing the group when the time allowed for an agenda item is over and it is time to move on.
- Refocusing the group if the discussion breaks into several different conversations.
- Managing the discussion of sensitive topics in a neutral manner.
- Preventing anyone from dominating the meeting or being ignored.
- Summarizing agenda points.

Managers can do several things to help ensure a successful meeting:

- Arrive early to ensure the meeting room is set up properly and that all materials needed for the meeting are ready.
- Have a sign-in sheet available, if needed, to create a record of who attended the meeting.
- Start on time. Do not punish employees who show up on time. After missing the start of a few meetings, those who show up late will likely get the message. If not, the manager should discuss the need for prompt attendance with those employees.
- Use and follow an agenda. Meeting participants become discouraged when a lot of time and effort are put into the creation of an agenda and then it is not used. Write the agenda on a flipchart or board and have extra printed copies available for employees who might have forgotten to bring theirs.
- Understand and refer to the objectives of the meeting. A brief reference to the objectives at the beginning of the meeting can help participants focus on them.
- Refer to items on the agenda. These items can be discussed in order and acted on.
- End on time. Attendees appreciate it when the meeting stays on track and ends at the scheduled time. When managers consistently end meetings on time, they are doing a lot to address one of the primary reasons that employees do not like meetings. Managers are showing the meeting participants that they know time is valuable and they respect the need for attendees to get back to their primary responsibilities.
- Use evaluation information for improvement. Employees appreciate a manager who tries to become more efficient at running meetings. Feedback about how meetings can be improved can be very helpful in better ensuring that they accomplish their purpose.

Manager's Memo

It may be strange to think about warm-up activities designed to introduce employees to each other. Employees in many establishments already know each other because they work together. However, in some large operations where employees always work the same basic schedule, it is more likely that some employees may not know others. Also, there may be times when managers and supervisors from different properties in a chain restaurant organization meet to consider common concerns.

What types of warm-up activities, if any, would you as a manager use in meetings for employees who already know each other?

Warm-Up Activities

Another important planning step involves determining whether any warm-up activities should be conducted at the start of the meeting. A **warm-up activity** is a quick exercise that prepares people to focus on the meeting and its objectives. If one is to be used, it is important to select something related to the meeting agenda and objectives so the activity has a useful impact on the participants.

Numerous warm-up activities can be designed to begin a meeting:

- **Introduction activities:** In these activities, participants pair up, ask each other a few questions, and then share this information with the group. This type of activity can be very useful when participants do not know each other.
- **Appreciation activities:** These activities can be used at recognition and reward meetings to show employees that their managers respect them and notice what they do.
- **Competitive activities:** These can be used at meetings involving sales campaigns or promotional contests in which managers reward teams with a prize for coming up with the best creative solution.
- **Team-building activities:** These can be used during various stages of team development to ensure the team is optimizing its performance. Chapter 5 stated that special meetings to build teams are important in the team development process. In these cases, team-building activities would not be used for warm-up purposes. Instead, they would be an important part of the meeting's objective.

Establishing Ground Rules

The meeting facilitator should begin the meeting by explaining his or her role and reviewing the agenda to ensure all participants know what will be discussed. While the agenda will have been circulated, experienced meeting managers know that some participants may not have carefully reviewed it.

Establishing ground rules is a critical part of every effective meeting. **Ground rules** are rules about how meetings are run, how participants should interact, and what behavior is acceptable. They may cover a wide range of concerns:

- Promptness
- Courtesy
- Breaks
- Interruptions
- Rotation of routine tasks such as meeting minute recorder or flipchart recorder
- Question-and-answer periods

Manager's Memo

Employee contests cause concern for many managers. They know an important key to success is that employees work together as a team. Some contests, however, make employees compete with each other. For example, servers may compete for the highest customer check average. One server wins and the other servers lose, and this does not emphasize teamwork.

An alternative is offering contests in which all employees on a team can win. For example, consider a contest in which every server with a customer check average above a certain amount, or who sells a certain number of bottles of wine per week or special desserts per shift, can "win."

When this type of contest is developed, team members have incentives to work together. Then recognition meetings can celebrate team victories and not embarrass employees who do not win.

THINK ABOUT IT . . .

What would you do if you were a meeting facilitator and realized you will not have time to cover the remaining agenda items? What might you do to help prevent this problem from occurring at future meetings?

New ground rules do not have to be developed for each meeting. In practice, there may not be a formal discussion about ground rules. Instead, ground rules develop over time, and procedures used in the past become the **status quo:** how things are normally done. Then meeting participants know what should and should not be done during meetings.

One important ground rule could address what to do about ideas or topics brought up that are important but cannot be addressed during the meeting. Perhaps, for example, there is not enough information or time, the right people may not be present, or the subject may not directly relate to the agenda topics. These items can be deferred to a future meeting when they can be adequately discussed. It is a good idea to note these topics as action items in the meeting minutes so they will be remembered. Then they can be added to the agenda for a future meeting.

Another ground rule that is essential to an effective meeting is setting time limits for discussions and sticking to them (*Exhibit 8.5*). If this is not done, the chances increase that there will not be enough time for items that follow on the agenda. Then the meeting facilitator has a tough choice to make: extend the existing meeting or place the items not discussed on the agenda for a future meeting. Neither of these alternatives may be a good one, especially if the items not discussed are of great importance.

Managing the Meeting

Throughout the meeting, each agenda item should be presented in the order it is listed. Depending on the type of action the item requires, the group should either discuss it, make a decision, or simply listen to the information being presented. Following each item, a question-and-answer period should be

Exhibit 8.5

allowed to ensure that everyone attending has understood the item. If the question-and-answer time becomes too long, some meeting facilitators add the topic "follow-up discussion" as an item for a future agenda.

During the discussion of some agenda items, action items will be identified. An **action item** is something that is part of an agenda item that requires some type of action. For example, an action item for a budget meeting might be to contact a vendor to learn the cost of a specific type of new equipment, or to contact the host of a planned banquet event to obtain additional information about his or her expectations.

The action item would be identified during the meeting and would be assigned to a specific person to collect and bring the information to a future meeting. The person who is given the action item to complete will then gather the information and include it in a report by an assigned deadline, or be prepared to discuss the new information at a specific meeting.

Meeting minutes will need to be taken at many meetings, especially when discussions and actions must be recalled for future activities and future meetings. Meeting **minutes** are a record of what is decided, what is accomplished, and what action items are agreed upon at meetings.

Meeting minutes can answer a number of questions:

- When was the meeting?
- Who attended the meeting?
- Who did not attend the meeting (if important)?
- What topics were discussed?
- What was decided?
- What actions were agreed upon?
- Who is to complete the actions and by when?
- Were materials distributed? If so, are copies available?
- Is there anything special that readers of the minutes should know or do?
- When and where is the next meeting?

It is probably not possible or even important to take down every point made during a meeting. Instead, the person taking minutes should concentrate on major issues and decisions. Brief notes about these matters can be made and then a more complete summary might be developed later. This should be done as soon as possible after the meeting so nothing will be forgotten.

OPEN FOR BUSINESS

RESTAURANT TECHNOLOGY

Technology has had a dramatic impact on meetings. For example, agenda drafts can be sent by email for comment and revision before a final draft is developed.

Presentation software can be used during information meetings, and electronic white boards or flipcharts allow information to be electronically recorded as it is written.

Persons taking minutes can use laptops and send minutes to attendees' stations almost before they return from the meeting. Attendees can use electronic copies that are easy to organize and file.

Meeting attendees who have been assigned action items can email their findings rather than make a presentation at a future meeting.

Almost every aspect of a meeting can be enhanced by technology. However, a facilitator must still keep meetings on track, and attendees must still provide creative ideas for decisions.

Exhibit 8.6

SAMPLE MINUTES FORMAT (BODY OF MINUTES)

Topic	Discussion	Action Item or Action to Be Taken	Person(s) Responsible	Timeline or Deadline

Exhibit 8.6 shows a possible format for the body of minutes. A form like this might be developed with the topics already included before the meeting begins (topics are included in the meeting agenda). Then notes can be taken about the discussion, action items, and persons responsible for each action.

Closing the Meeting

After all the agenda items have been considered, the meeting will come to a close. Final activities include reviewing all action items to ensure everyone understands what they are and who will be responsible for carrying them out. The meeting facilitator should briefly summarize the meeting for the group. By noting the decisions made, future agenda items, and any other issues, the manager gives the participants a chance to indicate their thoughts about the meeting's results. Before ending the meeting, the manager should thank the participants for attending and for their contributions. If necessary, the date and time for the next meeting should be determined.

MEETING EVALUATION AND FOLLOW-UP

The only way for managers to improve their ability to conduct meetings is to obtain feedback from participants. The purpose of a meeting evaluation is to learn what worked well in the meeting and to change things that did not work as effectively.

The evaluation can either use a form that participants complete, or it can be a feedback session in which the manager asks attendees a series of questions and writes down their responses. Whatever method he or she uses, the evaluation should be short and concise. *Exhibit 8.7* provides an example of questions a manager might ask in a meeting evaluation.

A final step in the meeting process is to write and circulate the meeting minutes. Ideally, the recorder should complete the minutes within a day or two and then distribute them to the participants. The minutes will then serve as a reference for participants to remember discussions, decisions made, and actions to be taken. For those who could not attend the meeting, the minutes will enable them to learn what happened.

Exhibit 8.7

SAMPLE MEETING EVALUATION FORM

MEETING EVALUATION SURVEY

FOR Weekly Preshift Staff Meeting

DATE October 11

Please take some time to fill out this short survey about today's meeting. Your feedback and comments will help us improve future meetings.

The meeting today was:

Unproductive	①	②	③	④	⑤	Productive
Not focused	①	②	③	④	⑤	Focused
Pace was too slow	①	②	③	④	⑤	Pace was too fast
Blaming individuals	①	②	③	④	⑤	Looking for solutions
Unreceptive to questions	①	②	③	④	⑤	Responsive to questions

Did we do the right things? How effective was the meeting?

How productive was the meeting?

What could we do differently to make it better next time?

When you are finished, please return this form to Janet White.

SUMMARY

1. **Explain the need for meetings to be effectively managed.**

   Managers facilitate information, problem-solving, brainstorming, and action meetings. All meetings must be effectively managed to minimize problems. Challenges include leaders not preparing, excessive and long meetings, lack of focus, undefined objectives, and topics not applicable to objectives. Other problems involve failing to solicit input from all attendees or ensure that the information is clear.

2. **Describe procedures for planning effective meetings.**

   Strategies for planning meetings include defining the objectives to be accomplished, using input from the management team and employees.

The meeting agenda should be based on its objectives and should include specific items with time limitations for discussion and action. The meeting should then be scheduled and any pre-meeting activities delegated.

3. **Explain procedures for conducting effective meetings.**

   The meeting facilitator is responsible for ensuring the meeting is effective, and especially that discussions focus on agenda items. Keeping the meeting on schedule is also necessary.

   Some meetings begin with warm-up activities to prepare attendees to focus on the meeting and its objectives. Ground rules must be established and followed to ensure that the behavior of all participants is acceptable. Each agenda item should be presented in the order listed, and action plans must be determined for those items that require follow-up. The meeting can be closed with a review of action items and a summary of decisions made. If necessary, a date and time for the next meeting can be announced.

4. **Suggest procedures required to evaluate and follow up on meetings.**

   Feedback is required to determine how to improve meetings in the future. A final step in the process is to write and circulate minutes. They will serve as a reference to remember meeting discussions, decisions, and action items.

APPLICATION EXERCISE

You are a manager at the Hosh Avenue Grill. The establishment has been experiencing some theft for the past three weeks, and much of it may have occurred during the busiest hours of operation. The items stolen include frozen meat, prewrapped items placed at the register for guests to purchase, and items received but not yet placed in storage areas.

Items taken from inventory are matched with orders one week after the sale. The prewrapped items are kept in inventory until placed on the counter based on the par levels desired. Note: *Par levels are the quantity of products the operation wants to keep on hand at all times.* Employees enter and exit through an employee entrance, and they are not allowed to bring packages to work or take out packages when they leave. Personal items are kept in employee lockers.

The establishment's accountant has provided a report that indicates the costs of products that should have been used to generate sales. There is a difference of more than $500 over the past three weeks.

Your plan is to ask a team of employees to meet as quickly as possible to try to resolve this problem. You want to conduct a meeting that helps identify where the problem is occurring and how to stop it. However, the problem may be caused by one or more of the attendees.

Break into groups of three or four and complete the following tasks:

- Identify objectives to accomplish during the first meeting. Identify at least three issues to discuss.
- Write objectives that address each of the issues.
- Determine the most appropriate type of meeting for accomplishing these objectives.
- Create an agenda for the meeting.
- Identify employees or positions to participate in the meeting.
- Identify how long you think the first meeting should last.
- What materials, if any, would you distribute either before or during the meeting?

REVIEW YOUR LEARNING

Select the best answer for each question.

1. An emergency meeting is an example of what type of meeting?

A. Problem-solving meeting
B. Brainstorming meeting
C. Information meeting
D. Action meeting

2. Which item drives the meeting planning process?

A. The amount of time to be spent at the meeting
B. The objectives established for the meeting
C. The employees who will be in attendance
D. The employees assigned to present reports

3. Who should be invited to attend a meeting?

A. All employees from affected departments
B. Staff members critical to the meeting's purpose
C. Senior managers and supervisors
D. Staff members who expect to be invited

4. Why are meeting time limits for agenda items important?

A. They must enable all agenda items to be discussed.
B. They must enable all attendees to say everything they wish to say.
C. They must enable most items to be covered in one meeting.
D. They must be established according to Robert's Rules of Order.

5. What is the most important responsibility of a meeting facilitator?

A. Ensuring that those with the most knowledge speak the most
B. Stating positions on agenda items and seeking agreement
C. Maintaining the objective-based focus of the meeting
D. Ensuring that meetings always remain on schedule

6. What should meeting ground rules address?

A. Specified length of time for meetings
B. Who should normally conduct meetings
C. Expected behavior for meeting attendees
D. Type of agenda items that should be covered

7. What should meeting leaders do about important topics brought up that do not relate to the agenda?

A. Include them when planning a future meeting.
B. Discuss them immediately, depending on urgency.
C. Ask attendees to vote about the time frame for discussion.
D. Discuss them if they affect all attendees at the current meeting.

8. Which is true about a meeting's action items?

A. Action items are considered before topics not requiring action.
B. They should be discussed during at least two meetings.
C. Someone must be assigned to follow up action items.
D. There must be an action item for every agenda topic.

9. Who should summarize the meeting when it ends?

A. The person who takes the minutes
B. The person who facilitates the meeting
C. Each attendee from his or her viewpoint
D. The most senior-level employee present

10. Ideally, within how many days after a meeting should its minutes be distributed?

A. 1 or 2
B. 3 or 4
C. 5 or 6
D. 7 or 8

9 Leaders Manage Compensation Programs

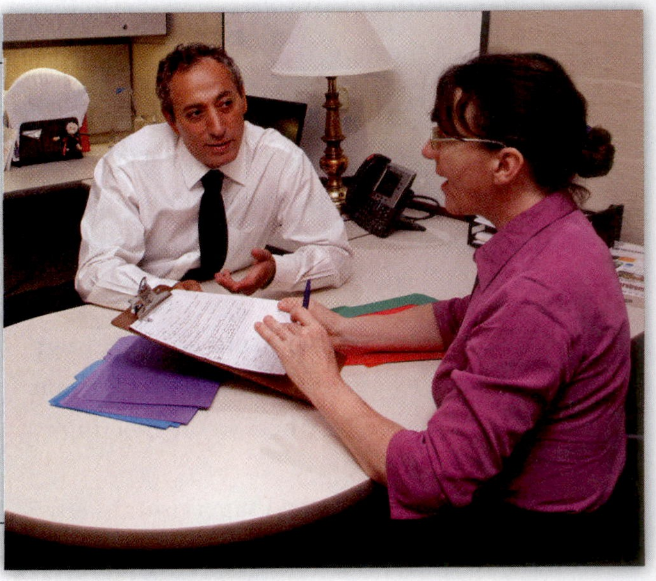

INSIDE THIS CHAPTER

- Overview of Compensation Challenges
- A Close Look at Compensation
- Federal and State Compensation Laws
- Factors Affecting Compensation
- Compensation Policies and Procedures
- Performance Appraisals and Compensation
- Payroll Services and Record Keeping

CHAPTER LEARNING OBJECTIVES

After completing this chapter, you should be able to:

- Explain how managers must balance the concerns of owners, employees, and themselves as they develop and manage compensation programs.
- Describe the three major components of compensation: wages, salaries, and benefits.
- Describe major requirements of federal and state compensation laws.
- Describe several of the most important factors that affect an operation's compensation cost.
- Identify basic procedures for developing and controlling restaurant and foodservice compensation policies and procedures.
- Explain how performance appraisals relate to compensation.
- Review procedures for processing payroll-related information and other information required for employee files.

KEY TERMS

anniversary date (employment), p. 247

benefits, p. 230

bonus (compensation), p. 230

collective bargaining agreement, p. 239

compensation, p. 230

competitive employers, p. 231

cost of living (COL), p. 246

defined benefit pension, p. 233

defined contributions, p. 233

Equal Pay Act, p. 234

exempt employee, p. 231

Fair Labor Standards Act (FLSA), p. 234

garnishment, p. 242

ghost employee, p. 250

gross pay, p. 230

Medicare, p. 232

merit pay plan, p. 242

outsource, p. 248

performance standard, p. 243

prime cost, p. 231

social security, p. 232

tip (compensation), p. 232

unemployment insurance, p. 232

withholding tax, p. 232

workers' compensation, p. 232

CASE STUDY

"We may have a problem, ladies and gentlemen, and I hope this meeting will be the start of our process to resolve it," said Vernette, the manager of Seashore Hills Restaurant.

"Well, I'll start the conversation because I know what it is about," said Federico, the kitchen manager. "I overheard two of my cooks talking about the wages received by some of their friends who are cooks in some of our competitors' restaurants, and it seems like our pay rates are pretty low."

After further discussion, Vernette heard similar stories from the head bartender and the dining-room manager.

"I might be taking too simple an approach on this," Vernette said, "but I wonder if our restaurant should be at the lower, middle, or higher end of the pay scale when compared to other restaurants?"

1. How would you respond to Vernette if you were one of her managers?
2. In addition to considering pay increases, what else can Vernette and her team do to address the compensation challenge?

THINK ABOUT IT . . .

Would you accept another job for 25 cents more per hour, $50 more per month, or $500 more per year? What other factors, aside from money, impact your decision to take a job?

OVERVIEW OF COMPENSATION CHALLENGES

Compensation is a topic of significant importance to almost everyone who works in any organization, including restaurant and foodservice operations. **Compensation** involves all of the financial, or money, and nonfinancial, or nonmoney, payments and rewards given to employees in return for the work they do.

The world of compensation management is much more difficult than it might appear. One may think, for example, that if an employee is paid $10 per hour and works 8 hours, it is easy to figure out that the employee has earned $80:

8 hours × $10 per hour = $80

In one respect, that is correct. The employee's **gross pay** would be $80, but that is the amount paid excluding contributions for payroll, social security, taxes, and other required employer payments. Compensation is also made more challenging by laws that impact what employees must be paid in certain situations.

In addition to gross pay, compensation includes **benefits:** employee health care, dental and vision insurance, vacation and sick leave pay, retirement contributions, and other benefits that may be paid wholly or in part by the employer to benefit the employees. Much effort is required, for example, to determine the best health insurance plan. These ever-increasing costs require decisions about who will be covered and how much the covered employees and the employer should pay to participate in the program.

How compensation programs are managed impacts the operation's culture as well as its profitability. Each major stakeholder will have concerns about compensation that pull in different directions:

- Employees want maximum compensation for the work they do. The more they do and the greater their responsibilities, the more compensation they think they deserve.
- The owner, whether an individual or a large corporation with investors, wants the maximum amount of profit. That goal is reasonable because investments must be repaid, expansion may be of interest, and there must be some reward for the financial risk taken to operate the business. If too much is spent on labor or on other costs, profit will be reduced accordingly.

The manager is caught between the employees and the owner. He or she wants the employees, especially the good ones, to be well paid. Also, the manager works hard to train and build a team and does not want to lose team members to other businesses that pay more. At the same time, some managers are paid a bonus based on meeting or exceeding specific financial goals. A **bonus** is an agreed-upon amount of additional compensation to be paid when specific financial goals are met.

Compensation is a sensitive issue from everyone's point of view. It is important that policies and procedures be developed and used consistently to manage compensation correctly and fairly.

A CLOSE LOOK AT COMPENSATION

There are two types of costs in any business: controllable and noncontrollable. Controllable costs are those that management can control. Noncontrollable costs are those that management cannot control. Labor is a controllable cost. It includes salaries, wages, tips, bonuses and merit pay, and commissions. At first, it may seem that some types of compensation such as for social security and unemployment compensation are not controllable because laws require that they be paid. However, they really are controllable because managers made the decision to hire the employees for which these types of compensation must be paid.

Labor costs are one of a restaurant or foodservice operation's two **prime costs:** the largest categories of costs. The other prime cost is product purchases. Labor costs must be carefully managed from establishing pay rates, to selecting and training employees, to scheduling hours of operation.

There are three broad types of labor costs, and each was defined in Chapter 6:

- **Wages:** The money paid to employees on the basis of the number of hours they work.
- **Salary:** The money paid to an employee on a per week, per month, or another basis that does not depend on the number of hours worked.
- **Benefits:** The money paid indirectly in support of employees for purposes such as vacation, sick leave, and health insurance, and to meet governmental requirements.

Wages, Tips, and Salaries

Employees in entry-level positions are typically paid wages. The amount of wages to be paid is influenced by numerous factors including federal and state laws, and it is also influenced by the wage rates of **competitive employers** who hire the same type of employees. It is important to note that a competitive employer may not be in the restaurant and foodservice industry. For example, retail stores and other service businesses often employ persons who could work in restaurant or foodservice positions (*Exhibit 9.1*).

Exhibit 9.1

Most salaried employees in restaurant and foodservice operations work in supervisory, managerial, or professional positions. They are paid on an annual or other basis and are generally exempt from overtime pay provisions. An **exempt employee** is one who does not qualify for overtime pay according to the Fair Labor Standards Act (FLSA). This federal law is discussed later in the chapter. Salaried employees receive the same amount of pay regardless of the number of working hours in the pay period. Requirements about rest breaks for salaried employees depend on the state. Salaried employees may be covered under other federal laws including the Americans with Disabilities Act, the Civil Rights Act of 1964, and Occupational Safety and Health Administration (OSHA) rules.

In addition to wages, many dining-room employees receive **tips:** money paid by customers in return for providing services. Tips are generally subject to **withholding taxes:** money taken from an employee's wages by an employer and paid directly to the government. Employees must report all tip income. Their employer, in turn, must collect income tax, employee's social security tax, and employee Medicare tax based on the tips reported by employees. Typically, these amounts are deducted from an employee's wages. Employers must generally ensure that the total income reported during any pay period is at least equal to 8 percent of the total revenue for the period. Since tips are considered employee income, they affect the minimum wage rate that must be paid to tipped employees.

Benefits

Restaurant and foodservice employees typically receive different salaries and wages based on their position and length of employment. However, some benefits are available to all full-time employees who have worked at the operation for a specific amount of time.

Some benefit programs are mandatory and are required by federal and state law:

- **Unemployment insurance:** A temporary source of income to eligible persons who lose their job that is funded with money paid by the employer while the person was employed.
- **Social security:** A supplemental retirement system that is funded by payroll taxes; a certain percentage of an employee's pay goes into a fund that provides benefits to current social security recipients.
- **Medicare:** A federal medical insurance program that primarily serves persons over 65 regardless of income, younger persons with disabilities, and dialysis patients. Medical bills are paid from trust funds into which covered persons have paid.
- **Workers' compensation:** A state-regulated insurance program that pays medical bills and some lost wages for employees who are injured at work or who have a work-related illness or disease.

In addition to benefits programs mandated by state and federal governments, there are numerous voluntary benefits that establishments can provide to attract and retain employees. Examples of these are shown in *Exhibit 9.2.*

Exhibit 9.2

EXAMPLES OF VOLUNTARY BENEFITS

Paid Leave for:

- Holidays and vacations
- Sick leave
- Jury duty
- Funerals
- Military
- Personal reasons including maternity and paternity

Unpaid Leave For:

- Maternity and paternity

Life Insurance Benefits:

- Employer-financed
- Partly employer-financed

Medical and Dental Care Benefits:

- Employee coverage:
  - Employer-financed
  - Partly employer-financed
- Family coverage:
  - Employer-financed
  - Partly employer-financed

Other Insurance Benefits:

- Sickness or accidents
  - Employer-financed
  - Partly employer-financed
- Long-term disability
  - Employer-financed
  - Partly employer-financed

Retirement Benefits:

- **Defined benefit pension:** A retirement plan in which the employer sets aside a certain percentage or amount of money to pay covered employees when they retire.
  - Employer-financed
  - Partly employer-financed
- **Defined contributions:** A retirement plan in which benefits depend on the contributions made to and the results of an employee's investments in stocks, bonds, mutual funds, and other alternatives.

Other:

- Reimbursement accounts
- Flexible benefits plans

Services:

- Tuition reimbursement
- Child care
- Elder care
- Financial services
- Relocation services
- Social or recreational programs

Managers have a role to play in managing benefit programs. In large restaurant and foodservice operations and many chain organizations, human resources staff often administers the details of benefits programs. However, a manager typically has certain responsibilities:

- Considering program benefits. Establishments typically try to match benefits offered by their competitors in or outside the industry.

Manager's Memo

Many employees think their total compensation is the wages or salary they are paid. Wise managers inform their employees about the value of benefits they receive in addition to salaries and wages.

For example, the cost of mandated benefits is approximately 15% of payroll in many states. Therefore, an employee receiving an hourly wage of $10.00 is really being paid $11.50:

$10.00 per hour × 115% = $11.50 per hour

Do you think about the value of benefits when you consider how much money you really make? Do most employees?

- Conducting meetings with employees to help determine preferred benefits and to discuss existing benefits. Some of these discussions occur at orientation programs for new employees. Additional information will be found in employee handbooks.
- Analyzing costs. Benefits costs can be significant, so the alternatives must be carefully analyzed.

FEDERAL AND STATE COMPENSATION LAWS

Managers are impacted by numerous factors as they establish pay rates for their employees. Laws implemented by the federal and state governments are among the most important of these factors. As with all other laws, managers must know and carefully follow all regulations that apply to their property.

Federal Compensation Laws

Minimum wage laws must be considered when compensation rates for positions are established. The federal minimum wage law falls under the **Fair Labor Standards Act (FLSA).** This law requires employers to pay nonexempt employees a minimum wage plus overtime for any time worked over 40 hours per week. The overtime premium is the hourly rate of pay plus 50 percent (time and one-half or 150 percent of the hourly rate).

This law has broad coverage and applies to most restaurant and foodservice operations. Even if an employer does not meet the broad tests for coverage, some of its employees may be covered individually under the law. Some exceptions apply to the FLSA for workers who are disabled or others working as trainees, full-time students, youth program and student learners, and independent contractors.

Tipped employees are covered by the FLSA, and they can be paid an hourly wage below the minimum wage rate if the amount of their tips plus the wages received are at least equal to the minimum hourly wage. If the tips are insufficient, then the employer must make up the difference to bring the employee's hourly pay up to the minimum wage.

Managers must be aware of the law and other details related to compensation and ensure they are reflected in the company's compensation guidelines, policies, and procedures as needed. One way to obtain more information is to go to *www.dol.gov/whd.*

The **Equal Pay Act** administered by the U.S. Equal Employment Opportunity Commission (EEOC) requires that men and women in the same workplace be given equal pay for equal work. The jobs do not need to be identical; they must only be substantially equal. All forms of pay are covered by this law

THINK ABOUT IT . . .

Many, if not most, establishments pay their employees more than the minimum wage. Do you think that minimum wage laws are a good idea? Why or why not?

including salary, overtime pay, and benefits. If the wages are not equal between men and women, employers may not reduce the wages of either gender to equalize the pay.

Restaurant and foodservice employees are generally qualified under the federal Family and Medical Leave Act (FMLA) if they work a specific number of hours for more than 12 months in a company with more than 50 employees.

State Compensation Laws

Many states have their own minimum wage laws. Some have a higher minimum wage than the federal law, while others require minimum wages that are the same or lower (see *Exhibit 9.3*). When employees are subject to both state and federal minimum wage law, they are entitled to the law that gives them the greatest benefit.

Exhibit 9.3

MINIMUM WAGE LAWS IN THE UNITED STATES*

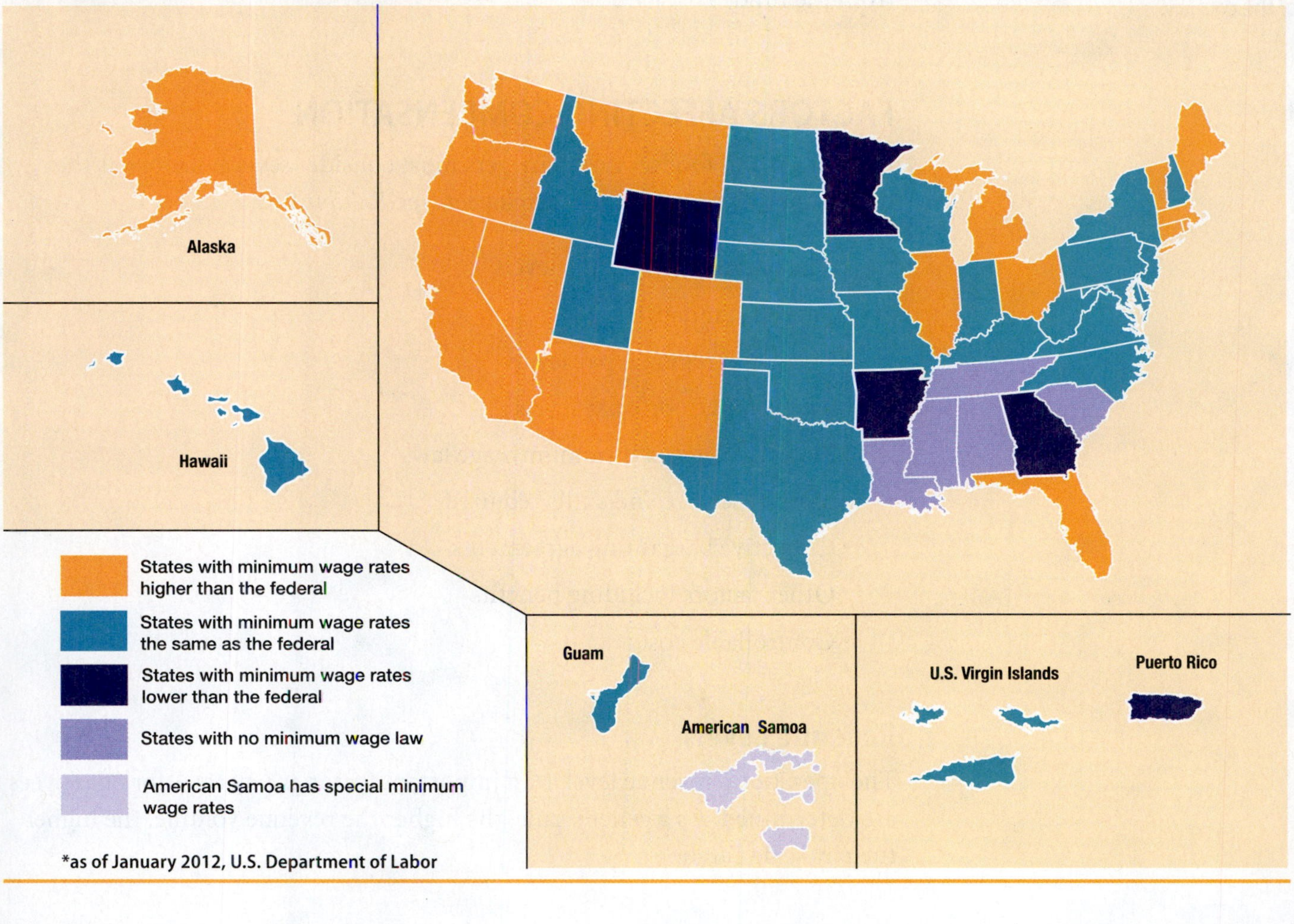

*as of January 2012, U.S. Department of Labor

Manager's Memo

Many cities and counties have adopted local living wage laws. These laws require employers receiving city contracts or city subsidies to pay wages to full-time employees that allow them to support themselves and their families at a subsistence level. Some of these laws include provisions requiring, for example, that businesses leasing land from the city or others that require city operating permits are covered by the law. Restaurant and foodservice operations would be affected by these regulations. This provides another example of a factor that can influence wages paid by managers in some areas of the country.

Workers' compensation laws are administered by the states to provide financial assistance to employees who are injured or disabled on the job. For example, California has a comprehensive state compensation program that is applicable to most employers. Its law limits the liability of the employer and employees. California law also requires employers to obtain insurance to cover potential workers' compensation claims. In addition, it sets up a fund for claims by employees whose employers have illegally failed to obtain the insurance.

Unemployment compensation programs are based on federal and state laws. They provide financial assistance for a specified time for workers whose jobs have been terminated. A combination of federal and state laws determines which employees are eligible for compensation, what amount they receive, and for how long.

Unemployment compensation programs are supported by a combination of federal and state taxes paid by employers into the fund that is used to pay employees. States base how much employers must pay on the amount of wages the employer has paid, the amount the employer has paid to the unemployment fund, and the amount the discharged employee has been paid from the fund.

FACTORS AFFECTING COMPENSATION

Restaurant and foodservice managers must consider several factors as they determine pay rates for their employees (see *Exhibit 9.4*):

- The operation's revenue levels
- Payroll standards
- Local and regional pay levels
- The competition's pay levels
- State and federal minimum wage laws
- Type of service and skills required
- Collective bargaining agreements
- Other factors including benefits
- Controllable costs

Revenue Levels

The operation's revenue level is an important factor as pay rates for employees are determined. As a general rule, the higher the revenue volume, the higher the pay scale can be.

Exhibit 9.4

FACTORS AFFECTING PAY RANGES

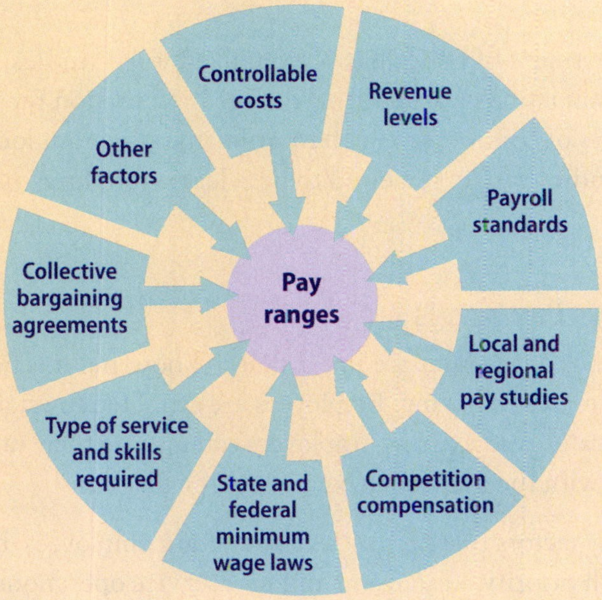

One reason for a higher pay scale is the frequent need to attract and retain a more knowledgeable and skilled team of employees. This is true for at least those in key positions such as managers, chefs, and line cooks. In other words, increased revenues in high-volume establishments yield more payroll dollars available to pay more employees and to pay higher rates to persons in several important positions.

Payroll Standards

Every operation should have a budget standard to let managers know how much of the total expected revenue can be spent for labor costs. These standards are expressed in both dollars of labor costs and in a labor cost percentage: the percentage of revenue that can be spent for labor. For example, if an operation's budget allows a 30 percent labor cost, this means that 30 percent of all revenue that is generated can be spent for compensation including benefits expenses.

When establishing pay ranges, managers must remember the total budgeted dollars available for payroll. They must also understand that these dollars are impacted by the actual amount of revenue. If they spend too much money for compensation, their budget goals will not be met. At the same time, if compensation levels are set too low, they will not be able to attract and keep the quality of employees they need to be successful.

Manager's Memo

Restaurant and foodservice managers know about a concept called economy of scale. This relates to the idea that there is typically a reduced cost per customer resulting from increased production because of operating efficiencies. For example, it takes the same amount of time to clean a steam kettle whether it was used to produce 25 portions of beef stew or 125 portions.

Do you believe that the labor cost per customer is normally lower in an establishment that serves 1,000 meals per day than in a similar establishment with a similar menu that serves 100 customers per day?

MANAGER'S MATH

Assume that Apple Orchard Restaurant has a budgeted (payroll) labor cost of 30% for a specific month and that its revenue for that month is $180,000. What should its monthly payroll cost be?

Revenue × Labor cost percentage = Monthly payroll cost

If revenue increases to $200,000, how much could be spent on the payroll?

Answers:
$180,000 × 0.30 = $54,000
$200,000 × 0.30 = $60,000

Local and Regional Pay Levels

Another factor to consider when establishing pay ranges relates to the going pay rates in the area. Wages for the same job vary widely across the country.

The U.S. Department of Labor has regionalized wage studies, and State Restaurant Associations normally have wage information for their state. Local chambers of commerce may have information about local pay rates. All of these studies can be reviewed to help learn about pay rates for specific areas.

Competition's Pay Levels

Regional and local wage rates are important to know, but it is best to know what the competition is paying. Employees are attracted to establishments with high pay rates, and existing employees often share their rates of compensation with their friends who are looking for jobs.

There are many factors that help attract and retain employees, but wages are normally a high priority. Restaurant and foodservice operations must offer competitive compensation to recruit the quality of employees needed to operate a successful business.

Manager's Memo

The Internet can help managers learn about compensation rates in the restaurant and foodservice industry. For example, type "restaurant wage rates" into a search engine and review some of the resources that you discover. Also, go to the Web site of the Bureau of Labor Statistics (*www.bls.gov*) and type "restaurant wages" in the search box on the home page.

Neither of these suggestions will provide detailed salary and wage payment data for your specific community or neighborhood. They will, however, provide some general information against which you may be able to benchmark.

Knowledge and Skills Required

Establishments with high customer check averages typically offer menu items and service styles that are more difficult to provide. This can require higher levels of employee knowledge and skills.

For example, the chef in a fine-dining restaurant requires a different set of skills than a shift leader at a quick-service restaurant (*Exhibit 9.5*). The knowledge and skills needed to be successful in each position are very different. Therefore, the pay range for each position must match the amount of education, training, and experience necessary to do that job. Pay ranges must increase as the standards of production and service rise.

Collective Bargaining Agreements

In some cases, an employee union represents restaurant or foodservice employees. Then a team of managers and another team representing employees will negotiate the pay scale for each job represented by the union.

When the negotiators reach agreement, the union members vote on the proposed contract. If both management and labor agree to it then the pay

Exhibit 9.5

ranges, along with other working conditions, become a binding contract or a collective bargaining agreement. A **collective bargaining agreement** is a legally binding contract between managers and the employees represented by a union. It defines employment conditions including wages and procedures to resolve disputes.

THINK ABOUT IT . . .

One establishment pays a high wage but has a "my way or the highway" attitude. Another establishment has a lower compensation rate but has a positive work environment. Which would you rather work for? Why?

Other Factors

Benefits are another factor that can influence compensation plans. An operation with an extensive program could have a lower pay range than an operation that offers little or no voluntary benefits. Some employees will work for less money if, for example, a company-paid health insurance plan is in effect. Managers offering benefits not available from their competitors must ensure that potential and existing employees know about these benefits and their financial value.

A property's location can be another factor. For example, an establishment that is not close to public transportation may have to pay more than a competitor that is. Operations located in downtown areas may have to subsidize employees who pay for parking, and this factor would influence compensation levels.

Operations Need Specific Pay Plans

There is no "one size fits all" plan when it comes to determining pay scale ranges. Even chain operations have different pay scales for different parts of the country. All of the factors just discussed should be considered before a pay policy is established. When the pay range is established, it must be fair for the employer and the employee.

After pay ranges are developed, most organizations review compensation guidelines annually. Inflation, changes in the marketplace, and economic forces can all affect an employee pay scale. By reviewing these annually, the operation will be better able to stay current with competitors and retain satisfied employees.

COMPENSATION POLICIES AND PROCEDURES

If there is one key word for establishing employee compensation policies and procedures, the word would have to be *fair*. Compensation management must be fair to the employees, the employers, and the managers. Plans must be consistently administered with equal consideration for all parties.

Compensation policies should be open and known to all concerned. Numerous problems can occur when information about pay scales and how they are determined is kept secret. While an individual's actual pay rate should be confidential, the pay ranges for the operation's various positions should be known.

Control Process for Compensation Policies

Policies and procedures for employee compensation must be controlled just like those for any other management concern. A typical control process for compensation policies and procedures is shown in *Exhibit 9.6*.

Exhibit 9.6

TYPICAL COMPENSATION CONTROL PROCESS

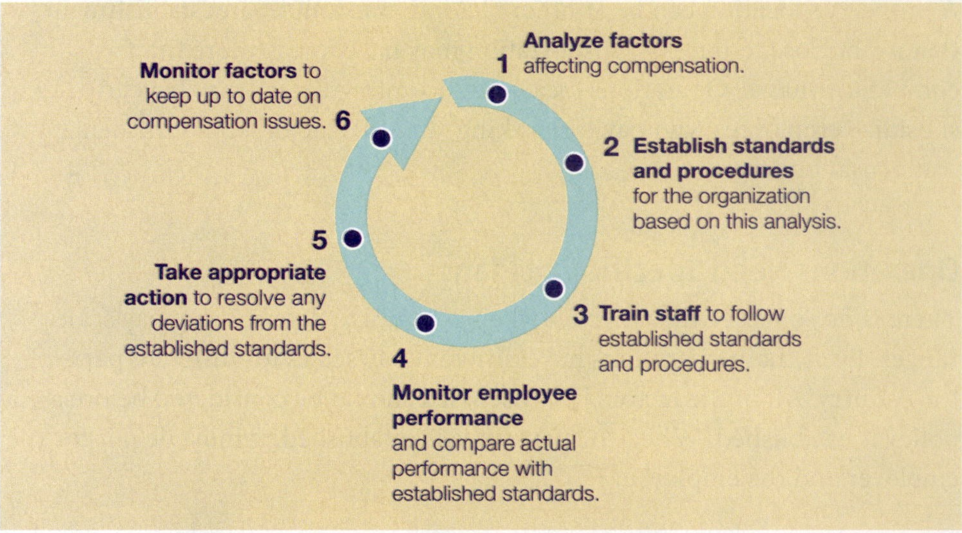

1 Analyze factors affecting compensation.
2 Establish standards and procedures for the organization based on this analysis.
3 Train staff to follow established standards and procedures.
4 Monitor employee performance and compare actual performance with established standards.
5 Take appropriate action to resolve any deviations from the established standards.
6 Monitor factors to keep up to date on compensation issues.

Exhibit 9.6 shows six steps:

- **Step 1:** Analyze factors affecting compensation. Some factors affecting compensation were discussed previously. The rates, once determined, will then change based on changing economic conditions and rates paid by other businesses that compete for the same employees. The analysis of pay rates in the community should be ongoing.
- **Step 2:** Establish standards and procedures based on the compensation analysis. Rates of pay and benefits must be determined. Numerous policies are necessary to ensure that compensation is managed consistently. Priority must be given to this task because of the numerous laws that must be followed and the concerns that can arise if employees view the management of compensation to be unfair.
- **Step 3:** Train staff to follow established standards and procedures. This training should begin when new employees attend orientation sessions. Information should also be provided during performance reviews if this is when employees are notified about pay increases. The employee handbook should detail compensation policies, and they should be updated as they change.
- **Step 4:** Monitor employee performance and compare actual performance with established standards. Each department will likely have a labor budget that identifies how much can be spent during the budget period. Most restaurant and foodservice operations require managers to seek approval about pay raises from their own manager, who typically has a big-picture overview of the operation's labor expense goals. If this policy is in place, monitoring of pay raises is relatively simple.

  Managers must also be concerned about the cost of benefits. They will likely spend time negotiating with providers, and they must consider the impact of rising costs on benefits that can be controlled by the property. Professional associations such as the National Restaurant Association provide members with updates on changes in federal or state laws that impact the cost of benefits.
- **Step 5:** Take actions to resolve any deviations from the established standards. These actions begin when budgets are developed and policies are established because these tools set the standards against which actual performance will be monitored. Employees must receive the pay to which they are entitled, and labor costs should not exceed budget standards. Problems that are noted must be resolved as quickly as possible to minimize unnecessary costs.
- **Step 6:** Monitor factors to keep up to date on compensation issues. This step is really the same as Step 1; compensation management is an ongoing responsibility. It involves much more than signing a contract for healthcare coverage or granting a pay raise to an employee for the next 12 months.

Manager's Memo

Assume a manager in a high-volume establishment grants an employee a pay increase of $25 per month. This will amount to an increase of $300 per year:

12 months × $25 per month = $300

The manager should consider that the pay increase is really much more. For example, if the employee remains with the operation for 10 years, the $25 a month increase amounts to $3,000:

10 years × $300 per year = $3,000

Managers must think of the long-term implications of many pay rate decisions. As with any financial decision, the increased expense should be offset by the value of the employee's contribution that is equal to or exceeds the increased expense.

Possible Compensation Policy Issues

Compensation policies help managers be consistent in how compensation programs are managed. The type and number of policies that are necessary depends on a manager's concept of the best way to treat all employees equally. For example, here are possible issues for which policies can be developed:

- Direct deposit of paychecks
- **Garnishment** (a legal procedure by which someone who is owed money can collect what is owed from an employee's wages)
- On-call pay and payments for work when called in
- Pay increases
- Promotions and reclassification
- Merit pay
- Confidentiality of compensation information
- Salary adjustments (effective dates)
- Salary deductions
- Salary structure
- Shift and weekend pay adjustments
- Time and record-keeping procedures

Not every operation will or should have policies about all of these issues. Some establishments may develop policies about other compensation matters. The need depends on the manager's concerns about important topics that should not be left to the judgment of individual managers.

Management of Compensation Increases

How do managers determine the amount of pay increases that employees should receive? Many operations have **merit pay plans.** These are programs that offer incentives for employees to improve performance and increase productivity. The concept of merit pay relates to a fundamental ethic that workers should be paid on the basis of their skills and performance. Another underlying premise to this type of compensation is that it can motivate some employees.

Merit pay plans need guidelines and policies to help ensure they are administered consistently and fairly. Since merit pay is based on skills and performance, there is a need for objective measures of performance to determine which employees are eligible. Without these measures, it is extremely difficult to relate pay to performance. Once these guidelines have been established, it is essential that they be consistently followed to ensure fairness and continued motivation.

Exhibit 9.7

FACTORS TO CONSIDER IN MERIT INCREASES

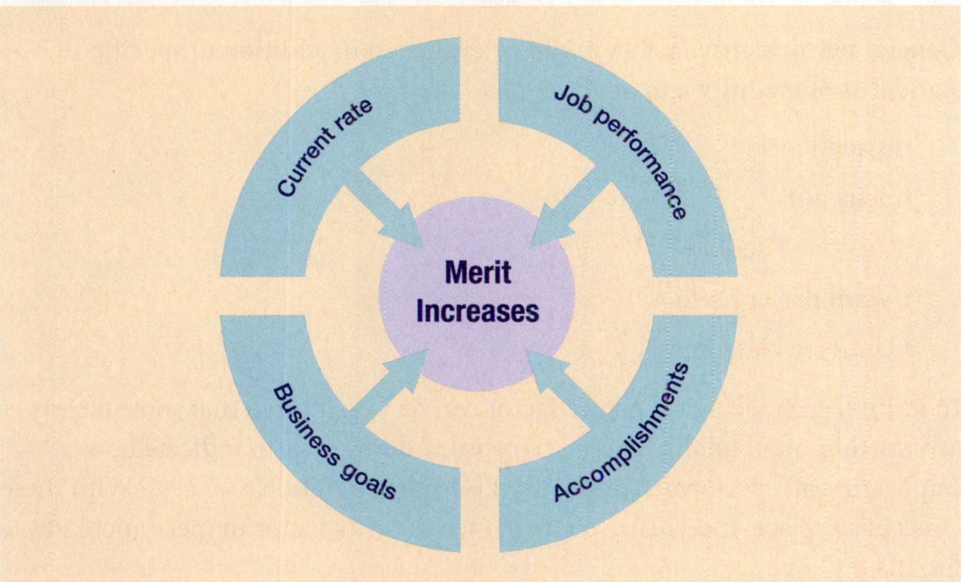

Some factors to include in merit pay policies are noted in *Exhibit 9.7*:

A salaried or hourly employee who meets or exceeds the property's standards for improved job performance, accomplishments, and contributions to business goals should be granted a merit increase within the pay range for the position. Merit pay policies apply to employees in full-time positions and should indicate if they also apply to part-time employees.

There are four factors involved in merit pay decisions:

- Job performance
- Accomplishments
- Current pay rate
- Contributions to business goals

JOB PERFORMANCE

Performance standards should be developed for each position. A **performance standard** is a measure set by managers that defines the expected quality and quantity of an employee's work. They should relate to the job description for each employee's position. For example, a server could be evaluated on the number of customers served per hour, his or her customer check average, and the number of customer complaints, if any. A line cook might also be measured by covers per hour, and the number of returned menu items could be a measure of work quality. Dish washers could be measured by

Exhibit 9.8

the number of racks correctly washed per hour (*Exhibit 9.8*). Employees who meet or exceed the performance standards for their position should then be considered for a merit increase.

General performance factors might be evaluated in addition to specific standards of quantity and quality:

- Attendance
- Behavior
- Customer service
- Team player outlook
- Uniform cleanliness

If desired, each job performance factor can be weighted so that some factors are worth more than others. The purpose of doing so is to indicate how important each performance standard is to the operation's success. With these concepts in place, measuring performance can be a factor in merit increases for all employees.

ACCOMPLISHMENTS

Sometimes employees go "beyond the call of duty" and do more than meet basic job performance standards. Examples of accomplishments include a chef who wins a medal in a local culinary competition, a server who organizes a food drive for homeless people, or a dish washer who suggests a new procedure.

These behaviors can be recognized in the operation's merit pay calculations. An employee who does his or her job well, and then does even more, is a valuable asset to the operation and should be paid accordingly.

CURRENT PAY RATE

Another factor to consider when determining pay increases is the employee's current rate of pay. If the employee is already at the top of the pay range for the position, a formal exception may be needed to allow higher pay. This topic is discussed in the next section.

It is also wise to confirm that the pay range for the position is still in line with what competitors are paying. While this may not be a problem if the pay range has been developed properly and reviewed on a routine basis, it should still be investigated.

CONTRIBUTION TO BUSINESS GOALS

Job performance, accomplishments, and current pay rate all consider merit increases from an employee's viewpoint. Business goals consider merit increases from the operation's perspective.

It should be clear that every establishment must have a labor cost standard that tells how much money can be spent on labor, and that this standard is identified in the approved budget. This labor standard must be considered when determining how much can be spent on merit increases. If the operation has had a good year, more money will probably be available for payroll. Then the employees who are meeting or exceeding expectations can share in the property's financial success. On the other hand, if the operation has not had a good year, merit increases should be given sparingly to help bring labor costs back into line with budget goals that consider profitability.

PUTTING IT ALL TOGETHER

Exhibit 9.9 shows a simple job performance score sheet for a server.

The score sheet in *Exhibit 9.9* indicates the job performance factors that will be used to determine the amount of merit increase for an employee in this position, shown in column 1. It also indicates the maximum rating (number of points) that an employee can receive for each factor, shown in column 2.

Exhibit 9.9

SAMPLE JOB PERFORMANCE SCORE SHEET

Employee Name:	Sally George	**Position:**	Server
Evaluation Period:	January 1, 2012–December 31, 2012		

1	2	3
A. Job Performance Factor	**Maximum Rating**	**Manager's Rating**
No. of customers served	10	10
Customer check average	10	10
Customer service skills	25	15
Attendance	15	15
Attitude	20	15
Team participation	20	15
B. Accomplishments	20	15
Designed a new series of table tents		
C. Contributions to Business Goals	20	15
	140	110

Merit Pay Increase Scale (Points)

0–90	0
91–105	1/3 of maximum amount
106–125	2/3 of maximum amount
126–140	maximum amount

Manager's Memo

This section has dealt with policies and procedures useful in considering pay increases for waged employees. However, the same basic factors can be used to assess salary increases for managers. For example, managers should also be held accountable for achieving standards and attaining goals.

Goals for many managers include responsibility for attaining food and labor cost percentages and revenue levels. These goals can be tied to the operation's budget or measured against last year's figures.

Other factors may also be evaluated, such as lowering employee turnover rates or developing a new local marketing strategy.

The score sheet also allows the manager to rate the employee on the basis of accomplishments (part B) and contributions to business goals (part C). It is important to note that plans for accomplishments and contributions to business goals can be determined in discussions with the employee at the time of performance appraisal. This will be discussed later in this chapter.

The bottom of the score sheet shows the merit pay increase scale for the server position. Sally received a score of 110 points. The scale indicates that she will be eligible for a merit pay increase equal to two-thirds of the maximum amount established for the position. The merit pay increase is in addition to any other pay increase given to all employees, such as one for cost of living. A **cost of living (COL)** pay increase relates to an index developed by the U.S. Bureau of Labor Statistics that reflects changes in the costs of items such as food, housing, and transportation to the average consumer.

Compensation Exceptions

As with many policies, there can be exceptions. A common problem arises when an employee does not receive a merit increase because he or she is at the top of the current pay range. Past merit increases may have moved him or her to the top of the pay range more quickly than expected. Also, the employee could have been hired at or near the top of the pay range because of outstanding experience. Either way, the person is a valued employee and, if possible, should be considered for an exception to the operation's compensation policy.

Payroll Information Is Private

Payroll information should be kept confidential. Rumors about pay can hurt employee morale and can even set up an "us" against "them" mentality toward management.

THINK ABOUT IT . . .

In your last job, were you aware of what other employees were paid? Did you feel that you were being treated fairly? Should pay information be shared with other employees? Why or why not?

The easiest way to avoid this pitfall is to restrict access to payroll information. The only people who should have access to payroll information for the entire operation should be specific managers and the person writing the payroll checks. Payroll processing is increasingly done by a service provider outside the establishment. This will be discussed later in this chapter.

In establishments with high revenue volume, there may be more than one manager involved in payroll decisions for specific employees. For example, a line supervisor could perform a performance review with a cook and recommend to the executive chef that an increase be given based on job performance. The executive chef would then take the recommendation to the general manager. All of these people need to keep payroll information confidential.

Any employee in a position that requires him or her to know other employees' pay rates should be counseled to keep the information private. Most record keeping is now done with a computer, so care is needed to ensure that information is not displayed on a screen while others can read it. Managers should not leave sensitive information displayed when they leave their office.

Each employee should be counseled about keeping his or her own pay rate confidential. The policy addressing this point should be discussed with each employee during orientation sessions. The consequences of violating this policy should also be explained. Be sure to follow any state and local regulations when determining policy violation tactics. The policy should be part of the employee manual, and each employee should sign a document indicating acceptance of the handbook including this policy.

PERFORMANCE APPRAISALS AND COMPENSATION

Performance appraisals should be conducted for time periods indicated in the applicable policy. While some operations require them quarterly (every three months), it is more common to conduct performance appraisals every six or 12 months.

If annual performance reviews are conducted, some operations' policies require that they coincide with the employee's **anniversary date:** the date that the employee began working for the establishment. This allows the managers to spread out reviews over the year. Doing so can result in a more thorough review for each employee because managers will not need to do numerous reviews at the same time.

When all performance appraisals are conducted over a short time period, it is usually done along with preparation of the annual budget. Knowing the dollar amount for payroll increases helps in estimating labor costs for the next year. However, budget planners can factor in a specific amount of payroll increase, such as an increase of 2 percent of current payroll, and conduct performance appraisals throughout the year. Regardless of timing, it is important for managers to establish and follow a schedule for performance appraisals.

Basic procedures for planning and conducting performance appraisals were presented in chapter 4. Employee compensation is usually discussed during these sessions.

Since employees are concerned about their pay, many managers discuss this topic at the start of performance appraisal sessions. Others schedule two performance appraisal sessions for each employee and discuss pay in the first session. Scheduling separate sessions has an advantage: it removes the discussion about pay from other aspects of performance appraisal. It does, however, require more time.

Manager's Memo

Most students have completed a special project or even a college course and have missed a higher grade by only one or two points. Discussions with the instructor about raising the grade make you happy if they are successful and perhaps frustrated if they are not successful.

You can imagine that the same type of discussion can occur between an employee and his or her manager when the rating given is just short of that required for a higher pay raise. In this case, the concern is about money rather than just a grade or score. Managers must be aware of these types of employee concerns and must be able to justify performance ratings given.

The job performance score sheet shown previously in *Exhibit 9.9* identified job performance factors for each position and allowed consideration of accomplishments and contributions to business goals. A score sheet can be completed by the manager and given to employees before their performance appraisals. They can then do a self-analysis of their performance and bring this information to the performance appraisal meeting. When the job performance factors relate to the tasks in the employee's job description, it is possible to discuss performance of job tasks at the same time that performance is evaluated for pay increases.

Managers can take steps to make employee performance easier to measure in future performance appraisal sessions. For example, the manager can make suggestions about what a server can do to minimize common customer complaints. A line cook can be told about problems servers have made when orders are picked up, and the cook can be advised on how to resolve the problem. As managers make notes about these conversations, it will become easier to evaluate performance during the next appraisal period and to justify the ratings given.

Some managers use performance appraisal meetings to focus on what the employee is doing wrong. A better approach is to identify problems, if any, and to work with the employee to develop a corrective action plan. When this is tied to the possibility of a pay increase, many employees will want to change their work habits.

PAYROLL SERVICES AND RECORD KEEPING

Employee payroll involves several tasks:

- Determining each employee's gross pay (pay before deductions)
- Determining the amount to be withheld from employee pay for various taxes and charges
- Determining the amount of mandated benefits to be paid for each employee
- Calculating the employee's share of voluntary benefits costs
- Completing forms to be sent with payments to government agencies for mandated withholding taxes

Payroll Services

The restaurant or foodservice manager can hire an employee to do all accounting-related tasks if it is a full-time job, or he or she can outsource the payroll task. The term **outsource** refers to using an outside provider to do work that could otherwise be done by an employee. Many managers use bookkeepers or contract with a bank to provide payroll services. Another alternative is to use a payroll services company.

Some companies provide “one-stop shopping” and can help managers with all of their compensation-related responsibilities. Employees can be paid with a paycheck, direct deposits can be made, or employees can receive debit cards. Payroll information can be given to the service provider by hardcopy, over the Internet, or even with a mobile payroll application.

Payroll service providers can calculate federal, state, and local taxes due for each employee and the operation, and these can be deposited along with paperwork required to meet the current regulations. Some services even have an automated poster update service to help managers ensure that they have the most recent federal and state labor law workplace posters that are required (*Exhibit 9.10*).

Some payroll services also provide human resources information for managers who do not have access to this specialized assistance. For example, they can provide human resources standards that can be used for benchmarking, and a help desk for telephone and email questions about human resources matters. They can also assist in developing employee handbooks, provide alerts when employment laws change, and help managers understand federal and state employment laws.

Should restaurant and foodservice managers use these types of services? That decision must be made by each manager. However, the many compensation and human resources tasks must be done by someone, and managers should decide who is best to do them for their specific operation.

Exhibit 9.10

Manager's Memo

Today, compensation-related information is processed by computer for almost all establishments. Some managers believe that computers do not make mistakes, and they do not carefully check computer-generated information.

In fact, computers may make "mistakes," and the information used for computer processing can include errors. It is necessary to routinely check computer-generated information, including that related to compensation, against the data used to generate the information.

Record-Keeping Tasks

Records provide the information needed for payroll or human resources information systems. Each operation's policies and procedures will guide how this information is collected.

PROCESSING PAYROLL AND BENEFIT INFORMATION

Employees are eligible for vacations and sick leave based in part on how long they have worked for the operation, and the gross wages of nonsalaried employees are based on the number of hours they worked. Managers should work with department heads to develop systems to ensure that the number of hours worked by employees who receive wages is accurate. They should routinely monitor employees' reports of actual hours worked against scheduled hours.

Managers and supervisors should routinely review employee paycheck data to confirm there are no processing errors. They may also personally distribute paychecks to ensure there are no **ghost employees,** persons who receive paychecks who are not currently employed.

Information about employment dates must be accurately and clearly posted in employee files because this information drives decisions about vacation and sick leave times, and other factors where seniority may be important. Policies relating to vacations and other leave time must be developed, kept current, and communicated to all employees.

Restaurant and foodservice establishments should have clear and concise policies that address the guidelines and procedures used to process payroll and benefits information. Managers should inform employees about these policies and consistently follow them to best ensure that problems do not occur.

Some managers also give copies of benefits information to the employees. They can then review and verify the information or point out potential problems that may require further review and analysis.

PROCESSING HUMAN RESOURCES INFORMATION

Employee personnel records are the central source of information about an employee's hire date, promotions, and other status changes including termination. Information in these records drives the development of necessary reports and decision making about the eligibility of employees for some benefits.

In small operations, managers may be responsible for entering and maintaining information in employee files. However, as the number of employees grows, this task may be delegated to another employee or outsourced.

Personnel records for all employees should be maintained in a centralized location within the organization. These files contain information that is important for management purposes and for complying with health department requirements. Training records such as for the National Restaurant Association's ServSafe food safety and ServSafe Alcohol programs can be retained in these files. Therefore, these records must be managed carefully and be under the control of one person.

Many operations use computerized systems to maintain human resources information. Procedures must be in place to identify what information is needed, how it should be entered into the records system, and how it should be maintained. Information in these systems should be entered completely and accurately and in a timely manner.

Employee records should be updated when necessary to accurately reflect changes. Routine system reports should be generated and carefully reviewed as a routine part of the manager's job.

PROCESSING HUMAN RESOURCES POLICIES

Many restaurant and foodservice operations have numerous policies relating to human resources. These policies can guide managers as they make employee-related decisions about numerous topics while treating all employees fairly and in the same way. Examples of policies that should be addressed include: vacations, sick leave, employee meals, performance appraisal procedures, uniforms, and employee parking.

Policies and procedures must be in place when, for example, employees request an unpaid leave under FMLA, request a leave of absence with or without pay, or sustain injuries on the job for which workers' compensation may be due.

Policies and procedures for some types of human resources actions, such as FMLA and workers' compensation, are affected by requirements of regulatory agencies. Those for other human resources actions such as requests for leave of absence and vacations are established by the operation.

In all cases, managers must know how to process the required forms and to update employee records. Procedures for these types of actions should be standardized, and processing must be done completely, accurately, and in a timely manner according to human resources policies and federal and state employment laws when applicable.

After records and systems are updated to reflect the actions taken, reports should be generated and audits should be undertaken to confirm that the database of human resources information is accurate.

THINK ABOUT IT . . .

More paperwork becomes necessary as more employees are hired. How much time do you think managers spend on human resources forms that could be spent on other activities if employee turnover were reduced?

SUMMARY

1. **Explain how managers must balance the concerns of owners, employees, and themselves as they develop and manage compensation programs.**

   How compensation programs are managed impacts an operation's culture and its profitability. Owners require a profit, whereas employees should receive fair compensation. Managers must strike a balance between owners and employees because they know that good employees are important.

2. **Describe the three major components of compensation: wages, salaries, and benefits.**

   Employee compensation is made up of wages, salaries, and benefits. Wages are paid to employees based on hours worked. Salaries are paid on an annual or other basis and do not depend on hours worked.

   Some benefits are mandated by federal and state laws including social security, workers' compensation, and unemployment. Others are voluntary including healthcare coverage, vacations, educational assistance, and other programs, the costs for which may be shared by the operation and participating employees. Employees may not be aware of the costs incurred to provide benefits.

3. **Describe major requirements of federal and state compensation laws.**

   The federal minimum wage law falls under the Fair Labor Standards Act (FLSA). Most employees must be paid a minimum wage plus overtime for any time worked over 40 hours per week.

   Many states also have applicable laws. When employees are subject to both state and federal minimum wage laws, they are entitled to the greater benefit. States also administer workers' compensation and unemployment compensation programs. These have significant impacts on an operation's costs, and managers must know and carefully follow laws regulating these programs that apply to them.

4. **Describe several of the most important factors that affect an operation's compensation cost.**

   These factors include the volume of the operation's revenue and its payroll standards along with local and regional pay levels and the amount competitors pay. Other factors include the knowledge and skills required of employees, collective bargaining agreements, if applicable, and other factors including benefits.

   Managers must ensure that pay ranges are fair for to the employer and employees. Pay ranges are frequently reviewed annually and adjusted as necessary to stay current with competitors and to retain satisfied employees.

5. **Identify basic procedures for developing and controlling restaurant and foodservice compensation policies and procedures.**

   Compensation is best controlled when the factors that affect it are known and when standards and procedures drive how the process is managed. Managers must monitor employee performance, take corrective action to maintain standards, and know about compensation issues that impact cost as well as regulatory requirements.

   Many operations have merit pay plans that offer incentives for employees. Factors used for these programs must be measurable and employees must know what they are. Merit pay factors typically include job performance, accomplishments, current pay rates, and employee contributions to business goals.

6. **Explain how performance appraisals relate to compensation.**

   Employees are typically informed about compensation increases during performance appraisal sessions. These meetings should focus on the extent to which employees met or exceeded agreed-upon standards. These sessions should also be used to set expectations for the next appraisal period.

7. **Review procedures for processing payroll-related information and other information required for employee files.**

   Much time and information is required to process payroll and maintain the records to support it. Some operations employ persons to do this work, and others outsource it. Wages and salaries, along with employee and employer deductions for mandated and voluntary benefits, must be calculated. Monies withheld and employer contributions must be sent to federal and state agencies as required.

   Effective policies and procedures must guide collection of payroll information and processing of benefits. Basic human resources information such as new employees and terminations must be correctly processed and confidentially maintained in employee files.

APPLICATION EXERCISE

You are the new manager of Ramble Woods Restaurant, which has a team of six salaried managers, about 75 full-time waged employees, and 15 part-time waged employees.

You have been employed about two months and have been careful not to make changes right away. Instead, you have learned how things are currently done and what problems are occurring. You want to gradually roll out some new compensation procedures to address your concerns.

Break into teams of three and brainstorm solutions for the following issues. If time permits, make a report of the team's suggestions to the class.

1. Employees paid on an hourly basis check in and check out with the supervisor on duty, who maintains a handwritten log of these times. The supervisor's signature is required to confirm the information is correct.
2. While there are written and circulated policies about vacation time and sick leave, managers pride themselves in being "flexible." For example, if employees become eligible for a one-week vacation several weeks from now, a manager might grant the vacation early if an employee makes a vacation request.
3. The operation employs a bookkeeper who works approximately 20 hours weekly on payroll and other compensation-related issues. He will soon be retiring. What factors should the manager consider as she decides whether to hire another part-time accountant or to contract with a payroll service?

REVIEW YOUR LEARNING

Select the best answer for each question.

1. **Which item is considered a prime cost?**
   A. Labor cost
   B. Supply cost
   C. Utilities cost
   D. Depreciation
2. **When federal and state laws differ, which minimum wage applies?**
   A. The state minimum wage
   B. The federal minimum wage
   C. The average of the two wages
   D. The law with the higher wage
3. **Which law requires a minimum wage be paid to covered employees?**
   A. Family and Medical Leave Act
   B. Fair Labor Standards Act
   C. Social Security Act
   D. Equal Pay Act
4. **How does the federal minimum wage law affect tipped employees?**
   A. It generally does not apply to tipped employees.
   B. It allows the manager to set the minimum wage.
   C. It applies without considering the amount of tips.
   D. It allows tips to be counted as part of employee pay.
5. **What does a performance standard measure?**
   A. The experience of an employee
   B. The quality of an employee's work
   C. The responsibilities of an employee
   D. The compensation an employee receives
6. **Which item is a voluntary benefit?**
   A. Life insurance
   B. Social security
   C. Workers' compensation
   D. Unemployment compensation
7. **Which is a mandatory benefit?**
   A. Healthcare insurance
   B. Paid vacation time
   C. Social security
   D. Paid sick time
8. **Which information is a key factor in determining merit pay?**
   A. Contribution to goals
   B. Date of employment
   C. Level of experience
   D. Position title

9. **The best way to ensure payroll information is kept private is to**
   A. terminate any employee sharing it.
   B. maintain it in an off-site location.
   C. require managers to maintain it.
   D. limit employee access to it.

10. **How often should performance appraisals generally be conducted?**
    A. Every 1 to 2 months
    B. Every 3 to 4 months
    C. Every 4 to 6 months
    D. Every 6 to 12 months

FIELD PROJECT

Part IV

1. Consult the manager of a local establishment to answer questions on compensation programs.

2. Determine how important the pay is for a higher-level position as employees consider whether they would like to prepare for the position.

3. How does the manager explain the benefits of challenges and greater opportunities to help the operation as an incentive for employees to participate in professional development programs?

4. How would the manager react if an employee completed a significant professional development activity and then told that manager that he or she would receive higher compensation elsewhere for the same position?

5. What is the relationship between compensation and professional development for the establishment's employees?

10 Employee Retention and Terminations

INSIDE THIS CHAPTER

- Leadership Strategies to Enhance Retention and Productivity
- Progressive Discipline Procedures
- Employee Terminations
- Unemployment Compensation

CHAPTER LEARNING OBJECTIVES

After completing this chapter, you should be able to:

- Describe leadership strategies to enhance employee retention and productivity.
- Explain common procedures used in progressive discipline programs.
- Describe procedures for voluntary and involuntary termination.
- Explain the basics of unemployment compensation.

KEY TERMS

COBRA, p. 272
exit interview, p. 269
insubordination, p. 267
involuntary termination, p. 266
probation (progressive discipline), p. 263
progressive discipline, p. 260
separation checklist, p. 272
structured interview, p. 270
terminable act, p. 267
unstructured interview, p. 270
voluntary termination, p. 266
W-2 income tax form, p. 275
"warm-body" syndrome, p. 258
wrongful discharge, p. 267

CASE STUDY

"Angelo, we've talked about this informally, and now I want to have a more formal discussion. That's why I've called you to my office," said Constance, the manager of Tiptonville Bistro.

"What do you think other servers think when you leave early saying that you're ill? This happens about once a week. It always seems to be after a rush when there is a lot of after-shift work because we didn't have the normal slowdown time," she continued. "Do you think it is fair to have your team be short one member when they do cleanup?"

"I can't help it if the hard work and long time on my feet make me feel very tired and even sick," replied Angelo. "There is nothing I can do about it!"

"Well," said Constance. "Dino, another server, told me that he saw you at a bar later on a night when you had to leave early. I think we need to agree right now about what we can do to resolve this problem."

1. Assume that Angelo asked you, the manager, what your suggestions are. What would you say?

2. Assume Angelo agreed to your suggestions, returned to work, and repeated the same actions on a shift the next week. What would you do?

Manager's Memo

Many restaurant and foodservice operations have seasonal business variations, and some new employees will likely need to be hired during busy times. As a result, some managers want to minimize the efforts required to select these new employees. However, managers must always try to ensure that the employees who are hired are trainable and want to assume the responsibilities. This means finding employees with the right attitude. It can be difficult to determine a potential employee's attitude. However, the difference between needing a job and wanting a specific job can make a significant long-term difference in an employee's job performance.

LEADERSHIP STRATEGIES TO ENHANCE RETENTION AND PRODUCTIVITY

Earlier chapters have presented numerous suggestions that managers can use to effectively supervise their employees. These suggestions are important because staff members are the restaurant and foodservice operation's most important resource. The establishment's goals cannot be attained or, at least, cannot be maximized without the benefits of dedicated team members who want their employer to be successful.

Strategies to gain the commitment and support of employees are not expensive to implement. In fact, many of the most important strategies cost nothing at all. For example, no costs are incurred when a manager smiles, says a friendly "hello," and expresses a genuine "thanks" at the end of a tough workday (*Exhibit 10.1*). The benefits—including more satisfied customers, greater productivity, fewer defects, and lessened employee turnover—cannot be measured.

Managers begin their relationship of trust and respect with employees when new staff members are selected. They then maintain a professional relationship with them throughout their career with the organization.

Select the Right Employees

Some managers use the **"warm-body" syndrome** when they make hiring decisions. The warm-body syndrome refers to the idea that any employee is better than no employee, so a fast selection is made.

Exhibit 10.1

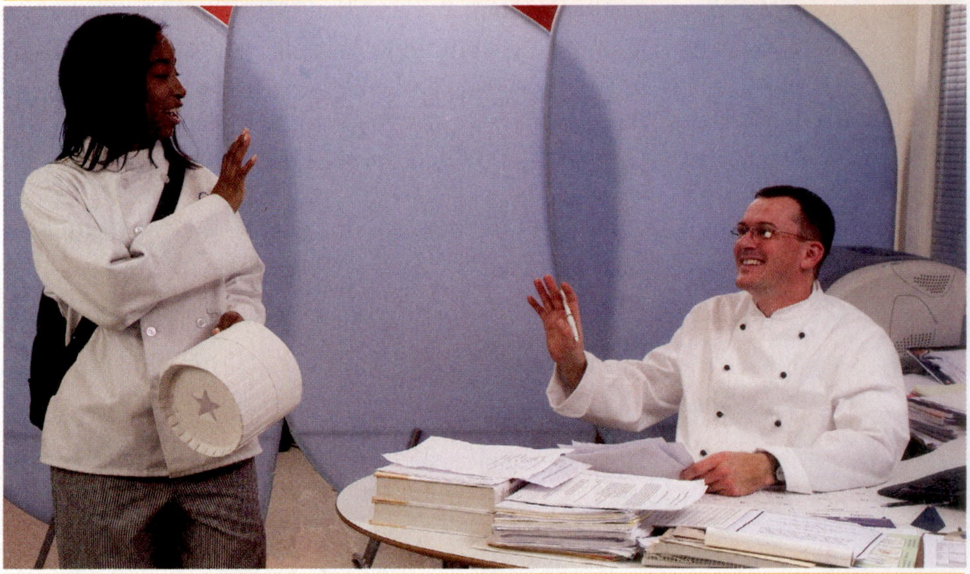

In fact, not everyone can easily perform all of the tasks in any restaurant or foodservice position. Even if they could, some people do not want to.

The manager should take a reasonable amount of time to recruit employees for vacant positions. In addition to learning about applicants so the best decision can be made, it is also important for candidates to learn about the operation.

Should an applicant for a dish-washing position know that an additional job task is cutting the grass? Does the establishment require servers to mop the floors? Must cooks wash pots and pans? Do storeroom staff need to use a computer for inventory or other purposes? Each of these tasks can be a surprise to a new employee, who might not have accepted the position if he or she had known about all of the responsibilities.

Train Correctly

Recall that training requires planning and cannot just involve a new employee shadowing an experienced employee. This common but ineffective training method has at least two shortcomings: It allows the possibility of the new employee learning incorrect procedures, and it suggests that the manager is not really concerned about the new employee's success.

Supervise Effectively

As previously mentioned in this book, there are several management strategies that can provide opportunities for employees to become motivated, to work as contributing members of the team, and to be allowed to make decisions that affect them. Performance appraisal, career planning, and ongoing coaching activities have all been discussed because they have an impact on employee performance and attitude.

Managers who help their employees find pride and satisfaction in their work and who genuinely respect their staff reap numerous benefits. They improve customer experiences and increase profits. They also reduce employee turnover costs, especially those that cannot be easily calculated, as they help employees do their jobs.

Be an Employer of Choice

Remember that an employer of choice is one where employees enjoy their work and encourage their friends and family to seek open positions in the organization. Almost by definition, employers of choice have fewer terminations than do other employers that do not consistently offer an enjoyable work experience.

THINK ABOUT IT . . .

The first weeks on the job provide many experiences that will impact an employee's interest in remaining on the job. What are some things managers should do to help new employees feel comfortable?

Manager's Memo

Interactions between managers and employees have evolved over the years. Many managers used to believe that employees did not want to work. Their job as managers was to closely direct their employees so work was done exactly as required. Later, managers recognized the benefits of a more participative leadership style in which employees can help make decisions about work procedures they will use and the problems that must be resolved.

Leadership styles are still evolving. In many restaurant and foodservice operations, managers train their employees to meet performance standards and work with employees to determine specific goals. Then the managers get out of the way and let the employees assume their responsibilities. Of course there is still follow-up evaluation and coaching, but the value of the employees is recognized by the extent to which responsibilities are delegated.

> **Manager's Memo**
>
> Restaurant and foodservice operations compete with employers in other businesses for employees in many positions. Sometimes it is difficult to find good employees, and managers wonder what they can do.
>
> Managers can use three basic strategies to ensure they always have the employees required. First, they can keep the employees they already have by reducing terminations. Second, they can increase productivity so they will require fewer labor hours for the work that must be done. Third, they can recruit from nontraditional employee markets such as those with physical or mental disabilities, who can be excellent employees after some job accommodations are made, or after special training is provided. Another group to consider is "empty nesters." These are persons returning to the job market after raising children.

Treating employees fairly is part of the organizational culture of employers of choice. Managers in these organizations treat their employees in the same way that managers want to be treated by their own supervisors. They see the benefits that arise when employers and employees work cooperatively in a "win–win" environment.

PROGRESSIVE DISCIPLINE PROCEDURES

Sometimes even the best managers encounter challenges with some employees. They may be caused by things that the manager does or does not do or by the actions of the employees. Managers must correct these problems, and a well-planned and implemented progressive discipline strategy is often the best way to do so.

What Is Progressive Discipline?

Progressive discipline assists an employee in improving his or her performance by bringing it up to established standards. Does the employee need to be retrained? Would coaching by a manager or another employee be beneficial? Would additional tools or equipment help? Does the employee have the ability and interest to perform the job? Would he or she benefit from a transfer to another department? These are the types of questions a manager should ask as progressive discipline actions are considered.

Progressive discipline has several objectives:

- Prevent or minimize misunderstandings between the employee and the manager.
- Ensure the employee is given specific evidence of unacceptable performance, guidelines for improvement, assistance as required, and sufficient time and opportunity to improve.
- Reduce the number of situations that result in terminations.
- Ensure that documentation is available to support the organization's position in the event that a terminated employee later brings a complaint.

Some employers use a formal progressive discipline process to discipline employees for improper behavior including failure to follow company policies. At these companies, the disciplinary process consists of a series of steps that may include coaching, oral warnings, written warnings, probation, and final warnings before termination. Other establishments make provision for other steps including suspension, often without compensation, and demotion to a position with lesser responsibilities and pay.

Sometimes an employee's behavior or a policy violation makes it necessary to terminate an employee immediately. Defining the actions that may result in immediate termination, as well as the management procedures for enacting an immediate termination, must be carefully developed and should also be addressed in the establishment's progressive discipline program. This topic will be discussed later in this chapter.

Common Steps in Progessive Discipline

This section reviews the first three steps commonly included in a progressive discipline program: oral warning, written warning, and probation. Each step has the same basic goal—to improve the employee's performance and to retain the employee.

The fourth step, termination, is a major concern. Hopefully, it can be avoided as the first three progressive discipline steps are implemented. There are many procedural and legal concerns applicable to termination, and the topic is addressed later in this chapter.

ORAL WARNING

The first step in the progressive discipline process is to discuss the problem informally but directly with the employee. When discussing performance with an employee, there should be two-way conversations and agreement between the manager and the employee. These discussions should not be one-way directions given by the manager. The outcome should be a program designed to bring the employee's performance up to standard.

For example, a discussion could clarify a misunderstanding between the employee and manager, or it could result in the manager assisting the employee in improving the quality or quantity of work. Examples include an employee with an untidy uniform or one who chews gum in public areas when the establishment is open.

The progressive discipline discussion should cover several items:

- Identification of the problem and its apparent causes
- The employee's role in solving the problem
- Specific actions to be taken by the employee and the manager
- A timetable for assessing progress
- Notice of the specific disciplinary action that will occur if performance does not improve

Manager's Memo

Many restaurant and foodservice managers recognize the importance of obtaining qualified legal advice when planning and implementing progressive discipline programs. This advice is very important as later stages are considered, including probation and termination. Employee lawsuits are always a possibility, and compliance with the law as well as consistency in the disciplinary actions used for different employees are very critical.

Managers in unionized operations must also be aware of and always comply with aspects of the union agreement that address employee discipline. It is likely that there will be specific procedures that must be addressed, including interactions with union officials.

Exhibit 10.2

PROGRESSIVE DISCIPLINE REPORT

[redacted]

Progressive Discipline Report

Employee ______________________ Position ________
Store/Location ______________________________
Supervisor ______________________ Date ________

Copies to: General Manager, Personnel File

The following serves as written documentation to the above employee for the incident(s) described below.

CURRENT INCIDENTS
Describe the situation (behavior, performance, policy violation, etc.) that occurred. Include date(s), time(s), location(s), people involved, witness, effects of the incident on the staff member's work or other staff members, and all other relevant circumstances or contributing factors. Please provide specific examples, whenever possible.

PREVIOUS INCIDENT(S) CORRECTIVE ACTIONS
List type of action (verbal warning, written warning, etc.), offense, and date for any previous incident.

GOALS AND TIMEFRAME FOR IMPROVEMENT
What specific actions—within what timeframe—are to be accomplished to improve behavior or performance? Within five (5) working days, supervisor and staff must jointly submit a personal development plan to address each of the crucial areas. This plan may be submitted under separate cover.

CONSEQUENCES
What will happen if the staff member fails to meet the goals set within the designated timeframe?

PLANNED FOLLOW-UP REVIEW DATE(S)
After each follow-up meeting, the supervisor provides a written summary to the employee and HR.

Progressive Discipline Report

FOLLOW-UP COMMENTS
The supervisor summarizes the employee's progress and determines if he or she is in good standing, or if further disciplinary action is required.

Date ____________
Comments ______________________________

STAFF MEMBER'S COMMENTS (Attach additional pages if needed.)
The employee may submit a response within five (5) business days.

Supervisor's signature ____________ Date ______
Division/Department head signature ____________ Date ______
*Staff member's signature ____________ Date ______
Human Resources signature ____________ Date ______

*Staff member's signature, with date, indicates the employee met with the supervisor indicated to discuss the incidents cited; it does not necessarily signify that the employee agrees with the Counsel and FeedBack report. In addition, this form does not alter the "at will" employment relationship in any way.

The manager should also keep a record of all formal or informal discussions with the employee by using a form such as that shown in *Exhibit 10.2*.

Note that the progressive discipline report in *Exhibit 10.2* records important information:

- Date the conversation took place and the individuals involved
- Nature of the problem in specific detail
- Corrective actions agreed to by the employee and manager
- Date for follow-up and progress report completion

When the manager initiates these steps, further action usually is not necessary.

WRITTEN WARNING

When a performance situation becomes more serious, the manager must take more formal action. These actions should include the second step in progressive discipline: a written warning with a formal meeting with the employee.

This meeting should be held privately in the manager's office. The written report serves as documentation and should be the focus of the formal meeting. At minimum, the documentation should include several pieces of key information:

- The date and time of the meeting
- A clear statement of the problem
- A comparison of the employee's behavior against the standard or expected behavior
- A plan of action to improve the performance or solve the problem
- The expected outcome that can be evaluated in a measurable way
- A deadline for achieving these results

The report should be reviewed with the employee, who should be allowed to express his or her thoughts about the report in writing (*Exhibit 10.3*). The report should then be signed and dated by the employee and the manager and placed in the employee's personnel file. Examples of behavior that could result in a written warning are excessive absenteeism or failure to follow a manager's instructions.

PROBATION

If the first two steps in a progressive discipline program, oral and written warnings, are not effective, the manager must then move to the third step. **Probation** is a specific time period during which an employee must consistently meet job standards or other reasonable conditions imposed by their manager as a condition for continued employment.

Manager's Memo

Failure to meet job standards is a typical reason for disciplining employees. However, to implement discipline, job standards must be developed and known by employees. Employees must be trained and given the resources needed to attain the expected job standards. The standards must also be consistently and fairly enforced.

Job standards should be objective and measurable. All employees should be evaluated by how well they perform the tasks in their job description. They should not be evaluated on the basis of how their performance compares to others working in the same position. Without job descriptions and standards, managers have little, if any, justification when disciplining or terminating employees for poor job performance.

Exhibit 10.3

Manager's Memo

As is true in all other businesses, some restaurant and foodservice employees have substance abuse challenges. These can lead to problems such as no-shows and late arrivals, failure to meet reasonable quality and quantity work standards, and conflicts with other employees. In extreme situations, employees may even report to work when under the influence of alcohol or other substances.

Company policies may indicate what managers should do in these cases. However, the corrective actions agreed upon to address performance problems may involve activities beyond the ability of the manager to assist. For example, enrollment and continued participation in a community-based substance abuse program might be an appropriate activity. Few, if any, managers are trained counselors who can address these kinds of problems.

The employee should be informed about disciplinary probation with a written notice. The notice should provide an explanation of the reason for the probation and the length of the probationary period. It should also include a corrective action plan that must be successfully completed during the time of probation.

The manager should meet with the employee to discuss the details of the disciplinary action probation. At this time, the employee should be asked to sign the probation notice to confirm that he or she has been informed of the action. A copy of the probation should be placed in the employee's personnel file.

During the time of the probation and at the end of the probationary period, the manager should meet with the employee to review performance improvements. If, at the end of the probationary period, the employee has not met the performance improvement requirements detailed in the probation notice, he or she will be terminated.

Improvement Timelines

The first three steps in progressive discipline focus on encouraging employees to improve their performance. Thought must also be given to the amount of time that will be allowed for the employee to meet improvement goals.

Time frames must be reasonable. They should provide enough time for the employee to improve, but they must also recognize that the operation is affected until the performance goals have been met. Managers must be careful as they consider how long they are going to allow a part of the operation to be substandard.

For example, assume the problem involves a line cook who always takes too long to turn out orders. This issue would probably need to be corrected more quickly than a server who is slow in serving guests. The line cook affects the entire operation, whereas the server affects only one station. While both problems must be corrected as soon as possible, one problem is more serious.

Consistent Management Actions

All workplace rules and standards must be clearly written and comply with legal standards. For example, there cannot be one set of rules for an older worker and a different set for younger workers. Likewise, there cannot be one set of rules for males and another set of rules for females.

In addition, managers must apply the rules consistently. One manager cannot loosely interpret them while another manager enforces them to the letter. Achievable and measurable goals, rules, and standards are easier to consistently enforce than are those that are not measurable.

Helping Employees Be Successful

Managers have the responsibility to help their employees improve. They must discover why employees do not meet the standards and then assist them in finding a solution. They should also be available as the employee tries to implement the solution.

For example, assume a salad prep employee can barely keep up with customer demand on the salad bar. The manager notices the employee is chopping large quantities of celery, onions, and green peppers by hand. The manager asks why the employee does not use the cutter-mixer and learns the employee does not know how to use it and is fearful of the sharp blades.

The manager instructs the employee in the safe use and cleaning of the machine and eases the employee's fear of operating it. The time saved by using this equipment solves the problem of late-arriving salads, and the unsatisfactory performance has been eliminated.

EMPLOYEE TERMINATIONS

Employee terminations affect the customers, the employees, and the establishment's profitability. Hopefully, the manager's actions, including those discussed in this book, can help keep termination rates low.

Operating Impacts of Termination

Employee vacancies caused by termination must be filled. Hopefully, employees who leave voluntarily will provide one or more weeks' notice so procedures to fill the position can begin. If so, the strategies used for routine recruitment and selection will be helpful. However, there will likely be times that a new employee will not be found and almost certainly that a new staff member cannot be trained in a short time period. Therefore, even in the best case, operating challenges will occur.

The manager can schedule extra hours for existing employees if a termination occurs on short notice. Perhaps, for example, a part-time employee will work a few extra hours until a permanent replacement for the terminated employee can be found. Some managers are lucky enough to have "on-call" persons who will fill in when additional assistance is needed. Regardless of the strategies used, managers will frequently have to be creative in scheduling required hours until a new staff member is able to work to job standards.

Managers have some ability to determine when they will terminate an employee as part of a progressive discipline process. While there is never a good time, a manager may determine in some cases that it is better to delay

Manager's Memo

The preceding salad-prep example poses an interesting question: Who is responsible for the problem of slow food preparation? Is it the employee who does not produce the ingredients on a timely basis, or is it the manager who has not taught the employee how to use the equipment?

The chief executive officer (CEO) of a well-known hotel chain once made the remark, "My managers cause the vast majority of all of the problems in my organization." Many managers believe that if they could recruit and retain good employees, most of their problems would be resolved. However, managers must take responsibility for helping their employees be successful. Whose fault is it if service is slow because there are not enough servers, if equipment breaks down because preventive maintenance is not implemented, or if the kitchen fails a sanitation inspection?

THINK ABOUT IT . . .

When employees must be terminated because of a lack of work or funding, managers often provide advance notice to the employees. What are possible advantages and disadvantages to this policy?

termination for a short time rather than to have it occur, for example, immediately before a busy period. Many factors can influence the manager's decision such as the availability of other employees, the type of work done by the departing employee, and the type of performance problems that were experienced.

Voluntary Termination

Voluntary termination occurs when an employee, for his or her own personal reasons, decides to leave the organization. This can occur for many reasons: desiring to change careers, finding a better position in another organization, retiring, starting a family, leaving the area, or returning to school.

Voluntary termination is often both a happy and a sad occasion. Managers are happy for the person leaving but, at the same time, they are losing a valuable member of their team.

Fellow employees are also affected when someone leaves. They may have developed professional and personal friendships with the departing employee, and they may be uncertain about how they will get along with his or her replacement. Employees may also have concerns about needing to do more work until the new employee has been selected and adequately trained.

This type of turnover is expected and cannot be avoided. Voluntary termination is generally easier to manage than termination resulting from progressive discipline procedures, although both types have challenges. All operations should have written policies and procedures regarding both voluntary and involuntary terminations. These guidelines should support a legal defense in the event a former employee either files for unemployment or sues.

Managers should conduct an exit interview with employees who leave voluntarily and also complete a separation checklist. Both of these activities are discussed later in this chapter.

Involuntary Termination

Involuntary termination is a situation in which managers terminate an employee for one or more of these four reasons: lack of work for the employee, lack of funding, unsatisfactory performance, or violation of a company policy. In other words, unlike voluntary termination, which generally occurs to benefit the employee, involuntary termination is done for the well-being of the organization.

The decision to terminate an employee should be made only after thorough consideration of the facts and circumstances leading to the decision. Prior to an employee being terminated, focused efforts should be made via the progressive discipline steps covered earlier in this chapter to make that person a productive member of the team, or to find another position for him or her.

Manager's Memo

What does it cost when one employee leaves the organization? Some of the costs can be easily calculated. Examples may include the time spent by an existing employee to interview job applicants, to complete paperwork for recently hired employees, and to conduct orientation and training sessions.

Unfortunately, many costs, including those that may be the highest, are difficult to calculate. Consider, for example, the cost of employees who know they are leaving and do not care if they provide poor service to customers. Consider also the costs incurred by new employees who want to do well, but are unable to meet performance standards until they gain necessary knowledge and skills.

While not every cost associated with employee termination can be identified, managers know that costs exist and recognize that they are likely to be significant. This knowledge provides an additional incentive for doing everything possible to reduce employee terminations.

THINK ABOUT IT . . .

You need to terminate a server but there is a large group reservation in two days. The server has issues with other dining-room staff but is great with customers. Do you delay the termination?

Managers know their investments in the employee will be lost on termination. Also, there could be significant costs associated with recruiting, hiring, and training a new employee. Additionally, significant time and legal costs can be incurred in possible cases of wrongful discharge. A **wrongful discharge** claim is a legal action taken by a former employee against a previous employer. It alleges that the discharge was in violation of state or federal antidiscrimination laws, public policy, or an implied contract, agreement, or written promise.

THINK ABOUT IT . . .

Imagine that you are a manager, and you know that a job applicant was terminated at another establishment for poor performance. Would you be willing to hire this applicant? Would your willingness depend on the reason for termination?

COMMON CAUSES

Involuntary termination can occur as the final step in a progressive discipline program or it can occur as the result of a terminable act. A **terminable act** is an action by an employee that typically causes immediate termination. The following behaviors are among those that usually justify discharge without going through an extensive progressive discipline process:

- Disruptive or destructive behavior
- **Insubordination** (failure to follow reasonable instructions)
- Theft of the operation's or customer's property or funds
- Harassment of employees or customers
- Alcohol or illegal drug abuse
- Inappropriate conduct toward coworkers or customers
- Conduct harmful to the company's image either on or off the job

Some organizations have identified other terminable acts. Owners or managers may wish to seek legal advice when identifying terminable acts. All such violations should be identified and explained in writing in the employee handbook. Employees should be required to sign a document showing their agreement. As with any worker dispute, violations of company policy should be documented in writing and kept on file in case of later legal proceedings.

Lack of work or funding are other reasons for involuntary termination. If an employee is facing a layoff because of lack of work or lack of funding to keep the person employed, the manager should attempt to find suitable employment for the person within the organization. This strategy is probably most useful in a chain organization that may have better-performing units relatively close to the property with financial problems. If the organization is large enough, the human resources department may be able to assist the employee in finding an opportunity that matches his or her skills.

REAL MANAGER

MANAGE EMPLOYEE TERMINATIONS

Terminations are never easy. They affect morale. They affect people and families. In June 2000, I began working at a bakery and café in New Orleans. I also managed the catering department and room service for the adjacent hotel. It was not uncommon to see celebrities and politicians on a daily basis—anyone from Steven Spielberg to Lil Wayne would dine in my bakery. I worked there for five years. On January 11, 2005, my district manager called me into his office to inform me that I was being terminated. I was told that it was strictly a cost-saving move; my salary had exceeded the range for the pay scale in my position. To say I was devastated would be an understatement. I had been working all my life, had never been fired, and all of a sudden it was all gone.

This experience helped me understand what it really means to terminate someone. It's always hard—whether the termination is deserved or not. It impacts the employee and his or her family. Explain the termination in a way that will be constructive. In many cases, you can offer suggestions as to what the employee might do or what resources might be available. Above all, be patient. This is a hard process for both the employee and the manager.

Finally, managers of financially successful restaurant or foodservice operations may involuntary terminate underperforming employees and those who violate company policies. The manager, department head, supervisor, or others including a human resources representative in a large organization should have first implemented activities to identify performance deficiencies and determine ways to address them.

If a skills mismatch has been identified, the employee may be offered a transfer to a new position. If an employee's performance continues to be unsatisfactory after repeated warnings and even probation, then termination procedures should be initiated.

TERMINATION PROCESS

The same basic steps should be used to terminate employees for voluntary or involuntary reasons:

- **Step 1:** Identify the cause for terminating the employee. There should be a legal, policy-based cause for which the employee is being terminated. When the reason is voluntary, the cause relates to personal reasons of importance to the employee.

  When the reason is involuntary and relates to lack of work and funding, there will be adequate operating and accounting data to support the termination decision. When the reason involves inadequate performance or behavior, the employee's file should include documentation about the activities undertaken as part of the progressive discipline process.

  Additionally, there should be company handbook or policy information to support the termination. Managers should confirm that the termination cause is legal and in line with company policy, and that all proper procedures including warning, write-up, and probation have been taken.

- **Step 2:** Ensure that proper documentation has been completed as part of the disciplinary process. Laws and company policies will dictate the type of documentation needed. This information will be found in the company handbook or policy, and other required information such as performance appraisal and disciplinary documentation should be in the employee's personnel file. It is important to confirm that the correct procedures and documentation are being followed. Managers should also confirm that the actions taken in this instance are consistent with similar situations in the past.

- **Step 3:** Obtain necessary approvals and seek legal advice, if necessary, for termination. Company policies should address this point. Managers often seek legal advice to confirm that the cause, applicable disciplinary process, and documentation are sufficient to justify termination.

- **Step 4:** Assemble termination package documents and information. Payroll and benefit concerns, necessary forms, and other activities should be considered.
- **Step 5:** Conduct the termination meeting. The meeting should be conducted in private with a third-party observer acting as a witness. The manager should review all necessary information and documentation to be fully prepared for the meeting. Remember that its purpose is neither to place blame nor to allow the employee to request a second chance. Instead, the manager should restate the specific reason for the termination and go over necessary documentation with the employee.
- **Step 6:** Ensure that the employee surrenders company property and receives his or her personal property, if any.
- **Step 7:** Make adjustments to security as needed. The terminated employee should be escorted outside the establishment. Door locks and computer passwords that were previously accessible to the terminated employee should be changed as necessary. Many operations have policies that provide specific information about this requirement.

EXIT INTERVIEWS

Exit interviews are used to help managers learn about any employee concerns, reasons for leaving, and suggestions about how the company can improve. Exit interviews should be conducted for several reasons:

Exhibit 10.4

- To determine the real reason an employee is leaving and to retain a desirable employee whenever possible
- To discover any grievances the employee may have regarding work conditions so that corrective action can be taken
- To retain the goodwill of the employee and his or her family and friends toward the organization (*Exhibit 10.4*)
- To learn about any difficulties the employee may have had regarding his or her supervisor

Information from effective exit interviews can be helpful in many ways:

- Reducing turnover
- Developing procedures to improve employees' work experiences
- Identifying any broad employee-related issues that should be addressed
- Assisting the departing employee's manager with developmental needs, if necessary
- Improving the effectiveness of general management practices
- Identifying and addressing any problems within a department or the organization

An exit interview can point out unknown problems and opportunities to management. Some employees are not comfortable discussing complaints, observations, or concerns with their current manager. If employees are concerned that their input is not wanted, this may contribute to the turnover rate.

In contrast, someone who is leaving the company has little to lose and is more likely to speak frankly with a manager. The employee's comments could offer insight into concerns such as unpopular company procedures, insufficient pay scales, inadequate working conditions, dissatisfaction with other employees, and favoritism.

Keep in mind during the interview that if the departing employee does not like a situation or policy, many other employees may not like it either. While some employee comments may be incorrect or overstated, it is still important to listen carefully to learn about situations that may exist.

Exit interviews can use a free-flowing **unstructured interview** approach, in which the manager conducts a conversation with the employee without using any prepared questions, or a **structured interview** approach, in which the manager asks a set of specific questions.

Three basic types of questions can be used in an exit interview:

- **Open-ended:** These are questions that ask for more than a one-word response and permit a free expression of ideas.
- **Close-ended:** Close-ended questions are those for which there are only short-answer responses or yes-or-no answers.
- **Multiple-choice:** These include questions that ask the departing employee to select the response that best represents his or her thoughts.

Exit interview questions can be oral or written. Many managers use elements of both structured and unstructured interviews in their meeting with employees.

A properly conducted exit interview can be a powerful tool that provides insight into the operation's organizational culture. On the other hand, some exit interviews could be just the opposite. The departing employee could have been happy working at the organization and have few, if any, complaints. This observation will support the continuation of current policies and procedures.

Exhibit 10.5 shows sample exit interview questions. Not all of these questions would be asked of each employee. Instead, the questions used would be based on company policy or the factors causing the employee to leave. The employee might complete the exit interview as a written interview, or the person conducting the interview might ask the questions and record the employee's responses on the interview form.

Exhibit 10.5

SAMPLE EXIT INTERVIEW QUESTIONS

Listed below are samples of the types of exit interview questions that employers commonly ask departing employees.

Open-Ended Questions

- What would you improve to make this company's workplace better?
- What could your immediate supervisor do to improve his or her management style?
- Based on your experience with us, what do you think it takes to succeed at this company?
- How do you generally feel about this company?
- What does your new company offer that this one does not?

Close-Ended Questions

- Did you receive sufficient feedback about your performance between merit reviews?
- Were you satisfied with this company's merit review process?
- Can this company do anything to encourage you to stay?
- Before deciding to leave, did you investigate a transfer within the company?
- Did anyone in this company discriminate against you, harass you, or cause hostile working conditions?

Multiple-Choice Questions

U = Unsatisfactory F = Fair S = Satisfactory G = Good E = Excellent

- Pay levels at this company were generally ____
- The amount of training I received when I first came here was ____
- The extent to which I had the opportunity to use or develop my potential was____
- The level of cooperation among the employees in my department was ____
- Generally speaking, I would rate this company as ____ to work for
- The level of concern for employees here was ____
- As compared to other companies, our benefit package was____

Written Questions

- What did you like most about working here?
- What did you like least about working here?
- What are your suggestions for improving this company as a place to work?
- Any other additional comments?

The manager conducting the exit interview must be a good listener and encourage the employee to share opinions. If the employee feels uncomfortable during the interview, he or she will not be completely honest.

The employee might be given some options about who will conduct the interview. For example, the interviewer could be the employee's immediate manager, the department head, or even the general manager. Some employees may provide more information when interviewed by a top-level manager because the employees may believe that their comments will be taken seriously by upper-level management.

> **Manager's Memo**
>
> Employees with good performance records are excellent candidates for rehire. They are trained and know the company's procedures and will likely experience a short learning curve to meet required job standards. A learning curve is the amount of time required for an employee to master a skill.
>
> Managers should document the exit interview and their opinion about whether the employee is a candidate for rehire. If the employee was marginal, this should be noted as well. This is important because managers, like employees, may resign for promotions or other opportunities. Documented records can then help the next management team make better employment decisions about applicants with previous experience at the property.

The interview should be held in a location in which the employee is most likely to feel comfortable and provide honest responses. It should occur shortly after the employee's resignation notice so that the employee may be more willing to provide valuable responses.

The employee should be informed that all information obtained from the exit interview will remain private and secure with the interviewer and other managers. At the completion of the interview, the employee can be asked to provide any additional input that may not have been covered in the questions.

A sample exit interview form is shown in *Exhibit 10.6*. The exiting employee could complete it, or the manager conducting the interview could ask the questions and record responses on the interview form.

Use of the exit interview form, along with any notes by the manager conducting the interview, may provide information useful in identifying problems contributing to employee turnover.

Separation Checklists

Completion of a separation checklist is an important component of the voluntary and involuntary termination process. A **separation checklist** is a list of activities to be completed for employees who are leaving the organization. *Exhibit 10.7* on page 274 shows a sample employee separation checklist.

When you review Exhibit 10.7 it will be helpful to know some additional information for activities 1,2, 4, 5, 7, and 8:

- **Activity 1. Accrued vacation or sick leave calculated and paid according to policy:** The amount of vacation and sick leave, if any, and any other financial benefits due to the departing employee must be calculated and paid according to the operation's policy.
- **Activity 2. Employee reference release signed:** The employee should be required to complete an employee reference release form if he or she will be using the operation as an employment reference and wants the manager to provide information to a potential employer.
- **Activity 4. COBRA information provided:** **COBRA** refers to the Consolidated Omnibus Budget Reconciliation Act. It gives workers who lose health insurance benefits the right to continue group health benefits for limited periods under certain situations. These situations include voluntary or involuntary job loss, reduction in hours, transition between jobs, and other life events. Former employees who are qualified may be required to pay the entire health insurance premium up to 102 percent of the cost to the plan.

Exhibit 10.6

SAMPLE EMPLOYEE EXIT INTERVIEW FORM

Employee name: ________________________ Date: ____________

Interviewed by: ________________________ Employee ID no. ____________

1. What factors influenced you to accept your position with us? (Check all that apply)

☐ Compensation ☐ Fringe benefits ☐ Location ☐ Reputation of the organization

☐ Career change ☐ Job responsibilities ☐ Schedule ☐ Other: ____________

2. Why are you leaving? (Check all that apply)

☐ Compensation ☐ Fringe benefits ☐ Location ☐ Reputation of the organization

☐ Career change ☐ Job responsibilities ☐ Schedule ☐ Other: ____________

3. What is your level of satisfaction about your experience with the organization?

Very Unsatisfied — Very Satisfied

① ② ③ ④ ⑤

4. What did you find least satisfying about your experience with the organization?

____

____

____

____

____

5. Do you think you were treated fairly on your performance reviews? ☐ Yes ☐ No

6. Were you told about opportunities for advancement? ☐ Yes ☐ No

7. Would you recommend us as an employer to your friends and family? ☐ Yes ☐ No

8. Please give us any other feedback you would like to provide to help us improve as an employer.

____

____

Thank you for answering these questions.

Exhibit 10.7

SAMPLE EMPLOYEE SEPARATION CHECKLIST

Employee name: ______________________ Employee ID no.______________

Last date of employment: ______________________

Separation Activities	Completed	Manager's Initials	Comments
1. Accrued vacation or sick leave calculated and paid according to policy.	☐ Yes ☐ No		
2. Employee reference release signed.	☐ Yes ☐ No		
3. Exit interview completed.	☐ Yes ☐ No		
4. COBRA information provided.	☐ Yes ☐ No		
5. Company property returned (if applicable). ☐ Keys ☐ Uniforms ☐ Tools ☐ Company identification ☐ Other: ______________ ☐ ______________ ☐ ______________	☐ Yes ☐ No		
6. Repayment of any advances collected.	☐ Yes ☐ No		
7. Verification of emergency contact information or address: ______________ ______________ ______________ ______________	☐ Yes ☐ No		
8. Final paycheck received.	☐ Yes ☐ No		

This is to certify that all of the above separation activities have been completed.

____

Employee's Signature Date

____

Manager's Signature Date

Important: This completed employee separation checklist should be placed in the employee's human resources file.

- **Activity 5. Company property returned:** Departing employees must return company property. This includes such things as keys, tools, uniforms, and corporate identification. The restaurant or foodservice manager should have a procedure in place to document property in employees' possession, and this information should be included in employees' human resources files (*Exhibit 10.8*). On termination, all company property should be returned.

Exhibit 10.8

- **Activity 7. Verification of emergency contact information or address:** Employers will be required to send former employees copies of their W-2 tax forms. A **W-2 income tax form** is an information return completed by employers and sent to the federal taxing authorities. It is used to report wages and salaries paid to employees and the taxes withheld from them. The employer must send copies of the federal W-2 form and applicable state and local tax forms to employees. Emergency contact information provided by a departing employee may provide a more permanent address that can be used to contact former employees.
- **Activity 8. Final paycheck received:** Some companies have a policy of not issuing the employee's final paycheck until all company materials have been returned. It is important to confirm that this action is within the guidelines of applicable state laws before implementing such a policy.

Note that the employee separation checklist should be signed by the departing employee and his or her manager after verifying that all necessary separation activities have been completed. The completed employee separation checklist should be placed in the employee's human resources file for future reference.

UNEMPLOYMENT COMPENSATION

Recall from Chapter 9 that unemployment compensation is a program administered at the state level following federal guidelines to provide benefits and income to workers who become unemployed through no fault of their own.

Although there are similarities among states, there are also differences. The examples that follow apply to most, but not all, states. Current information specific to a location can be found by typing "unemployment compensation in [specific state name]" into a search engine.

- Benefits are based on a percentage of earnings over a 52-week period, up to a maximum amount determined by the state.
- Benefits are paid for a maximum of 26 weeks in most states. However, the time has ranged up to 99 weeks in many states during difficult economic times.
- Recipients must be unemployed through no fault of their own and meet the eligibility requirement as determined by state law.

- Recipients can appeal if they are denied benefits.
- Employers have an assigned tax rate based on their average annual taxable payroll, unemployment claims against their account, and taxes previously paid.
- If an employer has been at the maximum rate for a specified time, a surcharge can be added to the rate.

Managers must know about the definition of eligibility and the assigned tax rates specified in their state's unemployment compensation laws.

Each state's definition of eligibility requires that potential recipients be unemployed through no fault of their own. However, the meaning of that concept can be open to interpretation. When an employee files for unemployment compensation, the state agency gathers information from the employee and the employer and determines whether the employee is entitled to compensation.

As stated previously, every action taken by management regarding an employee who does not meet the company's performance or other standards should be put in writing and signed by both the employee and a manager. When presenting or appealing a case, the manager can then use the written documents to reinforce the operation's position. Either side can appeal the decision.

Documentation is also important for assigning a tax rate because, in most states, the rate is based on the number of claims a business has against its account: the more claims, the higher the rate. By working with employees and coaching them, there will be fewer terminations. By documenting everything in writing, there will be fewer claims against the business.

THINK ABOUT IT . . .

In today's business world, being unemployed at some point is not uncommon. Have you or someone you know filed for unemployment compensation? What was the process? How did the employer respond?

SUMMARY

1. **Describe leadership strategies to enhance employee retention and productivity.**

   Managers cannot control many causes of voluntary termination. However, they can have an impact on reasons such as dislike of management strategies and workplace procedures. Also, managers can eliminate some problems that lead to poor job performance and involuntary termination.

   Managers must select the right employees and train and supervise them appropriately. Management practices must allow employees to find pride and satisfaction in their work. One way of doing this is to treat employees consistently and fairly. Managers can create a reputation for their property as an "employer of choice" in which employees tell their friends and family members about the benefits of working at the organization.

2. **Explain common procedures used in progressive discipline programs.**

   All restaurant and foodservice operations should have written policies and procedures relating to an effective progressive discipline program. Some employers use a formal progressive discipline process that consists of a series of steps that includes coaching, oral warnings, written warnings, probation, and termination. An oral warning is all that is necessary to encourage many employees to improve. Written documentation or probation may be necessary for others.

3. **Describe procedures for voluntary and involuntary termination.**

   Voluntary termination occurs when an employee decides to leave for personal reasons. Involuntary termination occurs when managers terminate an employee for one or more of several reasons. One reason is that the employee commits a terminable act that causes immediate termination. Examples include disruptive or destructive behavior, harassment, and theft. Other reasons for involuntary terminations include lack of work or funding, unsatisfactory performance, or violation of a company policy. Employees should be given opportunities to improve through the establishment's progressive discipline program.

   Several steps should be used to terminate employees. The cause for termination must be identified, and proper documentation must be completed. Necessary approvals for termination must be obtained and termination package documents compiled. The termination meeting is followed by activities to ensure that the employee surrenders company property or receives personal property. The final steps involve making adjustments to security as necessary and reviewing operational procedures involved in the cause for termination. Employees should complete an exit interview to help managers learn more about any concerns, reasons for leaving, and suggestions about how the company can improve.

4. **Explain the basics of unemployment compensation.**

   Unemployment compensation is a program administered at the state level according to federal guidelines. It provides benefits and income to workers who have become unemployed through no fault of their own. There are numerous provisions to the laws that vary between states. Documentation of terminations is important to explain performance problems in support of the operation's termination decision and to help reduce the number of claims against the business.

APPLICATION EXERCISES

Exercise 1

You are the owner and manager of an establishment known for good food and service. You credit your employees for much of your success. One of your cooks consistently turns out meals quickly and accurately. He gets along well with coworkers. His only problem is that he is sometimes late or misses work because of a drinking problem. You have talked to him about this problem, and he has promised to do better.

After work one evening, he stops for a few drinks and while driving home, he hits a parked police car. Although no one is injured, the incident makes the local paper. Your establishment's name is mentioned several times in the article. The day the employee returns to work you terminate him because he promised he would control his drinking, and because you believe the reputation of your restaurant has been hurt.

1. Was termination the correct response? Why or why not?
2. How much control should an operation have over its employees' off-duty activities?
3. What is an employee's responsibility to his or her employer?
4. Could this situation have been prevented? If so, how?

Exercise 2

Break into groups of two for two role-plays. In one, you will play the role of a restaurant or foodservice manager, and in the other you will be the employee.

When you role-play the manager, select one of the following situations and plan how you will conduct the meeting. Consider how the employee might react and what your response would be. Each situation should take three to five minutes.

Situation 1	Situation 2	Situation 3
The manager must put an employee on probation because he or she is slow at busing tables.	The manager must terminate an employee who was seen on camera stealing expensive food items.	The manager must inform an employee that he or she has to stop breaking dishes or be terminated.

After the role-play, share your thoughts, feelings, and insights with either the class or your partner using the questions that follow. Then switch positions and role-play the other position using a different situation.

1. Employee: Did the manager do a good job of informing you about the situation?
2. Employee: How could the manager have improved the initial communication of the situation?
3. Manager: Did you feel the employee was justified in his or her reaction to your message?
4. Manager: What might you have done differently to get a better reaction?

REVIEW YOUR LEARNING

Select the best answer for each question.

1. **Unemployment compensation laws are regulated at what governmental level or levels?**
   A. Federal and state
   B. State and local
   C. Federal
   D. State

2. **What is the purpose of an employee exit interview?**
   A. To learn if the employee will stay if a higher wage is paid
   B. To determine the actual reasons why the employee is leaving
   C. To find out who should be blamed for the employee's departure
   D. To discover which competitor the employee will now work for

3. **What type of message should be given to the employee by the person conducting an informal discussion about a performance problem?**
   A. You will receive no merit pay until your problem is resolved.
   B. You could improve your performance if you changed your attitude.
   C. We must identify your performance problem and the reasons for it.
   D. You have a performance problem, and you need to resolve it.

4. **Activities to be completed by employees leaving the organization are included in**
   A. an employee reference release.
   B. an exit interview survey.
   C. a property release form.
   D. a separation checklist.

5. **Which should be included in a progressive discipline report?**
   A. Corrective actions agreed to by the employee and manager
   B. Date of the employee's previous performance appraisal
   C. Revenue dollars lost because of the employee's behavior
   D. Date of the employee's initial employment at the establishment

6. **What is an example of a terminable act?**
   A. Failure to follow a procedure
   B. Theft of operation property
   C. Overportioning of entrées
   D. Dress code violation

7. **What is the term for an action taken by a former employee against an employer alleging that the termination was in violation of antidiscrimination laws?**
   A. Work severance claim
   B. Discharge of trust claim
   C. Illegal termination claim
   D. Wrongful discharge claim

8. **What is one objective of a progressive discipline program?**
   A. Provide incentives for employees to work harder.
   B. Reduce the need for employee retraining programs.
   C. Reduce situations that result in involuntary terminations.
   D. Eliminate those employees who do not improve quickly.

9. **What is the first step in a progressive discipline program?**
   A. Formal meeting
   B. Termination
   C. Oral warning
   D. Probation

10. **When should a terminated employee be given his or her final paycheck?**
    A. During the required exit interview
    B. One week after the last day of work
    C. At the start of the termination meeting
    D. When all operation property is returned

FIELD PROJECT

Becoming a Manager and a Leader

Managing a restaurant, foodservice, or hospitality operation and leading people are not easy tasks. Today, it is even more difficult due to the uncertainty of the economy, competition, and changes in the workforce pool. It takes leaders at all levels of the organization to determine how to best align what appear at times to be conflicting demands with various teams to achieve results, all while attending to and balancing personal and professional satisfaction. In addition, those in leadership positions must always evaluate these factors with the highest ethical standards.

The process of leadership and management development is greatly facilitated with feedback and coaching. Feedback is needed because it is often difficult for individuals to see themselves clearly and to honestly evaluate how they come across to others. Feedback that is solicited from those with whom you work or have a relationship with, and that is offered in a factual, noncritical way, is essential to determining those leadership skills that need the most development.

This field research project is designed to provide you with an opportunity to obtain feedback from others in the field, as well as to promote insight and to encourage you to ask questions. This guide focuses primarily on personal capabilities and competencies in becoming an effective manager and leader in the hospitality and restaurant industry. This project is designed to provide a composite picture of your current skill sets in areas discussed in this guide. In addition, it will also require you to reflect on this feedback, analyze it in terms of your strengths and weaknesses, and put together an action plan that can help you improve your leadership and management skills as part of your professional development.

Assignment

One of the most effective ways to learn about your skills as a manager and a leader is through feedback using a 360-degree feedback process. Successful leaders recognize that they must continually enhance and sharpen their leadership skills. They must focus their ability on achieving the organization's vision and mission through credible actions, authentic relationships, and clear communication of the company's strategic direction and goals.

1. Complete the "360 Shared Leadership Development Assessment Tool" on yourself.
2. Identify between five to seven individuals that you will ask to complete the same tool, providing you with feedback from their perspective. The individuals need to be in the following categories:
   - Who is your supervisor/manager? Ideally, ask your current boss. If you currently are not employed, ask a past boss or a professor or instructor to provide you with feedback. This person should, however, know you beyond just general encounters as a student.
   - Identify two to four other employees at your same level. These individuals should be your peers at your workplace. In most cases, they would be at the same level or perform the same functions as you do. If you are not employed, ask close friends who know you well.
   - Identify one to two other employees who have reported to you in the past. These individuals are often classified as subordinates to your function. However, if you have not had anyone report to you either regularly or on a team, you could also ask someone who is fairly new in a similar position to yours who is familiar with your work. If you are not currently working, you can ask fellow students who know you to complete the assessments on you as well.
3. Make copies of the assessment tool and distribute it to the individuals you have asked and who have agreed to provide you with feedback. You should ask them to complete it as soon as possible, but no later than one week from when they received it.

4. Once you have received all the feedback tools back, use the "Individual Feedback Analysis Worksheet" to enter the raters' scores.
5. Add the scores across each row and enter the total. Then divide this total by the number of raters to get the average score. Enter the average in the appropriate cell on the worksheet.
6. Compare the ratings you have recorded (i.e., self versus others). Some questions you should ask yourself are:
    - Is there congruity between the scores?
    - How varied are the results?
    - What four to five areas have the highest average scores? (Congratulate yourself on these scores and make a note to continue to engage in these successful kinds of activities or behavior.)
    - What four to five areas have the lowest average scores?
    - Prioritize the four or five areas in terms of relevance to what you currently do or aspire to do.
    - Read the specific feedback for these ratings. You may want to go back to your raters and ask for more specific feedback (i.e., why they think you are a "1" or "2" in that particular area).
    - Ask your raters for specific strategies or actions that you might take to improve in these areas.
7. Focus on two to three of the relevant areas that are in need of most improvement. Develop an action plan using the "360 Individual Action Plan Worksheet." This plan should include the area of improvement, the improvement goal you are setting for yourself, the strategy or action for improvement, resources needed, time frame, and method of evaluation.
    - Use one action plan worksheet for each area you have selected. It is important that you use a systematic process to ensure you reach your improvement goals.
    - Create a SMART goal for each of the selected improvement areas.
    - Identify the strategies and actions you will need to take. You should be answering the following questions: What? When? Where? How?
    - Identify the resources you will need.
    - Identify a time frame for each action and a target completion date.
    - Identify the measures you will use to evaluate your success.
8. Write a one- to two-page report that explains why you selected these two to three areas for improvement. Include your action plan along with this report and give it to your instructor for additional feedback. The report should include the following topics:
    - Background information on who completed the assessments
        1. Not specific names, but positions, titles, or general categories such as close friend, fellow student, team member, supervisor, or crew member
        2. Number of years this person knows you
    - Description of why you selected these two to three areas for your action plan
    - Description of why these are important to your current professional development or work experience
    - Explanation of how you will evaluate the outcome of your action plan. Be sure to include:
        1. What data you will collect to analyze?
        2. From whom?
        3. When?
        4. How?
        5. What are significant milestones in the action plan?

360° Shared Leadership Development Assessment Tool

Name of person being rated:

Name of person doing the rating:

Date:

Following are twenty skill set areas that represent knowledge, skills, abilities and attitudes of successful leaders. Along with the skill set categories are several descriptions of what this skill set represents. Please read the description of each skill set, and then rate the individual identified above using this rating scale:

5 = Exceptional

4 = Very good

3 = Good

2 = Needs improvement

1 = Weak

Also, please provide any written comments that provide additional insights into your rating. These comments are very helpful in interpreting the scores.

360° SHARED LEADERSHIP ASSESSMENT TOOL		
Skill Set	**Rating (1–5)**	**Written Comments**
1 Vision ☐ Has a clear vision about what needs to be accomplished ☐ Understands an organization's deeper purpose ☐ Articulates the vision to others		
2 Mission and Goals ☐ Values and understands the mission statements of the company ☐ Sets realistic goals that reflect the mission of the company ☐ Communicates the impact of his or her job and that of others on the company's mission		

360° SHARED LEADERSHIP ASSESSMENT TOOL		
Skill Set	**Rating (1–5)**	**Written Comments**
3 Ethics and Personal Integrity ☐ Models integrity in daily interactions ☐ Asks questions to determine ethical decisions ☐ Says "thank you" for assistance ☐ Shows respect of others		
4 Written Communication ☐ Writes clearly ☐ Identifies appropriate channels to communicate written messages ☐ Documents problem solutions and policies		
5 Oral Communication ☐ Engages in open communication ☐ Informs others about the what and why of a message ☐ Communicates in a language the audience understands ☐ Uses appropriate telephone skills in dealing with others		
6 Communicating Expectations ☐ Provides advice or assistance to help me complete tasks ☐ Communicates expectations ☐ Keeps me informed related to our work together		
7 Active Listening ☐ Asks for input and is receptive to ideas ☐ Encourages other points of views to be shared ☐ Listens carefully and attentively to me ☐ Paraphrases or repeats points back to ensure they understand speaker's point		

360° SHARED LEADERSHIP ASSESSMENT TOOL		
Skill Set	**Rating (1–5)**	**Written Comments**
8 Teamwork ☐ Actively shares information with team ☐ Does all possible to help team accomplish goals ☐ Shares recognition willingly with team ☐ Discourages we-they attitude		
9 Reliability ☐ Consistently fulfills commitments made ☐ Accepts personal responsibility and ownership for projects ☐ Follows through with task in a timely manner ☐ "Pitches in" when needed to meet deadlines		
10 Nurturing ☐ Visibly shows they care about and are interested in others ☐ Exhibits empathy for variety of personality types ☐ Offers praise and positive feedback on work well done ☐ Makes me feel like an essential member of the organization		
11 Interpersonal relations ☐ Establishes trusting relationships, makes me feel comfortable ☐ Treats everyone fairly ☐ Delivers on promises and commitments		
12 Motivating ☐ Creates a safe and fun environment for others ☐ Avoids embarrassing others ☐ Treats others with respect ☐ Recognizes others achievement		

360° SHARED LEADERSHIP ASSESSMENT TOOL		
Skill Set	**Rating (1–5)**	**Written Comments**
13 Problem Solving ☐ Follows appropriate processes and systems to get at root causes ☐ Demonstrates flexibility in identifying solutions ☐ Selects best solutions based on facts and priorities ☐ Encourages risk taking		
14 Decisiveness ☐ Seeks input on decisions that others will be affected by ☐ Bases decision on facts and priorities ☐ Makes effective and timely decisions		
15 Conflict Management ☐ Tries to resolve issues in an objective open manner ☐ Handles complaints professionally ☐ Provides mediation, does not take sides		
16 Productivity/Contribution ☐ Adds overall value to company's products and services ☐ Uses time productively ☐ Produces results that need little revision		
17 Delegating ☐ Understands the capabilities of others ☐ Empowers others after appropriate training ☐ Defines delegated task clearly ☐ Follows up and coaches as needed		

360° SHARED LEADERSHIP ASSESSMENT TOOL		
Skill Set	**Rating (1–5)**	**Written Comments**
18 Feedback ☐ Manages by "walking around" to learn work status ☐ Solicits input from internal and external customers concerning satisfaction ☐ Provides appropriate and timely feedback to others ☐ Distinguishes between good and poor work and takes appropriate action		
19 Meetings ☐ Participates constructively in team meetings ☐ Conducts or facilitates meetings effectively ☐ Follows agenda items to keep focus		
20 Professional Development ☐ Stays knowledgeable of changes in industry to benefit organization ☐ Participates in various associations or industry organizations ☐ Networks with other professionals		

INDIVIDUAL FEEDBACK ANALYSIS WORKSHEET										
Skill Set	Raters' Scores							Total	Average	Notes
	1	2	3	4	5	6	7			
1 Vision										
2 Mission and Goals										
3 Ethics and Personal Integrity										
4 Written Communications										
5 Oral Communications										
6 Communicating Expectations										
7 Listening										
8 Teamwork										
9 Reliability										
10 Nurturing										
11 Interpersonal Relations										
12 Motivating										
13 Problem Solving										
14 Decisiveness										
15 Conflict Management										
16 Productivity/ Contribution										
17 Delegating										
18 Feedback										
19 Meetings										
20 Professional Development										

STRATEGY OR ACTION TO TAKE FOR IMPROVEMENTS			
Action	**Resources Needed**	**Begin Date**	**End Date**

EVALUATION				
What data is collected?	**From whom?**	**When?**	**How?**	**Significance?**

GLOSSARY

Action item (meeting) A part of an agenda item that requires some type of action.

Action meeting A brief meeting, often with just a few employees, that addresses and resolves a problem so action can be taken right away.

Action plan A series of steps that will be taken to resolve a problem.

Adjourning (team development) The fifth stage of team development, which occurs when the team has achieved its purpose and members move on to other tasks.

Agenda A list of topics that will be considered at a meeting.

Alternative (problem solving) A possible solution to a problem.

Anniversary date (employment) The date that the employee began working for the establishment.

Arbitration A process in which a neutral third party listens and reviews facts and makes a decision to settle a conflict.

Authority Formal power within an organization.

Benchmark A standard by which something can be measured or judged.

Benefits A service or right provided by an employer in addition to wages or salary, including employee health care, dental and vision insurance, vacation and sick leave pay, retirement contributions, or other benefits paid wholly or in part by the employer.

Boilerplate A term that relates to portions of contracts that do not change when they are used with different parties.

Bonus (compensation) An agreed-upon amount of additional compensation to be paid when specific financial goals are met.

Brainstorming A way to collect ideas in which each team member makes suggestions without comment from the others.

Brainstorming meeting A meeting that develops a list of ideas or creative solutions to an issue confronting the operation; its purpose is to collect ideas, not to make a decision.

Business plan A statement of goals and activities to be addressed within the next 12 months to move the operation toward its mission.

Cause (problem solving) The actions or situations that create a problem.

Certification A process that requires an employee to demonstrate a high level of skill and to meet specific performance requirements by participating in a rigorous process to become certified.

Chain of command The way in which authority flows from one management level to the next.

Coaching An informal process that reinforces positive job performance and corrects negative performance; it involves considerable listening skills, patience, and focus.

COBRA (Consolidated Omnibus Budget Reconciliation Act) A law that gives workers who lose health insurance benefits the right to continue group health benefits for limited periods under certain situations.

Collective bargaining agreement A legally binding contract between managers and the employees represented by a union. It defines employment conditions including wages and procedures to resolve disputes.

Communication The process of sending and receiving information by speech, gestures, or writing to receive a response or action.

Compensation All of the financial, or money, and nonfinancial, or nonmoney, payments and rewards given to employees in return for the work they do.

Competitive bids Prices requested for items of the same quality from a specified number of vendors to determine the lowest price.

Competitive employers Employers who hire the same type of employees as the establishment.

Conflict resolution Processes that encourage finding solutions to problems before more formal grievance procedures are needed.

Constructive feedback Feedback that focuses on specific aspects of performance and can be positive, such as emphasizing desired performance, or negative, such as addressing performance that should be improved.

Contact list A list of key persons to be notified in the event of an emergency.

Contingency plan A document that outlines actions to take in the event of an emergency or an unexpected event.

Controlling The basic management activity that involves determining the extent to which the organization keeps on track of achieving goals.

Coordinating The basic management activity that involves arranging group efforts in the best way.

Core value A key element of an operation that indicates the most basic reasons the business exists.

Cost of living (COL) A pay increase related to an index developed by the U.S. Bureau of Labor Statistics that reflects changes in the costs of items such as food, housing, and transportation to the average consumer.

Crew schedule A chart that informs employees who receive wages about the days and hours they are expected to work during a specific time period.

Critical incidents Events that need to be recorded for historical purposes in case of a potential claim or lawsuit.

Cross-functional teams A team of employees from different departments who consider problems that impact their areas and the operation as a whole.

Cross-training Training an employee to do work that is not normally part of his or her position.

Debrief meeting A session in which the team leader asks all team members to evaluate all aspects of a project after it is completed.

Delegation The process of assigning authority to employees to do work that a manager at a higher organizational level would otherwise do.

Departmental (team) goal A goal that is set at the second highest level in the operation.

Discrimination Treating persons unequally for reasons that do not relate to their legal rights or abilities.

Embezzlement The crime of stealing money or property from the person or business who lawfully owns it.

Emergency A sudden or unexpected situation that can cause injury, death, or property damage, or interfere with normal activities.

Emergency meeting A type of action meeting that occurs when some type of emergency has occurred and immediate action must be taken.

Employee absence policies Guidelines and procedures that explain how employees must tell managers if they are unable to work.

Employee development program An organized series of actions planned to expand an employee's skills and knowledge.

Employee turnover rate The percentage of the total number of employees who must be replaced during a specific time period such as a month or a year.

Environmental noise Any sound, such as loud talking or blaring radios, that interferes with communication.

Equal Pay Act A federal law that requires that men and women in the same workplace be given equal pay for equal work.

Esteem needs Needs that focus on how people feel about themselves and how they think others feel about them.

Evacuation The process of removing customers and employees from the building when an emergency occurs.

Exempt employee An employee who does not qualify for overtime pay according to the Fair Labor Standards Act (FLSA).

Exit interview An interview with an employee who leaves voluntarily to help managers learn about any employee concerns, reasons for leaving, and suggestions about how the company can improve.

External communication Communication that builds the customer base and helps build and maintain the establishment's desired identity throughout the community.

Facilitator Someone who runs a meeting.

Fair Labor Standards Act (FLSA) A federal law that sets minimum wage, overtime pay, equal pay, record-keeping, and child-labor standards for covered employees.

Family and Medical Leave Act (FMLA) A federal law that allows eligible employees to take off an extended amount of time for medical and other personal reasons; it applies to businesses employing 50 or more persons.

Feedback The way in which a person responds when he or she receives a message.

Floater An employee who can perform more than one job on a regular basis.

Forming (team development) The first stage of team development, in which team members get to know each other and learn what they will have to do to reach their assigned goals.

Fringe benefits Money paid indirectly in support of employees for purposes such as vacation, holiday pay, sick leave, and health insurance.

Functional team A team of employees from the same area or department who perform the routine tasks in their job description.

Garnishment A legal procedure by which someone who is owed money can collect what is owed from an employee's wages.

Ghost employee A person who receives a paycheck but is not currently employed.

Gross pay The amount paid excluding contributions for payroll, social security, taxes, and other required employer payments.

Ground rules (meeting) Rules about how meetings are run, how participants should interact, and what behavior is acceptable.

Harassment Unwelcome conduct based on race, color, religion, sex (including pregnancy), national origin, age (40 or older), disability, or genetic information.

Herzberg's two-factor theory A theory that identifies two different sets of factors that can motivate (**motivation factors**) and demotivate (**maintenance factors**) employees.

High-performance team A team whose members have an intense interest in helping make decisions and develop plans to assist the operation in reaching its goals.

Hostile environment (sexual harassment) An environment that is sexually demeaning or intimidating (creating fear).

Incentive A factor such as recognition or wanting to be part of a group that makes employees act in ways that help them reach personal goals.

Income statement A summary of the establishment's profitability during a certain time period.

Individual performance goal A goal that focuses on each employee's personal efforts.

Information meeting A meeting that shares communication such as project reports and updates or one used for orientation and training.

Insubordination Failure to follow reasonable instructions.

Interdepartmental communication Communication that occurs between employees in different departments.

Internal communication Communication that relates to messages of all types sent by managers to all employees.

Interpersonal communication Communication that involves speaking to one or a few individuals who are standing or sitting close to each other and providing immediate feedback.

Intranet A system that allows employees and teams to use the company's private communications network to share information and ideas.

Involuntary termination A situation in which managers terminate an employee for one or more of four reasons: lack of work for the employee, lack of funding, unsatisfactory performance, or violation of a company policy.

Job description A listing of the tasks that a person working within a position must be able to perform.

Job specification A listing of the personal requirements needed to successfully do the tasks listed on the job description.

Labor cost The money and fringe benefit expenses paid to the employees for the work they do.

Leadership The ability to inspire and motivate employees to act in ways that are in line with the vision of an organization and that help accomplish its goals.

Legal liability Liability that occurs when an establishment is legally responsible for a situation.

Line position A position ranging from the establishment's owner or manager, to department heads such as the kitchen or beverage manager, to entry-level employees such as servers and bartenders.

Line-up meeting A brief training session held before a work shift begins.

Listening The ability to focus on what a person is saying to understand the message being sent.

Long-range plan A statement of goals and the activities necessary to reach them that can be used over the next three to five years to move the operation toward its mission.

Maintenance factor (two-factor theory) Things that, if not taken care of, can make employees unhappy and prevent them from doing a good job.

Manage by walking around The process of moving around the restaurant or foodservice operation constantly, praising workers who perform well and correcting employees if work is not being done correctly.

Management Using what you have to do what you want to do.

Management schedule A schedule that shows days and times managers are expected to work.

Manager's daily log A log containing information that affects the operation, including what happened during each shift. It is useful for reviewing situations and noting problems, and for capturing facts that can protect the establishment from legal liabilities.

Marketing plan A calendar of specific activities designed to meet the operation's revenue goals.

Maslow's hierarchy of needs A theory that identifies five basic human needs, which typically arise in a certain order. As soon as one need is fulfilled to the desired extent, a person is motivated to fulfill the next need.

Master schedule A schedule that allows managers to determine the number of employees needed in each position and the total hours that persons in these positions should work.

Media policy A strategy developed to guide interactions with newspaper, television, and radio reporters about an establishment's response to an emergency.

Mediation A process in which a neutral third party facilitates a discussion of difficult issues and makes suggestions about an agreement.

Medicare A federal medical insurance program that primarily serves individuals over 65 regardless of income, younger persons who are disabled, and dialysis patients.

Mentor Someone who can serve as a wise adviser for an employee.

Merit pay plan A program that offers incentives for employees to improve performance and increase productivity.

Message channel The way in which a message is communicated; it can be through spoken or written words, graphics such as diagrams or photos, or nonverbal actions including body motions.

Message content The information sent by the sender to the receiver.

Message context The surroundings or environment through which a message travels.

Minutes A record of what is decided, what is accomplished, and what action items are agreed upon at meetings.

Mission statement A statement that refines an operation's vision statement by stating the purpose of the organization to employees and customers.

Motivation The process of providing a person with a reason to do something.

Motivation factor (two-factor theory) Things that motivate people. Motivation factors can be personal and difficult to measure.

Negative discipline Actions that discourage improper worker behavior.

Negligence A legal term that indicates a failure to use reasonable care as a manager, which is grounds for legal action.

Negotiation A discussion between involved persons with the goal of reaching an acceptable agreement.

Networking A process in which several people build relationships to help with career advancement and keep updated about the industry.

Nonverbal communication Movements and body language used to convey a message.

Norming (team development) The third stage of team development, in which team members settle their differences and develop more trusting relationships.

"No-show" An employee who, when scheduled to work, neither tells the manager he or she will not work nor reports for his or her assigned shift.

Operating budget A financial plan that estimates the revenue to be generated, the expenses to be incurred, and the profit, if any, for a specified time period.

Organizational culture The beliefs, values, and norms shared by workers in the organization that are then passed on to new employees.

Organizational goal A goal at the highest level, focusing on broad statements of what the entire operation wants to achieve.

Outsource Using an outside provider to do work that could otherwise be done by an employee.

Overtime (control) The number of labor hours worked in excess of scheduled hours.

Overtime (legal) The number of hours of work, usually 40, after which an employee must receive a premium pay rate.

Performance standard A measure set by managers that defines the expected quality and quantity of an employee's work.

Performing (team development) The fourth stage of team development, in which team members begin to depend on each other and can effectively analyze and solve problems together.

Personnel file A file that is maintained for each employee and contains confidential documents including employment application, emergency contact form, disciplinary action history, and current personal information.

Petty cash fund A predetermined amount of money that is used to make relatively infrequent and low-cost purchases for an establishment.

Physiological needs Needs that relate to the body and include food, water, air, and sleep.

Point-of-sale (POS) system A system that collects information about revenue, number of customers, menu items sold, and a wide range of other information that is helpful for management decision making.

Policy A planned course of action for an important activity that provides a general strategy for managing that activity.

Positive discipline Actions that encourage desired worker behavior.

Preventable emergency An emergency that may be prevented from happening, such as a fire or foodborne illness.

Preventive maintenance Procedures that follow a manufacturer's instructions about how to keep equipment in good working order.

Prime cost The largest category of an operation's costs.

Probation (progressive discipline) A specific time period during which an employee must consistently meet job standards or other reasonable conditions imposed by his or her manager as a condition for continued employment.

Problem solving A well-thought-out process that uses a logical series of activities to determine a course of action.

Problem-solving meeting A meeting held to consider and resolve one or more problems; it may involve discussing, analyzing, and reviewing alternatives, and deciding what actions should be taken.

Problem-solving team A temporary team of employees selected to solve a specific problem.

Professional development The actions people take to further their careers.

Progressive discipline A process that involves a series of punishments that become more serious as unacceptable performance continues.

Quid pro quo (sexual harassment) Sexual harassment that occurs when one person asks for or expects an action of a sexual nature from another person in return for that person's employment or advancement.

Receiver The person or persons for whom a message is intended.

Resources The food and beverage products, money, time, equipment, energy, and work methods that can be used to reach goals.

Responsibility The obligation that workers have to their own bosses.

Robert's Rules of Order A set of rules for conducting meetings in an organized way that allows everyone to be heard and to make decisions without confusion.

Safety needs Needs concerning those things that make people feel secure or keep them safe.

Salary A fixed amount of money for a certain time period that does not vary, regardless of the number of hours worked.

Sales forecasts Estimates of future sales based on sales history information.

Sales history Information about the number of customers who have visited the establishment on different days in previous weeks that can be used to forecast customer counts for future dates.

Scheduling The process of determining which employees will be needed to serve the expected number of customers during specific times.

Self-actualization The drive to do the very best that one can do, which can make people push themselves, learn new things, and be creative.

Self-directed team A small group of employees who manage many daily issues within their functional team with little supervision.

Sender The person who sends a message to a receiver.

Separation checklist A list of activities to be completed for employees who are leaving the organization.

Sexual harassment Unwelcome behavior of a sexual nature that interferes with an employee's job performance.

Shift leader An employee who receives wages and, in addition to his or her regular tasks, trains new employees, answers work-related questions, and performs other functions assigned by managers.

SMART goal A goal that is SMART is specific, measurable, achievable, relevant, and timebound.

Social needs Needs that involve interaction with others, including love, belonging, and friendship.

Social security A supplemental retirement system that is funded by payroll taxes; a certain percentage of an employee's pay goes into a fund that provides benefits to current social security recipients.

Staffing The job of recruiting and selecting new workers, making job offers, and orienting the new employees.

Staff position Technical, advisory specialists such as accountants and purchasing personnel whose jobs are to provide good advice to the actual decision makers employed in line positions.

Stakeholder The persons who affect or are affected by the establishment. Stakeholders include owners, managers, supervisors, employees, and customers.

Standard operating procedure (SOP) A written description or list of steps that tells how to correctly perform a task.

Standardized recipe A set of instructions used to produce a food or beverage item.

Standards Baselines of quality and quantity that can be compared to actual operating results.

Status quo How things are normally done.

Storming (team development) The second stage of team development, in which the reality of what the team is expected to do becomes clearer and some conflicts between team members may begin to surface.

Strategic priority An operation's highest-level concern for employees to address.

Strategy A plan of action to reach a goal.

Stress management A process managers can use to identify what causes them stress in the workplace or in their personal lives.

Structured interview An interview in which the manager asks a set of specific questions.

Subpoena A legal notice that requires certain documents be provided to a court of law.

Suggestive selling A strategy for encouraging guests to order products or services they may not have been aware of or intending to purchase.

Supervisor A first-rung manager who directs the work of entry-level employees on his or her team.

SWOT analysis An analysis that identifies an operation's strengths and weaknesses and examines its opportunities and threats.

Tabled (agenda item) Held over for another meeting.

Table turn The number of times a table is used during a specific meal period.

Task analysis A process for identifying each task in a position such as cook or server and determining how the procedures in a task should be done.

Task breakdown An explanation of how to perform each of the procedures that make up a task.

Task list A list that indicates all tasks included in a position.

Team A group of people who work together to complete a task or reach a common goal.

Teamwork The act of cooperating and working together to complete tasks and reach common goals.

Terminable act An action by an employee that typically causes immediate termination.

Time management Planning and using procedures and tools to increase a person's efficiency and productivity.

Time-off request policy The procedures and guidelines that employees should follow when they want time off from work.

Tip (compensation) Money paid by customers in return for providing services.

Unemployment insurance A temporary source of income to eligible persons who lose their job that is funded with money paid by the employer while the person was employed.

Unity of command principle The principle that each staff member should have only one boss.

Unpreventable emergency An emergency that cannot be prevented, such as a natural disaster.

Unstructured interview An interview in which the manager conducts a conversation with the employee without using any prepared questions.

Value The relationship between what is paid for something and the quality of the product or service that is received.

Value statement A set of standards that guides restaurant and foodservice operations, which is the foundation for developing the vision statement and mission statement.

Variance The difference between a budgeted expense and an actual expense.

Vision statement A statement based on an establishment's value statements that describes what it wants to become and why it exists.

Voluntary termination A situation in which an employee, for his or her own personal reasons, decides to leave the organization.

W-2 income tax form An information return completed by employers and sent to the federal taxing authorities that is used to report wages and salaries paid to employees and the taxes withheld from them.

Wages Monetary compensation for employees who are paid on the basis of the number of hours they work.

Warm-body syndrome The idea that any employee is better than no employee, leading to a fast hiring decision.

Warm-up activity A quick exercise that prepares people to focus on the meeting and its objectives.

Withholding tax Money taken from an employee's wages by an employer and paid directly to the government.

Work ethic A set of values based on the idea that there are benefits to work that include strengthening character.

Workers' compensation A state-regulated insurance program that pays medical bills and some lost wages for employees who are injured at work or who have a work-related illness or disease.

Workplace ethics Rules of appropriate behavior toward others at work.

Wrongful discharge A legal action taken by a former employee against a previous employer, alleging that the discharge was in violation of state or federal antidiscrimination laws, public policy, or an implied contract, agreement, or written promise.

Zero tolerance A policy that allows no amount of harassing behavior.

INDEX

D

E

F

G

H

I

J

L

M

N

O

P

U

V

W

Z